Effective Presentations

Melanie Morgan, Ph.D. | Jane Natt

2016–2017 Edition

VAN-GRINER

Effective Presentations

Melanie Morgan, Ph.D.
Jane Natt
2016–2017 Edition

Printed in the United States of America
10 9 8 7 6 5 4 3 2 1
ISBN: 978-1-61740-052-0

Van-Griner Publishing
Cincinnati, Ohio
www.van-griner.com

CEO: Mike Griner
President: Dreis Van Landuyt
Project Manager: Maria Walterbusch
Customer Care Lead: Julie Reichert

Natt 052-0 Su16
169940
Copyright © 2017

Brief Contents

1 Introduction to Presentational Speaking 1

2 Audience Analysis 21

3 Selecting the Topic and Purpose 45

4 Introductions and Conclusions 65

5 Organizing the Presentation 95

6 Supporting Evidence and Research 109

7 Outlining the Presentation 137

8 Informative and Special Occasion Speaking 157

9 The Persuasive Process 187

10 Strategies for Persuasive Presentations 211

11 Delivering the Presentation 227

12 Presentation Aids 243

13 Presenting as a Group 267

14 Presenting Outline 283

15 The Question-and-Answer Session 317

R References 327

I Index 359

A Forms and Assignments A1

Table of Contents

1 Introduction to Presentational Speaking
1

Objectives 1

Presentational Speaking and Career Success 3

What Is Presentational Speaking? 3

Presentational Speaking Is More Inclusive 3

Presentational Speaking Is Less Formal 4

Presentational Speaking Is More Interactive 4

Presentational Speaking Reaches a Smaller Number of Individuals 4

Characteristics of Effective Presentational Speaking 4

Good Presentational Speaking Is Goal-Directed 5

Good Presentational Speaking Is Audience-Centered 5

Good Presentational Speaking Is Ethical 6

Plagiarism 6

Types of Plagiarism 7

The Presentation Process 12
  Selecting the Topic 12
  Determining Your Purpose 12
  Researching Your Presentation 12
  Organizing Your Presentation 13
  Practicing the Presentation 13

Anxiety and Speaking 14
  What Is Communication Apprehension? 14
  Addressing Communication Apprehension 15
    Skills Training 15
    Systematic Desensitization 15
    Cognitive Restructuring 18
    Visualization 18

Conclusion 19

Key Terms 20

2

Audience Analysis
21

Objectives 21

The Importance of Audience Analysis 22

Demographic Audience Analysis 23
  Age 24
  Sex and Gender 24
  Geographical Location 25
  Group Affiliation 25
  Socioeconomic Factors 26

Psychological Audience Analysis 27
  Audience Attitudes 28
  Favorable Audiences 29
  Hostile Audiences 30
  Neutral Audiences 31
  Audience Motivation 31
  Audience Knowledge 34
  Audience Mood 35

Environmental Audience Analysis 36
  Physical Setting 36
  Occasion 36
  Time of Day 37

Order of Speakers 37
Time/Length of Presentation 38
Technology 38

Audience Adaptation before the Presentation **39**
Direct Methods of Audience Analysis 40
Indirect Methods of Audience Analysis 41

Audience Adaptation during the Presentation **42**

Conclusion **42**

Key Terms **43**

Exercises **43**

3

Selecting the Topic and Purpose
45

Objectives **45**

Do You Have a Choice? **46**

Qualities of a Good Topic **47**
Your Topic Interests You 47
Your Topic Interests Your Audience 47
Your Topic Is Significant 48
Your Topic Is Fresh 48
Your Topic Can Be Covered in the Allotted Time 48
Your Topic Is Audience Appropriate 49
Your Topic Can Be Easily Researched 50
Your Topic Is Timely 50

How to Select a Topic **50**
Personal Experience 50
Personal Interests 51
Current Events 51
News Releases, News Services, and Newsletters 52
Internet Searches 54
Weblogs 54
Social Media 56
Other Sources 57

Narrowing the Topic **57**
The General Purpose 58
The Specific Purpose 59
Qualities of a Well-Written Specific Purpose Statement 59

Expressed as a Full Declarative Statement 59
Limited to One Distinct Idea 60
Clear and Precise 60
Thesis Statement 61
Guidelines for a Thesis Statement 61
Anatomy of a Thesis Statement 62

Conclusion **63**

Key Terms **64**

Introductions and Conclusions
65

Objectives **65**

Introductions **67**

Objectives of an Effective Introduction **67**
Capturing the Attention of Your Audience 68
Story/Narrative 68
Quotation 76
Interesting Fact or Statistic 76
Use Technology (Audio/Visual Aids) 76
Attention-Getters for Outside the Classroom 77
Compliment the Audience 77
Refer to Recent Events 77
Solicit Participation 78
Attention-Getters to Avoid 78
Questions 78
Jokes 79
Hypothetical Situations 79
Considerations in Choosing an Attention-Gaining Device 80
Consider Building Identification with the Audience 80
Consider the Tone Your Presentation Is Trying to Establish 81
Consider Your Time Restrictions 81
Consider Your Strengths as a Speaker 81
Consider the Audience 81
Consider Your Topic 81
Establishing Credibility 82
Relating the Material to the Audience 83
Announcing the Topic and Previewing the Main Points 84

The Conclusion **85**

Objectives of an Effective Conclusion 85
   Restating the Thesis and Main Points 86
   Ending with a Clincher or Memorable Thought 86
     Referring Back to the Attention-Getter 86
     Quotation 87
     Call to Action 87
   Common Conclusion Pitfalls 88
     Ending Abruptly 88
     Drawing It Out 88
     Introducing New Arguments and Points 88
     Leaving Conclusions Implicit 88

Example Introduction and Conclusion 89
   Introduction 89
   Conclusion 90

Conclusion 91

Key Terms 91

Exercises 92

5   Organizing the Presentation
95

Objectives 95

Why Organization Is Important 96

Organizing the Body of Your Presentation 97
   Main Points 97
     Number of Main Points 98
     Organization of Main Points 98
       Spatial 98
       Chronological 99
       Problem-Solution 99
       Causal Pattern 100
       Topical 100
     Characteristics of Good Main Points 101
       Main Points Should Be Balanced 101
       Try to Use Parallel Wording 102
   Supporting Evidence 102
   Transitions 104
     Directional Transitions 104
     Signposts 105

Internal Previews 105
Internal Summaries 105
Transitioning within Main Points 106

Conclusion **106**

Key Terms **107**

6 Supporting Evidence and Research
109

Objectives 109

Why Supporting Evidence Is Important 110

Types of Supporting Materials 111
Statistics 111
Tips for Using Statistics 112
Make Sure Statistics Are Representative 112
Understand What the Statistics Mean 113
Explain the Statistics 113
Localize Statistics 113
Limit Your Use of Statistics 114
Round Off Statistics 114
Identify the Sources of Your Statistics 114
Examples 115
Brief Examples 115
Extended Examples 116
Hypothetical Examples 116
Tips for Using Examples 117
Make Examples Vivid 117
Make Sure Extended Examples Have a Beginning, Middle, and End 117
Practice Delivering Extended Examples 117
Select the Right Example 117
Select Appropriate Examples 118
Testimony 118
Expert Testimony 118
Peer Testimony 118
Prestige Testimony 119
Tips for Using Testimony 119
Quote or Paraphrase Accurately 119
Use Testimony from Unbiased Sources 119
Cite the Credentials of Your Sources 120
General Tips on Using Supporting Material 120
Use a Variety of Types of Supporting Material 120

Use a Variety of Sources for Supporting Material 121
Use Consistent and Complementary Supporting Material 121

Where to Find Supporting Material **121**
Libraries 121
Interviews 122
Websites 123
Weblogs 123
Social Media 126
News Releases 128
Books 128
Reference Works 129
Magazines, Newspapers, and Broadcast Outlets 129
Government Documents 131
Academic Journals 131
Evaluating Information Sources 132
Authority 132
Accuracy 132
Objectivity 133
Relevancy 133
Variety 133
Level of Information 133

Citing Your Evidence during the Presentation **134**
Books 134
Journal or Magazine Articles 134
Newspapers 134
Interviews 135
Websites 135
News Releases 135

Conclusion **136**

Key Terms **136**

Exercises **136**

7

Outlining the Presentation
137

Objectives **137**
Why Outlining Is Important **138**
Ensures Organization 139
Balances the Presentation 139
Identifies Evidence 139
Assesses Quantity 139

Allows for Flexibility 140
Allows for Instructional Feedback 140

Formatting the Preparation Outline **140**
Full Sentences 140
Appropriate Symbolization 141
Effective Subordination 141
Coordinated Points 142
Specific Purpose and Thesis Statements 143
Transitions 143
Reference Page 144

Putting the Outline Together **144**

The Speaking Outline **146**
Guidelines for the Speaking Outline 147
Be Brief 147
Follow Structure of the Preparation Outline 147
Include Supporting Materials 147
Be Legible 147
Provide Delivery Cues 148
Usually Use Note Cards 148
Frameworks vs. Outlines 148

Conclusion **149**

Key Terms **149**

Donating to Soles4Souls **150**
Introduction 150
Body 150
Conclusion 152
References 152

Sample Speaking Outline **153**

8 Informative and Special Occasion Speaking 157

Objectives **157**

Informative Speaking **159**
Types of Informative Speaking 159

Informatory Presentations **160**
News Presentations 160
Relevance 161
Surprise Value 161

Factuality 164

Comprehensiveness 164

Instructional Presentations 165

Explanatory Presentations **167**

The Simple Explanation 169

Explanatory Presentation Obstacles 173

Difficulty Understanding the Use of a Concept or Term 175

Understanding Complex Structures or Processes 176

Hard-to-Believe Phenomena 180

Special Occasion Speaking **182**

Speech of Introduction 182

Speech of Acceptance 184

Speech of Recognition 185

Speech of Welcome 185

Conclusion **185**

Key Terms **186**

Exercises **186**

The Persuasive Process
187

Objectives 187

Differences between Informative and Persuasive Presentations 189

Persuasive Speaking Asks the Audience to
Choose between Two or More Alternatives 189

Persuasive Speaking Demands More Thorough Audience Analysis 190

Persuasive Speaking Makes More Demands of an Audience 190

Persuasive Speaking Has a Higher Ethical Threshold 190

What Is Persuasion? **190**

The Process of Persuasion 191

Targets of Persuasion 191

Beliefs 192

Attitudes 192

Behaviors 193

Goals of Persuasion 193

Creating 194

Reinforcing 194

Changing 194

The Elaboration Likelihood Model **195**
   Applying the Principles of the ELM 197
Social Judgment Theory **198**
   Applying Social Judgment Theory 198
Organizing the Persuasive Speech **199**
   Presentations Concerning Questions of Fact 199
      Organizing the Presentation 200
   Presentations Concerning Questions of Value 201
      Organizing the Presentation 202
   Presentations Concerning Questions of Policy 203
      Organizing the Presentation 205

Conclusion **208**
Key Terms **209**

10 Strategies for Persuasive Presentations
211

Objectives **211**
Ethos, Logos, and Pathos **212**
   Using Ethos in Your Presentation 213
      Tips for Enhancing Ethos 214
   Using Logos in Your Presentation 215
      Deductive Reasoning 215
         Tips for Using Deductive Arguments 215
      Inductive Reasoning 216
         Tips for Using Induction 217
      Analogical Reasoning 217
         Tips for Using Arguments by Analogy 218
      Causal Reasoning 218
         Tips for Using Causal Arguments 219
   Fallacies 220
      Argument Ad Hominem 220
      Bandwagon 220
      Slippery Slope 221
      False Dilemma 221
      Straw Person 222
      Red Herring 222
   Using Pathos in Your Presentation 222
      Language 223
      Supporting Evidence 223

Delivery 224
Visual Aids 225
Enhancing the Use of Pathos 225

Conclusion **225**

Key Terms **226**

11 Delivering the Presentation
227

Objectives **227**

The Importance of Good Delivery **228**

Characteristics of Effective Delivery **229**
Effective Delivery Is Conversational 229
Effective Delivery Is Natural 229
Effective Delivery Is Varied 229
Effective Delivery Enhances the Message 230

Methods of Delivery **230**
Impromptu 230
Guidelines for Impromptu Speaking 231
Manuscript 232
Memorized 232
Extemporaneous 233

Vocal Delivery **233**
Vocal Variety 233
Volume 233
Rate 234
Pitch 234
Pauses 235
Vocal Nonfluencies 235
Enunciation 235
Pronunciation 235

Physical Delivery **236**
Gestures 236
Movement 237
Eye Contact 237
Facial Expression 238
Appearance 238
Speaking with a Translator 239

Practicing the Presentation 240

Conclusion 242

Key Terms 242

12

Presentation Aids
243

Objectives 243

Functions of Presentation Aids 244

Increase Clarity and Retention 244

Increase Presentation Effectiveness 245

Increase Speaker Effectiveness 245

Types of Presentation Aids 246

Numerical Charts 246

Parts of a Whole 247

Item Comparison 248

Time Series Comparisons 249

Text Charts 250

Maps 251

Diagrams 251

Photographs 252

Audio/Video 252

Creating Multimedia Presentations 253

Advantages to Using Presentation Software 253

Types of Presentation Slides 253

Using Presentation Software Effectively 254

Slides Are Not Designed to Tell the Entire Story 254

Too Much Text 254

Phrase Headlines 255

Reliance on Bulleted Lists 257

Take Advantage of the Build Feature 258

Keep the Slides Simple 258

Use Slides Only When Needed 259

Use Effective Design Principles 259

Avoid Special Effects 259

Avoid Standing in the Shadows 259

Tips for Designing Presentation Aids 260

Prepare Presentation Aids Carefully 260

Choose Fonts Carefully 260

Use Color 262
Keep Presentation Aids Simple 262

Tips for Using Presentation Aids **263**
Avoid Using the Chalkboard 263
Practice, Practice, Practice 263
Have a Backup Plan 263
Stay Focused on Your Audience 263
Avoid Passing out Presentation Aids 264
Display Presentation Aids Only When Explaining Them 264
Explain Your Presentation Aids 264

Conclusion **265**

Key Terms **265**

13

Presenting as a Group
267

Objectives **267**

Preparing and Delivering the Group Presentation **268**
Group Conflict 268

The Preparation Stage **269**
Choose a Leader or Point Person 269
Establish the Goal 270
Conduct Research 272
Assign Tasks 272
Stay on Task 274
Develop the Presentation Template 274
Design Presentation Format 275
Introductions 275
Speaker Transitions 275
The 10-Minute Rule 275
Question-and-Answer Session 276
Practice the Presentation 276
Make Contingency Plans 276

The Actual Presentation **277**

The Business Presentation **277**
The Status Report 278
Three Components of Status Reports 278
Overall 279

Milestones 279
Issues 280

Working in Multicultural Groups 281

Conclusion 282

Key Terms 282

14 Presenting Online
283

Objectives 283

Presenting Online 284
Benefits of Online Presentations 285
Cost Savings 286
Time Savings 286
Green 286
Faster Decision-Making 287
Effective Coordination 287
Types of Online Presentations 287

Synchronous Presentations 288
Planning the Synchronous Presentation 289
Setting 290
Lighting 290
Camera Angles 290
Framing 291
Backgrounds 291
Colors and Wardrobe 291
Content 292
Delivering the Synchronous Presentation 293
Eye Contact 293
Movement 293
Voice 294
Posture 294
Behavior 294

Presenting to a Global Audience 294
Selecting Supporting Material 295
Constructing Your Presentation 295
Delivering Your Presentation 295

Asynchronous Presentations **297**
Planning the Asynchronous Presentation 298
Writing the Script 299
Recording the Asynchronous Presentation 300
The Format of the Asynchronous Presentation 300
Opening 300
Slides 301
Speaking 301
Conclusion 301
Working Together 302

Challenges of Online Presentations **303**
Challenges of Synchronous Presentations 303
Technical Difficulties 303
Technical Expertise and Extra Planning 303
Delivery Challenges 305
Interactivity 305
Environmental Constraints 306
Infrastructure 307
Challenges of Asynchronous Presentations 307
Permanency 307
Accessibility 308
Interactivity 309
Presentational Aids 309

Common Tools for Online Presentations **309**
Using Slide Presentation Software in Online Presentations 310
Creating Slides for Online Use 311
Using Audio/Video/Chat Software for Live Presentations 313
Using Skype for Live Presentations 313

Conclusion **314**
Key Terms **314**
Exercises **314**

15 The Question-and-Answer Session 317

Objectives **317**
Guidelines for an Effective Q&A **318**
Prepare for the Q&A 318
Anticipate Questions 318
Have a Plan 319

Answering Questions 319
   Keep Answers Concise and Direct 319
   Repeat Each Question 320
   Listen to the Entire Question 320
   What If I Don't Know the Answer? 320
   What If No One Asks a Question? 320
   What If I Can't Understand the Questioner? 321
   What If a Group Member Provides Wrong Information? 321
   What If Someone Asks a Question Clearly Answered by the Presentation? .. 321
   With Whom Should I Make Eye Contact? 321
   Dealing with Difficult Audience Members 321
   Stay Confident 322
The New Backchannel 322
   The Online Question-and-Answer Session 324
Provide Closure 326

Conclusion **326**

Key Terms **326**

REFERENCES
327

INDEX
359

FORMS AND ASSIGNMENTS
A1

CHAPTER 1

Introduction to Presentational Speaking

Objectives

After reading this chapter, you should be able to

◎ explain the differences between public speaking and presentational speaking;

◎ explain the elements of effective presentations;

◎ understand the different types of plagiarism;

◎ describe the presentational process;

◎ define communication apprehension; and

◎ describe methods for addressing communication apprehension.

Each summer and fall, perennial Big Ten football powerhouses like Michigan State and Ohio State put their players through grueling pre-season training camps. But for some players, the most difficult drill happens off the field: public speaking.

Both schools require seniors to give 15-minute speeches in front of their teammates and coaches on a non-football topic. Spartans defensive lineman Lawrence Thomas told *The Wall Street Journal* in 2015 "It's scarier than playing before a packed house on national television. You go up there and see all those eyes at you."[1]

At Ohio State, they even video the speeches so the players can recognize delivery errors and adjust accordingly. The goal is to increase players' confidence, which might encourage them to speak up in team settings, in classes, with media, and in other communication settings.

Athletic teams are recognizing what employers have known for a long time. Every year the National Association of Colleges and Employers (NACE) conducts a survey asking employers to rank the most important skills or qualities for job candidates. The results from NACE's Job Outlook 2015 indicate that employers are looking for leaders who can work effectively on teams and have strong communication skills.[2] The results of this year's survey are not unique. Communication skills have consistently ranked near the top in importance to employers in this annual survey. The *Wall Street Journal* also reports that the ability to articulate your ideas is vital to getting a job.[3] These findings indicate how important good communication skills are to your success in finding your first job and succeeding once you are hired.

Although your first job may seem a long way away at this point, you cannot underestimate the importance of strong presentational skills for your success in the workplace. This course will provide you with the basics that you will need to succeed in presentational speaking. Not only will you learn theories and skills that are vital in the workplace, but those skills will also serve you well in other courses you take while in college.

Many of the courses you take at the university level will require some type of presentation. Use these presentations as practice for the presentations you will make later in your career. All of the strategies and skills you learn in this course will be valuable and applicable to the speaking you will be required to do while in college, whether that speaking occurs in the classroom or as part of a membership you have in some organization. Perhaps you will become president of your sorority or fraternity and will be required to deliver presentations to raise money, increase membership, or even remain in good standing with the university. The skills you learn in this course will help you achieve those goals.

This course and text are designed to present communication theories and research to help you learn the fundamentals of presentational speaking. As part of this process, various guidelines will be presented on how to prepare presentations. Some of these guidelines are very specific. Elements of the presentations will be required to contain particular features. Sometimes, students report that these requirements seem constraining. However, research has shown that these guidelines work in almost all speaking contexts. You cannot go wrong if you use the fundamental guidelines this book and course advocate. Once you become an accomplished speaker, you learn which of the guidelines can be broken or adapted to specific speaking situations. Until then, these guidelines will serve you well and help ensure that your presentations are successful.

Presentational Speaking and Career Success

As mentioned at the beginning of this chapter and as the *Wall Street Journal* reports, the ability to clearly articulate your ideas is vital to obtaining employment.[4] The ability to make effective presentations is important for employment. Job candidates who can differentiate themselves in terms of oral communication skills and teamwork skills are at an advantage in the job market.[5]

Good speaking skills may help you land that important job, and they also get you promoted once you are in the organization. In fact, organizational recruiters report that the fear of public speaking is one of the most common career-stoppers in America. Alan Greenwald, a partner at Bresner & Associates, a company that helps executives with presentation skills, says, "Being a poor speaker is the principal reason people don't make it into the executive ranks."[6]

So now that you know how important good speaking is to career success, it is also important to know that potential employers have been less than impressed with the communication skills their employees are currently bringing into the workplace. An article in the *Pittsburgh Post-Gazette* reports that although communication skills are usually the most desired skills, they are often the weakest skills potential employees bring to an interview.[7] The website JobWeb reports similar findings. Use the information in this course to your advantage. Take risks and try the methods and suggestions this course offers. This is a safe place to build these important skills. Take advantage of this opportunity so that you can arrive at your employment interviews with strong presentation skills.

Tip

Knowing how to deliver a good presentation is crucial in all areas of business. Without good presentational skills, it is very difficult to become a true leader.

Jelena Nikodijevic | Senior Consultant | Service Innovation | Deloitte Services, LP

What Is Presentational Speaking?

By now you have determined that **presentational speaking** is unavoidable and also essential to success. No matter how much you dread it, it is an inevitable part of academic and professional life. This book has been referring to presentational speaking, not public speaking. So what are the differences? Let's examine some of these differences now. The popular TED talks (TED.com) are a great example. Participants can range from experts in their fields offering advice to everyday people sharing their stories.

Presentational Speaking Is More Inclusive

Public speaking can be thought of as a grand presentation. By public we usually mean it is a presentation that affects the community at large. The audience will include a "public audience." Staff meetings don't fall under this category. However, if you have ever attended a staff meeting, you know that the ability to present one's ideas in an organized and effective fashion is important. Presentational speaking includes more typical types of situations that people commonly face. Therefore, the term *presentational* includes both the public type of presentations we often see politicians making and those smaller types of presentations that occur within organizations. The popular TED talks (TED.com) are a great example. Participants can range from experts in their fields offering advice to everyday people sharing their stories.

Presentational Speaking Is Less Formal

Public speaking usually occurs in a formal setting. Speakers are behind podiums and microphones. They are usually dressed in formal attire. Speakers deliver their presentations from a prepared manuscript, and the presentation is rather scripted—meaning that there is little room for spontaneity.

Presentational speaking can occur around a table while everyone is seated. The speaker doesn't necessarily have to stand up to address the audience. Most likely, the presentation will be delivered from an outline rather than a manuscript; therefore, the situation is much more relaxed and allows for informality.

Presentational Speaking Is More Interactive

The reliance on manuscript delivery usually means that public speeches rarely adapt to the needs of the audience. Audience members often have little chance for interaction with the speaker, although they can usually stop the speaker during a presentation and ask questions if they feel they need to. The extemporaneous delivery style of presentational speaking, on the other hand, allows the speaker the spontaneity to talk to the audience and adapt the presentation to audience members' needs.

Presentational Speaking Reaches a Smaller Number of Individuals

Presentations are often made to smaller audiences than public speeches. Public speeches usually reach multiple audiences through a variety of mediums. They may be videotaped for replay, and the actual words delivered in the presentations are transcribed so that they can be reprinted in the newspaper. So, while you may not be able to see the president deliver his State of the Union Address, you may be able to see it replayed on television or read the transcript in the newspaper. This extra distribution has the ability to reach a very wide audience.

Characteristics of Effective Presentational Speaking

Now that you know how important presentational speaking is and how it differs from public speaking, let's examine the three essential factors that will make your presentations effective. We will refer back to these elements throughout the entire book. They will help guide you in making many of the decisions that you need to make when preparing for a presentation.

Good Presentational Speaking Is Goal-Directed

Good speaking is goal-directed. Each time you address an audience, you should be extremely clear regarding the purpose of your presentation. What exactly are you trying to convey? What are you hoping to achieve? Are you trying to explain a procedure to a group of colleagues, update your staff on new developments in your product line, or persuade a client to change operating systems? Whatever the purpose, the content of your presentation should be driven by your goal. Every decision you make about what to address or what to include in the presentation should be based on the overarching goal of your presentation. If the material you are considering using doesn't support your goal, don't use it.

Presentations that aren't goal-directed seem muddled and often ramble. The message is unclear, and audiences often leave wondering what they should take away from the presentation.

> **Presentations that aren't goal-directed seem muddled and often ramble.**

Before beginning the preparation process, have a firm idea of what you want to achieve in the presentation. After ensuring that the goal is appropriate for the audience and the situation, use it as your guide. Your goal or purpose should drive every decision you make during the preparation process. If you follow this guideline, you will be on the road to delivering a presentation with a clear message that your audience can follow.

Good Presentational Speaking Is Audience-Centered

Good presenters are always aware of their audience. One of the differences between strong speakers and average speakers is the ability to relate and adapt to their audience. You have to know your audience in order to reach them. If you are delivering a sales presentation to potential clients, hoping to sell them a new computer operating system, and you know little about the types of features that will be most useful to them, you will probably lose the sale.

To be successful as a speaker, you must know the attitudes audience members hold about your message and be able to strategically plan for possible differences between your position and theirs.

Being audience-centered means that you should think of your audience while planning the presentation, but you should also respond to the audience during the presentation. Watch for audience feedback, and adapt your message as needs change. For example, if you notice that audience members seem confused by some statistical data you just presented, stop the presentation, and explain it in a different way.

This speaker must tailor her delivery style to an audience of school children.

The bottom line: Good presentations are those that relate to your audience. It is important to make sure that, as a speaker, you are connecting with your audience. If you fail to achieve this connection, it is unlikely that you will achieve your presentation's goal or purpose. Therefore, keep your audience in mind at every step of the presentation.

Good Presentational Speaking Is Ethical

While the goal of your presentation may have great significance to you personally, you have a responsibility to your audience to pursue that goal in an ethical manner. As the expert on a given topic, you have great power over your audience. Audience members trust you to provide them with good, solid evidence and sound reasoning. Providing them with anything less is unethical. If you are asking audience members to change the way they eat, then it is important that you present all of the evidence so that audience members can make an informed decision about a change in their diet. This means using supporting evidence that is timely and from respected sources and refraining from fallacious reasoning (see Chapter 10).

Additionally, make sure that the goals of your speech are ethical. You don't want to ask anything of your audience members that could potentially cause them harm. This becomes particularly important for classroom presentations. It is unethical to advocate any behavior that may cause potential harm to audience members. While a presentation on how to make a fake ID may appeal to an audience of traditional-age college students, making fake IDs is illegal. If audience members actually engaged in this behavior, they could be arrested and face serious legal ramifications. Therefore, stop and ask yourself what you are advocating. If it could potentially cause harm to audience members, pursue another topic.

> **Make sure that the goals of your speech are ethical.**

Ethical speakers are always prepared. As we discuss later in the book, it is a waste of time for you and the audience both if you arrive at a speaking engagement unprepared. If audience members don't get what they are expecting from your presentation, they will be disappointed. More importantly, it is essential that you have prepared thoroughly and are competent to speak about the topic you are addressing. If you are not fully informed about your topic, your presentation could be misleading to audience members and cause potential harm.

Ethical speakers are also honest. Be truthful in what you say. This means reporting statistics in a straightforward manner that your audience can understand, quoting experts accurately, citing sources correctly, using examples that are typical rather than unusual, and using sound reasoning.

Don't make promises your presentation can't deliver. Don't tell audience members that you hold the key to all of their dating happiness if you don't. Be realistic in what your presentation can accomplish.

Plagiarism

As an ethical speaker, it is important for you to know exactly what plagiarism is so that you can avoid it. **Plagiarism** is taking someone else's words or ideas and claiming them as your own. Plagiarism is a rising problem on college campuses.[8] It is a serious offense with stiff penalties. It can result in a variety of consequences that range from failing the assignment in question to being expelled from the university. It can even keep you from being accepted to a university. Blair Hornstine had been accepted to Harvard University. However, after her acceptance, she was found guilty of plagiarizing materials for articles she wrote for her hometown newspaper. Harvard then revoked her acceptance. She claimed that she was unaware that she had committed plagiarism and that it was due to poor journalistic training and inexperience. However, Harvard did not see it that way and stood by its decision to revoke her admittance.

Plagiarism isn't only an issue on college campuses and universities. Republican U.S. Sen. Rand Paul of Kentucky, a 2016 presidential hopeful, was mired in a huge plagiarism scandal in 2013. Journalists said he used material verbatim from news stories from *The Associated Press,* articles in Wikipedia, and other websites in his speeches without giving credit. They also accused Paul of using exact wording from studies by such organizations as the Heritage Foundation and the Cato Institute in his book without citing the authors. Paul eventually admitted to "improperly using footnotes."[9]

Plagiarism can carry severe punishment in the organizational world. Defense contractor Raytheon Co.'s board decided it would not give Chairman and Chief Executive William Swanson a salary raise and reduced his incentive-stock compensation when it was uncovered that Swanson plagiarized parts of a management booklet, "Swanson's Unwritten Rules of Management," the company gave away free on its website.[10]

Plagiarism can also have direct financial consequences. Sam Smith, a noted musician, was accused of a type of plagiarism, or in this case copyright infringement, by fellow musicians Tom Petty and Jeff Lynne. Sam Smith's 2014 hit "Stay With Me" was found to have similarities to their song "Won't Back Down." In an arrangement, between the artists, Petty and Lynne were added to the song's credits and now share in the royalties enjoyed by the tune. Although Smith argues that the plagiarism was unintentional, there were severe consequences and ultimately he had to share the credit for the song.[11]

As these presenters demonstrate, competent speakers use evidence accurately throughout the presentation.

You may have also heard of another similar situation where the artists who wrote the song "Blurred Lines," Robin Thicke, Pharrell Williams, and T.I., were sued by the late Marvin Gaye's estate over plagiarism. The "Blurred Lines" songwriters lost their lawsuit and were ordered to pay the estate $3.7 million. In both of these examples, plagiarism had expensive consequences. While these aren't typical for your experiences in college, plagiarism–intentional or not–can have severe consequences.[12]

As you have seen, plagiarism carries serious consequences. To avoid plagiarism, you must understand exactly what counts as plagiarism. Sometimes, a simple misunderstanding about what constitutes plagiarism can get someone into deep trouble. Students may be unfamiliar with how to cite an original document and simply misunderstand when it is appropriate to give someone else credit. Familiarize yourself with the following types of plagiarism so that you can ensure that you avoid it in your own work.

Types of Plagiarism

Misrepresentation   Misrepresentation occurs when you take something someone else has written and claim it as your own.zThis is the most blatant type of plagiarism, and it is often what people think of when they use the term *plagiarism*. Buying a speech or paper on an Internet site, taking an assignment from a file, or having someone ghostwrite your assignment are all examples of misrepresentation. Also referred to as "cloning," this is the most frequent and problematic type of plagiarism based on a recent worldwide survey.[13]

Misrepresentation is a serious offense within the academic community and the larger community as a whole. Some students who engage in misrepresentation do so because they are dishonest. Other students wait too long to complete an assignment and then realize at the last minute that they have not allowed themselves enough time. They then may take the work of a former student, put their name on it, and turn it in.

Make sure you don't get yourself into a similar situation. You would be better off not turning in the assignment than suffering the consequences of academic dishonesty.

Copy-and-Paste or Cut-and-Paste Plagiarism   Unlike misrepresentation, which involves pirating your entire presentation from one source, **copy-and-paste** or **cut-and-paste plagiarism** consists of taking chunks of information from one or from several sources and patching it together in one document. It can range from a sentence or two to whole paragraphs. Cut-and-paste plagiarism is more common today for two reasons: First, word processors make it easy to cut and paste things into our documents, and second, the Internet provides access to a wealth of information on any topic. Instead of taking the ideas of other individuals and putting them into their own words and providing proper citations, or putting the information in quotation marks and providing proper citations, individuals engaged in cut-and-paste plagiarism paste the text verbatim into the new document and do not give any credit to the original author.

If you take exact wording from a source, the information you quote must be contained within quotation marks and cited within the document or speech where it appears. It is not sufficient to solely cite, in the bibliography, the material you directly copied, although it is necessary. A direct quotation must be cited in the outline or speech as you use it. For example, suppose you wanted to use the following quote in a presentation you were giving. Assume that the quote was going to appear in both your outline and the spoken presentation. To avoid plagiarism, the following citation would be necessary in the outline:

> **Resources on Plagiarism**
>
> ◎ http://owl.english.purdue.edu/owl/ resource/589/01/
> ◎ http://www.indiana.edu/~wts/ pamphlets/plagiarism.shtml

> "ASD begins before the age of 3 and lasts throughout a person's life. It occurs in all racial, ethnic, and socioeconomic groups and is four times more likely to occur in boys than girls." (Centers for Disease Control, 2007, p. 34)

The complete reference to the source of the information would also appear on your reference page or bibliography in American Psychological Association (APA) style. The following spoken citation would be necessary within the speech:

> Quoting a 2007 report from the Centers for Disease Control, "ASD begins before the age of 3 and lasts throughout a person's life. It occurs in all racial, ethnic, and socioeconomic groups and is four times more likely to occur in boys than girls."

Just like your assignments in other classes, your presentations must be combined with research and your own ideas. You should conduct sufficient research and be involved enough with your topic that you can write a presentation that not only conveys information from experts, but also provides your own perspective on the topic. Simply cutting and pasting information from online resources is not good enough. A presentation composed of a series of direct quotes is not your original material, even if all of your quotations are cited properly. You must combine information you find with your own insights and ideas.

Incremental Plagiarism   Sometimes plagiarism occurs because we just fail to give proper credit for small parts of the presentation. This is usually a result of misusing quotations or paraphrasing incorrectly, and is termed **incremental plagiarism.**

Assume that you plan to give a speech on discrimination related to obesity. You find the following quote regarding a study on the American Obesity Association's website:

> Things are not better in higher education, including evidence of a reliable pattern between Body Mass Index (BMI) and financial support for schooling. Results from one study show that normal weight students received more family financial support for college than did overweight students who depended more on financial aid and jobs. This was especially pronounced among women. Differences in family support remained after controlling for the parent's education, income, ethnicity and family size.

You like the quote because it conveys how prevalent and insidious this type of discrimination can be. If you wanted to use this information as it is, you would need to document it with quotations in your outline and introduce it verbally in your speech in the following way:

Sometimes plagiarism occurs because we just fail to give proper credit for small parts of the presentation.

> Quoting the American Obesity Association's website regarding a recent study, "Things are not better …"

You have made it clear that these ideas belong to someone else, and you have given credit to the original author or organization. If you had decided to paraphrase the passage instead, you would simply restate or summarize the ideas in your own words. But you must remember that these ideas are not your own. Even though you have restated the ideas presented on the American Obesity Association's website, they are not original, and you must still give credit to the author.

Here is an example of how that passage may be paraphrased and documented orally during your presentation.

> According to the American Obesity Association's website, discrimination isn't limited to the workplace. A study found that obese college students receive less financial assistance from their families than do comparable students of normal weight. This finding is robust, even after controlling for things such as family education and income.

While the ideas from the website are now presented in your own words, it would still be plagiarism if you failed to credit the website for the ideas. Notice how this phrase begins by stating the originating source. It is clear that the material that follows was derived from information provided in American Obesity Association materials.

You would not use quotation marks in the outline, since you are not quoting directly. But you would still need to cite the originating source. The following example shows how to document the paraphrased ideas presented on the website in your outline:

> According to the American Obesity Association's website, discrimination isn't limited to the workplace. A study found that obese college students receive less financial assistance from their families than do comparable students of normal weight. This finding is robust, even after controlling for things such as family education and income (American Obesity Associations, 2005).

Although incremental plagiarism can be accidental, the consequences are just as severe as if it were intentional. Be careful and err on the side of caution. If you have any questions about how to document a citation, speak to your instructor.

Excessive Collaboration   Sometimes, we ask our friends or family to read something we have written for class and make suggestions for improvement. Other times, however, we sit down and write the assignment with our friend or family member. While the first example is acceptable, the second is considered **excessive collaboration,** and you can no longer claim the work as solely your own.

Several semesters ago, two students from this course were discussing their first persuasive presentation assignment. Since they were both volunteers at the local Humane Society and wanted to persuade more students to volunteer, they decided to share information they found while researching. They even shared their outlines with each other and decided on the best main points and subpoints together. SafeAssign, the plagiarism detector, then flagged those outlines as having similar content and wording. The students were called in to a conference, where they admitted to sharing research and writing the outline together. However, the assignment was not a group assignment, and the students were found guilty of academic dishonesty and punished accordingly.

The previous was an example of excessive collaboration. However, that doesn't mean you can't, for example, give your speech in front of friends and ask for feedback. Just be careful that when you ask for feedback or advice from friends that the work remains your own. Plagiarism can be a serious infraction with undesirable consequences. Try to prevent it at all costs. If you are in doubt about how to cite a reference or how to handle a particular piece of reference material, ask your instructor. It is much better to be safe than sorry.

Collaboration is a great way to get feedback on your work. Just be careful that when you ask for feedback or advice from friends that the work remains your own.

Self-Plagiarism   When Robert Barbato of the E. Philip Saunders College of Business at Rochester Institute of Technology was accused of plagiarizing his own work, he said: "I can't plagiarize myself–those are my own words."[14]

But not everyone agrees. Self-plagiarism has become a controversial topic. As the name indicates, self-plagiarism occurs when an author re-uses previously published material without revealing that it is not new. A more common name is text recycling.[15] Portions of text from a previous paper, article, or publication of any kind are included in a new paper, article, or publication. No references are provided to the previous publication.

This has become an issue, especially in the scientific and academic communities. Some scientists argue that because they study the same content over and over, it is only natural that they will repeat themselves sometimes. They say it is unavoidable. And, since they spent time discovering how to best relay the information the first time, there is no need to change the wording.

However, some believe this is an ethical situation and disagree. In fact, more and more academic and technical journals are actually pulling articles that have been found to contain self-plagiarism.[16] And the advent of text similarity software paired with an increase in electronic publishing has made it easier to identify copied text. Most journals now subscribe to such plagiarism detection software. Still, many publications are just now realizing that more concrete guidelines need to be established for self-plagiarism.

Self-plagiarism can call other aspects of a person's work into question. In 2011, up and coming science jour-nalist and *New Yorker* writer Jonah Lehrer was accused of self-plagiarizing. He was accused of using passages from older books and articles in newer ones. While the *New Yorker* kept him on with a reprimand, an ensuing investigation triggered by the self-plagiarism revealed he has also fabricated some aspects of articles. He was then fired.

"Where most of the world seems to be getting a better handle on the concept of traditional plagiarism, with self-plagiarism, much like collusion, there's still a lot of debate, discussion and resolution to be had," said Jonathan Bailey, a copyright and plagiarism consultant who writes for *Plagiarism Today*.[17]

Self-plagiarism is prohibited in COM114. This means that you cannot misrepresent work you have previously done as being new for 114. No parts of outlines or presentations from previous semesters or other classes can be used again in 114.

Additional Considerations Regarding Plagiarism   Plagiarism isn't limited to written words. Copyright issues are also important considerations. The use of graphs, pictures, charts, and so on can also present ownership issues when utilizing PowerPoint or some other presentation software during a speech. Unless you create a graphic yourself or it is owned by the company or group you represent, you must cite the source for that graphic on the slide. If you adapt a graphic from any source, you must state in the citation that the graphic is "based on" or "adapted from" a given source.[18] Careful attention to these details should help you protect yourself from any accusations of plagiarism or misuse.

As we have discussed, ethics are extremely important to good presentational speaking, whether we are talking about collecting supporting materials or about giving proper credit to those sources. Another ethical issue similar to plagiarism is **fabrication.** You fabricate when you make up support for your presentations. You fabricate when you manipulate support to benefit your argument. You fabricate when you include citations to non-existent sources. You fabricate when you attribute material to a source knowing that information is not found in that source. You fabricate when you include testimony from non-existent interviewees. You fabricate when you pad your bibliography with references you did not use. And you fabricate when you present as factual information you have manipulated to serve the purposes of your speech.

In a previous semester, a student in this course wanted to give a speech on why homework was actually harmful to college students. She presented a lot of statistical support from several sources on why too much homework was harmful to elementary-age students. Her instructor informed the student that this was an invalid analogy: Elementary-age students and college-age students were not similar. When the student gave her presentation, she still included the statistical support; she simply neglected to mention that it was about elementary-age children. This was unethical, and a form of fabrication.

Plagiarism can be a serious infraction with undesirable consequences. Try to prevent it at all costs.

Ethical issues have consequences for you as a speaker and for your audience. As an effective speaker, you should make every effort to be ethical in every aspect of the presentation process. At each step in the deci-sion-making process, ask yourself: Is this the most ethical decision I can make? If not, reconsider.

The Presentation Process

Now that you know what presentational speaking is, why it is important, and what makes it effective, it is time to examine an overview of the presentation process. Just how do you write and deliver a successful presentation? The following section presents a brief introduction to the steps in this process. It does not address everything you need to know about making good presentations, but it will get you started.

Selecting the Topic

Sometimes, you are asked to deliver a presentation based on specific knowledge that you possess. In this particular situation, the topic is selected for you. The tricky part in this situation is adapting the topic to the particular audience that you will address. Imagine that you are an IBM representative making a sales presentation to the client's engineering department; your presentation would look very different from the same presentation made to the accounting department. Or, at least, it should look very different, if you have adapted to the various needs of these diverse audiences. After all, these two audiences have different needs, interests, and motivations, and the two presentations should reflect these differences.

Sometimes, however, topic choice is left up to the speaker. In this class, you will have to address the parameters of the assignment, but your topic will be more or less up to you to determine. When faced with this situation, you have to consider two things. First, you have to choose a topic that will be interesting and important to your audience, and second, you have to adapt this topic to meet their needs. More detail on this process is provided in Chapter 2.

Determining Your Purpose

Once you have selected your topic, you should determine exactly what you want to achieve with your presentation. Do you want to increase the audience's understanding of the topic, or do you want to encourage them to try something new? You need to concentrate on what is realistic for you to achieve in one presentation and then focus all of your energy and preparation into achieving that goal.

Researching Your Presentation

At this point, you need to determine what type of evidence is required to reach your goal. Answers to the following questions can help you determine what type of evidence you might need. Exactly what type of audience are you facing? Are they hostile, captive, motivated, knowledgeable, and so on? What types of evidence are they going to find most compelling and useful? Will narratives be more persuasive, or would statistics be more convincing?

All claims and arguments need to be supported by evidence. By performing a thorough audience analysis, you can have a much better idea of what type of supporting evidence is going to work best in your particular situation.

The Presentation Process

Select the Topic
- Pick a topic based on your interests, expertise, and the audience's interest.
- Adapt that topic to the specific needs of your audience.

Determine the Purpose
- Write your specific purpose statement.
- Write your thesis statement.

Research the Presentation
- Determine what evidence you need to reach your goal or purpose.
- Collect a variety of types of supporting material.

Organize the Presentation
- Decide on your main points.
- Choose an organizational structure.
- Arrange supporting material.
- Create a preparation outline.

Practice the Presentation
- Construct a speaking outline.
- Refine delivery.
- Check the length of the presentation.
- Practice in front of an audience.

Organizing Your Presentation

Once you have collected your supporting evidence, you are ready to decide on an organizational structure. Using a framework or an outline, you begin developing main points and arranging your supporting material. After you have completed the body of the presentation, you craft the introduction, form the conclusion, and complete the reference list.

Practicing the Presentation

At this point in the presentation process, you are ready to construct a speaking outline and begin the practice sessions. One of the most important details to assess at this point is whether or not the presentation is adhering to the time constraints. Practice as much and as often as you can. Rehearsal in front of an audience is one of the best methods of practice. Speakers who practice their presentations enjoy more success.

Now that you have an overview of the process, you are almost ready to begin writing your first presentation. However, one final issue needs to be addressed: nervousness. Feeling some amount of stage fright is normal. After reading the following section on communication anxiety, you should be ready to jump in and get started.

Anxiety and Speaking

Many people report feeling anxious about speaking in front of an audience. It is an extremely common fear. In fact, Mark Twain has supposedly said, "There are two kinds of speakers, those who are nervous and those who are liars." There is probably some truth to this statement. Everybody gets a little nervous when they have to face an audience. The *Washington Business Journal* reports that the fear of public speaking has enjoyed a top spot in Gallup polls for years. Many people report being more frightened of giving a speech than of heights, spiders, snakes, thunderstorms, or even death. In fact, people report that they would rather work math problems in front of others than speak in front of them.[19] As you can see, fear of delivering a presentation is a normal anxiety. So if you feel anxious, you aren't alone. The good news is that there is a large body of research devoted to this topic. And the research has identified many methods that you can use to manage this fear. The first step in reducing anxiety, however, is understanding exactly what it is. So, let's start there.

What Is Communication Apprehension?

Communication apprehension has been defined as "the fear or anxiety associated with real or anticipated communication with others."[23] As you can see from this definition, the fear of public speaking is just one small part of communication apprehension. Individuals can feel anxious about communicating across a wide range of contexts. Some of us may feel more anxious in communication situations that involve one-on-one interactions. Others may not feel anxious while delivering a presentation to a large group of people but are nervous about communicating with a small group of individuals. Still others may feel anxious when thinking about almost any communicative event. So, as you can see, communication apprehension is broad and extends across a wide array of contexts and situations. However, we are only interested in the apprehension related to the public speaking context, and so we will focus our energy on this area.

You can experience communication apprehension in one of two ways. First, the communication apprehension you experience may be trait-like. With this type of communication apprehension, you are likely to feel anxious when delivering a presentation of any kind, to any type of audience, under any circumstance.[24] In other words, public speaking in general makes you anxious.

> **Fear of delivering a presentation is a normal anxiety. So if you feel anxious, you aren't alone.**

The second type of apprehension you can face is situational. This means the current speaking situation makes you nervous, not public speaking in general. There is something unique about this particular speaking situation that makes you nervous or anxious. Maybe you are a little less prepared than usual and so you feel more anxious, or the outcome of the presentation may have serious consequences and so you feel more nervous than usual. Perhaps the audience is particularly knowledgeable about your topic and that makes you a bit anxious. You are anxious because of something unique to the situation.

You can assess your level of communication apprehension by filling out the Personal Report of Public Speaking Anxiety (PRPSA) developed by communication researcher James McCroskey. It can give you a very good idea of how much anxiety you feel across speaking contexts.

Regardless of the type of apprehension you experience, there are methods for addressing it. Next, we discuss the four most popular methods.

Addressing Communication Apprehension ——————

Skills Training

Skills training, or courses such as this one, can actually alleviate anxiety for some people. One source of anxiety results from what researchers call a skills deficit. If you perceive that you lack the appropriate skills necessary to succeed in a speaking situation, you will likely experience some anxiety.[25] For example, if you are worried about your ability to organize a presentation and deliver it dynamically, you will naturally be nervous when making the presentation. By taking a course such as this, you are eliminating the source of the problem—the skills deficit—by acquiring the appropriate skills. Once you have the ability to learn the theory and guidelines, practice speeches, and receive feedback, you will feel trained and competent in your ability to effectively deliver a successful presentation.

If you experience anxiety due to a skills deficit, then you are in the right place. The knowledge and experience you will acquire in this course may help alleviate your fear and allow you to feel comfortable facing speaking situations after completing this course. For skills training to be effective, however, there must be a high level of commitment on the participant's behalf.[20]

Systematic Desensitization

Systematic desensitization is the most popular method used in the communication field to treat communication apprehension.[21] It is designed "to alter the negative and unconscious association between some aversive stimulus (e.g., public speaking) and anxiety."[22]

Systematic desensitization involves two primary steps. First, a series of deep muscular relaxation techniques are taught. Second, visualization is used to simulate the participation in various communication situations while in a deep state of relaxation. The visualization progressively becomes more and more threatening. Once you can remain in a relaxed state while envisioning a scenario, you may move on to a more threatening one. For example, imagine delivering a presentation to your best friend. If you can remain calm while picturing this scenario, you can move to the next one and the next, which increasingly become more threatening. The last situation you are asked to visualize is the most threatening and would look something like this: "You are ready to appear on a television show and give a speech, but you lost your notes."[26]

Systematic desensitization is extremely effective both in the short term and over time. Studies have concluded that 90% of the individuals who receive this treatment reduce their communication apprehension levels. Of those participants who are extremely apprehensive, 80% report that after completing this treatment, they are no longer categorized as highly apprehensive.[27]

Personal Report of Public Speaking Anxiety (PRPSA)

Directions: This instrument is composed of 34 statements concerning feelings about communicating with other people. Indicate the degree to which the statements apply to you by marking whether you (1) strongly disagree, (2) disagree, (3) are undecided, (4) agree, or (5) strongly agree with each statement. Work quickly; just record your first impression.

1. _____ While preparing for giving a speech, I feel tense and nervous.
2. _____ I feel tense when I see the words *speech* and *public speech* on a course outline when studying.
3. _____ My thoughts become confused and jumbled when I am giving a speech.
4. _____ Right after giving a speech, I feel that I have had a pleasant experience.
5. _____ I get anxious when I think about a speech coming up.
6. _____ I have no fear of giving a speech.
7. _____ Although I am nervous just before starting a speech, I soon settle down after starting and feel calm and comfortable.
8. _____ I look forward to giving a speech.
9. _____ When the instructor announces a speaking assignment in class, I can feel myself getting tense.
10. _____ My hands tremble when I am giving a speech.
11. _____ I feel relaxed while giving a speech.
12. _____ I enjoy preparing for a speech.
13. _____ I am in constant fear of forgetting what I prepared to say.
14. _____ I get anxious if someone asks me something about my topic that I do not know.
15. _____ I face the prospect of giving a speech with confidence.
16. _____ I feel that I am in complete possession of myself while giving a speech.
17. _____ My mind is clear when giving a speech.
18. _____ I do not dread giving a speech.
19. _____ I perspire just before starting a speech.
20. _____ My heart beats very fast just as I start a speech.
21. _____ I experience considerable anxiety while sitting in the room just before my speech starts.
22. _____ Certain parts of my body feel very tense and rigid while giving a speech.
23. _____ Realizing that only a little time remains in a speech makes me very tense and anxious.
24. _____ While giving a speech, I know I can control my feelings of tension and stress.

Personal Report of Public Speaking Anxiety (PRPSA)—Continued

25. _____ I breathe faster just before starting a speech.
26. _____ I feel comfortable and relaxed in the hour or so just before giving a speech.
27. _____ I do poorer on speeches because I am anxious.
28. _____ I feel anxious when the teacher announces the date of a speaking assignment.
29. _____ When I make a mistake while giving a speech, I find it hard to concentrate on the parts that follow.
30. _____ During an important speech, I experience a feeling of helplessness building up inside me.
31. _____ I have trouble falling asleep the night before a speech.
32. _____ My heart beats very fast while I present a speech.
33. _____ I feel anxious while waiting to give my speech.
34. _____ While giving a speech, I get so nervous I forget facts I really know.

To determine your score on the PRPSA, complete the following steps:

1. **Step 1:** Add the scores for items 1, 2, 3, 5, 9, 10, 13, 14, 19, 20, 21, 22, 23, 25, 27, 28, 29, 30, 31, 32, 33, and 34.
2. **Step 2:** Add the scores for items 4, 6, 7, 8, 11, 12, 15, 16, 17, 18, 24, and 26.
3. Complete the following formula: **PRPSA = 72 – Total from Step 2 + Total from Step 1**
4. Your score on the PRPSA can range between 34 and 170:

34–84   indicates a very low anxiety about public speaking.

85–92   indicates a moderately low level of anxiety about public speaking.

93–110   suggests moderate anxiety in most public speaking situations but not so severe that the individual cannot cope and be a successful speaker.

111–119   suggests a moderately high anxiety about public speaking. People with such scores will tend to avoid public speaking.

120–170   indicates a very high anxiety about public speaking. People with these scores will go to considerable lengths to avoid all types of public speaking situations.

You can also take the assessment online at: http://www.wadsworth.com/communication_d/templates/student_resources/053455170X_sellnow/psa/main_frame.htm.[28]

Cognitive Restructuring

Another method for reducing communication anxiety is **cognitive restructuring** or **cognitive modification.** This method assumes that individuals' fear of public speaking stems from irrational thoughts they have about themselves and their ability to perform effectively. These irrational thoughts or beliefs are attacked and replaced with more appropriate thoughts. Once the illogical thoughts disappear, so, too, should the communication apprehension.[29]

Cognitive restructuring is administered in five or six one-hour sessions that extend across several days or weeks. The treatment typically involves four steps. First, participants are introduced to the method. Second, participants are asked to identify their negative self-statements or illogical beliefs. Some examples might be "I can't ever think about anything to talk about when making my presentations," or "The audience will find me boring." The leader of the session explains the illogical nature of these thoughts to participants. Third, participants are asked to replace these thoughts with more appropriate ones: "I have something valuable to offer to my audience," and "My audience will find my presentation topic interesting." Finally, the participants are required to practice these coping strategies or replacement messages.[30]

Research regarding cognitive restructuring has demonstrated that it is useful in reducing self-reported levels of apprehension. Its success rates are similar to those of systematic desensitization.[31]

Current research indicates that a combination of these three treatments—skills training, systematic desensitization, and cognitive restructuring—is the most effective treatment in reducing self-reported communication apprehension.[32]

Visualization

The final method for reducing apprehension is **visualization.**[33] The theory behind this treatment is that some speakers exhibit anxiety because they simply cannot envision themselves being successful in a speaking situation.[34] Visualization asks participants to imagine the day on which they are going to speak. They are told to imagine the entire day, from the moment they get up in the morning to the moment they finish their presentation. They are to imagine that everything they do that day goes extremely well. Participants are even asked to imagine being congratulated by their classmates or business colleagues for their successful presentation.[35]

Visualization has also been found to be effective in reducing self-reported communication apprehension.[36] Visualization techniques are also associated with enhanced speaking performance. Students who were exposed to visualization were perceived as less rigid than students who did not receive visualization treatments.[37] However, this method is best suited to individuals whose mental-imaging ability is high. These individuals are able to visualize themselves in certain situations more easily than others.[38]

Communication apprehension related to public speaking is a common phenomenon experienced by almost all of us. However, it can be problematic for individuals who experience it at high levels. By using the techniques described in this chapter, you can begin to cope with your fear.

Spotlight on Research

Virtual Visualization

Another type of visualization is currently being implemented to assist anxious speakers. This type of visualization takes advantage of virtual reality. Virtual reality actually immerses an individual in the speaking situation to simulate the experience. Current research seems to indicate that the fear of public speaking can be reduced if individuals are exposed to "virtual audiences" and asked to deliver presentations to avatars, or virtual audience members. Anxious speakers can reduce their apprehension after as few as four exposures to the virtual audience. One study found that virtual reality therapy worked better than simple visualization alone at increasing self-confidence and reducing public speaking anxiety.

Virtual visualization has been found to be as successful as cognitive behavioral therapy or cognitive restructuring. However, therapy has a high drop-out rate. One study found that half of the participants seeking therapy for communication anxiety dropped out of therapy, while none of the participants enrolled in the virtual reality treatment dropped out. At the moment, it shows real promise in its treatment for anxiety.[39]

Conclusion

Presentational speaking is vital to your organizational success. Remember, the guidelines outlined in this book are appropriate for both public speaking and presentational speaking situations. Regardless of your speaking situation, a presentation that is goal-directed, audience-centered, and ethical has a good chance of being successful. By understanding what counts as plagiarism, you have a much better chance of avoiding this kind of ethical dilemma. The presentational speaking process is quite manageable as long as you take the time to prepare. Even those of us who experience a little stage fright can deliver extremely effective presentations if we follow the guidelines discussed in this chapter.

Key Terms

Characteristics of
effective speaking

Cognitive restructuring
(or modification)

Communication
apprehension

Cut-and-paste plagiarism

Excessive collaboration

Fabrication

Incremental plagiarism

Misrepresentation

Plagiarism

Presentational speaking

Skills training

Visualization

CHAPTER 2

Audience Analysis

Objectives

After reading this chapter, you should be able to

- ◎ explain why audience analysis is important;
- ◎ explain and apply demographic audience analysis;
- ◎ explain and apply psychological audience analysis;
- ◎ explain and apply environmental audience analysis;
- ◎ explain and apply learning styles;
- ◎ adapt to different environmental constraints when speaking;
- ◎ use direct and indirect methods to gather material about an audience;
- ◎ explain how a speaker can adapt to the audience before the presentation; and
- ◎ explain how a speaker can adapt to the audience during the presentation.

Famed director Quentin Tarantino is no stranger to public speaking. But that doesn't mean he doesn't make mistakes sometimes.

During the 2016 Golden Globe Awards ceremony, Tarantino was giving a speech of acceptance for "Best Original Score–Movie" on behalf of absent composer Ennio Morricone, who had composed the music for Tarantino's movie "The Hateful Eight." In his speech, Tarantino praised Morricone by saying, "When I say favorite composer, I don't mean movie composer–that ghetto. I'm talking about Mozart, I'm talking about Beethoven, I'm talking about Schubert. That's who I'm talking about."

Many in the diverse audience quickly reacted unfavorably to his use of the word "ghetto." Presenter and actor Jamie Foxx, an African-American, even referenced it when he returned to the microphone. In addition, social media lit up with Tarantino's decision to use "a racist term."

Technically, Tarantino used the word correctly. Ghetto can mean "an isolated or segregrated group." Academics have been known to use the word when referring to disciplines that don't receive enough funding. But Tarantino was not at an academic conference. He was at an awards show that was televised worldwide to millions of people. And he failed to account for how a diverse audience might react to his use of a word that to most references a physical location and oppression. His message of praise for his composer was lost amid the furor.

The presentations you make may not be as public or as open to criticism as those of an entertainer. But you have the same goal: You don't want your main message to be lost because of a mistake, such as word selection, that could have been avoided with some forethought. It is still imperative that you analyze your audiences. It is fundamental to your success as a speaker. The following chapter will provide guidelines and recommendations that will aid in the analysis of your audiences.

The Importance of Audience Analysis

As mentioned in Chapter 1, **audience analysis** is essential to a successful presentation. You have little, if any, chance of achieving your presentational goals if you don't adapt your message to the needs of your audience. As a speaker, you need to be able to answer the following questions about your audience members:

◎ What is the position of the audience on my topic?
◎ What are the interests of my audience?
◎ How knowledgeable is the audience about my topic?
◎ Why is my audience here?
◎ What are the demographics of my audience?

The answers to these questions help you craft a message tailored to your specific audience. By focusing on the audience's needs and specific characteristics and attitudes, you have a much better chance of achieving the purpose of your presentation.

Good audience analysis allows you to achieve your goals because it assists you in identifying with your audience. **Identification** is the process of expressing ideas and beliefs that you and your audience share.[1] It builds common ground and helps you establish a relationship with your audience. Being audience-centered also ensures that you won't alienate or offend your audience. We live in a diverse world with people from many different backgrounds. Acknowledging this diversity shows that you respect your audience and that you have high ethical standards.

Word selection is closely related to that identification process. It signals how you identify your audience, and it may affect how you are identified by your audience.

First, it's very important to make sure you are choosing words that your audience can understand. You have to make a judgment early on whether the audience members are capable of understanding the words you will be using. In this way, you are identifying your audience as either expert, or novice, or somewhere in between. Here you will be making an assumption as to their expertise based on your analysis. Nothing will lose an audience more than to talk over their heads. If you think an audience may struggle with certain words, construct your presentation in such a way as to avoid language that may cause a problem in understanding. By the same token, you don't want to offend an audience with your word selection. Experts don't need you to "dumb down" your language choices.

Second, **word selection** can affect your credibility as a speaker. If you use special terminology well, your audience will identify you as an expert.[2] However, if you have difficulties using a term (including pronunciation), it could label you as incompetent or amateurish in your audience's mind.

It is important to note that, although you must adapt your message to your audience, you don't simply tell audience members what you think they want to hear. It is not necessary for you to change the focus of your message so that your audience automatically agrees with you. Nor is it necessary to present a point of view that you don't believe. But you do want to present a message that your audience can "hear." By understanding audience members' positions, beliefs, and attitudes, you can construct messages that will allow audiences to listen and think about what you have to say, rather than shutting down and tuning you out.

Three types of audience analysis will aid in your planning process: demographic analysis, psychological analysis, and environmental analysis. Each is described in the following sections.

Demographic Audience Analysis

One method of analyzing an audience is to examine the demographics that characterize a particular audience and then adapt the presentation to the characteristics associated with those demographics. **Demographics** are the traits that describe your population or audience. Demographics may include age, gender, religion, geographical location, group membership, sexual orientation, ethnicity, occupation, and many other characteristics.

At one time, demographic audience analysis was the primary tool used in assessing an audience. However, we now know that we cannot make accurate assumptions about individuals just because they belong to a particular group. Just because an audience member is female doesn't mean that she enjoys decorating or shopping. You simply cannot make those types of assumptions. Placing too much emphasis on demographic audience analysis can lead you to stereotype your audience. If audience members feel stereotyped, they will likely react negatively to your presentation. However, if used with caution, demographic audience analysis can inform certain aspects of your presentation.

Let's examine a few of these categories in order to understand how you may utilize them to prepare your presentations. While there are many other demographic categories that this chapter does not address, the analyses of these other categories are similar to the examples discussed here.

Age

Age is one of the most helpful of the demographic categories. It is important for you to stop and think: "What are the ages of the individuals who will make up my audience?" We can predict with certainty what events a particular cohort has experienced. For example, we know that young people growing up in the late 1920s and early 1930s were deeply affected by the Great Depression. Therefore, any presentation concerning finances would have to take that event and the effects on that generation into account when putting together the presentation.

> By knowing the age of your audience members, you also can predict basic concerns they may have.

First, we can use age to predict with certainty what events a particular cohort has experienced. For example, we know that experiences such as 9/11 have a deep effect on a generation of individuals. Events such as these shape the way they view life. To individuals who experienced 9/11, national security is a big issue. So if you were planning to speak to a group of 9/11-era individuals on relaxing airport safety regulations, you might need to adjust your presentation to address their specific fears. Second, age can be used to gauge need. Say you were planning a presentation about managing money. Audience age would play a big role in your topic selection. A college-age audience might be looking for advice on how to pay off student loans. An older audience might want tips for how to save for a house down payment.

By knowing the age of your audience members, you also can predict basic concerns they may have. For example, college students planning vacations in March or April have an interest in spring-break vacations. They are interested in "hot spots" and economical destinations. An audience of professionals planning vacations in March or April is probably not interested in this type of vacation planning. In fact, this age group would probably want to avoid any "hot" spring-break destination. Therefore, any presentation made by a travel agent would have to take these differences into account.

Age is such an important variable in adapting to audiences that Beloit College publishes a "Mindset List" for each entering freshman class. This list is compiled to help professors relate to their students. It explains how they may view the world differently from individuals born in different age cohorts because of changes in the world. (You can visit this list at http://www.beloit.edu/mindset/.)

Sex and Gender

Sex, which is biologically assigned at conception, consists of the physiological and anatomical characteristics that make someone male or female. There are particular topics that are relevant to only one sex or the other. For example, only men can get prostate cancer. Only women can be physically pregnant. However, these topics can be adapted so that there is relevant information for each sex in your audience. For example, Jill gave a speech on breast cancer. Although this is a disease that normally only affects females, Jill presented some evidence about male breast cancer as well, thereby making her speech relevant to both sexes in her audience.

Gender is more complicated. Gender is more psychological and emotional than physical and refers to an identity that is socially constructed throughout an individual's lifespan.[3] Research on gender indicates that individuals today can feel masculine in some aspects of their lives and feminine in other aspects. So although an individual's sex may be female, she may approach relationships in life with more traditional masculine behaviors. For example, she may be highly independent and less emotionally expressive. Therefore, simply approaching an all-female audience with the assumption that they all view relationships in the same way or feel the same way about domestic responsibilities is a mistake. The gender differences in this all-female audience would cause them to react very differently to this topic. As a speaker, it is important that you are aware of these issues and refrain from alienating certain segments of your audience by stereotyping them based on gender differences.

Geographical Location

The part of the country or world an individual comes from is also part of demographic audience analysis. Individuals are often characterized by certain traits, based on where they were born or raised. For example, people from the southern region of the U.S. are assumed to have a variety of attributes that individuals from other parts of the United States are not assumed to possess. Southerners are often thought of as slow-talking, conservative, warm, and friendly, among other characteristics. Adapting your presentation to a group of Southerners based on your stereotyped expectations would be a big mistake. People living or raised in one geographical location are extremely diverse. While it may be safe to assume that individuals who live along the Gulf Coast would be concerned with hurricane safety, it would not be safe to assume they will all vote Republican or are conservative.

Group Affiliation

Group affiliation is another demographic that may inform your presentation preparation. If it is possible to discern what groups your audience members belong to, you will have a better chance of reaching them. Belonging to particular groups may indicate interests or particular positions on topics.

> You have to respect differences and approach your presentation in a way that respects diverse views and opinions.

For example, you may learn that many of your audience members belong to the American Legion. This is a veterans' organization committed to community service. Membership includes males and females who have served in the U.S. military during wartime. Learning that a large proportion of your audience belongs to the American Legion could be extremely helpful. This is a patriotic organization. It would be safe to assume that most members would not support burning the American flag. This group is also extremely supportive of the military and would be unlikely to support antiwar sentiment.

Sometimes, you get lucky and are asked to speak to a group that shares an affiliation. For example, you may be asked to present an informative talk on increasing study skills to a group of fraternity pledges on campus. Knowing that this group shares this affiliation will tell you a great deal about them. You can use this information to tailor your message to the needs of this particular audience and their situation. This adaptation makes the information in your presentation more relevant and beneficial to them.

More often than not, the individuals that make up your audience will belong to many diverse groups and share little in common in terms of group affiliation. In that case, you have to respect differences and approach your presentation in a way that respects diverse views and opinions.

Socioeconomic Factors

Socioeconomic factors include occupation, income, and education, all of which can influence the way an audience responds to your message.

For example, individuals' occupations can consume a large portion of their identity, affecting the way they think about certain topics and determining the types of interests they have. A group of teachers will have different concerns than a group of doctors regarding managed care. Doctors are interested in how managed care affects their practice, while teachers are more concerned with how managed care will affect their insurance premiums and the level of care they receive from their physicians. Therefore, knowing this information in advance can facilitate the adaptation of your presentation.

Common Demographics Used in Audience Analysis

- Group affiliation
- Age
- Sex
- Geographical location
- Gender
- Socioeconomic factors

The amount of income individuals earn can also have an impact on their attitudes, beliefs, and behaviors. Imagine giving a tax-planning seminar to a group of individuals who earn less than $35,000 a year vs. a group of individuals who earn over $200,000 a year. This difference in income would greatly affect the material you address in your presentation because tax planning guidelines differ, depending on income. While someone with a large income may be interested in tax shelters, this type of tax planning would not be appropriate for someone with a lower income.

Knowing the amount of education audience members have can also be beneficial in adapting your message to fit their interests. Knowing, for example, that most of your audience did not complete college can help you adapt your message. If you are presenting material on saving for your children's college education, certain aspects of the college experience would need to be explained to this audience—for example, that the cost of textbooks is not included in the cost of tuition. Presenting the same topic to a group of individuals with undergraduate and master's degrees would be different. They already know the ins and outs of higher education, and this background information would not be necessary for them to understand your message.

As with any other demographic category, you should be careful not to stereotype audience members based on their level of education. For example, just because you are speaking to a group of individuals with Ph.D.s, it is not safe to assume that they all enjoy classical music or listen to National Public Radio. The same can be said for a group of individuals who did not attend college; they may enjoy and be patrons of the arts, even though their educational background may not indicate such.

One aspect of demographic audience analysis that cannot be overstated is that you should be extremely careful about stereotyping your audience. Nothing is more patronizing and alienating to audience members than to feel they have been marginalized. So, while it is important that you know about demographic audience analysis, use it with caution. Some of the other types of analyses discussed in this chapter may prove more useful to you.

Psychological Audience Analysis

In the previous section, we discussed how you might adapt your presentation based on the traits or group memberships of audience members. There is more to audience analysis than simply examining demographics, however. Understanding why audience members are there, how they think about your topic, and how motivated they are about your material are all important **psychological factors.** A good psychological audience analysis asks, what attitudes do audience members hold in respect to my topic? That is, how favorable, or unfavorable, is their reaction to my position? What is their motivation for attending my presentation, and how much do they know about my topic? By answering these questions, you can better anticipate and adapt to their interests and needs. In the long run, you will be more successful as a speaker if you engage in a thorough psychological audience analysis.

Ethically Speaking

The Dangers of Demographics

As discussed in the chapter, stereotyping audience members based on demographics can be patronizing and offensive. But alienating your audience isn't the only problem it can cause. Analyzing an audience strictly in terms of demographics can also raise ethical concerns. Sometimes, we omit or limit certain types of information when addressing specific groups because we assume that the information we have to share is irrelevant to them or they just wouldn't be interested. Often, this overlooked information can have real consequences for a particular group of individuals.

This exact situation has recently been covered in the news media concerning older women and their health. Sexually transmitted diseases are on the rise among older women.[4] One speculation for this increase is lack of health campaigns or sex education programs that target this particular demographic or age group. Often, we make the assumption that older women aren't engaging in sexual activity and if they are, they already understand the rules for "safe sex." So, public health officials didn't believe that this group had a need for this information. Obviously, this wasn't the case and women's health is suffering because they lack the information they need to make educated decisions in this area of their lives. Older women report that they do not have the skills to discuss "safe sex" with their partners or with their physicians and they need information on how to have these tough conversations.[5]

So, as this example illustrates, it is important that you carefully consider demographic analyses in constructing your presentations to ensure that you make decisions that don't alienate your audience or limit information that may have important implications for their health or well-being.

Audience Attitudes

One of the most important aspects of audience analysis is assessing what attitudes audience members hold about the information you are planning to present. An attitude is an individual's evaluation of an object, event, person, policy, and so on.[6] In other words, attitudes express how positively or negatively you feel about a particular object, person, policy, and so on. Here are some examples of attitudes:

- ◎ My university's course registration system is cutting-edge and extremely efficient.
- ◎ Daily exercise is beneficial to well-being.
- ◎ College internships are excellent methods to secure permanent employment.
- ◎ Rain harvesting is good for the environment.

Attitudes are different from values. **Values** are ideals that we hope to achieve and underlie specific attitudes.[7] They are more global and abstract than attitudes.[8] Examples of values include equity, wisdom, democracy, and justice. These values then shape the attitudes we hold about affirmative action, assisted suicide, or gay marriage, for example. For instance, an individual's views on justice and equity might predispose him or her to have a positive attitude toward policies that allow for gay marriage.

> **Attitudes express how positively or negatively you feel about an object, person, policy, and so on.**

At this point you may be asking yourself, why should I be concerned with attitudes? You are probably thinking that you are more interested in the actual behaviors of a particular audience. After all, you want a particular audience to vote for your candidate or buy your company's software. Your concern is understandable. However, attitudes and behaviors are intertwined and actually work together. In order to affect the behaviors of audience members, you must first understand their underlying attitudes.

Let's briefly examine this relationship. Research has demonstrated that we are most comfortable when our behaviors and attitudes are consistent.[9] For example, if we hold the attitude that daily exercise is healthy, and we engage in a regular exercise routine, we feel good. However, if we hold this same attitude but fail to exercise regularly, this mismatch between our attitude and behavior can be psychologically uncomfortable. When this mismatch occurs, we are motivated to change either our attitude or behavior so that they are more aligned or consistent. So, many times, if we can predict audience members' attitudes on a given issue, we may also be able to predict their behaviors.[10]

Let's examine how this might work in terms of speaking. Let's assume that you want to increase usage of the campus co-recreational facilities. You are going to speak to a campus service organization, and you hope to persuade organization members to take advantage of the many services the co-rec provides. You know from your audience analysis that only 15% of audience members are currently involved in an exercise regimen. You also know that audience members believe that exercise is good for them or healthy. That's where you start—with this positive attitude toward exercise. Reinforce the attitude that audience members hold about health and physical activity. Next, emphasize the difference between their attitude and their current behavior. Explicitly point out that although they believe in the exercise/health-benefit relationship, few of them are actually engaging in exercise. Then call for them to attend a class or event at the co-recreational facility on campus. This attitude/behavior issue is further discussed in Chapter 9, but for now it helps us understand the role of attitudes in relation to audience analysis.

Audience members' attitudes regarding your position as a speaker can be placed in three broad categories. Sometimes, audience members are favorable to your position and in complete agreement with the ideas you present. Other times, their attitudes are in direct opposition to your own. And sometimes, they have yet to form any attitude at all on your topic. Whether you are delivering an informative or persuasive presentation, there are strategies for dealing with each of these types of audiences, as described in the section that follows.

> ... attitudes and behaviors are intertwined and actually work together. To affect the behaviors of audience members, you must first understand their underlying attitudes.

Favorable Audiences

The easiest audience to face is a favorable audience. Speakers are usually relieved to learn that they will be addressing an audience that holds attitudes similar to their own regarding the topic at hand. Audiences who share our attitudes are called favorable or friendly audiences. Sometimes, speakers wonder why they should even address a favorable audience. After all, you already share the same beliefs. However, there are many reasons to address a favorable audience, as discussed below.

Increase Commitment   With a favorable audience, your goal is to reinforce your position, and thereby, the position of audience members (see Chapter 10). They are already on your side; you just want to reinvigorate them. Basically, you act as a cheerleader explaining why audience members are right to feel or act the way they do. They are already excited about the issue on which you will speak, so you want to reaffirm their commitment and keep them motivated. This is what typically occurs at campaign rallies. The audience members already support the candidate or the party, and the goal of the rally is to keep them committed or even increase their commitment.

Inoculation   Speaking to a favorable audience is also a chance to protect audience members against counterpersuasion. We are bombarded with messages every day. Some of those messages may run in opposition to the attitudes we currently hold. Therefore, they have the potential to move us from our current positions. To guard against this process, remind audience members of the strengths related to their own position or attitudes, and demonstrate the weaknesses in opposition arguments. This process is called inoculation.[11] Inoculation is extremely powerful. Sometimes, people agree with you but haven't heard other positions. You have the opportunity to educate them in a way that makes them both more informed but also more confident in their current belief that they share with you. You see inoculation at work in political campaigns. At campaign rallies, candidates often make statements such as, "My opponent will tell you I am weak on crime. Let me show you the evidence that clearly proves this statement is false." These politicians have now inoculated their supporters against their opponent's argument, should they be exposed to it at a later time.

Increase Involvement   Addressing a friendly audience is also an opportunity to get audience members more involved in the issue. Maybe they hold consistent attitudes with your position but don't engage in any relevant behaviors. Take this opportunity to get them to engage in consistent behaviors. For example, assume that audience members are supportive of your particular candidate but don't currently volunteer in your candidate's campaign. Use your presentation to motivate your audience to become directly involved. Ask them to hand out fliers, make telephone calls, or simply run errands. It can be a great opportunity to strengthen their involvement and commitment.

Hostile Audiences

Sometimes, audience members are on your side, and sometimes, they just don't see things the way you do because they hold different attitudes. Audiences who are unfavorable to you or your position are called **hostile audiences.** None of us wants to face a hostile audience, but sometimes it is unavoidable. The good news is that research has shown that individuals perform better when they perceive the audience to be nonsupportive, rather than supportive.[14] So, even if you do have to face a hostile audience, odds are you will rise to the challenge and present more effectively.

If you have adequately prepared for the presentation, you will rarely, if ever, be surprised by a hostile audience. More than likely, you will be warned in advance so you can prepare for the challenge. Several strategies can make facing hostile audiences easier.

First, stress commonalities between you and audience members, or your position and the position they hold. Again, this increases identification and can be an effective tool in establishing a relationship between the speaker and audience members. Here is how it works: Assume you are trying to persuade audience members to build a community center, and they are opposed because of a potential increase in taxes needed to fund the center. You might express that everyone there wants what is best for the children in the community. It is safe to assume that audience members will be in favor of programs that enhance the welfare of local children. This is something you all agree upon and have in common. The disagreement lies in the approach to funding these programs. So start from a position where you both agree. Try to find an attitude that both you and audience members share and then move to positions where there are disagreements. The more similarities that audience members perceive between their position and yours, the more likely they will respond favorably to your presentation.

Second, take small steps with a hostile audience and set modest goals. You aren't going to persuade audience members who are pro-gun control to donate money to the National Rifle Association, but you might get them to listen to your position and at least understand why you believe the right to purchase arms without waiting periods is important. As we discuss in Chapter 9, persuasion is a process. Don't get overly ambitious in one presentation. Set realistic goals and proceed incrementally. This is essential with a hostile audience.

Third, acknowledge the differences explicitly between your position and that of audience members. This demonstrates to audience members that you respect and understand their position. This may encourage them to listen fairly to your point of view, and it establishes your trustworthiness.

Tip

One strategy I use for a hostile audience is to try to disarm them. I try to mention up front that I may not be an expert, and I may have a lot to learn from them. This establishes that I am not arrogant and that I need their input. Most audiences appreciate that honesty and the opportunity to help teach me. Also, if I feel the audience may be reluctant, I try to structure the presentation as a discussion.

Jay Fehnel | Owner | Johan Advisors, LLC

Spotlight on Research

Inoculation Theory

In an influential research article, McGuire and Papageorgis demonstrated the advantages of refuting opposing viewpoints.[12] In their study, they gave some subjects arguments that supported common cultural truisms, such as "you should brush your teeth three times a day." Other subjects received the same argument, as well as an opposing viewpoint that was then refuted. Those receiving the supporting argument plus the refutation of the opposing viewpoint were better able to resist later arguments challenging the truism. McGuire and Papageorgis argued that this resistance is analogous to medical inoculations, where a weakened form of a virus could protect against a stronger version of the virus later on. In other words, participants in the study were "inoculated" against later persuasion attempts and more immune to counter persuasion. This is an important strategy for you to consider when you face a favorable audience that may be exposed to counter positions at a later date.[13]

Neutral Audiences

A **neutral audience** has yet to form an attitude about your topic. Audience members are a blank canvas, so to speak. With neutral audience members, you have some latitude of movement; they can be persuaded.[15] If you are facing neutral audience members, it is important for you to determine why they are neutral about your topic. Is the information new to them and they are simply unfamiliar and have yet to form an attitude, or are they apathetic? Once you are able to answer these questions, you can begin preparation of your presentation.

If audience members are simply uninformed about your issues, present them with the facts and material relevant to your topic. Once you have informed them about the topic, then you can draw out the conclusion you are working toward.

If audience members are apathetic, they just don't care. You will need to focus on increasing the relevance of the topic to them. Why is it important? We elaborate on this idea in the next section regarding audience motivation.

Although many of the examples discussed in this section regard persuasion, audience members' attitudes also play an essential role in informative presentations. Even in informative presentations, audience members' attitudes may interfere with their ability to listen and process the information in your presentation.

Audience Motivation

Sometimes, audience members are highly interested in the material you present and actively listen to every aspect of your message or presentation. They carefully consider all of your arguments, analyze your supporting material, and critically examine your credibility. Audiences who are engaged at this level are called **motivated audiences.** Other times, audiences are less interested in your material and therefore less likely to put forth much effort into critically examining or thinking about the messages you are presenting. These types of audiences are called **passive audiences.**

Knowing whether audience members are highly motivated or less motivated can be a big help in crafting your presentation. It can dictate specific strategies you might use in your actual presentation.

Motivation ultimately depends on how involved audience members are with your particular topic. **Involvement** is the personal relevance a topic holds for an audience member. For example, if you are delivering a speech about a proposed increase in the university's tuition to an audience of current students, involvement is extremely high. A change in the cafeteria menu at a local high school in your city, however, is a topic with which this same audience would have little involvement. Audience members are unlikely to be affected by changes in a high school menu; however, they will be greatly affected by an increase in tuition at the university. Therefore, their level of motivation to process the material on each of these two topics is very different.

When topics are highly relevant to audience members, they are motivated to engage in a good deal of thinking about the messages presented on that particular topic. This means they will actually devote a good deal of mental energy to thinking about the ideas you present. They will critique arguments more closely and pay attention to the minute details in the presentation. As a speaker, you must be even more attentive to the quality and strength of your arguments when dealing with motivated or involved audiences.[16]

If audience members have low involvement and motivation, and are passive, as with the example of the menu changes in a local area high school, they will be less motivated and therefore less likely to spend large amounts of mental energy in processing the material you present.[17] Rather than exerting the mental energy to elaborate on each of the ideas you present, they sit back and rely on cues for making decisions. For example, instead of examining the strength of each argument you present, they may only notice the number of arguments or the length of those arguments. This doesn't mean that you can be less prepared; it just means that you should refocus the type of supporting material you choose to use. Less-involved audiences are going to be more interested in supporting evidence that is easier to process. LaShara, a former student, used this strategy and focused on a narrative rather than on solely hard evidence such as statistics to keep her audience motivated.

> **Knowing whether audience members are highly motivated or less motivated can be a big help in crafting your presentation.**

LaShara presented a speech on Chronic Traumatic Encephalopathy to her class audience. Her audience had little motivation for processing complex messages on this topic as many did not even know what it was. Chronic Traumatic Encephalopathy, or C.T.E., is a close relative of Alzheimer's disease believed to be caused by repeated blows to the head received in sports like hockey or boxing. LaShara could have explained the medical causes of this disease or even cited the statistics associated with C.T.E. However, she decided to tell the emotional story of Derek Boogaard, a professional hockey player, who died at the age of 28. Derek Boogaard was trained to be a hockey "enforcer" or fighter for his team. He was 6'4" at age 13 and he loved hockey more than anything. He had one dream, to play for the National Hockey League, but his only way in was to fight. He was drafted and eventually earned the nickname "Boogeyman." He was a legendary tough guy in the NHL, but the fighting took its toll and eventually, his life. LaShara used this tragic story weaved in and out of her presentation to keep her audience motivated and emotionally tied to the topic.

A key factor in determining audience members' motivation for your topic is to examine why they are in the audience. Are they captive or voluntary? **Captive audiences** are forced to attend your presentation. They may include employees required to attend a training presentation or students in a classroom audience. In both of these examples, audience members are there by force. In one case, they could lose their job if they don't attend, and in the other, they could receive a failing grade.

Other audiences are voluntary. Members of **voluntary audiences** attend a presentation because they are interested in the material you are going to present or are interested in you as a speaker. Understanding the differences between these two types of audiences is critical when planning your presentation.

Captive audience members, by definition, are tougher to reach. You have to work harder at gaining their attention and making the presentation relevant to them and their needs. You must be able to convince these audience members that you have something that will benefit them. Be explicit; tell them directly how they will benefit from listening to your presentation. Once you have managed to capture their attention, you must work hard to keep it.

Members of a voluntary audience are less daunting. They are attending your presentation because they are interested in your topic or your expertise. Therefore, it will be relatively easy to gain their attention. These audience members arrive motivated and interested in your material. It is still important to use good evidence and sound reasoning. However, it will not be as difficult to engage them with your information.

Professionally Speaking

Adapting on the Fly

Rusty Rueff is past CEO of SNOCAP and former Executive Vice President of Human Resources for Electronic Arts (AE), an interactive entertainment software company. Currently, he advises and invests in a number of companies. He is an emeritus member of the Board of the San Francisco based American Conservatory Theatre (A.C.T.). He is also the Board Chairman Emeritus of The Grammy Foundation in Los Angeles.

Adapting to an audience during a presentation is always a difficult. Last year, I was asked to speak at a conference of pastors who were gathering at Indiana Wesleyan University. I was the "outside of the box" speaker as I am not a pastor. I live in the Bay Area, and I am just a businessman who happens to know something about technology and how to use it to reach younger people. I was billed as somewhat of a futurist. What I didn't realize was that my "futuring" was being presented to a number of people who, by necessity, were operating in the past and not even to today's technology standards. They received my presentation with great excitement, but also with great frustration. They wanted to do what I presented, but would not be able to do so, so they started to tune out. I could see it in their eyes as I was presenting. It was about 200 people and I could feel it in the air. What I had to do was slow my presentation and step away from my content as a recipe and make it more a set of ingredients for them to determine their own "meal." Once I did that, about 20 minutes into the hour, the rest went well.

As Rueff notes, it is extremely important to monitor your audience during the presentation and make important adaptations that will make your message more memorable or effective to your specific audience. Good audience analysis doesn't stop when you begin to speak but continues throughout your presentation.

Audience Knowledge

The amount of familiarity audience members have with your topic is another important consideration in psychological audience analysis. Are audience members experts, or are they novices? It can be very irritating for a knowledgeable audience to attend a presentation and learn nothing new. Likewise, it can also be frustrating for novices to attend a presentation and feel like everything was above their heads.

Adapting to Different Audiences

Attitudes

Supportive
- Reinforce their current position.
- Inoculate the audience against counter persuasion.
- Build involvement.

Hostile
- Find common ground that you share with audience members.
- Set extremely modest goals.

Neutral
- For uninformed audiences, focus on educating them on the issue.
- For apathetic audiences, focus on establishing relevance.

Motivation

Motivated
- Provide very strong evidence.
- Be thorough in your treatment of the material.

Passive
- Emphasize your credibility and expertise.
- Refine delivery and involve the audience.

Knowledge

High
- Don't waste audience members' time with rudimentary information.
- Be sophisticated in your approach to the material.

Low
- Don't patronize audience members; assume they are intelligent.
- Focus on one or two key areas audience members need to know to begin to understand your position.

If audience members are unfamiliar with the topic you are presenting, start with the basics. Explain technical terms, and use organizing analogies and directional transitions (see Chapter 9) to enhance their understanding. Even if you know that audience members are unfamiliar with the material you are presenting, be careful not to patronize them. Assume that they are bright and intelligent. As you move through the presentation, check for understanding; if they are following along, you can adjust your material to meet their needs and increase the complexity if necessary.

Knowledge also becomes an important variable when you consider what type of evidence and reasoning to use. Audiences that are extremely knowledgeable about a given topic are able to engage in more issue-relevant thoughts.[18] This means that if audience members are knowledgeable on your topic, they can easily process the material you present because of their familiarity with the topic, even if your material is extremely complex. Knowledgeable audiences depend more on the quality of your arguments and rely less on details such as number of sources, length of argument, and how much they like you as a speaker[19, 20] to make their judgments about your presentation.

Audience Mood

We've all been in "bad moods." Think about how receptive you are during such times to people trying to persuade you to change something, give something up, or learn something difficult. Not very, right? In fact, research shows us that "the presence of a good mood enhances a listener's receptiveness to a speaker's message." That's why keeping an audience's mood in mind can help presenters.[21]

We cannot determine the mood of every individual in a presentation. That's simply not possible. But it is possible to use some of the same audience analysis techniques we've discussed to help determine an audience's mood. Was there just a recent tragedy in the area? A big layoff at a major employer? A fatal accident involving young people? By the same token, what might have occurred that has the audience in a more favorable mood? Good community economic news? A big victory by a local sports team? And obviously some environmental factors like those discussed later in the chapter (is the audience in a bad mood because they had to give up their day off to attend your presentation) can influence mood as well.

Pre-existing moods can have practical implications for a presenter. Research in health communication, for example, informs us that audiences in negative moods are more interested in hearing about how to prevent things from happening. Those in a more positive mood want to know how to detect if something is wrong. Such knowledge could influence what information a presenter wants to highlight.

In addition, research shows us that people in positive moods pay more attention to whether information is relevant to them or not than those in negative moods. You will really have to focus on relating your information specifically to a happy crowd!

Environmental Audience Analysis

In addition to analyzing the different characteristics of your audience, it is also important to examine the environment that will surround your audience. Just where will you be speaking, and how will that affect your audience's ability to relate to you?

Physical Setting

Where will you be making your presentation? Will your audience have comfortable seating? Will the setting be formal, as in a large lecture hall, or will it be informal, as in a conference room? All of these factors will affect your audience and will require adaptation on your part. Always try to visit the actual place where you will be making your presentation. If this is not possible, ask the person who is scheduling or arranging your presentation to describe the accommodations.

> ### Considerations in Environmental Audience Analysis
>
> - ◎ Physical setting
> - ◎ Length of presentation
> - ◎ Time of day
> - ◎ Occasion
> - ◎ Order of speakers

If you will be speaking outside, it is unlikely that you will be able to use audiovisual equipment. PowerPoint® slides will not be visible outdoors, even if you have the equipment available to you. You will also be competing with the environment. If it is a beautiful spring day after a cold, drab winter, audience members may find it difficult to concentrate on what you say. How might you accommodate this? Some type of novelty in your presentation may help you overcome this distraction.

If the room is large, you will need to speak louder so that audience members in the back can hear you. You may even consider wearing a microphone. Large rooms also suggest more formality. Speakers are required to be more formal in large settings. Think about your own experiences. Classes conducted in standard classrooms are usually more informal than those conducted in large lecture halls.

If you notice that your audience is uncomfortable due to the room's environment, you will want to shorten your presentation. The attention of audience members who are sitting in uncomfortable chairs or having to stand in the back of the room will wander. Make accommodations during your presentation if you sense that audience members are uncomfortable.

The physical setting can enhance a presentation but if a speaker is not careful, the physical setting can also provide distractions.

Occasion

The occasion also can require adaptation on your part as a speaker. Why are you being asked to give this presentation? Is this part of a sales presentation? Are you being asked to reveal changes as part of an organizational restructuring? The occasion will dictate how you will approach the topic. For example, organizational restructuring makes employees very nervous. Their jobs are potentially at risk. Therefore, you would approach this occasion very differently than if you were speaking to commemorate the anniversary of the organization. In terms of the occasion, think about what audience members are expecting and feeling and how those expectations can be incorporated into the presentation.

Time of Day

The time of day that you deliver your presentation can also affect your audience. You want to prepare for audience members' reactions and adapt your message to best engage them. If you are asked to deliver a briefing at 11:30 a.m., you can anticipate that audience members will be hungry and looking forward to lunch. You would want to keep your comments short and to the point. If you continued your presentation well after the noon hour, you would lose your audience. Audience members would be distracted and thinking, "When will this presentation be over so I can get some lunch?"

Similarly, speaking right after an audience has returned from lunch also can have profound implications on your presentation. Audience members are often sleepy after eating a large meal. Therefore, you must plan very engaging and exciting material if you are making a presentation right after the lunch hour. What can you do to get your audience involved? Some type of activity might be necessary when facing this situation. For a very important presentation, it might be better to try to alter the circumstances rather than adapting your presentation to increase the likelihood of achieving the desired impact.

Order of Speakers

The order that you speak can be important in terms of audience analysis. Do you speak first, or are you sandwiched between many speakers? The first speaker in a series of presentations enjoys the advantage of facing a fresh audience. Fresh audiences are usually engaged and alert early in the program, and therefore likely to focus on the material presented.

The opposite is true if you speak last or near the end of a series of speakers. Your audience will be fatigued and less likely to expend a great deal of effort processing your message. Use strategies for reinvigorating the audience. Involve audience members, and use an animated delivery style. Use narratives, and avoid long lists of statistics or other information that may be difficult to process. If there is a question-and-answer session, your audience may be too tired to participate. Their questions may have already been answered by previous speakers. If there aren't a lot of questions, don't worry. It probably has more to do with fatigue than your actual presentation.

If you find yourself speaking in the middle of a program, use that to your advantage. Relate material other speakers have presented to your own. You can use their information as context for your own material. Demonstrate how your material and ideas relate to all the others, and try to synthesize the main ideas of the previous speakers to give your audience the "big picture" of the topic being addressed.

Speaking order can have an impact on your presentation. Take this into consideration when you are planning your talk. By making a few minor adjustments, you can better meet the needs of your audience. Audience members will appreciate it, and your presentation will more likely have the impact you want to achieve.

Time/Length of Presentation

Students often complain about the time restrictions associated with their presentational assignments. What you may not know is that speakers in the real world face similar constraints that have real implications. Will Miller, Ph.D., comedian and motivational speaker, says that "the time restrictions I face from my clients are very real. If I go over my allotted time, audience members will start to leave. They have other engagements, and their schedules are very tight. If I go under my allotted time, audiences feel they haven't gotten their money's worth."

When speakers exceed their time constraints, they send several negative messages. First, they are communicating that their message is more important than everyone else's. After all, when they go over their time limit, they are taking time away from another speaker. This implies that they think that their material is more important. If they are the only speaker, they show a lack of respect for the audience by failing to recognize that audience members have other commitments and obligations. Second, exceeding a time constraint demonstrates incompetence. It implies that the speaker was unable to adapt the material to the situational constraints.

As Will Miller suggested, falling far short of your time limit is problematic as well. If audience members pay to listen to an hour-long presentation on gardening and the speaker only talks for 20 minutes, audience members will feel cheated. Even if the material the speaker presented was valuable, audience members may not appreciate it because the entire presentation failed to meet their expectations.

It is the speaker's responsibility to adhere to the given time constraints. Whenever accepting a speaking engagement, always make sure you understand the time constraints. Determine whether the time constraints include a question-and-answer session. During your presentation, keep an eye on the clock. Ultimately, it is your responsibility to ensure that you stay within the time limit.

Technology

As a speaker, it is important that you understand what technology you will have available to you and plan accordingly. But no matter how well you plan, there can always be technical difficulties. "The show must go on," so to speak. So, have a backup plan. If the bulb of the LCD projector burns out, you will need to be able to give your presentation without the use of visual aids. You can always print transparencies for use with an overhead projector as a backup (see Chapter 12 for more discussion). However, projectors can be difficult to find, and the venue you are speaking at may not have one available. Be flexible and plan for every contingency.

Speak with the event coordinator about what technologies will be available. Some questions that you will want to ask include:

- ◎   Will I have a lectern?
- ◎   Will I have an LCD projector?
- ◎   Will I have access to a computer, or should I bring my own?
- ◎   Will the room have Internet access?
- ◎   Will I have a microphone? Is it cordless?
- ◎   Will I have a cordless mouse?

Knowing what technologies are available to you will help you plan your presentation more effectively. Remember, utilize the technology to better meet the needs of your audience. If it doesn't enhance your message, you really don't need it.

Professionally Speaking

Audience Adaptation Is a Responsibility

Charles Catalono, Ph.D., is the Director of Worldwide Franchise Communications for Ethicon Endo-Surgery (EES), which is part of the Johnson & Johnson family of companies. His primary focus is on communication to the organization's employees.

Public speaking is fundamental to what I do. I routinely have to present strategic communications plans to small groups and prepare presentations for senior executives to deliver at company-wide town hall meetings.

To borrow a phrase from marketing communications, audience analysis is always "top of mind" for me whenever I'm preparing a presentation for myself or others. It has to be. Having the opportunity to deliver a presentation is a privilege. I think speakers sometimes forget this. That being said, speakers have a responsibility to make their presentations special for their audiences and to also make effective use of their audiences' time.

I always begin planning presentations with a clear purpose in mind by asking myself the following questions: Why have I been asked to present? What do I hope to accomplish? What's the reason I'm presenting? These questions seem simple, but in my experience they're often overlooked, especially as people advance in their careers and juggle the challenges associated with balancing their personal and professional lives.

I tailor my remarks based upon the answers to the questions above, the time I have to speak, and the audience to whom I'm speaking. Remember, your presentation should be special for your audience and make effective use of their time. Your goal should be to "light them up" with interest, excitement, and passion.

The fundamentals you learn in a course like this are essential to effective speaking. They'll be important to you throughout your career.

Audience Adaptation before the Presentation

Now that you know many of the important ways to adapt to your audience, you may be thinking, "How will I get this information? How will I know the demographics of my audience and how motivated they will be to process my presentation?" There are direct and indirect ways of gathering this information.

Direct Methods of Audience Analysis

One of the best ways to gather information about your audience is through **direct methods.** These include directly asking your audiences about who they are and what characteristics they possess. Interviews, focus groups, and surveys are some of the traditional tools used in gathering information directly from your audience.

Direct Methods of Audience Analysis

- ◎ Interview   ◎ Focus groups
- ◎ Surveys

Interviews are conducted one-on-one with audience members. You should prepare a list of questions in advance that includes both closed- and open-ended questions. **Closed-ended questions** limit responses to a specific range of answers. An example would be, "Do you exercise regularly?" The respondent only has two choices: yes or no. **Open-ended questions** allow respondents the freedom to answer any way they choose. An example would be, "Describe your exercise routine." By including open-ended and closed-ended questions in your interview, you will be able to get better and more varied information about your audience.

Technically Speaking

Using Twitter to Determine Audience Position

Speakers often struggle to determine what an audience thinks about their topic or what specific attitudes they might hold toward the topic. Sometimes it's hard to determine which of the issues surrounding the topic are most important and which don't hold much interest for an audience. Nothing can substitute for getting direct access to your specific audience and asking them "what do you think about …?" However, we rarely get that kind of access to an audience before we arrive to deliver our presentation. One social media tool that can facilitate this process is Twitter. Although Twitter limits "tweets" or posts to just 140 characters, you can learn a lot about what topics people are interested in and how they think or feel about particular issues by reading their tweets.

There are a couple of different ways that you can use Twitter to help understand the issues surrounding a particular topic. First, you can search Twitter for a specific topic you are researching. Let's assume you are preparing a speech on homeschoolers participation in public school athletic programs. From examining all the posts related to homeschooling and playing high school sports, we can learn how divided people are on the topic. We can learn what the arguments are for supporting homeschoolers participation in high school athletics and the arguments against it. By examining the posts thoroughly, we are able to gauge rough leanings of those engaged in the debate. This information goes a long way in helping you understand how concerned parties (parents, students, school administrators, community members, etc.) are leaning on the issue. By following the links embedded in these tweets you can learn even more about specific attitudes and opinions of concerned parties.

Second, if you are a big Twitter user yourself, you can tweet to find out what your followers think about a particular issues. For example, you can tweet, "Do unpaid internships take advantage of workers?" Although far from scientific, the tweets from your followers can provide some insight into what they are currently thinking on the topic and may provide valuable insight into the analysis of your audience.

The **focus group** differs from the interview in one substantial way: The number of people involved at one time is much larger. A focus group is a group interview facilitated by one leader. Focus groups usually range in size from three to twelve individuals. They are advantageous because the group can often think of ideas or issues that individuals may not think of alone. However, some individuals may be hesitant to speak up in a group setting. Compared to individual interviews, focus groups allow you to collect more information in less time. So, from a preparation standpoint, they may be more efficient.

Surveys or **questionnaires** are other direct methods of collecting information about your audience. Surveys allow you to collect a large amount of information in a relatively short amount of time. Polls that political candidates distribute are examples of surveys. You can use the e-mail tool in Blackboard to distribute questionnaires to your classmates. You can also use Facebook and Twitter to poll audiences (see Technically Speaking box). This is a quick and easy way for you to collect information on your classroom audience.

Many times, direct methods such as the preceding are not feasible. This kind of research takes time and money. Usually, investment in this type of research is only conducted if the stakes are high, such as for corporate takeovers, political presentations, and new product launches, just to name a few.

While direct methods are the most effective for gathering information about your audience, they aren't always available to you as a speaker. If you are unable to gather information directly from your audience, indirect tools for audience analysis are helpful and are discussed next.

Indirect Methods of Audience Analysis

Indirect methods of audience analysis involve collecting information from any source but your audience. You might ask the contact person who invited you to speak for some information about the group. This is one of the best methods of collecting information about your audience. Contact people know a great deal about the group and have a good idea of what the group is expecting from you as a speaker. You can also ask individuals who have spoken to the group before to help you understand the characteristics of the group. They can give you a very good preview of how the audience will likely respond.

Indirect Methods of Audience Analysis

- ◎ Interview the individual arranging the presentation.
- ◎ Interview other speakers who have addressed the group.
- ◎ Examine organizational websites and social media sites.
- ◎ Examine organizational pamphlets and other materials.

I recently delivered a presentation to a large group of students at a local university. After speaking with the contact person who arranged the presentation, I asked several people who had previously addressed this group to give me some advice on how best to approach this audience. All of them gave me some great information, but the most helpful was that this particular audience tended to be a rowdy crowd. This enabled me to plan for this possibility. I knew that my presentation style would have to be more relaxed and involve the audience from the very beginning. If I had arrived at the speaking engagement and found the audience a bit wild, I would have been unprepared for this outcome. Knowing this information beforehand was extremely helpful.

You can also examine promotional materials associated with the group you will be addressing. If you have been asked to make a presentation for your company to a potential client, you will want to read every newspaper article about that client, visit the client's corporate website, read their Twitter feed, and visit their Facebook page. Anything you can learn about the client will help you adapt to the client's needs.

Audience Adaptation during the Presentation

It is also important that you continue to adapt to your audience as you make your presentation. Stay tuned to audience feedback. Don't get so engrossed in your presentation that you fail to recognize subtle messages from the audience. Audiences send a variety of messages to a speaker during a presentation. The messages can indicate confusion, boredom, or nods of agreement.

You can make adaptations during your presentation to help facilitate your presentation's effectiveness. If audience members seem confused, stop. Go back and explain that part of the presentation again. Try using a different explanatory strategy this time. If audience members still seem perplexed, ask them what seems to be causing difficulty. You may not be able to deliver the presentation as you had expected, but it is much better to ensure that audience members are following you.

If your audience seems bored, try picking up the pace of the presentation. This may mean that you simply speed up the delivery.

However, other situations may call for you to cut portions of the presentation. A second strategy is to use more narratives and capitalize on good delivery skills. Stay away from using statistics and facts that are not completely necessary. Make sure that you are making good eye contact and using a varied delivery style. You can also try to involve audience members: Ask for a show of hands, or call on someone directly. This will help you regain audience members' attention.

Conclusion

Audience analysis is fundamental to a successful presentation. As we have discussed in this chapter, a speaker can use a variety of methods to adapt a presentation to an audience. Demographic analysis provides a general understanding of an audience and includes items such as age, gender, sex, socioeconomic status, culture, religious background, and sexual orientation. However, demographic audience analyses are limited in nature. Be careful not to marginalize your audience by stereotyping them. More sophisticated approaches to analyzing your audience include psychological approaches. Understanding what attitudes audience members hold about your message, why they are in your audience, and what they know about your topic are all important. Environmental audience analysis helps you adapt to the situation that surrounds your audience. Be prepared by assessing the room or venue in which you will speak. There are many methods for collecting the information you will use for audience analysis. Indirect and direct methods for collecting information can be insightful, so take advantage of both. It is also important to remember that audience analysis isn't only conducted before the presentation. You must continue to analyze and adapt to audience members' needs during the presentation as well.

Key Terms

Attitude

Audience analysis

Captive audiences

Closed-ended questions

Demographics

Direct methods

Favorable audiences

Focus groups

Friendly audiences

Hostile audiences

Identification

Indirect methods

Inoculation

Interviews

Involvement

Motivated audiences

Neutral audiences

Open-ended questions

Passive audiences

Psychological factors

Questionnaires

Surveys

Values

Voluntary audiences

Word selection

Exercises

1. Visit an organization's website and/or obtain printed materials (pamphlets, mission statements, ethics codes, brochures, etc.) for the organization. Using the materials as a basis for demographic and psychological audience analysis, try to decide what kind of audience you would be giving a presentation to and how this would affect your choice of presentation materials and your goals for the speech. Possible organizations include American Association of Retired Persons (http://www.aarp.org), the Red Hat Society (http://www.redhatsociety.com), New Chauncey Neighborhood Association (http://www.newchauncey.org), Young Democrats of America (http://www.yda.org), College Republicans (http://www.crnc.org), Future Farmers of America (https://www.ffa.org), the Sierra Club (http://www.sierraclub.org), or the Audubon Society (http://www.audubon.org).

2. Advertising is a profession that makes extensive use of audience analysis. Choose an issue of a popular magazine like *Newsweek, Sports Illustrated, Scientific American, Rolling Stone, Good Housekeeping,* etc. From that issue, select three advertisements to analyze. Try to determine who the target audience was, what attributes of the target audience the advertiser appealed to, and what type of analysis (demographic, psychological, or environmental) the advertiser relied most heavily on.

3. Explain a technological term like Cloud Computing or Twitter to the following audiences: a classroom of second graders, your grandmother's bridge club, a group of Liberal Arts professors. Think about how you would make changes to these presentations for each of these audiences.

4. Jermaine has been invited to speak to a group of young entrepreneurs as part of their annual conference. He is one of seven business executives who will present during the day's activities. When Jermaine arrives to the auditorium, he learns that his presentation is scheduled fourth, right before the participants will be breaking for lunch. Using the guidelines in this chapter, what advice would you have for Jermaine in this situation?

CHAPTER **3**

Selecting the Topic and Purpose

Objectives

After reading this chapter, you should be able to

- ◎ explain the qualities of a good topic;
- ◎ identify methods for choosing a topic;
- ◎ identify differences between general and specific purpose statements;
- ◎ identify differences between the specific purpose statement and the thesis statement; and
- ◎ construct effective general purpose, specific purpose, and thesis statements following the criteria outlined in the chapter.

A decision by Liberty University, an evangelical Christian school in Virginia, to invite then presidential candidate Donald Trump to speak at the school's opening convocation on Martin Luther King Day in 2016 brought complaints from some students and alumni. They pointed to Trump's controversial remarks about minorities—he had touted plans to deny Muslims and Mexican immigrants entrance to the U.S. and had made some disparaging comments about women—during his campaign as being the antithesis of King's philosophies.

The school defended the pick, saying: "I think this one was picked to afford Mr. Trump the opportunity to, among other things, honor Dr. King."[1]

But King did not figure prominently into Trump's speech. In fact, he did not deviate much from the usual stump speech he gave at all his other rallies. He only acknowledged King when he bragged about the 11,000 people who turned out to hear him—even though attendance is required of students at the convocations.

"Did we break the record?" he asked. "So we'll dedicate that to Martin Luther King, a great man."[2]

Overall, the audience reacted politely to Trump's speech. But he never got the loud, passionate reception he usually got at his campaign rallies. In fact, many in the audience expressed displeasure with his speech. Russell Moore, a Southern Baptist leader, reacted: "This would be hilarious if it weren't so counter to the mission of the gospel of Jesus Christ."[3]

Many saw this as an opportunity for Trump to reach a religious conservative audience that, to that point in the campaign had been favoring some of his primary opponents. But his decision not to pick a speech topic to reflect the tenets of MLK Day and his audience actually worked against him.

Do You Have a Choice?

Although selecting a topic is a large part of the presentation-making process in this course, you will rarely have to pull a topic out of thin air for presentations outside of the classroom. When you are invited to give a presentation out in the local community, or are required to present material as part of a job, for example, it's likely your topic will be predetermined for you. That is, you will most likely be invited to speak because of your expertise, and your only decision will be how to address the topic in a given situation with a particular audience.

Many times, however, while your topic is set, you will need to decide how to narrow that topic. Often, that will provide you with some choices. For example, as an avid cycler, you might be invited to speak to a local civic group about your interest. At that point, you know the subject of your presentation: cycling. Now, you must refine and adapt your presentation topic to the situation. Will you talk about cycling equipment? How to get started in cycling? Safety in cycling? The history of the sport? In addition, if you are asked to speak to two local groups within a relatively short time span, you don't want to give the same presentation again. Some members of the second audience may have attended your previous presentation. That means you will need to refine the topic yet again.

In this course, we sometimes limit your choices to help you focus on the assignment itself. Choosing the right topic is an important process that takes time and effort. This chapter provides steps to assist you in selecting a topic. If you follow the guidelines, it will be easier for you to select an appropriate topic you are excited about. Later in the chapter, we discuss how to narrow your topic and develop effective purpose and thesis statements for your presentation. The information contained in this chapter refers both to specific presentations you have been assigned in this course and other types of presentations you might be asked to give in other courses, at work, or on behalf of an organization you might belong to.

Let's begin by discussing the characteristics of a good topic.

Qualities of a Good Topic

Your Topic Interests You

The topics that you choose for your presentations in this course should be interesting and important to you. Because you will spend a good deal of time working on each presentation, the topic you choose needs to be in an area that you find compelling and interesting so that it continues to motivate you throughout the entire speech-planning process. Planning the presentation will be difficult if you do not find your topic interesting. In addition to keeping you motivated, your topic choice must also be able to motivate the audience. If you have little interest in the topic, it will be obvious to audience members and they will have little interest as well. How can you expect to motivate an audience to listen and be excited about a topic that you do not find interesting?

Your Topic Interests Your Audience

Your topic must be one that the audience finds interesting, compelling, and useful. As we have discussed in earlier chapters, the audience's motivation to process the information in your presentation is extremely important.[4] Although you may find the topic engaging and interesting, you must find a way to connect that topic with audience members so that they will be motivated to think about your message. No topic will interest every member of your class. Audiences are interested in new information that they can use. For example, in this course, most of your audience is made up of students who are roughly the same age and in the same situation as you are. Many are hoping to find great jobs after graduation and are preparing for that goal. Therefore, an instructional presentation on how to sign up for the job counseling service on your campus would be very useful to your particular audience.

Spotlight on Research

Your Topic Must Be Relevant

As you ponder what topic your audience might find interesting, keep in mind that research has shown that making the topic relevant to the audience is a key determinant in interest. But how do you determine if your topic is relevant? John Keller's ARCS Model of Motivational Design puts relevance into easy-to-understand terminology. According to Keller's model, to make a topic relevant, you need to

- ◎ tell the audience how the new learning will use their existing skills;
- ◎ tell the audience what the subject matter will do for them today;
- ◎ tell the audience what the subject matter will do for them tomorrow.[5]

Your Topic Is Significant

Your topic should be significant and worthy of being addressed in public. Is it a topic that audiences feel is worthwhile? While you may make the best lasagna in the world, sharing this information with your audience in this particular environment is not necessarily significant. You should share information that will actually have an impact on your audience. Even in an organizational setting, you want to make sure that the topic you select is significant enough to warrant your audience's time. When employees take time out of their schedules to listen to a presentation, they are taking time away from other tasks. Therefore, make sure that when you ask for your colleagues' time and attention, you have something valuable and insightful to offer them.

Your Topic Is Fresh

Last year, a student in this course interning at the student co-recreational facility was assigned the task of coming up with ideas for two 15-minute presentations to give to incoming first-year students during orientation week activities. The student proposed sessions on the importance of eating a good breakfast and the importance of getting enough sleep. Both were soundly rejected by the supervisor. Why? Because these are what are referred to as "stale" topics, or topics that most audience members already know quite a bit about. For instance, we all know it's important to eat a good breakfast. You grew up with your mother telling you this. And there is scientific research to back up the benefits of eating a healthy breakfast. But it's nothing we haven't heard before. No audience member wants to sit in a presentation and hear information that he or she already knows in some way or another. Make sure your topic is fresh—something that will make your audience say, "I didn't know that." If your topic isn't fresh, you need to find another topic. The former student, for example, revised her session to inform first-year students about the nutritional differences between popular breakfast bars—a common "breakfast" item for students living in dormitories. This was a fresh take on a stale topic.

The most important part is to remember that they are probably not just like you. So you need to focus on how you can make your comments most compelling to them, not you.

Jay Fehnel | Executive Coach| Kensington International

Your Topic Can Be Covered in the Allotted Time

The topic you choose for your presentation must also fit the time constraints of the situation. In today's frantic pace, we all have limited amounts of time we can devote to messages. The same is true for our audiences. Consequently, we are often constrained by time in speaking situations. More often than not, you will be given a time frame in which your presentation must fit. This time frame may be as short as a few minutes or as long as several days. Think about the topic you would like to address and determine whether you can adequately do that topic justice in the time frame available.

Jodie, a previous student in this course, wanted to instruct her audience how to construct a webpage from scratch. She had a 3- to 5-minute time frame to present this information in an asynchronous presentation. While timely and interesting, creating a webpage is a difficult and timely process with many intricacies. Jodie simply did not have time to adequately address this issue in a meaningful way to a novice audience. After doing initial research, she quickly realized that this was not a topic well suited to the time. In the end, Jodie showed her audience how to set up a webpage using a free content management system like Wordpress, which is much simpler and could be done thoroughly in the allotted time frame.

As discussed in Chapter 2, always adhere to your time limits. Speaking for longer than your allotted time may be perceived as rude and inconsiderate by an audience. It shows lack of respect for audience members, and it has ethical implications. The same is true for speaking for less than your allocated time. If you are hired to deliver an hour-long presentation on investing in today's markets and you only speak for 20 minutes, you will be perceived negatively and damage your credibility for future presentations. Your audience will feel shortchanged and cheated. Respect your time constraints by choosing a topic that can be adequately addressed within your time restrictions and practice to ensure that your presentation comfortably fits the parameters of the time frame.

In addition, many controversial topics do not lend themselves to short speeches. For instance, in a classroom speech, you aren't going to persuade a longtime Republican to vote for the Democratic Party candidate. Take a look at your topic. Can you realistically expect to achieve your purpose in the allotted time? If not, you need to redefine and adapt, or else pick out a new topic. Perhaps you could attempt to convince the audience to attend a speech by your candidate instead.

Your Topic Is Audience Appropriate

Previously in this course, a student asked to give a persuasive speech on why the United States deserved the terrorist attacks of September 11, 2001. While Purdue University does have a Free Expression Policy (http://www.purdue.edu/purdue/about/free-speech.html), there are exceptions. One exception allows the rejection of free speech in order to protect students' safety. It was deemed in this incident that the student giving the speech might be in danger from other students still traumatized by the attack. In addition, speech topics may be rejected in order to "prevent disruptions."

Speech topics may also be rejected if they encourage audience members to participate in illegal activities. Remember, good presentational speaking is ethical. You cannot be an ethical speaker if you encourage a captive audience to behave in an unethical manner.

On a more basic level, however, you should think about your audience first when choosing a speech topic. While you might be passionate about an alternative religion or reproductive issues, for instance, will a majority of audience members be offended or made uncomfortable by your presentation? If that's possible, the topic is not a good choice.

In addition, many topics you might enjoy might be a little too difficult to share in a setting such as a classroom. Your interest in the intricacies of chemical engineering research might be too technical a topic to try to pass on to a group of lay students.

Your Topic Can Be Easily Researched

The topic you select for this class should also be easily researched. It should be a topic with a wide availability of resources, including traditional print media, such as books, magazines, and newspaper articles; personal interviews; and so on. If you are having a difficult time generating material for the topic you have chosen, move on to another topic. If the research materials you are finding for your topic are old and do not fit the criteria for the assignment, then the topic may not be novel and informative enough to meet the criteria of the assignment. Ideally, your support for your topic should be no older than one year. If you can't find enough recent research, chances are that your topic is stale.

Your Topic Is Timely

A good topic is also timely. This means that it is relatively new or presents new information on an old topic. If you do not have new information to share with an audience, your topic will not be perceived as pertinent or useful. During the research phase of the planning process, make sure that you find new information and development within the field you are researching. If you are having difficulty finding material that is new and novel for you, perhaps this topic isn't well suited for the presentation.

For example, you might find the topic of Alzheimer's disease interesting and even know a friend or family member suffering from the disease. While most audience members are aware of what the disease is and the symptoms that accompany it, new breakthroughs regarding Alzheimer's are being discovered daily. A presentation that focuses on the new developments would be timely for your audience. A presentation that simply describes the disease would not.

How to Select a Topic

Now that you know the characteristics of a good topic, let's examine strategies to help you select a topic. If you follow the tips presented in this chapter, the process will be a snap.

Personal Experience

One of the best suggestions for choosing a topic is to select something from your own personal experience. Think about something that you know a lot about. We feel more comfortable in front of an audience when we know a lot about the topic on which we are presenting. In addition, speaking on a topic about which you already have knowledge makes the process easier. Do you have hobbies or special interests that would make good presentational topics? For example, Will, a student in this course, was an avid NASCAR fan. He capitalized on his passion and knowledge of racing by informing audience members of ways they could volunteer at the Indy 500. Use your areas of expertise to help choose a topic. Perhaps you took an excellent course on campus that led to some personal benefit for you. Tell your audience about the course or even persuade them to take it. Do you have a job that could provide interesting material? What about trips you have taken? What are your passions?

Spotlight on Research

Anxiety Over Topic Selection

If you feel anxious about choosing your topic, you are not alone. Research has indicated that students feel a great deal of stress and anxiety about choosing topics for any assignment. However, this same research has indicated that social interaction can actually help reduce the stress and anxiety many students feel about this process. In addition to getting feedback from your classmates during in-class activities, discussing your ideas with a roommate, family member, or friend can actually help you narrow the topic and feel good about your choice. The people in our social networks are sometimes better equipped to recommend good directions for a topic. So when choosing a topic for this course or any presentation, also talk to your friends and family about your ideas. They can be a valuable support during this phase of the preparation process.[6]

Personal Interests

Another good way to choose a topic for this course is to investigate something in which you have always been interested. Consider topics that fascinate you but that you have never had a chance to pursue. See the assignment as a way to investigate a topic that has always sparked your interest but that you've never had the time to explore. You might think about other courses you are currently taking. Are there issues mentioned in those classes that you would like to know more about? If so, these issues may make excellent topics for presentations in this course.

Current Events

Other good places to look for topics are newspapers, talk radio programs, news magazines, news networks such as CNN or MSNBC, news portals such as Google News (http://news.google.com/), National Public Radio (NPR), and news programs such as *60 Minutes*. Topics presented in the media are usually being discussed in society; therefore, these topics tend to be relevant for audiences and are significant and timely. Topics currently being covered in the news are also easy to find, so it may simplify your research process.

Most news sources have their own websites that are easily accessed and easy to read. In addition, most of them break that news into categories. For instance,

Sources for Current Events

- ◎ Google news: http://news.google.com
- ◎ Yahoo news: http://news.yahoo.com
- ◎ Newspaper List: http://www.usnpl.com
- ◎ CNN: http://www.cnn.com
- ◎ National Public Radio: http://www.npr.org

on CNN's website (http://www.cnn.com), news is broken down into such categories as U.S., Money, Tech, Health, Justice, Politics, and Entertainment. This makes it easy to search for events in areas in which you have an interest. The same thing is true for Google News. Most of the day's largest stories are broken into categories for easy perusal.

In addition to being relevant and timely, current events may also lend themselves to being localized for a presentation. **Localizing** is a term used in mass communication when events that are taking place elsewhere are examined for their status or effect at the local level. For instance, Elton, a former student, wanted to persuade his classmates to donate their game meat to "Hunters Feed the Hungry." The nonprofit provides venison and other game meat to shelters and food banks. Through his research, Elton was able to discover that more than 40 shelters in the state accept game meat through the program, including the largest local shelter. Using this localized information made his plea more relevant to the audience.

News Releases, News Services, and Newsletters

News releases are communications from for-profit and nonprofit companies as well as private and governmental entities that are directed at members of the news media. Most news releases claim to have some "news value" and are an attempt to garner media attention for a new product, event, discovery, and so on. Just as news releases can be a good source of story ideas for journalists, they can also be the source for a good topic for either informative or persuasive presentations.

News releases can be easily located. Both Google and Yahoo redefined the term *news* to allow news releases

Sources for News Releases

◎ PR Newswire: http://www.prnewswire.com/news-releases/
◎ Census Bureau: http://www.census.gov/newsroom/releases/
◎ EurekAlert!: http://www.eurekalert.org/

to be displayed in search results along with news stories. Other sites are designed solely for the purpose of making releases readily available to both the media and the public. PR Newswire (http://www.prnewswire.com/news-releases/) is one of the more popular sources and reports an average of more than 1.2 million hits per month. On this site, in addition to browsing all news releases, you can browse news releases by category.

PR Newswire

In addition, most governmental, political, business, and organization websites make their news releases available online on their respective sites. Many of the sites have entire pages dedicated to releases. Most of these pages are headlined "newsroom" or "media." For example, the Census Bureau's newsroom (http://www.census.gov/newsroom/press-releases.html) is a popular site for journalists because of the large number of releases put out by the bureau. The Census Bureau's newsroom is accessible to everyone, as most are, and not just the news media. In addition, the Census Bureau also breaks down its news releases by date and by categories such as health, business, families, economy, etc. to further aid topic selection.

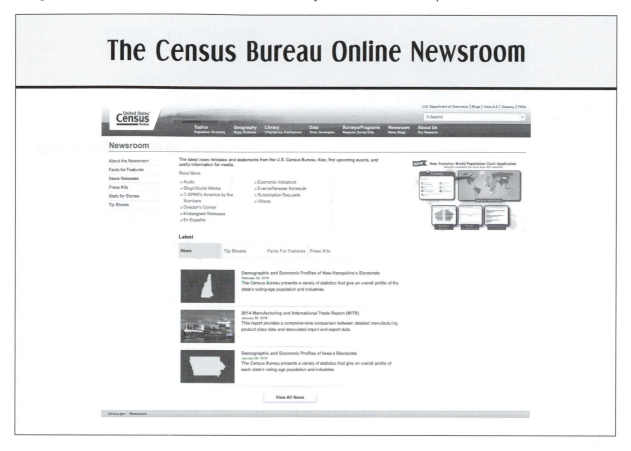

There are also many "specialized" news releases and news services that focus on a particular area. For instance, the sites EurekAlert! (http://www.eurekalert.org/) and Science Daily (http:// www.sciencedaily.com/) feature news releases and news stories highlighting new scientific developments. Such new developments in the areas of science, agriculture, medicine, and technology often make interesting informative or explanatory speeches. Science Daily even breaks its news stories and releases into eight major areas, such as Health & Medicine, Computers & Math, and Plants & Animals, which are then further subdivided into up to 40 subcategories. On a recent day, for instance, Science Daily featured a news release about how stress in your early years can lead to cardiovascular disease when you get older. This could make an excellent informative topic for a health presentation to a college-age audience.

Finally, most companies and organizations have their own newsletters to keep customers and supporters informed on the latest products, developments, research, and so on. Many are mailed; others can be found on the home page of the organization. E-mail newsletters, such as that produced by *BusinessWeek*, are also becoming more popular. Interested parties can sign up online and electronic newsletters arrive in your e-mail. *BusinessWeek* offers interested parties a choice of eight newsletters, including BW Insider, a weekly recap of the top business stories, and Technology Insider for up-to-date tech news. Here at Purdue, for instance, the

College of Technology and the Regenstrief Center for Healthcare Engineering are just two departments that put out electronic newsletters. Newsletters are not produced as frequently as news releases; many are monthly or quarterly. However, they can still be good sources of topic ideas.

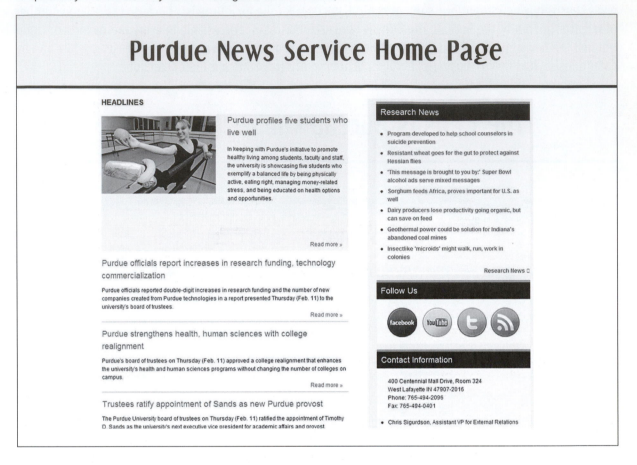

Internet Searches

You mainly think of using an Internet search engine such at Google or Bing to find support for a topic. But you can also use the Internet to help you decide on a topic. Pick a topic you are interested in. Type it in to Google search. What happens? Google will return a variety of webpages about areas within that topic, and recent reports in news outlets that feature the topic. Chances are information on one of those pages might make an interesting presentation.

Weblogs

Weblogs, or blogs as they are more commonly called, are regularly updated, self-published, online journals. Posts are in reverse chronological order and can contain original reporting, commentary, hyperlinks to news items and other sites, personal narratives, and even photos and video.

Weblogs began as a form of online personal diaries, but today, many newspapers, organizations, and corporations operate weblogs as alternative sources of news delivery. Numerous studies, with disparate results, have attempted to count the number of blogs and bloggers worldwide. The *New York Times* currently features more than 60 blogs, on topics from fashion to food to politics, on its website.

The *New York Times'* Weblogs Home Page

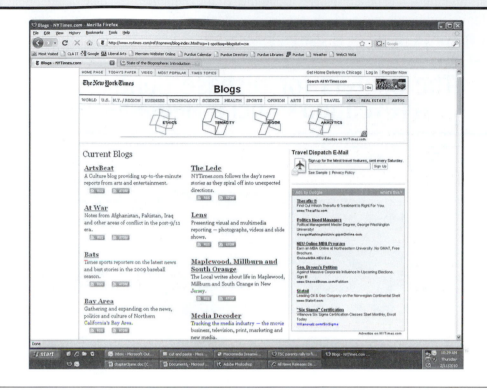

According to a 2012 "State of the Blogging World Report,"[7] there are an estimated 31 million bloggers in the United States. While that number has waned significantly in recent years, most top news organizations, businesses and nonprofits maintain blogs that are legitimate sources of information. The top blogging sites, such as NBC, CNN, Dow Jones, TED, and even Auto Trader, report more than 528 million page views every month. Some top news sources, such as the Huffington Post Mashable, are only in blog format.

Not all blogs are professionally maintained, however. With the advent of do-it-yourself platforms like Wordpress and Blogger, anybody can have a blog. Wordpress reports that its bloggers make more than 500,000 new posts a day, which result in almost 400,000 daily comments.[8] That doesn't mean that you can't use information you might find on an enthusiast's blog. For example, presentations on hobbies can benefit from real people stories and tips you might find on someone's blog. Just use the same common sense and tips to evaluate a blog that you do when looking at any web-based source.

Weblog Sources

◎ Blog search engine:
http://blogsearchengine.org

◎ Google's blog search engine:
http://blogsearch.google.com/?hl=en&tab=wb

Because the format of blogs allows for quick updates on breaking stories and links to additional sources on the topics, they can be an excellent source of ideas for presentations on current national news events and trends.

According to the Poynter Institute, reporters are using blogs to publish news or events that don't fit in routine articles.[9] Blogs also allow reporters to publish breaking news ahead of a print run and to link to additional information on a topic. Finally, unlike traditional news stories, blogs often contain commentary and opinions of the authors and those who post responses to comments. These opinions can help gauge public sentiment on current topics and trends and guide persuasive arguments. Blogs are an excellent additional tool to use for audience analysis.

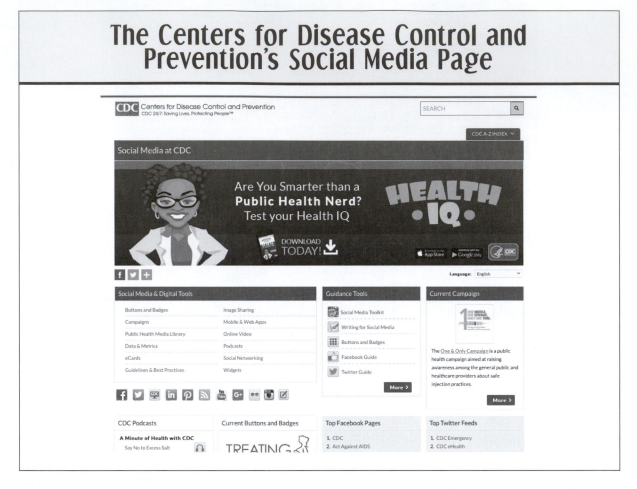

Even journalists use weblogs to get ideas. A new survey released as part of an ongoing research project by Marketwire[10] found that weblogs are a regular source for journalists. More than three-fourths of journalists indicate that blogs are helpful in giving them story ideas, story angles, and insights into issues.

Social Media

As the popularity of social media expands, more and more entities are turning to programs such as Twitter and Facebook to get their news out. Currently, Facebook has more than 1.5 billion active pages, including those of businesses and organizations. Meanwhile, there are now more than 300 million active Twitter users.[11]

The Centers for Disease Control in Atlanta has an entire newsroom dedicated to social media. Twitter, Facebook, YouTube, and other social media became main outlets to get out updates about the H1N1 flu, especially to younger audiences. Purdue University now has a Twitter page[12], a Facebook page[13] and an Instagram account to update students, faculty, alumni, prospective students, and area residents.

The Tippecanoe School Corporation's Save Our Schools Facebook Page

Social media resources are a great place to find out about grassroots movements whose actions and ideas would make interesting speeches. Here locally, for example, Tippecanoe School Corp. parents rallying to save programs in the face of budget cuts took to Facebook and created their own Save Our Schools Facebook page. The page served many functions, including exchange of ideas, announcements, and updates.

Other Sources

Sometimes, all we need is a little inspiration to get going. One technique is to brainstorm on ideas related to a topic in which you have a general interest. For instance, your general interest in sports might lead you to think about exercising, which leads you to think about common stress injuries, which leads you to wonder how casual exercisers can protect themselves. At this point, a possible topic for an informative speech is beginning to form. You might also use such tactics as going to the library and looking through the book stacks in areas related to your interest. You will often find interesting books that could form the basis of a presentation.

Narrowing the Topic

Once you have selected your topic, you must narrow that topic to fit the situation. A common mistake is attempting to make a presentation on a topic that is too broad, which usually results in a superficial treatment of the topic. There is simply not enough time to address the topic in detail. Try to avoid this pitfall by focusing in on a particular aspect of the topic that you can develop in detail. Consider the following example:

Sarah had her heart set on pursuing health-care reform as the topic of her presentation in her health communication class. After determining that she could not adequately address the important issues related to this topic in the 3–5 minutes allotted, she found an interesting alternative: student insurance options at her own university. She was still able to pursue her original interest in healthcare, but with a new spin that would both easily fit her time constraint and be highly relevant for her audience.

The General Purpose

After you have selected and narrowed your topic, it is time to begin thinking about the **general purpose** or overarching goal of your presentation. Effective presentations have a strong sense of purpose. Planning your purpose is one of the most important steps in your presentation.

Traditionally, the general purpose of a presentation falls into three categories: to inform, to persuade, or to entertain. Because presentations with the goal of entertaining are not generally a focus of introductory speaking classes, they are not addressed here.

If your general purpose is "to inform," you will be providing the audience with new information to create understanding. **Informative presentations** describe, explain, or demonstrate something. Your role in this type of presentation is that of a teacher. If you do not present new material or enhance your audience's understanding of a topic, you have failed to meet the general purpose of the presentation. Informative presentations are discussed in greater detail in Chapter 8.

As this attorney demonstrates, persuasion asks the speaker to advocate a particular position or course of action.

If your general purpose is "to persuade," you will basically act as an advocate or leader in your presentation. The goal of a **persuasive presentation** is to influence the attitudes, beliefs, or behaviors of your audience.[14] You will go beyond presenting information and will actually advocate a particular position or course of action regarding that information. (Persuasive presentations are discussed further in Chapter 9.)

Although the framework just provided is useful in getting you started, it is a bit oversimplified. The purpose of a presentation is usually never strictly informative or persuasive. For example, a successful persuasive presentation often has to be entertaining in order to win the audience over. A speech that is persuasive will also contain some informative elements.

Although the general purpose often is assigned in this course, it is important to remember that in presentations outside of this course, it is your responsibility to determine the purpose of your speech—whether to inform or to persuade. Sometimes, the same topic will be persuasive for one audience and informative for another. It is your role as an effective speaker to determine what the situation calls for and to make the appropriate decisions in those circumstances.

The Specific Purpose

In order to further refine and focus the scope or goal of your presentation, you need to develop your specific purpose statement. The specific purpose statement simply refines your general purpose to make it more specific. The **specific purpose statement** conveys what you want your audience to walk away from the presentation knowing or feeling. It expresses exactly what you hope to accomplish in the speech:

- ◎   To inform my audience (to explain or to instruct) …
- ◎   To persuade my audience …

To be effective, a specific purpose statement must meet the following guidelines: It must include the audience in the statement, it must be written as a full infinitive phrase, it must be written as a full declarative statement, it must contain one distinct idea, and it must be clear and precise. Each of these guidelines is discussed next, along with some examples.

Qualities of an Effective Specific Purpose Statement

- ◎   Written as an infinitive phrase
- ◎   Expressed as a full declarative statement
- ◎   Limited to one distinct idea
- ◎   Clear and precise

Qualities of a Well-Written Specific Purpose Statement

Written as a Full Infinitive Phrase   An **infinitive phrase** consists of the word *to* plus a verb. In this case, the verb will either be *inform* or *persuade*. Examples:

- ◎   **Ineffective:** Nutrition
- ◎   **Better:** To inform my audience about the new food pyramid issued by the U.S. Department of Agriculture
- ◎   **Ineffective:** Photomicrography
- ◎   **Better:** To explain to my audience the difference between photomacrography and photomicrography

The ineffective examples do not adequately address what the presentation hopes to accomplish. While they announce the topic, they do not provide enough detail to indicate the direction of the presentation. Remember–the specific purpose statement guides the direction of your presentation. It is a tool used to refine and focus your material. If you cannot identify the exact content of the presentation, the specific purpose is not adequate. The effective examples provide a clear description of where the presentation is headed.

Expressed as a Full Declarative Statement

Examples:

- ◎   **Ineffective:** What is nanotechnology?
- ◎   **Better:** To inform my audience about the latest advances in nanotechnology

- ◎ **Ineffective:** Do you need to get a flu vaccine?
- ◎ **Better:** To persuade my audience to get a flu vaccine

Specific purpose statements written in the form of a question do not clearly indicate the goals of the presentation. While they introduce the topic, they do not provide enough information to reveal what the presentation expects to achieve. Similarly, specific purpose statements that are expressed as fragments also present problems. They do not give enough information about the direction of the presentation.

Limited to One Distinct Idea

Examples:

- ◎ **Ineffective:** To persuade my audience to become active in campus organizations and to reside in on-campus housing
- ◎ **Better:** To persuade my audience to become active in campus organizations
  or
- ◎ **Better:** To persuade my audience to reside in on-campus housing

- ◎ **Ineffective:** To persuade my audience to fill out the census and to become active in the Big Brothers/ Big Sisters organization
- ◎ **Better:** To persuade my audience to fill out the census
  or
- ◎ **Better:** To persuade my audience to become active in the Big Brothers/Big Sisters organization

While the ineffective examples are written as declarative statements and infinitive phrases, they contain more than one distinct and unrelated idea. In each of these examples, it would be better to break them into two separate specific purpose statements, one of which could then be chosen as the focus of the presentation.

Clear and Precise

Examples:

- ◎ **Ineffective:** To persuade my audience to support equality
- ◎ **Better:** To persuade my audience to support new additions to Purdue's Nondiscrimination Policy
- ◎ **Ineffective:** To inform my audience about technology in the college classroom
- ◎ **Better:** To inform my audience how to use the new technology Hotseat that integrates social media to help students participate in class

The ineffective examples above are too general. The specific purpose statement is a tool that assists you in determining what should and should not be included in your presentation. These examples do not provide guidance in this area. They are too vague and nonspecific. Equality for whom? What about technology? The history, current uses, new developments, novel uses, or perhaps popularity? The ineffective examples are too broad and do not provide guidance in focusing the presentation. The better examples, however, are appropriate in focus and provide enough detail to assist in the preparation of the presentation.

Thesis Statement

Once you have written a good specific purpose statement that meets all of the criteria outlined previously, you are ready to construct your thesis statement. The **thesis statement** further refines your purpose for the presentation and is a summary of the main idea of your presentation. It announces your topic and previews the main points of the presentation. It acts as a guide for your audience. A strong thesis statement makes it easier to organize the information that follows because you will be able to relate the information back to that strong thesis.

The primary difference between the specific purpose statement and the thesis statement is that the specific purpose statement is what you expect to accomplish in your speech, while the thesis statement is what you will actually

> **The thesis statement announces your topic and previews the main points of the presentation.**

say to introduce your topic and main points in the introduction of your speech. Keep referring to your thesis statement as you construct your presentation. It will keep your presentation on track. If the materials you find don't relate back to your thesis, they probably don't belong in your presentation.

There are several guidelines you should use as you prepare your thesis statement, and these are discussed next.

Qualities of Effective Thesis Statement

- Is expressed as a full declarative sentence
- Is limited to one idea
- Fits the speech purpose
- Is constructed with clear and concise language and structure

Guidelines for a Thesis Statement

Is Expressed as a Full Declarative Sentence   The thesis statement should be expressed in a complete declarative sentence and not as a question or an incomplete sentence. As with the specific purpose statements, full declarative sentences are better suited to detail the path of the presentation. Examples:

- **Ineffective:** How was the H1N1 vaccine developed?
- **Ineffective:** Developing a vaccine
- **Better:** The H3N2 vaccine introduces a weakened or killed germ into your system that prompts your body to produce antibodies. These antibodies stay in your body, giving you immunity.

Is Limited to One Idea   Similar to the specific purpose statement, if your thesis contains more than one distinct idea, the focus of your presentation will be unclear. Remember, you have a very limited amount of time to address your audience. Within your allotted time frame, you cannot address more than one main idea sufficiently. Examples:

- ◎ **Ineffective:** Our oceans are being destroyed by overfishing, pollution, and the importation of alien species.
- ◎ **Better:** Destructive alien species are being transplanted to our oceans through two primary means: ballast water and ocean litter.

The first thesis is too broad. Too many causes of destruction are being covered in this presentation. The presentation will be more effective if the focus is on only one of these types of destruction.

Fits the Speech Purpose   As you learned in this chapter, each speech has a general purpose or overarching goal. Your thesis should state that purpose—whether that is to inform your audience, or instead, persuade them. So make sure if you plan to inform your audience about a controversial new treatment that you don't end up advocating for that treatment in your thesis. You don't want to word your thesis to encourage your audience to get that treatment in an informative speech. Examples:

- ◎ **Ineffective:** College students should get a hepatitis B vaccine to ensure they don't contract this serious disease.
- ◎ **Better:** Hepatitis B is a serious disease that affects the liver and can be prevented through a vaccine.

Is Constructed with Clear and Concise Language and Structure   As is addressed in Chapter 4, it is more difficult for an audience to follow a verbal message than a written one. It therefore becomes important that your thesis be stated as clearly as possible so that you can enhance your audience's ability to understand the message. This means using simple grammatical structure and avoiding overly complex sentences. It also means using language that is concise and not figurative. Examples:

- ◎ **Ineffective:** We live in an exciting time characterized by many new advances in ophthalmology that are paving the way for revolutionary treatments for eye diseases that could rob us of those beautiful sunsets we all enjoy watching.
- ◎ **Better:** New advances in ophthalmology are leading to changes in both prevention and treatment of eye disease.
- ◎ **Ineffective:** Backpacks can damage young adults' spines. By placing too much weight in their backpacks, students create stress on their back; this may lead to spinal injuries. Young adults can avoid injury by properly using their backpacks.
- ◎ **Better:** In order to avoid back injury, practice safe backpack use by following these four easy steps: choose right, pack right, lift right, and wear right.

Anatomy of a Thesis Statement

Kaley is a health and kinesiology major at Purdue. She's trying to decide on a topic for a required presentation in her "Health Behavior and Promotion" class.

Start with Your Topic Idea   After perusing current event websites such as CNN.com and Google's Science News, Kaley decides to combine her interest in health with current events and give a presentation on the H3N2 flu.

Narrow Your Topic   As Kaley examines recent articles, she finds a variety of possible ideas for her presentation: the scope of the flu, its worldwide impact, its evolution, current medical research on the disease. In the end, she decides that localization will work best for her topic. She knows that Purdue University's Student Health Services, or PUSH, recently announced that H3N2 vaccines were available to all university students. She therefore decides to give her presentation on the H3N2 vaccine.

General Purpose Statement   First, she must decide whether she wants to inform her audience of something (e.g., how the vaccine works, how the vaccine was developed) or persuade them of something (e.g., that the vaccine is safe or unsafe, that they should or should not get the vaccine).

After conducting her research, she decides to get an H3N2 vaccine. That experience helps her decide that she wants to persuade her classmates to do the same.

Her general purpose then become to persuade.

Specific Purpose Statement   This is exactly what Kaley wants her audience to walk out of the room thinking. She wants them to leave the room thinking that they should go to PUSH and get an H3N2 vaccine.

So her specific purpose statement becomes "To persuade my audience to get an H3N2 flu shot."

Thesis   Now that she knows the goal of her speech—to persuade her audience to get an H3N2 flu shot—she has to decide exactly how she is going to put that goal into words. That's what the thesis statement does; it puts your goal into words. It is that statement you will actually deliver in front of your classmates. In her thesis statement, Kaley will need to not only announce that goal but also preview any main points that support her goal. In other words, she wants them to get an H3N2 vaccine, but why?

What are the advantages of getting a flu shot? What hesitations might they have that she needs to overcome? Her research has shown her that the H3N2 flu is a serious disease, especially for the college-age group. The vaccine is a safe way to cut down the chances of getting the flu. However, her research also tells Kaley that some people question the safety of the flu vaccine.

So her thesis statement becomes "College students should get an H3N2 vaccine because it is a safe way to protect themselves from this possibly deadly disease."

Conclusion

This chapter covered the major factors associated with selecting a topic and defining the purpose of the presentation. Many of you are likely struggling with this very issue as you prepare for your class presentations. As indicated earlier, topic selection is not as difficult in professional life as it is in a somewhat artificial classroom environment. However, topics need to be relevant, timely, and appropriate, regardless of the circumstances. This chapter overviewed qualities of a good topic and where to look for topic ideas. It then outlined how to identify and construct the general purpose and the specific purpose and thesis statements will guide the rest of the presentation's development. By creating these statements, you now have a guide that will help you identify important resources, conduct research, and organize information for your presentation.

Key Terms

General purpose statement

Infinitive phrase

Informative presentation

Localizing

Persuasive presentation

Specific purpose statement

Thesis statement

Weblogs

CHAPTER 4

Introductions and Conclusions

Objectives

After reading this chapter, you should be able to

- ◎ identify the five components of an effective introduction;
- ◎ compose an effective introduction;
- ◎ identify the three components of an effective conclusion; and
- ◎ compose an effective conclusion.

Paul Smith, the former associate director of Procter & Gamble's market research, tells the story of how a workplace experience radically changed his approach to presentations.[1] He had spent three weeks assembling a 20-minute presentation that consisted of 30 PowerPoint slides for the CEO of P&G and his team of managers on why Smith's team needed more funding for new market-research techniques. During the presentation, however, then-CEO A.G. Lafley turned his back to the screen and stared at Smith the whole time, ignoring the PowerPoint.

"It didn't occur to me until later that he did that because he was more interested in what I had to say than in what my slides looked like," Smith said the *Wall Street Journal.*

Smith said today he uses "far fewer slides and a lot more anecdotes." He said he begins with a story to get his audience's attention and then peppers additional stories throughout that his audience can relate to. As a result, he says he has had more success getting his ideas across. He noted that after making these adjustments, subsequent presentations to Lafley's group resulted in managers paying closer attention, asking more questions, and providing better feedback.

The ability to craft narratives is a presentation tool that's more useful that PowerPoint mastery, said Lafley, author of *Lead with a Story: A Guide to Crafting Business Narratives That Captivate, Convince, and Inspire.* That's why companies such as Federal Express, Kimberly-Clark and Microsoft are teaching executives to use narratives as a way to improve workplace communication.[2] And it's why it's a skill stressed in this course and in this chapter. As Lafley noted, narratives are a particularly effective way to begin, and end, your presentation.

As a speaker, it is essential that you carefully plan the first and last minutes of your presentation so that you can get the most from your audience. The first two minutes of your presentation are extremely important. This is when you gain the attention of your audience and set the tone for everything that follows. In this chapter, we talk about two key elements of the presentation: the introduction and the conclusion. We will discuss the importance of starting strong and taking advantage of the **primacy effect.** Audiences remember what they hear first, but you need to end strong, as well. Audiences also tend to remember the last thing they hear, which is referred to as the **recency effect.** You want to leave your audience with something to remember.

Tip

While some audience members may be forgiving of a rocky introduction, most will not. So it's important that your introduction be engaging and brings the audience to a level of wanting to know more.

Professionally Speaking | Amy Stoehr | Founder and Director | Real Estate Masters Guild

It should be noted here that even though the introduction and conclusion are important aspects of the presentation, we don't begin the writing process there. It is essential that the body of your presentation be crafted before thinking about the introduction or the conclusion. You simply cannot craft an effective introduction unless you have clearly formulated or articulated the body or main ideas of the presentation. After you have a firm grasp on the main ideas you want to share with your audience, you can then begin to design the introduction. Same with the conclusion: You simply cannot write an effective conclusion until you know what you are going to say in the body of the presentation. The conclusion simply sums up your main ideas. If the main ideas are yet to be formalized, then the conclusion cannot be written. This chapter will provide you with guidelines and helpful hints to make the most of those key opening and closing moments of your presentation.

Spotlight on Research

The Importance of Introductions

How important are the opening minutes of your presentation? Let's turn to educational research for the answer. In one study, students were asked to write summaries of presentations. The results showed that students recalled most information from the first five minutes of the presentation. Another study focused on audience attention levels. It showed that students' attention levels dropped dramatically throughout a lecture. In fact, students retained 70% of the first ten minutes of a lecture, but only 20% of the last ten minutes. This is why it's so important to give your audience a strong thesis statement and to preview the main points in your introduction. These will aid your audience in organizing, and thus retaining, all of the information that follows.[3]

Introductions

As you may recall from earlier chapters, for people to expend significant energy processing your message, two things must be in place: They must be motivated to process the message, and they must be able to process the message.[4] It is during your introduction, the first few moments of your presentation, that listeners make critical assessments about how important and understandable your message will be. If they do not perceive that your presentation will be relevant to them and that they will be able to understand or follow your presentation, then they may tune out.

The introduction in any speech sets the tone for the rest of the presentation. The **introduction** gains the attention of your audience, introduces the speaker and establishes their credibility, relates the topic to the audience, and prepares the audience for the rest of the presentation by announcing and previewing the topic and the main points. For some of your COM114 assignments, you will not need a full, traditional introduction, but it is important you know all of these elements. You cannot overestimate the impact the introduction will make on your audience. First impressions are extremely powerful. Don't underestimate them.

Objectives of an Effective Introduction

An effective introduction in any presentation should:

- ◎ Capture the attention of your audience.
- ◎ Establish your credibility as a speaker.
- ◎ Relate the material to your audience.
- ◎ Announce the topic of the speech.
- ◎ Preview the main points of the speech.

All of these components must be addressed in the introduction of the presentation in order to achieve maximum effect. The speaker must also be able to accomplish all of these components or goals within the allotted time frame. As David Murray, editor of *Vital Speeches of the Day*, argues, you have to get to the point right away or you will lose your audience. A guideline for the length of an introduction is that it should be about 10% of the total speaking time. For example, if you have been asked to deliver a seven-minute presentation, your introduction should last about 45 seconds. Let's examine each of the five goals of an effective introduction so that you can get a better idea of how these components fit together.

Capturing the Attention of Your Audience

The opening remarks in a presentation—the first few phrases that a speaker utters—set the tone for everything that will follow. Therefore, the attention-getter or opening is extremely important. The **attention-gaining device (attention-getter)** is the tool a speaker uses to gain immediate attention from an audience. It can be a story, quotation, fact, statistic, or any one of the other suggestions made in this chapter. If you are unable to capture audience members' attention early in the presentation, it is very difficult to get them to focus on your topic. Therefore, your choice of attention-gaining devices is important.

> The opening remarks in a presentation set the tone for everything that will follow.

Regardless of the type of presentation or the situation, whether it is a sales presentation or a classroom presentation, you will always want to begin with an attention-getter. For some presentations outside the classroom, such as when you are an invited guest, you will want to take the time to thank the group for inviting you and then launch into your attention-getting device. This is not the case in your classroom presentations, however. You do not want to thank your classmates for attending a presentation they are required to attend! There are many devices or strategies that you can use to capture attention inside the classroom. We will review several of the most popular and then examine additional tactics that work better in more professional settings.

Story/Narrative

When author Roald Dahl (*Charlie & the Chocolate Factory, James and the Giant Peach*) jumped in to the debate about whether children should be vaccinated against childhood diseases in England in 1989, he did so in an open letter to parents on his website. The letter began:

> Olivia, my eldest daughter, caught measles when she was seven years old. As the illness took its usual course I can remember reading to her often in bed and not feeling particularly alarmed about it. Then one morning, when she was well on the road to recovery, I was sitting on her bed showing her how to fashion little animals out of coloured pipe-cleaners, and when it came to her turn to make one herself, I noticed that her fingers and her mind were not working together and she couldn't do anything.

> "Are you feeling all right?" I asked her.

> "I feel all sleepy," she said.

> In an hour, she was unconscious. In twelve hours she was dead.

The measles had turned into a terrible thing called measles encephalitis and there was nothing the doctors could do to save her. That was twenty-four years ago in 1962, but even now, if a child with measles happens to develop the same deadly reaction from measles as Olivia did, there would still be nothing the doctors could do to help her.

On the other hand, there is today something that parents can do to make sure that this sort of tragedy does not happen to a child of theirs. They can insist that their child is immunised against measles. I was unable to do that for Olivia in 1962 because in those days a reliable measles vaccine had not been discovered. Today a good and safe vaccine is available to every family and all you have to do is to ask your doctor to administer it.

It is not yet generally accepted that measles can be a dangerous illness. Believe me, it is. In my opinion parents who now refuse to have their children immunised are putting the lives of those children at risk. In America, where measles immunisation is compulsory, measles like smallpox, has been virtually wiped out.

Here in Britain, because so many parents refuse, either out of obstinacy or ignorance or fear, to allow their children to be immunised, we still have a hundred thousand cases of measles every year. Out of those, more than 10,000 will suffer side effects of one kind or another. At least 10,000 will develop ear or chest infections. About 20 will die.

In 2015, after a measles outbreak in the United States was tied to an unvaccinated child at Disneyland, proponents of vaccines quoted Dahl's letter as part of a nationwide campaign to convince all parents that vaccines were safe and necessary.[5]

What made Dahl's letter so effective an appeal decades after he wrote it? It was the emotional story of his daughter that all parents could relate to. Notice that even before he shared the startling statistics of the dangers of measles, he got our attention through his compelling narration of his daughter's contraction, recuperation, relapse, and subsequent death.

One of the best ways to build a relationship immediately with your audience is to begin with a story or narrative. *Forbes* magazine tells us that in business, "learning to tell stories to capture, direct and sustain the attention of others is a key leadership skill. It also greatly helps anyone presenting in front of an audience."[6]

With practice, you can learn to use stories as not only a way to gain attention but also to provide support for key points throughout presentations (see Chapter 6). "I will jam pack a keynote with stories and examples, and will still get questions from the audience to hear more," said Kristi Hedges, a speaker and author of *Power and Presence: Unlock your Potential to Influence and Engage Others.*[7]

Yet most people avoid this presentation device because they do not believe they are good storytellers, or because they do not believe they have good stories to tell. Learning to tell stories is a skill worth developing, however. That's because audiences have been conditioned to listen and learn from stories.

The Science of Stories   Why is that? Why does a story have such an effect on our learning and understanding? We can turn to the neurosciences—which deal with the structure and functions of the brain—for the answer.

When we listen to a presentation that is over-reliant on text visual aids—such as a long PowerPoint presentation with bulleted lists—the language processing areas of our brains, where we decode words into meaning, get activated. But that's all. When we tell a story, not only are the language processing parts of our brain activated, but any other areas of our brain that we would be using to experience the event in the story get activated as well.[8]

Simply put, our brain is responding to fictitious events as if they were real. In one scientific study, researchers placed participants in a functional magnetic resonance imaging (FMRI) machine to watch how participants' brains responded while viewing a story. They found that "the brain doesn't look like a spectator; it looks more like a participant in the action."[9] The vivid simulation of reality produced "runs on minds of readers just as computer simulations run on computers."[10] You have likely experienced this firsthand. Remember the last time you saw a horror movie in a theater? How did you and your fellow audience members react? Did you scream? Jump in your seat? Throw your hands up in the air to protect yourselves from a chainsaw that wasn't really there? Stories hook us because, at least in our brain, whatever is happening in a story is happening to us and not just to them. In other words, a story is the only way to activate parts of the brain so that a listener turns the story into their own.[11]

The ability to make such connections is not lost on many professions. For example, many advertisers have turned to stories to sell products or ideas. A study by the Nielsen research group found that consumers want a more personal connection when they gather information.[12] As a result, you get advertisements such as the popular Budweiser beer commercials that tell the story of a friendship between a Budweiser Clydesdale horse and a puppy. These ads have proved to be among the most popular Super Bowl commercials because they tug at our hearts.

Stoytelling Rules

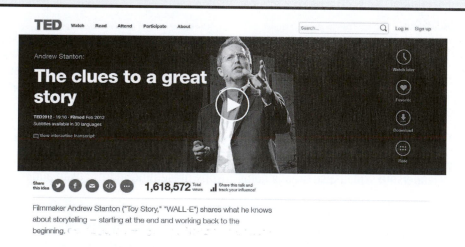

Filmmaker Andrew Stanton ("Toy Story," "WALL-E") shares what he knows about storytelling — starting at the end and working back to the beginning.

Andrew Stanton, the Pixar writer and director behind both Toy Story and WALL-E, talks storytelling rules in his popular TED Talk, "The clues to a great story."[13]

1. **Make me care.** From the beginning, a story has to draw the sympathy of the audience.
2. **Take me with you.** He says that a story is a promise of a journey you will take with the storyteller.
3. **Be intentional.** The protagonist must have a motivation driving them toward a goal.
4. **Let me like you.** The audience has to relate to and appreciate the character's struggle.
5. **Delight me.** Charm, fascinate your audience. Make them forget for a moment and be inside your story.

Psychologists call this "**narrative transport.**"[14] This occurs when the audiences' emotions become entwined with those of the narrative's characters.

Such familiarity is found to help audience members relate to and believe the information to be more important. One study found that prior knowledge and experience can affect just how profound this immersive experience is.[15] Participants were asked to read a short story about a gay man attending his college fraternity's reunion. Those who had family or friends who were gay, or those who had past experiences in fraternities or sororities, reported higher transportation. They also were more likely to perceive the story and its elements to be real. "Familiarity helps, and a character to identify with helps," said study author, psychologist Melanie C. Green.[16]

That doesn't mean that stories won't have an effect on an audience that has not had similar experiences. Stories also have been proven to increase empathy in audiences.[17] Empathy is the ability to put ourselves in someone else's shoes. This can be especially helpful when you are presenting information on situations with which audiences may not have much experience. Think of the American Red Cross attempting to raise money for victims of a natural disaster. Since the target audience is not actually affected by the disaster, and possibly may never have experienced such a loss, stories will be critical in getting an audience to walk in the shoes of families whose lives were destroyed by this natural disaster.

Story Recall   It is also easier for us to remember stories than facts. Whenever we hear a story, we want to relate it to an existing story we already have. When we search for a similar experience in our brains, we activate a part of the brain called the insula. The insula appears to be activated during a wide array of events. "Depending on whom you ask, the insula is involved in pain, love, emotion, craving, addiction, the enjoyment of music, or even the tasting of wine."[18]

Also, a story can be broken down into a connection between a cause and effect, which is how our brains are wired to think.[19] We think in such narratives all day long. When we shop at the grocery store, we are already in our minds cooking the food, and serving it to our friends, and having a nice dinner, or we are remembering the last time we made a particular food and what happened when we did. "We make up stories in our heads for every action and conversation."[20]

In fact, one study found that personal stories make up 65 percent of our conversations.[21] One researcher even went so far as to call our brains "insanely greedy for stories." "We spend about a third of our lives daydreaming—our minds are constantly looking for distractions—and the only time we stop flitting from daydream to daydream is when we have a good story in front of us."[22]

Using a Story as an Attention-Gaining Device   When using a story or narrative as an attention-gaining device, keep several tips in mind.

◎ First, the story must relate directly to the topic of the presentation. Even the most interesting irrelevant stories can leave an audience going: "Why was I just told that?"

◎ Second, it must be brief. We often ramble as we tell stories. In a presentation, we do not have that luxury. Remember, the AG is only part of the whole Introduction, and the Introduction is only 10 percent of your entire presentation. Leave out unnecessary details or parts of the story. One to two minutes is the longest a story should be no matter how long your presentation is. In a three minute speech, you would have only about 20 seconds for an attention-gaining narrative.

- ◎ Third, a simple story is much more successful than a complex one. The simpler the story, the more likely your audience is to remember it. And make sure you use simple language.
- ◎ Fourth, a story must be delivered well (see Delivering the Story on page 72).
- ◎ And finally, the story must have good structure.

Good Story Structure   A good story has a beginning, middle and end. That's called pacing. Audiences process information more effectively when stories build toward a conclusion.[23] So it's important that the story have a clear structure and closure. It is possible to split the story parts among your presentation. You could have the start and middle in your introduction, for example, and your end in your conclusion. But you must have a complete story. We must get from "Once upon a time" to "They lived happily ever after" in the same presentation.

But there is more to the structure of a good story, even a short one, than that. Just because a story has a beginning, middle, and end doesn't mean it's a good choice for your presentation. There are other elements to consider as you structure your story, whether it be your attention-getter or a supporting point in your presentation:

- ◎ **Clear Purpose:** It should be readily clear to the audience why you are telling this story at this point in your presentation.
- ◎ **Match Your Stories to Key Points in Your Presentation:** Audiences remember more when you combine narratives with other forms of support. So as you are constructing your presentation, consider if a story would help support your main points in addition to all the statistics, survey results, and expert testimony you found. The best supporting points combine multiple forms of support.
- ◎ **Common Reference Points:** As you structure your story, be sure to highlight any similarities or common experiences with the audience. This could be as simple as age, gender, or employer, or as complex as a shared life experience or a common goal.
- ◎ **Details:** You should have enough visual descriptions that the audience can picture what you are picturing. We remember best what can be seen, heard, touched, and personally experienced.
- ◎ **Perspective:** A good story puts information in perspective. It doesn't replace information. When you use a story as support in a presentation, the story doesn't replace your need to state your main points and subpoints. Tell me first what this story is illustrating.
- ◎ **Emotion:** A good story highlights and/or evokes emotions. This allows your audience to relate on a personal level to the subject of the story.
- ◎ **Action:** Make something happen in your story in a specific time and place. Conflict. Achievement. An action is necessary for your story to advance toward completion.

Delivering the Story   As stated previously, many of us avoid stories as a presentational device because we are not sure how to tell them well. Here are some tips that when used will help you feel more confident in delivering a narrative:

- ◎ **Practice Telling Your Stories:** "A good story is one you are comfortable telling."[24] If audiences perceive you are forcing a story, they won't believe it. The reason professionals can weave such stories that hold our attention is because they are likely telling stories they have told before. Practice does make perfect. So you need to practice telling your stories just as you would practice any other aspect of your presentation.

◎ **But Don't Be Robotic:** You don't want to practice your story so much that is comes out sounding over-rehearsed and memorized. Stories should sound more spontaneous, more sincere. Don't write it out word for word and then memorize it. You will definitely want to deliver a story from key words only.

◎ **Length:** Your story cannot be so long as to detract from the actual presentation itself. It should support, but not overwhelm, your point. Remember, as an attention-gaining device, a story should be short.

Finding Stories   Right now many of you are saying, "But I don't have that many experiences to share." It's important to remember that there are many sources of narratives for your presentations:

◎ **Personal Stories:** You have had some experiences that you could share with others. Because these are personal stories, you will be able to relate them with great passion. As you think about your presentations, think about related experiences you have had that you can share with your audience.

◎ **Interviews:** You can interview others to extract stories from them. These could be family members, friends, professors, even strangers. Many people will be happy to share stories with you.

◎ **Media:** Newspaper and magazine articles are a great source of personal stories. Using a database like LexisNexis, or visiting a newspaper's website, you can put in key terms and find news articles that contain interviews with real people who have shared their personal stories with reporters.

◎ **Internet:** Nonprofit organizations and companies know the power of a good story. Research in advertising shows that audiences respond more positively to advertisements in narrative form compared to more linear ads that highlight arguments for a product.[25] Chances are many of these organizations have stories and testimonials on their websites that you could share in your presentations.

◎ **Recycle Stories:** It's perfectly fine to retell or adapt stories you have heard others tell. But it is unethical to pass off someone else's story as your own. Make sure when you retell a story, you make it clear that it didn't happen to you. "One time, my friend Jane …" or "Susan Smith was a teacher when she …" makes it clear to listeners that you are sharing Jane's and Susan's stories. This does not diminish the effectiveness of the story.

◎ **Story Log:** In a professional setting, it's a good idea to keep a list of possible narratives. Get in the habit of jotting down situations in which you had a success or failure. This way, when called upon to make a presentation, you will have a ready list of possible stories to include.

Here is an example of a narrative taken from Natalie's informative speech on e-lectures:

> Medical school interviews forced senior Brad Burmeister to miss three days of classes last semester. He had to rely on a friend's notes to pick up cellular and molecular biology concepts. As he attempted to copy and translate his friend's notes, Brad realized that he and his friend had very different styles of note-taking and that these notes would be of little use to him. Brad felt that he missed out on some very important competencies because he had to miss class to attend the medical school interviews. It would have been an easier and better method, he argued, to have those lectures from class available on the Web, through audio and video recordings.

Natalie uses this story to immediately involve the audience in the topic. Audiences can relate to the plight of a student who had to miss class and got behind because of it. Here is another example of a personal narrative told by Lupe encouraging her classmates to take a class online:

When I decided to return to school to get my degree, I eagerly explored the school's online course catalog to pick out my courses. But my feeling of excitement quickly subsided when I saw that most of the courses I needed conflicted with my "day job." I thought this meant that it was going to take me twice as long to get my degree, and I was discouraged. But then, someone pointed out that many of the courses I couldn't take in a "brick and mortar classroom" were available through our college's distance learning program. Now, I'm enrolled in two classes instead of one, and on my way to earning my degree sooner.

Spotlight on Research

We know that language choice is a key element in effective storytelling. We want to choose words that create strong emotions and produce vivid images for our listeners. But one study has found that some words have become so overused that they've lost their ability to produce reactions.

A study by scientists in Spain found that our brain has learned to ignore certain overused words and phrases. Specifically, researchers found that such words failed to activate the brain's frontal cortex–the area of your brain responsible for emotions.

For example, figures of speech like "a rough day" or "stinking mad" or "smelled fishy" or a "hard life" are so familiar that they are treated simply as words. Keep this in mind when constructing your narratives.[26]

Here are a few more examples taken from industry speeches, which are considerably longer than your classroom assignments, allowing for longer attention-getters. The first example uses a different type of story, a folktale, to convey the thesis and main points of a presentation and was delivered by Deborah A. P. Hersman, chair of the National Transportation Safety Board.[27]

Once upon a time ... three goats, Siksik, Mikmik, and Jureybon were grazing on a stony hill. Scenting them, a hyena lopes up. "Siksik," calls the hyena. "Yes, sir," says the goat. "What are those points on your head?" "These are my little horns, sir." "What is that patch on your back?" the hyena asks. "My hair, sir." "Why are you shivering?" roars the hyena. "Because I am afraid, sir." With that, the hyena gobbles him up. The hyena turns to Mikmik, who answers just as his brother, with the same tragic result. Next, the hyena approaches Jureybon. The hyena asks, "What are those points on your head?" "Why those are my trusty sabers!" "And the patch on your back, what is that?" "My sturdy shield!" Jureybon replies. To the hyena's last question, "Why are you shivering?" Jureybon snarls, "Shivering? I'm shaking with rage to throttle you!" Jureybon advances on the hyena, who runs for his life. Jureybon springs after him, slits open his belly, and frees his brothers. He saw what happened, learned from it, and adapted to prevent it from happening again. And that's what I will talk about tonight: accident investigation–its past, present and how it must adapt in order to play an even more pivotal role in creating civil aviation's safer and stronger future.

As you notice, the story or fable is succinct and the lessons learned lead right into the presentation. Ms. Hersman continues to refer back to the story as she builds her major points in the presentation.

In the next example, Dr. Clare Gerard delivers an address to the annual Primary Care Conference in Liverpool, England, and begins her speech with this personal story:[28]

I'd like to tell you a story about a GP, a radiologist, a pathologist, and a psychiatrist. Sounds like the first line of a joke, but it isn't. The GP was me. We were having dinner with our children at an open-air opera in Germany. The place was packed. Everyone was having a good time, when the dreaded happened. Out of the corner of my eye, I saw an elderly man fall headfirst into his plate. The four of us looked at each other. We knew our meal was over and we swung into action. Each working to type: the psychiatrist tending to the man's wife; the radiologist searching for a defibrillator; the pathologist pounding on the poor man's chest; me, giving mouth-to-mouth. From the way he keeled over, it was obvious he was dead. But we knew there was still plenty for us to do. We had to comfort his distressed wife. And we had to keep the crowd calm for 30 minutes, till the paramedics arrived. When it was over, my 15-year-old son turned to me and said: "I want to be able to do that." "Do what?" I asked him. "Care for people," he said. His reply surprised me. Not just because impressing teenage children isn't easy, but also because what impressed him wasn't the glory and the drama of our public display of medical skill. No. What impressed him was our simple act of caring.

Dr. Gerard went on to encourage her audience to remember their story—why they wanted to be a doctor—and to persuade them not to forget to *care* in this day and age of medical economics.

When using a story or narrative as an attention-getting device, keep several tips in mind. First, the story must relate directly to the topic of the presentation. Second, it must be brief. We often ramble as we tell stories. In a presentation, we do not have that luxury. Third, the story must have a clear beginning, middle, and end. Audiences process information more effectively when stories build toward a conclusion.[29] So it is important that the story have a clear structure and closure.

Ethically Speaking

Using Fictionalized Narratives

Anecdotes or narratives are a great way to start a presentation. As you have read, narratives can personalize your topic and build identification with your audience. But ethics requires that we reveal to our audience when a narrative is fictionalized. A fictionalized account may allow us to add more drama to a story, but if we don't tell the audience the story is a creation of our imagination, we are misleading them. This will damage our credibility. Our audience might feel betrayed when they discover that the character they were moved by does not exist. We can examine a recent incident of this in the publishing world. The television show *60 Minutes* revealed that the opening anecdote in the best-selling memoir *Three Cups of Tea* was manufactured. The author, philanthropist Greg Mortenson, opens with an account of getting lost while mountain climbing in rural Pakistan in 1993. According to the book, Mortenson wandered into the village of Korphe, where the residents nursed Mortenson back to health. It was their kindness that inspired him to build a school, the first of what he said were more than 170 his charity has constructed in that area of the world. But according to CBS, Mortenson didn't visit the village until 1994. Mortenson later conceded the opening anecdote wasn't literally true but "a compressed version of events." However, the damage had been done. Mortenson's credibility was called into question, as was the work of his charities.[30]

A story or narrative is often one of the best ways to start a presentation, especially for beginning speakers. Stories are interesting and effective in building identification with your audience. You really can't go wrong with a good story if you tell it with skill.

Quotation

Another common way to begin a presentation is by introducing a quotation. A famous quotation or a quotation from a well-known figure that relates to your topic can be a clever way to engage your audience. Audiences appreciate comments from individuals they respect. Again, as with a story or narrative, your quotation must relate directly to your material. It should be very clear to your audience why you are using the quotation. If you have to explain the relevance of the quotation to the topic of your presentation, it is probably not the best choice.

You also need to avoid quotes that have become obvious clichés. For example, consider the following quote from Ben Franklin: "Early to bed and early to rise makes a man healthy, wealthy, and wise." This overused quotation has become a cliché. In a presentation, you want to grab the audience with a powerful quote; this one probably wouldn't do the trick because we've all heard it before.

The following example demonstrates a more effective way to use a quotation: A physician addressing a civic organization was asked to speak about health information on the Internet.

He started his speech by saying, "Mark Twain once said, 'Be careful about reading health books. You may die of a misprint.' The same might be said of health sites on the Internet." He then went on to give a presentation on how to evaluate online health information sources. The quote worked well because it was relevant, humorous, from a well-known source, and appropriate to the audience.

Interesting Fact or Statistic

Sometimes the best way to introduce a topic is to surprise the audience in some meaningful way. This is often accomplished by sharing some interesting fact or statistic that startles or shocks the audience. Jane's informative speech on healthy lifestyle choices started this way:

> According to the University of Colorado's Wellness Center, two out of five women and one out of five men would trade three to five years of their life to achieve their weight-loss goals.

This is an alarming statistic. Jane used an interesting fact to engage and pique the interest of her audience and used it as a springboard for the rest of her presentation. Shocking facts and statistics, like this one, are easily found while you are conducting your research. Sometimes we overlook these pieces of information. Be alert–they can really add impact to the introduction.

Use Technology (Audio/Visual Aids)

Sometimes the old cliché "a picture is worth a thousand words" is true, and it is possible to grab an audience's interest by demonstrating an important part of your presentation visually. Jeremy, a student at the University of Louisville, was very involved in cheerleading. He delivered a presentation persuading his audience that the university should consider cheerleading a sport. He began his presentation by showing a video of the national championship routine of the University of Louisville coed cheerleading squad from the previous year. Audience members were dumbfounded. None of them had any idea of the level of athleticism these cheerleading routines required. The video was one of the most compelling pieces of supporting evidence used in Jeremy's presentation, and it had an even greater impact as an attention-getter.

There are a few guidelines to consider when using a video, audio, or any other multimedia device as an attention-getter. First, rather than simply pushing PLAY, introduce your presentational aid. Audience members need some introduction to prepare themselves for whatever it is you want to show them. If you start the media device without orienting the audience to it, the audience can end up missing half of the audio/visual presentation. Second, cue the video or media to its exact position. Beginning the media at the wrong spot is unprofessional.

Finally, you must have good working knowledge of the equipment in the room. Orient yourself to the equipment beforehand, or arrange to have a knowledgeable person there with whom you have discussed and practiced your presentation. If you have any doubts about how to run the equipment, choose another attention-getter. Your ability to use the equipment must be seamlessly incorporated into your presentation. Anything less is unprofessional. Remember, this is the first thing an audience sees of your presentation. If you have problems right from the start, your credibility will suffer.

Attention-Getters for Outside the Classroom

Your speaking situation will dictate what types of attention-gaining devices you should consider using. The previous examples work well in a classroom setting or with captive audiences. Additional attention-gaining devices are available for presentations in more professional settings with motivated audiences.

Compliment the Audience

When you are asked to address an audience outside of the classroom, it is nice if you can draw on some of the audience's previous successes and incorporate those into your opening. It demonstrates that you have done your research about this particular group, thereby enhancing your credibility, and it also relates the audience's experiences with the topic of your presentation.

Consider the following scenario in which this type of opening is appropriate: Imagine that you are a fifth-grade teacher addressing a group of parents about an upcoming field trip. One thing you know about this group of parents is that they have just completed a very successful fund-raising campaign. Compliment them on the successful campaign, and thank them for their hard work. Then you can address your primary goal of presenting information about the field trip by highlighting how the successful fundraising campaign has provided plenty of money to cover not only normal classroom expenses, but additional frills as well, such as the upcoming field trip.

Don't draw compliments out too long and don't feel compelled to compliment everyone in the room. This strategy should be executed quickly, get directly to your point, and relate back to the topic of the presentation.

Refer to Recent Events

When you make a presentation, remember that speeches never occur in a vacuum. Many outside events affect our daily lives. Events that are very important to your particular audience may have occurred recently. Perhaps their organization has just gone through a big organizational restructuring or has had a change in leadership. Or maybe the economy has particularly affected their industry. If you can relate these events to your presentation topic, it might be important to address them.

John C. Lechleiter, chairman, president, and CEO of Eli Lilly & Co., used this strategy when he addressed the Dallas Friday Group, a group of business executives in Dallas, Texas, shortly after the Rangers, the home baseball team, had lost the 2010 World Series.[31] He stated, "I have to console you about the Rangers–never count them out–they'll be back!" He went on to use the Ranger's statistics from the year to illustrate the main point in his speech.

This was a great strategy for Mr. Lechleiter to use to connect with his audience. He started with something familiar, the Rangers, and then used their season statistics as a mechanism for pulling his audience into his topic, medical spending.

Solicit Participation

Another way to get audience members excited about the presentation from the very beginning is to get them involved. Asking for a volunteer to participate in some aspect of a demonstration is a way to get the audience directly involved. Or you can ask audience members to perform a related task.

For example, a presenter was delivering a speech about longterm care facilities. She asked the audience to take out a sheet of paper and list the five most important things in their lives. Then she asked them to cross off three of those items. Audience members found this to be a difficult task. The speaker then explained that giving up those things most important to them (e.g., their homes, their pets) is exactly what individuals face when entering a long-term care facility such as a nursing home.

This attention-getting device fulfilled two goals for the speaker. First, by getting audience members involved in the presentation, she got their attention. Second, she aroused empathy for older adults who were facing these life-changing choices, which significantly affected the way the audience reacted to the entire presentation. Audience members were then able to take the perspective of the older adult, which was exactly what the speaker hoped.

Soliciting audience participation is an attention-getter that could backfire on you, however. You don't want to spend the opening minutes of your speech begging someone to volunteer. Make sure you try this attention-gaining device with a motivated audience. A captive audience is less likely to participate in such an attention-getter.

Attention-Getters to Avoid

Questions

Many presenters open by posing a question for their audience. Sometimes, this is a purely **rhetorical question,** which means that you do not expect a verbal response to the question you have posed. Rather, you only want audience members to think about the question you have raised. Sometimes, however, you want an answer from the audience. If this is the case, you ask a **direct question** because you desire a response. The response the audience provides may guide the way you adapt your presentation to that audience. Or perhaps you simply ask the question in order to get the audience actively involved.

Students sometimes open their presentations with questions because they think it is easy. This couldn't be further from the truth. Skilled use of questions is difficult. First, there is the risk that your audience won't care about the answer. For example, suppose you are delivering a presentation about a new process to genetically modify foods. You might begin the presentation with a question such as, "Have you ever wondered where some foods come from?" But what if audience members' answer is "no"? Maybe they haven't; maybe this is something they don't think would be appealing to them. If they can answer "no" to your initial question, why should they continue to listen to the rest of your presentation?

Second, dependence on an audience's response to a question attention-getter can be dangerous. David, a former student in a presentational speaking course, gave a speech on controlling the wild deer population. He began his speech by asking his audience a direct question: "What animal, reptile, or insect kills more Americans each year?" David had anticipated that audience members would offer many incorrect guesses before he dramatically revealed that the correct answer was wild deer. However, nobody in the audience offered a guess. Many audience members are reluctant to participate in such a way. As a result, David's planned big announcement was a flop, as was his attention-getter.

> **Not all attention-gaining devices will work in all settings.**

Another common flop is informal polls. Julie planned a speech on the condition of rental properties around campus. She first asked people to raise their hands if they thought their rent was fair. Next she asked them to raise their hands if they thought their rent was too high. However, out of a class of 28, only a couple of people raised their hands for either choice. Now what? Julie became flustered and was unsure how to handle this. Her presentation suffered as a result. Before using this method, ask yourself why you want to use it. If you don't have a good reason, choose another method for gaining attention.

Jokes

Humor is another commonly used device for beginning a presentation, but humor is tricky to use well, and there are many pitfalls. Some audiences react favorably to humor; others are offended. As mentioned in other chapters in this text, the global environment in which we now find ourselves operating is extremely complex. Cultural differences in global audiences add another degree of difficulty to using humor well. Unless you are extremely familiar with another culture, you simply cannot predict what an audience will find humorous, appropriate, or offensive.

If, after doing a thorough analysis of the speaking situation, you find that humor would be an effective way to engage your audience, you can begin by telling a funny narrative or example. You should not begin your speech by telling a joke. This is usually a sign that the speaker is a novice. Jokes also have the potential to alienate individuals in the audience. What is funny to you may be offensive to someone else. There are more sophisticated and appropriate ways to incorporate humor into the opening of your presentation.

Hypothetical Situations

The "imagine this hypothetical situation" is another commonly used device for beginning a presentation, but in reality it often is a weaker way to start. First, the speaker is oftentimes asking the audience to imagine a situation they can't possibly imagine. Emily, a student, was giving a useful information presentation on her university's grief counseling options. She asked her classmates to imagine they had just lost a child. Her 18-year-old classmates could not possibly know how this might feel. Similarly, David, who was attempting to persuade his peers to join the university's ROTC, asked them to imagine themselves in a firefight in Afghanistan. Again, his classmates, many of whom had never been out the country, could not possibly do so.

As stated previously in the narratives section, a stronger alternative to a hypothetical situation attention-getter would be to share a narrative from a real person who had actually experienced a situation. Don't ask your audience to imagine a made-up situation where a student must get a full-time job because of tuition increases. Instead, find a student who has taken on this added responsibility. Your audience will be more moved by a real person's trials than by those of your imaginary student. In many instances, you can find such narratives while doing research for your topic, in newspaper and magazine stories, or through interviews.

Considerations in Choosing an Attention-Gaining Device

At this point, you may be overwhelmed by the choices for beginning your presentation. You may be wondering where you should start and what you should choose. Guidelines that should help you in this phase of the presentation process follow. These guidelines consider criteria such as mood, time, audience, and your personal strengths.

Consider Building Identification with the Audience

Showing similarity with audience members is important, especially in persuasive presentations. Audience members need to see themselves as similar to the speaker in important respects, such as age, political views, or socioeconomic status. If you can highlight some of these similarities, it becomes easier for the audience to identify with you as the speaker and, ultimately, with the goal of your presentation.[32]

Almost any of the devices discussed above can be used to increase identification with an audience. Here is an example of how Bryan used a personal narrative to build identification with his classroom audience. He began his presentation by telling audience members that he used to be just like them—a college student strapped for cash and working at a low-paying, dead-end job—but that he was now a 21-year-old college student and a successful entrepreneur. He had begun his own necktie business and was currently earning $35,000 a year. He went on to give a persuasive presentation that encouraged the audience to become entrepreneurs.

But be careful. In 2011, actress Kim Delaney was asked to give a speech at the ceremony awarding the Liberty National Award to former defense secretary Robert Gates. She opened her presentation by sharing with her audience of military families and dignitaries what she said were her own experiences with the active-duty military. She talked about the struggles she and her husband went through during multiple deployments. She said she had watched hundreds of wounded soldiers come home, and had even attended the military funeral of her best friend's son. The problem: Delaney was actually referring to her character on the television series *Army Wives*, something she neglected to mention for several minutes to an obviously confused audience. Those in attendance at Delaney's speech were actual military families, who were insulted by her suggestion that she had been through what so many of them had and were unsure how to react. Her decision to try to use her television adventures to show similarity with the audience was inappropriate. She was actually escorted off stage before she finished her presentation. As Delaney discovered, you should not lie or mislead your audience in an attempt to build rapport with them. An audience who feels they have been misled will not be receptive.

Consider the Tone Your Presentation Is Trying to Establish

If your presentation has a somber tone, humor is not an appropriate way to begin. You want the attention-getter to match the overall tone of your presentation. Keeping the tone consistent in your presentation will help achieve optimal impact.

Consider Your Time Restrictions

Sometimes we can think of incredible attention-getters. However, they take up a large portion of time relative to our entire speaking time. Maybe you have a wonderful narrative that relates well to your subject matter; however, the narrative takes four minutes, and you can see no way to shorten the story and still achieve the desired effect. In this case, it may not be feasible to use the narrative. Remember, your introduction must contain an attention-getter, a credibility statement, a relevance statement, a thesis, and a preview in order to be effective. This is a good deal of material to cover, considering the time constraints and the 10% rule. You do not want your attention-getter to take up too much of your speaking time.

Consider Your Strengths as a Speaker

It is also important that you capitalize on your strengths as a speaker in the attention-gaining phase of your presentation. If you are a gifted storyteller, use a narrative to engage your audience. Think about what you do best, and capitalize on your strengths. Choose an attention-gaining device that is right not only for the topic and presentation, but also for you and your speaking strengths.

Consider the Audience

Always choose an attention-getter with your audience in mind. Audience analysis is important at every step in planning your presentation, even when planning the attention-gaining phase. Ask yourself, "How will my audience likely respond to this attention-getter?" To answer this question, you must also consider your relationship to the audience. Your role in relation to that of the audience is important.

Consider this example of a student who did not recognize her relationship to her audience: Mary was in her late 60s, while the rest of the class members were "traditional" college students, ages 18 to 23. She was delivering an informative presentation about sex education programs in public schools. In opening the presentation, she told a funny story about sex and condoms. Instead of laughing, audience members looked horrified. After the presentation, the students in her audience commented that it was almost as if their grandmother had told a dirty joke to their friends. It made them very uncomfortable. Mary had not considered how her relationship with the other students in the class might impact the effect of her attention-getter. Although the students may have found the same story funny from another student in the class, and even though they enjoyed and respected Mary as a classmate, her age in relation to theirs changed the impact of the humor.

Consider Your Topic

The attention-getter must also contribute to the development of the topic. Many times, students find an excellent example or startling statistic that they would like to use as their attention-getter, but it is only tangentially related to their topic. If this is the case, do not use it. The attention-getter should be the initial step in introducing your topic. The link between your attention-getter and your thesis statement should be extremely clear to your audience. If it is not, you need to consider another opening for your presentation.

Establishing Credibility

Once you have gained the attention of your audience, it is important that you establish your credibility as a speaker on the topic you are addressing. **Credibility** refers to an audience's perception of how believable a speaker is on a given topic. Sometimes the person who invited you to speak will establish your credibility in his or her introduction, and you will not have to devote time in your introduction to this step. More often than not, however, you will have to establish your credibility for yourself through a credibility statement. A **credibility statement** simply states what experiences or educational preparation you have had that make you an expert on this topic.

To construct your credibility statement, ask yourself what specific experiences, qualifications, or educational background provide you with authority on this particular topic. Whatever those qualifications may be, you need to describe them to your audience. This is the point in the presentation when you really want to sell yourself or the company you represent. You must accomplish this task in a modest manner, since being boastful could offend or insult your audience. However, you do want audience members to understand why you should be viewed as an expert. Research indicates that education level, occupation, and experience all work together to increase a speaker's expertise and trustworthiness.[33]

The following credibility statement was delivered in a presentation by Cynthia J. Starks, a professional speechwriter, to the Columbia Club of Indianapolis.[34] The Columbia Club is an organization that provides local business leaders with social networking opportunities. Ms. Starks's speech was titled "Harness the Visceral Power of Oral Communication."

> My name is Cynthia Starks and I've been writing speeches for men and women like you for about 25 years. I've been a speechwriter at IBM, United Technologies Corp., and Southern New England Telecommunications. I've written for business, government and education leaders, and, once, for the late Walter Cronkite.

By describing her industry experience, Ms. Starks answers the question of why her audience should listen to her. She describes specifically those aspects of her career that make her qualified to speak on this particular topic.

In the classroom, the speaking situation is a little different than presentations made to other groups. Although many of you will choose topics in which you have direct experience and educational credibility, some of you will not. You may choose a topic simply because you are interested in it. Perhaps you will have had no direct experience with your topic other than the research you did for the presentation. That is perfectly acceptable in this context. Simply tell your audience why you became interested in the topic and what you did in terms of research to prepare for the presentation. Consider the following examples from student speeches.

Keys to an Effective Introduction

- ◎ Always start with an attention-gaining device.
- ◎ Display enthusiasm for your presentation.
- ◎ Display a sense of control.

- ◎ Do not make apologies.
- ◎ Do not make promises your presentation cannot keep.

Tyrone delivered a speech on DNA profiling and included the following credibility statement:

> As a criminal justice student, I have always been interested in DNA profiling. This speech allowed me the opportunity to dive in and explore the issue a bit more critically through academic research and interviews, and I'd like to share what I discovered with you.

Relating the Material to the Audience

One important factor in motivating your audience to listen to your presentation is demonstrating how the subject relates to them and how they will benefit directly from the information you will impart.[35] A speaker can easily achieve this through a relevance statement. The **relevance statement** explicitly states the relationship between your topic and your audience. It answers the question, "What's in this for me?" It is important that you, as the speaker, answer this question for audience members. Do not leave this important step up to them. Give them a reason to listen. Be explicit. If they will be more organized as a result of your speech, tell them that. If they will be able to protect themselves from intruders, get better seats on an airplane, or even make a better cheesecake, tell them that. What will they get out of your presentation today?

While a relevance statement is important for all types of audiences, it is particularly important for the captive audience. Recall from Chapter 2 that captive audiences attend a presentation because they are required to do so. They have no choice. Their attendance is required, perhaps because of a job they hold or due to a course requirement they must fulfill. You have to work extra hard to motivate a captive audience to listen to and process your presentation.

Making your material relevant to your audience also has other benefits.[36] By increasing the relevance to your audience, you also increase the likelihood that your audience will comprehend and learn from the material that you present.[37]

Lupe, a former student, was encouraging her classmates to take an online course. Here is her relevance statement:

> I know many of you are handicapped as well when deciding on your schedule by either full- or part-time jobs. Bosses aren't always as flexible as we would like them to be, yet according to the U.S. Department of Education, 78 percent of undergraduates work.

As you can see, Lupe made this information relevant to her classmates not only by acknowledging that many of them work, but also by highlighting the problem of inflexible work schedules. She provides a solution to their problem—online classes.

Localizing a statistic, as discussed in Chapter 6, is another way to get your audience to care. Show them that your topic is affecting them right in their community. Don't just use national statistics and national or international examples. Bring your topic home to your specific audience. What are the statistics for members of your audience?

Marcus, a former student, did just that. He worked for an exterminator in the local area and wanted to deliver a speech on the prevalence of bed bugs. In order to get his audience to recognize the potential threat of bed bugs to them, he had to focus on local infestation rates and figures. He even provided evidence from earlier that week that bed bugs had been found in their own campus housing. This focus on the local prevalence of bedbugs made the potential threat much more real to his audience. By the end of his presentation, he had his audience in the palm of his hands!

Announcing the Topic and Previewing the Main Points

As discussed in Chapter 3, the **thesis statement** encapsulates the general message and previews the main points of the presentation. In effect, it announces the topic and the main ideas of your presentation. You deliver your thesis statement during the introduction of the speech so that you can prepare your audience for the rest of the presentation.

Although previewing your main points may be a bit uncomfortable, it is vital in helping audiences understand your message. Organizational structure in an oral presentation is not as apparent as it is in a written presentation. In contrast to a reader of "the printed word," an audience of "the spoken word" does not have the luxury of turning back a few pages in order to follow a point you have made. By previewing the main points of the speech, you help audience members to organize the presentation in advance so that they are prepared to listen when you get there. This repetition helps ensure that your message will be clear and that your audience can follow you.[39] Organizational cues, such as **preview statements,** help audiences retain and learn information,[40] so don't neglect this step.

Spotlight on Research

The Importance of Previews

The importance of previewing your main points in your introduction is supported by much research. In one interesting experiment, researchers wanted to examine the effects of previewing on children's comprehension of television storylines. The children were divided into two groups: One group simply watched an episode of a show; the second group was given a preview of the information in the episode before watching it. Then both groups were tested on what information was contained in the show. Those children who had the information previewed were better able to comprehend and retain factual information from the episode. In addition, the preview group retained more events that were central to the storyline, just as your audiences will be able to connect your evidence to your main points.[38]

Here is an example of an introduction for a speech, including its specific purpose statement:

Specific Purpose   To inform my audience about the injury treatment and prevention services offered by the University Recreational Sports Center.

Attention-Getter   As part of his renewed commitment to get in shape, Jason decided to train for the Indianapolis 500 mini-marathon. He began a daily workout routine. But his training kept getting interrupted by a nagging muscle injury that kept recurring. Jason was unsure how to get well and how to prevent the injury from coming back. As a student, he could have simply gone to the Co-Rec to get the help he needed, for free or little cost.

Credibility Statement   As a physical therapy major, I currently intern at the Co-Rec in the trainer division and know firsthand the many valuable services available to students.

Relevance Statement   You don't have to be training for a marathon to get injured. You can go down simply trying to lose a few pounds before swimsuit weather. The National Electronic Injury Surveillance System says there were almost 64,000 exercise-related injuries in our age group treated at emergency rooms last year.

Thesis and Preview Statement   The Recreational Sports Center offers an array of exercise-related injury treatment and prevention services as part of its promotion of active lifestyles. First, I will tell you how the Co-Rec can help rehabilitating that nagging injury you've suffered, and then I will tell you how the Co-Rec can help make sure you don't get injured again.

The Conclusion

Now that you understand the necessary components for constructing an effective introduction, let's examine how to prepare the final element in a presentation, the conclusion.

The **conclusion** is where you review the information you just presented and leave the audience with your final thoughts. An effective conclusion should achieve three objectives: First, you want to reiterate your thesis statement. Second, you want to review your main points. And finally, you want to leave your audience with a memorable thought or lasting impression; this is accomplished through a "clincher" and is discussed later in this chapter. (For some of your COM114 assignments, you will not need a traditional conclusion.)

The conclusion is the shortest major element in your presentation. It should consume approximately 5% of your total speaking time. Thus, if your presentation is scheduled to last seven minutes, your conclusion should take 20 to 25 seconds. If there were a motto for the conclusion, it would be, "Be clear, brief, and memorable."

The conclusion will be the last impression you make on your audience. As mentioned in the opening of this chapter, research suggests that what audiences hear last, they remember best.[41] Take full advantage of this opportunity to leave

> The conclusion will be the last impression you make on your audience.

your audience with a lasting impression. Many speakers depend on a solid introduction and body to get them through the presentation and pay little attention to the conclusion. These speeches tend to fizzle out. Don't let this happen to you. End your presentation with a bang.

Objectives of an Effective Conclusion

An effective conclusion in any presentation should

- ◎   restate the thesis;
- ◎   restate the main points; and
- ◎   end with a clincher or memorable thought.

Restating the Thesis and Main Points

The conclusion in a presentation "tells the audience what you've told them." That is exactly what you want to do. Take advantage of repetition. What you have a chance to repeat during your presentation, your audience will remember.[42] The more the audience can remember about your presentation, the greater your chances of achieving your presentation goals.

You will want to restate the thesis and the preview statement. This can occur in one step or two steps; you can combine the thesis and main points into one statement or separate them into two. You want the audience to leave your presentation with a clear sense of what you covered. This is where you provide them with that information.

Try to vary the words you use when restating your thesis and main points. You do not have to use the same language you used in the introduction. In fact, it is better if you don't. Rephrase them so that the message is still conveyed but in a more novel manner.

Sometimes, as we deliver a presentation, we are unable to cover all of the material we had hoped to present because of time or other situational constraints. It is important that the conclusion review only material you presented in the body of your presentation. Even those items that may have been previewed in the introduction, but were skipped due to situational constraints, should be omitted from the conclusion.

Ending with a Clincher or Memorable Thought

Just as you should fully engage your audience in the beginning of the speech, you should also seek to hold their attention at the end of your speech. The **clincher** is the final remark that you will make to your audience. It should be as compelling as your attention-getter. Give your audience something to think about. Don't let a great presentation fizzle with a weak ending such as, "Well, that's about it." There are many ways to end a speech, just as many as there are to begin a speech. Let's review some of the most common approaches.

Referring Back to the Attention-Getter

One of the most effective ways to end your speech and provide a sense of closure for your audience is to tie the speech back to your attention-getter. For example, if you have opened your presentation with a story, refer back to that story and end with an extension of that narrative. Scott Davis, chairman and CEO of UPS, demonstrates this strategy in a speech he delivered to the Americas Competitiveness Forum in Atlanta.[43]

He began the speech with a quote: "Over 300 years ago, in 1666, English poet John Dryden said, 'Trade, like blood, should circulate and flow freely.' That is a concept I think most of you share." He concluded with the same quotation: "In closing, let me leave you with a thought: John Dryden was right. 'Trade, like blood should circulate and flow freely.' Global trade is, indeed, a critical element—in my view the most important element—on our road to global prosperity and growth."

Keys to an Effective Conclusion

- ◎ Continue to make eye contact with your audience for a few seconds after the conclusion.
- ◎ Keep the conclusion brief.
- ◎ Refrain from adding new information in the conclusion.
- ◎ Stay composed as you return to your seat.

Quotation

As illustrated in the example above, it also is common to end a speech with a famous quote or a quote from a famous individual. If well chosen, this type of clincher can tie the ideas up nicely. As with using quotes in other parts of the presentation, speakers can benefit from a last additional boost to their credibility through their identification with the source of the quotation. As with attention-getters, avoid overly used quotations to end your presentation. You want to end with a memorable thought, not a stale one.

Call to Action

Many times at the end of a persuasive speech on a question of policy, a speaker will call the audience to action. In other words, the speaker will ask the audience to do something at the end of the presentation. Perhaps that call involves signing a petition, starting an exercise program, or voting for a proposal. Calls to actions are described in greater detail in Chapter 10.

In her call to action clincher, Lupe made sure she gave her classmates specific information they needed to find an online course to take:

> I want you all to go and look at the distance education's online catalog today. It's simple and easy to do. First, you can look for distance learning courses in the online course catalog by looking for course numbers followed by an X. Or, you can go to our college's website and type in "Distance Learning" to bring up the Distance Learning homepage. On the homepage, you can find a list of all available courses, plus other helpful information, such as Frequently Asked Questions and contact information if you have additional questions.

Sometimes students think that calls to action are only made in classroom speeches, but this is not the case. Let's look at the conclusion of Cynthia Starks' speech that we referenced earlier in this chapter.[44] She encouraged or persuaded business professionals to deliver more speeches:

> My call to action? I'm giving you a homework assignment. Sometime before bed tonight, take three minutes—just 180 seconds—to think about the answers to these three questions:
>
> 1. What audiences need to hear from me?
> 2. What goals can I accomplish by speaking to them?
> 3. Who can write the speech? The answer might be yourself, someone already in your organization, or a professional speechwriter you already know or one with whom you're willing to develop a working relationship.
>
> Don't put it off. "Carpe diem"—seize the day, seize the moment, seize the opportunity. And if you think you don't have time to give speeches, during 2009, John Lechleiter, Chairman, President and CEO of Eli Lilly, gave more than 100 internal and external speeches. How many speeches will you give in 2010?

Although you have many options when ending your presentation, think carefully about the option that would add the most impact to your presentation. All of the guidelines that apply to attention-getters also apply to clinchers. When choosing a clincher, make sure to

- consider the tone of the presentation;
- consider your time restrictions;
- consider your strengths as a speaker;
- consider your audience; and
- consider your topic.

Common Conclusion Pitfalls

The conclusion is the last chance you have to reiterate and drive your message home. It also leaves your audience with a lasting impression of you and your message. So you want your conclusion to be as strong and as impactful as it can possibly be. Here are some common mistakes speakers make in the conclusion, mistakes that you should avoid.

Ending Abruptly

Your audience should be prepared for your conclusion. You should use signposts and transitions (see Chapter 5) to indicate that you are wrapping up the presentation and entering the conclusion (i.e., in conclusion, to wrap things up, to sum up today's main ideas, etc.). Audience members should never be surprised to find themselves at the end of the presentation. Although the conclusion should be short, the audience should not feel that they were left hanging. The conclusion should provide nice closure for the speech and the ideas you worked to present.

Drawing It Out

Once you have transitioned to the conclusion, your audience will only provide you a limited amount of time to close it out. They are listening for summary material and if that isn't what they get, they tune out. When an audience hears those words that signal the speech is nearing an end, that's what they expect. If you violate these expectations, you will lose your audience. As mentioned earlier in the chapter, the conclusion should not exceed 5% of the entire length of your presentation. So make sure to be brief and clear.

Introducing New Arguments and Points

The conclusion's purpose is to summarize your main points and leave your audience with a final thought. You should not introduce new material that makes new arguments or adds any new points or ideas. Sometimes it is very tempting to throw in just one more idea that didn't seem to fit anywhere else. Simply review or reinforce what you have already shared and end with a memorable thought or idea.

Leaving Conclusions Implicit

As we discuss later in Chapter 10, conclusions should not be left implicit for an audience.[45] Tell your audience specifically what you want them to do, what you want them to believe, what you want them to feel, or what you want them to know. When you make the conclusions of your reasoning explicit, audiences know exactly what you want from them, and there is no room for confusion.

An effective conclusion can help maintain the impact of an effective presentation. To be successful, the conclusion must restate the thesis and main ideas of the presentation and provide a sense of closure for your audience. To help clarify how all of these elements come together, let's examine the actual introduction and conclusion of Manuel's informative presentation on the quiet sound technology of hybrid vehicles.

Technically Speaking

While you still want to end your virtual presentation with a memorable thought, remember that in the virtual context, participants can't walk up to you after the event to ask additional questions. So after your clincher, it's helpful to display your e-mail or Web address for about 30 seconds at the end of your presentation. This gives your virtual audience a way to continue the conversation, and it makes you seem more approachable and sincere about helping.

It is also important to remember that a virtual presentation isn't over until everyone has disconnected. So make sure that the comments you make after the presentation is over are comments you would want to share with your audience. Many speakers have been embarrassed by comments they have made after their presentation only to learn their virtual audience was still connected and could hear everything that was said.[46]

Example Introduction and Conclusion

Manuel's assignment for his introductory technology class was to inform his audience about a new technology. This is the introduction and conclusion to his classroom presentation.

Specific Purpose   To inform my audience about new technologies being developed to counter the danger to pedestrians and others from the quiet sound technology of hybrid vehicles.

Introction

Attention-Getter   My friend Luis has been deaf in one ear since he contracted scarlet fever as a child. He doesn't let that slow him down, though. He remains very active, riding his bike to campus and frequently jogging along city streets. But last year, as he jogged across a parking lot on campus, he ran in front of a Toyota Prius. The hybrid car was so quiet that it snuck up on Luis without him hearing. Although he escaped serious injury, he did end up on the car's hood. Now, imagine this scene unfolding all over campus involving students with disabilities who rely on sound to detect vehicles or students simply jamming to music on their way to classes.

Manuel tells a story about his friend Luis. It is a story that engages the audience from the beginning because it resonates with their lifestyles. The details of his story makes this narrative come to life and the audience is able to empathize with Luis.

Relevance Statement   The National Highway Transportation Safety Administration reports that 64,000 pedestrians are struck by cars each year. Many of those are college students who, while walking to and from class, carelessly cross a crosswalk preoccupied with their cell phones, MP3 players, or chatting with a friend. These tasks make it harder for everyone to detect a hybrid approaching an intersection or pulling out of a driveway.

> Manuel continues to keep our attention by reminding audience members the many instances they, too, may have been unable to hear a hybrid car approaching and providing statistics that make this topic relevant for the audience. It demonstrates that members of his audience are at risk, so they should listen.

Credibility Statement   As an automotive engineering major, I have been closely following the research to make hybrids more audible. I hope to be able to make automobiles safer for people with disabilities, such as my friend Luis.

> Manuel explains to his audience why they should listen to him about this topic. He explains that he developed an interest because of his friend's experience and his own potential risk.

Thesis Statement   While the quiet sound signature of a hybrid vehicle can be a danger to pedestrians, legislatures and car manufacturers are working diligently on so-called pedestrian protection packages to provide a solution.

> Manuel announces the topic of the presentation. The audience now understands where he is headed and what they can expect.

Conclusion

Review of Thesis   As stated before, legislatures and car manufacturers are working hard to find a solution to the dangers that the quiet sound signature of a hybrid vehicle can post to pedestrians.

> At this point Manuel begins his conclusion by simply reviewing his thesis sentence. This step helps encapsulate the entire presentation for his audience.

Review Statement   I hope you understand the dangers of these quiet hybrids, and are aware of the new technologies such as sensors and noise vibrators being developed to make these vehicles more audible to pedestrians who are blind or have difficulty hearing, children, bikers, and inattentive walkers.

> Manuel explicitly reminds his audience of his main points.

Clincher   My friend Luis is still running around campus each day. Now he's more aware of the dangers he can see and hear, and those that he can't. Hopefully, one day soon, he will have one less obstacle to dodge.

Manuel provides a nice sense of closure by tying the attention-gaining device used in his introduction to the ending of his speech. Not only does this choice add closure, but also reminds his audience just how relevant this topic is to college students.

Conclusion

Introductions are the first impression speakers make on their audience. The introduction must capture the attention of your audience, establish your credibility, provide relevance for your audience, announce your topic, and preview your main points.

The conclusion of your presentation is as important as the introduction. According to the recency effect, we remember best what we hear last. Therefore, the conclusion can be a powerful tool in reaching and persuading your audience. To be effective, your conclusion must review your thesis and main points, and provide closure for your audience with a clincher or memorable thought. Do not underestimate the power of the clincher. Too many presentations fizzle at this point, rather than ending with a bang.

Remember when choosing both your attention-gaining device and your clincher, keep in mind the tone of your presentation, your time restrictions, your strengths as a speaker, your audience, and your topic.

Introductions and conclusions, though brief, are very powerful tools within the overall presentation. They play valuable roles, and you need to take them seriously. First impressions and last impressions are important. Though introductions and conclusions are relatively short compared to the overall presentation, they can have a big impact on the overall presentation success.

Key Terms

Attention-gaining device (attention-getter)

Clincher

Conclusion

Credibility

Credibility statement

Direct question

Introduction

Narrative transport

Preview statement

Primacy effect

Recency effect

Relevance statement

Rhetorical question

Thesis statement

Exercises

1. Visit the 60-Second Science website: http://www.scientificamerican.com/podcast/60-second-science/. This site provides quick reports on scientific research every day through 60-second podcasts. Each podcast begins with an attention-gaining device and ends with a clincher. Examine several of these reports and catalog which devices you think work and which don't. Share your favorites with the class.

2. Using the guidelines in this chapter, critique the following introductions of informative speeches. What suggestions might you make for improvement?

Example A

Attention-Getter   What would you say if I had a way to prevent adolescent smoking, drinking, and drug addiction? According to a recent study, something as simple as eating family dinners nightly could do just that.

Credibility Statement   I am very interested in the influence of family in child development, and I have conducted research over this topic.

Relating to the Audience   Maybe you have been thankful for the time you had to eat meals together with your family. Or perhaps you feel as though you missed out by not having this opportunity. Whichever experience you had could have played a monumental role in the person you are today.

Thesis Statement   Frequent family dining has been found to profit children physically, mentally, and socially.

Example B

Attention-Getter   Imagine this: You take off from an airport in Chicago. Your destination is London, but on this flight, there will be no soda pop or pretzels served. Instead of this flight taking nine hours, it will now take less than 45 minutes.

Relevance Statement   The ability to fly in space economically could change the way you live.

Credibility Statement   I have traveled all over the world.

Thesis Statement   The Ansari X prize has begun a competition that will jump-start the space tourism industry and provide countless benefits.

Example C

Attention-Getter   According to NGA, there are a lot more overweight children now than in the 1970s.

Relevance Statement   CNN reports that students spend 2,000 hours a year in school; therefore, the schools have a huge influence with vending machines, menus, soda, and candy sales.

Thesis Statement   Obesity is an increasing problem and schools contribute and try to reduce the problem.

3. Using the guidelines in this chapter, critique the following introduction and conclusion. Remember to critique them as a unit rather than individually. What suggestions might you make for improvement?

Example

Introduction

Attention-Getter   I'm sure everyone has heard this quote before: "Enjoy yourselves, these are the best times of your life."

Credibility Statement   As a student, I have experienced firsthand the fun of college and the stress of college.

Relevance Statement   As we all know, college can be a great experience, and it can be stressful.

Thesis Statement   As college students' stress levels rise each year, we have to see that stress is bad and not be stressed.

Transition   First, I will discuss how stress develops in students' lives.

Conclusion

Restate Thesis   I have discussed what causes stress in college students' lives and how to alleviate that stress.

Clincher   Hopefully, you have learned how to avoid stress.

4. Using LexisNexis or another database in your library that indexes newspapers and magazines, search for stories about real people that would make good attention-getters for various presentations. Practice delivering these narratives.

5. Visit the following website and view Paul Conneally's presentation on Digital Humanitarianism: http://www.ted.com/talks/paul_conneally_digital_humanitarianism.html. Using the guidelines presented in this chapter, what suggestions would you have for improvement for Paul's introduction and conclusion? What were the strengths in his introduction and conclusion?

CHAPTER 5

Organizing the Presentation

Objectives

After reading this chapter, you should be able to

- ◎ explain the guidelines for arranging main points;
- ◎ identify the five types of organizational patterns;
- ◎ explain the four kinds of transitions; and
- ◎ discuss the importance of organization.

Chip and Dan Heath wondered why some ideas "stick" and others just don't. Even more interesting to these two brothers was why a false idea could actually supplant a true one. So, they began to research these issues and wrote an entertaining and informative book titled, *Made to Stick: Why Some Ideas Survive and Others Die.* The book eventually became a *New York Times* bestseller.

Speakers at all levels have difficulty determining how to begin and end their presentations. When faced with making a presentation, many individuals immediately start thinking about how they will start their presentation. How will they begin? We often get so overcome by how we will start that we neglect some of the important planning aspects of the presentation. We want to come out of the gate running, so to speak, and so we make fundamental errors by focusing on the wrong elements of the presentation.

The authors found that one of the most compelling factors of a memorable message is simplicity. They advise readers to deliver a message in a way that makes it easily accessible to the audience. They warn against "burying your lead."

Good organization will help you do just that. Well-organized presentations are simple and easy to follow, and the main ideas stand out. You don't want your ideas buried under a mountain of statistics or other evidence; you want them to "pop" for your audience. This chapter presents strategies that will help ensure that your message stands out for your audience because of its simplicity and accessibility.

Why Organization Is Important

Clear organizational structure benefits both the audience and the speaker. Some of these benefits include improved recall of the material presented, enhanced understanding of complex material, and increased speaker credibility.

> **Speakers who employ clear organization enhance their credibility.**

Audiences are more easily able to retain the information presented when there is a clear organizational structure.[1] One of the essential elements in being clear is the use of transitions, which we discuss later in this chapter. Transitions have a strong impact on an audience member's ability to recall content, so you want to make sure you take advantage of this organizing tool.

Complex material is also easier to understand when it is laid out in a clear fashion.[2] Research indicates that a clear organizational pattern marked with signposts and internal summaries (see the "Transitions" discussion later in this chapter) actually decreases the cognitive load audience members face when processing your material. In other words, you free up some of the working memory so that audience members can focus on the content. You do some of the work for them, which allows them to concentrate more closely on your message.

Finally, speakers who employ clear organization enhance their credibility as well.[3] Organized presentations appear more prepared and the speakers more knowledgeable.

Some of the speech types referenced here are not assignments in COM114. But you might be asked to create one in another course or for an internship or organization you belong to. Thus it is important for you to recognize how to organize multiple presentation types.

Organizing the Body of Your Presentation

Clear organization of a speech often makes the difference between an effective presentation and an ineffective one. One reason why organization is so critical in oral presentations is that the audience can't go back and revisit your ideas. Giving a presentation is very different from reading prose on a page. Audience members don't have the luxury of examining the material at their own pace or referring back to material that was already presented. Therefore, clear organization with good use of transitions is vital to a solid presentation. Attention to organization helps ensure that audience members understand your ideas and process them in the way you intended. In this chapter, we discuss how to organize the body of your presentation.

Speakers who want to help their audiences understand and retain new information need to pay attention to the fundamental concept of "chunking."[4] **Chunking** refers to the process of organizing small units of information into larger clusters. In terms of your presentations, think of putting your sub-subpoints and subpoints together into main points, and then those main points into a presentation body.

Chunking your material into more manageable units (subpoints, main points), helps the audience remember more. It also increases the amount of information that the audience members can be expected to retain and understand. In other words, you can share more information effectively.[5] As you continue to present information, your audience is able to recode any new information and assimilate it into information chunks you've already presented. Chunking is both a "triggering device" (helping you relate to previous material) and a "recall" device (as new chunks are presented, you recall previous chunks).[6]

Main Points

As mentioned throughout this text, the three main components in a presentation are (1) the introduction, (2) the body, and (3) the conclusion. The body is where you present the "meat" of your presentation. This is where you place the information you are trying to convey to your audience. To do this effectively, you divide your material into **main points.** Here is an example of how one student divided his material into main points.

Tip

By telling my audience in advance what to expect, it makes it more likely that they will stay engaged and follow the basic logic of the proposal.

Jay Fehnel | Principal and Owner | Johan Advisors, LLC

Specific Purpose   To explain to my audience how plants absorb non-mineral and mineral nutrients from soil.

Thesis Statement   Plants absorb non-mineral and mineral nutrients in two different ways. First I will explain how plants absorb non-mineral nutrients and then I will explain how plants absorb mineral nutrients from soil.

Main Points

1. Non-mineral nutrients, which are hydrogen, oxygen, and carbon, are absorbed by plants via photosynthesis.
2. Mineral nutrients, which are found in soil, are dissolved in water and then absorbed by plants via their roots.

These main points form the skeleton of the speech. At this point, we don't know much about the points this student is going to make. After deciding what your main points should be, you go back and provide supporting evidence for each of these main points.

Number of Main Points

How many main points should you have? In a classroom speech, you will need no more than three main points. Two to three points is a good rule for the amount of time you have to speak in the classroom. Even if you have an unlimited amount of time to address your audience, you will still want to limit your main points. Good presentations rarely have over four or five main points.

Spotlight on Research

Sharing Negative Information

It is possible that in the course of your careers you will need to share unpleasant information with your audience. A project has lost funding. Your school's test scores have fallen. Your nonprofit did not reach its fundraising goals. Research into composing negative messages focuses mainly on the benefits of using either the indirect (gradually lead into the bad news) vs. the direct (present the unfavorable message first) approaches. While both of these methods have qualitative support, research in organizational communication tells us of at least one alternative. Researchers found that the ability to transform negative events into positive opportunities for improvement (we didn't get funding for the new project so we can focus all our attention on making existing projects the best they can be) was a successful additional option to sharing bad news.[7]

Organization of Main Points

In what order should you present your main points? An organizational pattern can help you make that decision. An **organizational pattern** is a structure that delineates the nature of the relationship between your main points. There are numerous organizational patterns. In this text, we will discuss the most basic. As you become a more experienced speaker, you will add others to your repertoire or adapt the ones discussed here. Let's begin by discussing each of these patterns, along with suggestions for using them, followed by some examples from student presentations.

Spatial

The **spatial pattern** of organization is used when you want to demonstrate the relationship between your material geographically or directionally (e.g., top to bottom, inside to outside, left to right, etc.). This pattern can also be used when demonstrating how parts are related to the whole (e.g., parts of the skeleton, parts of the space shuttle).

Specific Purpose   To inform my audience about new fashion trends around the United States.

Thesis Statement   There are numerous new fashion trends springing up on the West Coast, on the East Coast, and in the Midwest.

Main Points

1.   The most popular trends along the West Coast this winter will be fake fur, the color purple, and boots.
2.   The most popular trends along the East Coast this winter will be tweed and short skirts.
3.   The most popular trends in the Midwest this winter will include anything leather and vintage T-shirts.

Chronological

The **chronological pattern** of organization arranges material in an ordered sequence. In other words, it follows a time line. This pattern is especially well-suited for historical topics and instructional presentations (e.g., "how to" presentations).

Specific Purpose   To instruct my audience on how to change a tire.

Thesis Statement   To change a flat tire safely, you will need to jack up the vehicle, remove the old tire, and replace it with a new tire.

Main Points

1.   First, you will need to use an approved jack to raise the vehicle .
2.   Next, you will need to remove the flat tire.
3.   Finally, you will need to fit the new tire.

Problem-Solution

The **problem-solution design** is the organizational pattern to use if your material clearly falls into two main points: a problem and a solution. The first main point focuses on demonstrating to the audience that there is a problem and the implications of that problem, while the second main point centers on explaining a workable solution to the problem. While problem-solution speeches can be used in either informative or persuasive situations, they are primarily used in persuasive presentations. Chapter 9 provides more information on the problem-solution speech design.

Specific Purpose   To persuade my audience that spam is a problem with some simple solutions.

Thesis Statement   According to Microsoft, 80% to 90% of all e-mails sent over the Internet are unwanted or spam. These e-mails have significant costs, but their impact can be reduced by following three simple steps.

Main Points

1.   Spam has many societal costs, but two of the most expensive are loss of productivity and the need for specialized equipment and software.
2.   Spam can be significantly reduced if we all follow these three recommended guidelines.

Here is another example from a different student on a speech about noise pollution.

Specific Purpose   To persuade my audience to protect themselves from the dangers of noise pollution.

Thesis Statement   Noise pollution leads to three primary problems, but by following a few easy guidelines, we can reduce our exposure.

Main Points

1. Noise pollution leads to three problems: annoyance, speech interference, and hearing loss.
2. Noise pollution can be prevented if we adhere to three easy guidelines.

Causal Pattern

Speeches organized using the **causal design** seek to establish a cause-effect relationship between two variables or events. Presentations arranged in this format have two main points. One main point centers on the causes, while the other main point addresses the effects. Speeches of cause and effect can be arranged in either of two ways: (1) cause, then effect; or (2) effect followed by cause. Here are examples:

Main Points

1. Strong storms called solar flares on the surface of the sun release large amounts of magnetic energy toward Earth.
2. Solar flares are so powerful they can damage satellites, cause power outages, and disrupt other electronic and magnetic equipment.

or

Main Points

1. The history of life on the planet Earth has been characterized by a series of major extinctions.
2. The cause of many of these extinctions has been traced to the impact of large meteors or comets.

Topical

Presentations that do not fall into one of the other organizational patterns described (spatial, chronological, problem-solution, or causal) usually fit within the **topical pattern.** The topic is subdivided into smaller parts or subtopics that then become the main points of the speech. The key to using the topical pattern successfully is ensuring that your topic divides into a set of main points that are logical and consistent.

Consider the following topical organization for a student speech that Nathan pursued last semester on the Hubble Telescope:

Specific Purpose   To inform my audience of a few of the major contributions of the Hubble Telescope.

Thesis Statement   The Hubble Telescope has refined our knowledge of the age of the universe and the rate at which it is expanding, as well as our understanding of dwarf planets.

Main Points

1. The Hubble Telescope has helped refine estimates of the age of the universe.
2. The Hubble Telescope has provided data that indicate that the expansion of the universe is accelerating.
3. The Hubble Telescope has also provided data that have increased our understanding of dwarf planets, such as Pluto.

Here is another example of a topical design:

Specific Purpose   To inform my audience about the different types of weight discrimination.

Thesis Statement   Individuals with a BMI of 30 or above are categorized as obese and, as a result, suffer job discrimination, financial discrimination, and even medical discrimination.

Main Points

1. Obese individuals report being passed over for promotions, teased and harassed while on the job, and even being fired due to their weight.
2. Financial discrimination is another type of discrimination experienced by obese individuals.
3. Recently, researchers have discovered evidence that obese individuals receive inferior healthcare as compared to their slimmer counterparts.

Characteristics of Good Main Points

Main Points Should Be Balanced

Balance means that you spend approximately the same amount of time addressing each of your main points. When you identify your main points, you are saying that these items are essentially equal in terms of importance. If that is true, you should spend roughly the same amount of time addressing each main point. Let's say that after examining your outline, you notice that your speech breaks down like this:

> **You should spend roughly the same amount of time addressing each main point.**

- ◎ **MPI:**   75%
- ◎ **MPII:**   20%
- ◎ **MPIII:**   5%

From this information, you can determine one of two things: First, you may not have developed the second and third points like they should have been developed. Perhaps you have focused too much energy and planning on the first main point. Second, perhaps you only have one main point. In this case, go back and look at your material and see if you can break it down differently. You may not have initially divided the material in the most effective way.

Your time allocation for each main point does not have to be equal. Spending roughly the same amount of time on each main point is sufficient. Here are a few breakdowns that give you an idea of how much time you might spend on each of your main points:

◎	**MPI:**	30%	◎	**MPI:**	30%
◎	**MPII:**	45%	◎	**MPII:**	30%
◎	**MPIII:**	25%	◎	**MPIII:**	40%

Try to Use Parallel Wording

Audience members find it easier to follow your speech if you use **parallel wording**–that is, the same phrasing–for your main points. For example, the following sets of main points demonstrate the difference between main points that are parallel in structure and those that are not. While both sets of points get the same ideas across, the first set of points is easier for audience members to follow.

All organizational patterns contain main points that should be balanced.

Effective

- ◎ **MPI:** A good night's sleep helps promote healthy glucose processing.
- ◎ **MPII:** A good night's sleep helps regulate a healthy weight.
- ◎ **MPIII:** A good night's sleep helps promote cognitive health.

Less Effective

- ◎ **MPI:** Glucose is converted to insulin more efficiently after a productive sleep period.
- ◎ **MPII:** Leptin, a hormone that regulates feelings of fullness and therefore regulates weight, is produced after a good night's rest.
- ◎ **MPIII:** Lack of sleep is associated with shrinkage in the right temporal lobe of the brain.

Of course, all materials will not allow themselves to be so easily organized into parallel structure. However, if you can use parallel wording, you should.

Supporting Evidence

The main points are just the skeletons of your presentation. The supporting evidence you provide for each of your main points will flesh out the body of your speech. One important aspect that beginning speakers often overlook is that the supporting material within each main point should be organized into subpoints. In other words, you should have an organizational pattern within each main point. So while your overall pattern may be topical, one main point and its supporting material or subpoints can be organized chronologically or spatially. Examine the organization of the main points and subpoints in the following excerpt. As you can see, the subpoints of main point I are arranged topically, while the subpoints of main point II are arranged spatially.

◎ **MPI:** Dangerous traffic signs are characterized by one of the following attributes.
1. Sign lettering is illegible.
2. The sign is obstructed.
3. The sign is missing.

◎ **MPII:** West Lafayette has many dangerous signs, and some of the most hazardous can be found at the following locations.
1. At the intersection of 3rd and Main, there are three illegible street signs.
2. In the older New Chauncey neighborhood, there are many obstructed signs.
3. On roads adjacent to Purdue's on-campus housing, there are many missing signs.

(Although not noted here, the student then provided statistics and other documentation to further support this material.)

Another key to remember is to make sure that all of your main points are supported. Sometimes, you will find that your material only supports a couple of your main points, leaving some of your arguments completely unsupported. Although the

> **Make sure that all of your main points are supported.**

material you have collected is related to your topic, it does not directly support all of your arguments. At this point, you may have to discard some of your research and go back to the library to collect more supporting material. One trip to the library or one massive search for supporting material is rarely enough.

Another mistake students commonly make is dividing their material incorrectly. There is a tendency to have too many main points and not enough supporting evidence or subpoints. Many times, the extra main points can be collapsed into subpoints that support two or three main points. Examine the following example:

◎ **MPI:** Volunteering at the humane society is fun.
◎ **MPII:** Volunteering at the humane society will make you feel good about yourself.
◎ **MPIII:** Volunteering at the humane society looks good on a resume.
◎ **MPIV:** Volunteering at the humane society will help you get references.

Although each of these main points supports the speaker's ultimate goal—to persuade the audience to volunteer at the local humane society—they do not stand alone. They can be collapsed into a more concise organizational pattern. It would make more sense to organize the speech in the following way:

◎ **MPI:** Volunteering at the humane society can benefit you personally.
   a. You will have fun volunteering.
   b. You will feel good about the work you do.
◎ **MPII:** Volunteering at the humane society can benefit you professionally.
   a. Your activities will provide you with real-world experience to list on a resume.
   b. Your supervisors can provide you with strong references from actual employers for future positions.

Transitions

Transitions are words, phrases, or sentences that show the relationship between ideas in your presentation. They are the elements that help your speech flow and allow listeners to follow you easily. Research suggests that the skillful use of transitions is essential to audience understanding.[8] Audience members also follow your organizational pattern more effectively and are more likely to remember the material that is close to a transition.[9]

There are four types of transitions: (1) directional transitions, (2) signposts, (3) internal previews, and (4) internal summaries. Transitions can be sentences, phrases, and, in some cases, a single word. Let's discuss each of these types of transitions, as well as strategies for using them effectively in your presentations.

Directional Transitions

Directional transitions are phrases that let your audience know that you are moving away from one idea and on to another. They contain two parts: First, they restate the information you are leaving, and second, they preview the information that is coming. *You must use a directional transition between each of your main points.* Here are some examples of directional transitions:

> **Now that you understand** the causes of poverty, **let's examine the effect** on our nation's youth.

> **As you can see,** internships are an important step in attaining future employment, **so** the university has implemented a process to aid in the search for these opportunities.

> **Now that we have examined** some of the problems associated with e-waste, it is important that **we explore** some possible solutions.

Spotlight on Research

Transitions Have Positive Impact

Researchers presented a lecture to 40 college students. The students were instructed to take notes during the lecture. When the lecture contained transitions such as directional transitions, signposts, and internal and external summaries, the students were able to take more notes than when the lectures did not contain transitions. Additionally, their notes listed more ideas from the lecture.

As you can see, using transitions can have a positive impact on your audience. A well-organized presentation that highlights transitions will improve your audience's ability to hear and understand the important points of your message.[10]

The key to using directional transitions effectively is to remind audience members of what they have just heard and then preview the upcoming point. Directional transitions are primarily used between each of the main points, but also can be used additionally to separate the introduction and the body, and the body and the conclusion. While it is necessary to include a directional transition between the main points of a presentation, you may also find it beneficial to use directional transitions within main points.

Signposts

Signposts are transitions that mark the exact location in the speech. They tell audience members where they are within the presentation. Here are some commonly used signposts:

- The first point …
- The second cause …
- In conclusion …
- The most important point …

Signposts are extremely helpful for the audience. They help organize the material in a way that is easy to follow. They commonly alert listeners that a speaker is moving from the introduction to the first main point, or that the speaker is transitioning to the conclusion. Students often overlook the importance of signposting. This is one of the easiest ways to assist your audience in following the information in your presentation.

Internal Previews

Internal previews preview material within the body of the presentation or even within a main point. Internal previews are not always necessary. However, if your material is lengthy and contains many small components and subpoints, or is complicated, an internal preview will enhance your audience's ability to follow your message. Here is an example taken from a student presentation:

> In examining the effects of e-waste, there are two problems: the use of landfills and the use of hazardous materials.

Sometimes, you can combine a directional transition with an internal preview. Here is an example of how that might look:

> Now that we understand how DNA profiling works, let's move on to the techniques of DNA profiling. [*directional transition*] I will examine two types of DNA profiling—PCR analysis and STR analysis. [*internal preview*]

Internal Summaries

Internal summaries are similar to internal previews except they remind the audience of what was just covered. Like internal previews, they should be used when the material you just presented was complicated, lengthy, or important. Here is an example:

> **Internal summaries are an excellent way to assist audiences in remembering your ideas.**

As you have seen, there are many reasons why plastic bags have become a problem for our environment. They are dispersed in large quantities, are disposed of carelessly, and are cheaper and hold less than paper or cloth bags, therefore increasing our consumption.

Internal summaries are an excellent way to assist audiences in remembering your ideas. By restating key material, you are able to reinforce the main ideas of the presentation.

Just as you can combine a directional transition and an internal preview, you can also combine an internal summary with other transitions. Here is an example:

> To reiterate, there are several problems with environmental tobacco smoke. [*internal summary*] First [*signpost*], it has been proven to cause cancer. Second [*signpost*], it increases heart rate and blood pressure. Third [*signpost*], it increases the likelihood of sudden infant death syndrome among babies. Now that you have a thorough understanding of the problem, let's examine some possible solutions. [*directional transition*]

Transitions become even more important when your audience is distributed, as in this photograph.

Transitioning within Main Points

Too often, students in this course focus on transitioning between the major parts of the presentation but ignore the fact that there is a strong need as well for transitions between subpoints and sub-subpoints. Without transitions, support can seem like an unrelated list instead of a cohesive argument. Here are some instances in which you might need to transition within a main point and suggested transitional language you can use:

- Transition to a supporting example: "For instance," or "As an example."
- Contrast two subpoints or two sub-subpoints: "However" or "The other argument."
- Show similarity between your subpoints or sub-subpoints: "Likewise" or "Similarly."
- Recall something in a previous subpoint or sub-subpoint: "Remember," or "Let's go back to."
- Show a cause-effect relationship between two subpoints or sub-subpoints: "Therefore," or "As a result."

Conclusion

Organization is vital to a successful presentation. Using the right organizational pattern (spatial, chronological, problem-solution, causal, or topical) is extremely important. Not only does organization affect the audience's ability to process your information, it also has implications for your credibility as a speaker. The number of main points, the way they are worded, and the skillful use of transitions are all important elements of effective organization. Don't overlook the importance of organization. Your audience will appreciate it, and your presentation will be more successful.

Key Terms

Balance	Internal previews	Problem-solution design
Causal design	Internal summaries	Signposts
Chronological pattern	Main points	Spatial pattern
Chunking	Organizational pattern	Topical pattern
Directional transitions	Parallel wording	Transitions

CHAPTER 6

Supporting Evidence and Research

Objectives

After reading this chapter, you should be able to

- explain why speakers need strong evidence;
- identify types of supporting materials;
- distinguish among types of examples;
- distinguish among types of testimony;
- understand how to evaluate supporting material; and
- identify sources for finding supporting evidence.

In a study conducted by Project Information Literacy,[1] students reported having an easier time finding information for personal use than conducting research for class.

One reason, the study found, is that students utilize a wider array of information sources when it comes to gathering personal information. According to the study, students don't stray too far from "tried and true" sources such as course readings, scholarly research databases, search engines, and instructors when conducting academic research. On the other hand, they are more likely to explore nontraditional sources such as Facebook, Twitter, and Weblogs when seeking information for personal use.

Another reason is that students are ignoring one of their best resources: their college's librarian. Librarians can direct students to new sources of information they might not have thought of, or might be unaware of, yet only 11% of students reported ever asking librarians for help when conducting academic research.

The study's authors said such a strategy "underscores the gap between the plethora of Web sources and rich information campus libraries make available to students and the sources students actually use."[2]

Why Supporting Evidence Is Important

The material or evidence you use to support your main points is actually the heart of your presentation, so your ability to find such support is critical to your success. Without credible and ample support, your thesis statement and all of your claims are just uninformed opinions. Students often complain about including supporting evidence in their presentations. They simply don't understand why they need to cite somebody else when they know everything there is to know about a topic.

Imagine you decide to speak on the benefits of Greek life. After all, you're an expert—you have been a member of a fraternity or sorority for over three years. While audience members may appreciate your personal experiences, they will also want to hear other evidence. After all, your personal experiences and those of your Greek brothers or sisters are somewhat biased. You can bolster your claims by providing statistics and testimony from national sources. What are the national statistics, examples, and so on, relating to Greek life and academic success, for example? Opinions can be supported by personal experience, but arguments need evidence, statistics, testimonials, and other support.

Depending on the presentation, you will need to use different types of supporting material in varying degrees to provide evidence for your main points or arguments. How much and what type of supporting material depends on a variety of factors, including audience knowledge of the topic (novice or expert), your own credibility on the topic (novice or expert), and the purpose of the speech (informative or persuasive).

For example, if a scientist were giving a presentation on the age of the solar system to other scientists in the field, the nature of the facts she discussed would most likely be the specific procedures and results of her own scientific studies. If the same expert were invited to give a presentation on this same topic to a lay audience, she would likely simplify the supporting material, focusing more on providing general information regarding her results. She would reduce the complexity of the statistics and procedures, and use more narratives and explanatory analogies regarding the formation of the solar system and why it is important to understand this subject in the first place. If a novice were to speak on this same topic, it would be important for him or her to systematically document what specific experts in the field believe about the age of the solar system. This would bolster the speaker's own credibility on the subject and demonstrate that he or she is basically summarizing and explaining the research and thoughts of experts. Novices essentially borrow the credibility of experts through the use of research.

Spotlight on Research

Supporting Evidence Can Aid Your Credibility

Often for your classes, you are assigned to give presentations about topics you might not have expertise in. By incorporating outside evidence into your presentation, you strengthen your arguments, and you also enhance your credibility as a speaker. Studies have shown that citing evidence within a presentation can improve audience perceptions of a speaker's expertise and trustworthiness.[3] Of course, perceptions of expertise and trustworthiness are only bolstered by high-credibility sources. Low-credibility supporting evidence does not generate this same effect. So while you might not be an expert in your topic, you can still be viewed as a credible presenter by your classmates based on the sources that you cite.

Each of these two presentations would be very different, primarily because they would use different types of supporting evidence to make claims about the topic. Ultimately, the supporting evidence makes the difference between a believable and interesting presentation and one that is uninformative or unimportant to the audience.[4] So it is important that you think critically about your situation, audience, and topic and choose the type of supporting evidence that will have the biggest impact in your presentation.

This chapter gives you an overview of the types of supporting evidence you will likely use as you begin to construct your presentations. It also provides you with information on where to find supporting material and how to evaluate it. These are skills you will use throughout your collegiate and professional careers. A 2016 study by Project Literacy reported that the ability to search for information and then use that information well, was the top skill new workers adapted from college.[5] So now is the time to learn this skill.

Types of Supporting Materials

Statistics

Statistics are an extremely powerful type of supporting evidence;[6] they consist of numerical facts that are used to describe a population or event. We hear and see statistics so often in our everyday lives that we expect them. They carry a great

> By using statistics, you can summarize a large amount of material in a concise manner.

deal of power and can be extremely persuasive. Just think about the number of statistics you read about or hear every day: The economy lost 7.9 million jobs during the recent Great Recession; the Harry Potter film series made $7.7 billion worldwide; obesity-related diseases cost Americans $147 billion a year. We feel secure using numbers. Statistics are especially useful in demonstrating trends, explaining relationships, and quantifying information. By using statistics, you can summarize a large amount of material in a concise manner.

Statistics provide compelling supporting evidence in your presentations. Consider the following two statements:

> Americans use a lot of plastic bags. This is a big environmental problem.

or

> According to a 2015 article on the website Scientific American, 100 billion plastic shopping bags are handed out in the United States annually. That's 332 per person or 1,500 per family. Yet a New American Media article in 2015 says less than 5% of these are recycled.

The second statement is much more compelling. It clarifies the point and adds strength to the argument. We have a much better idea of how big a problem plastic bags are and the impact they can have on the environment. When you effectively use statistics to bolster your argument, audiences are more likely to be persuaded, because the example becomes more vivid. Statistics can be used effectively to:

Describe Quantities   McDonald's is the third most popular brand on Facebook, with 57 million fans.

Demonstrate Trends   Snapchat is the fastest-growing social media, growing 57% to 200 million followers from 2014 to 2015.

Imply Relationships   People who consume diet sodas daily are 43% more likely to suffer from a stroke or heart attack than those who do not consume diet sodas.

Statistics aren't magical in and of themselves. They must be used well in order to be impactful. The following section will provide some guidelines for using statistics successfully.

Tips for Using Statistics

Make Sure Statistics Are Representative

One common flaw in the use of statistical evidence is that the data can be collected in unscientific ways. Every time you hear statistics, you should ask yourself the following questions: How were the data collected? How large was the sample size? Who were the participants in the study? Was the sample representative of the population it claims to represent? Who conducted the survey? When was it conducted?

Let's assume that you survey your peers in this class and then claim that 50% of the students surveyed at this university are dissatisfied with food services on campus. This is not a compelling statistic. The 25 students in your class are not a representative sample, and you cannot make this claim using the data you have collected. Your sample size is too small to be representative. In addition, because the individuals are all drawn from the same required class, they likely have characteristics that are unique to them. For example, they may come from a restrictive set of majors, and they may be primarily freshmen and sophomores. As an ethical speaker, you must ensure that your statistics truly represent what you claim.

Understand What the Statistics Mean

When using statistics, you need to have a reasonable understanding of which statistics are appropriate for making which types of claims. For example, if your sample size is relatively small, a single outlier (an extremely high or low figure) will influence the mean of the group more than it will the median. The mean and median are different ways of describing average or central tendencies within a set of data. They are often confused with each other. They both have their advantages and disadvantages, depending on the nature of the data being reported.

The mean is the arithmetic average of a collection of numbers, computed by adding them up and dividing by the number of cases in your sample. The mean can be very sensitive. For example, if you survey ten people and find that one of them makes a million dollars a year but that the other nine make around $50,000 a year, the mean salary will suggest that, on average, the sample makes approximately $145,000 per year. This statistic, while technically accurate, would lead audience members to conclude that the sample members make much more money than they really do.

The median, on the other hand, represents the middle value in a series of numbers. It is found by arranging a set of values in order and then selecting the one in the middle. (If the total number of values in the sample is even, then the median is the average of the two middle numbers.) In our example, the median income would be $50,500. This statistic indicates a much lower value than the mean and gives the audience a truer picture of the earnings of this sample.

Explain the Statistics

It is extremely important that you explain what the statistics mean to your audience. In other words, you need to relate the statistics to audience members and their particular context. One of the easiest ways to explain statistics is through visual aids. It is hard for audience members to visualize large numbers. However, if you can relate the information to something that is easy to visualize, they will have a much easier time following your arguments.

Sometimes, visual aids are not practical or aren't enough to explain a particular number. In that case, use analogies or examples that give those numbers more meaning for your audience. Consider the following example: "Australians alone consume about 6.9 billion plastic bags each year." That 6.9 billion is a hard number for audience members to visualize. Restate that number in terms they can understand. For example, you could say the following to explain the statistic: "Australians alone consume about 6.9 billion plastic bags each year; that's 326 per person." Sometimes, when numbers get very large, audiences have difficulty conceptualizing them.[7] If you provide audiences with some additional way to visualize a statistic, it will add impact to your presentation.

Localize Statistics

Whenever possible, you want to relate your statistics directly to audience members and their lives geographically.[8] What does a particular statistic mean for members of your audience and their particular geographical area? As mentioned in Chapter 3, this is called **localizing.**

> You need to relate statistics to audience members and their particular context.

Remember Elton, the former student who wanted to persuade his classmates to donate their game meat to "Hunters Feed the Hungry," a nationwide organization? Elton was able to find numerous statistics to help localize his plea, among them:

◎ Over the past 7 years, more than 280,000 pounds of meat have been donated, providing over 1 million servings of meat to soup kitchens and food pantries across Indiana.

◎ 100% of donations go the local community.

◎ 17% of Tippecanoe County residents are considered "food insecure."

These numbers bring his plea closer to home and make the numbers more relevant to his particular audience.

Using graphical representations of statistics is an effective way to utilize information in your presentations.

Limit Your Use of Statistics

Long lists of statistics get very tiresome for audiences to follow. Nothing will bore an audience faster than being bombarded with a list of statistics. Be strategic. Use statistics when you really need the added impact or when the type of audience you will be addressing demands it.

Round Off Statistics

Processing large amounts of numerical data is taxing to an audience. One way to simplify large amounts of data is to round off your statistics. Unless it is extremely important that your numbers be exact, round them off.

Identify the Sources of Your Statistics

The reliability of your numbers is only as strong as the source of those numbers. If any of your support can be discredited, it will make the audience question your other supporting material as well.[9]

> **Your statistics will carry more impact if you can relate them directly to your audience.**

In the 2012 Republican presidential primary, a statistic cited frequently by conservative candidate Rick Santorum attracted much attention. In his ads and during campaign stops, Santorum frequently repeated that "62% of kids who enter college with some kind of faith commitment leave without it." As you can imagine, such an astounding statistic garnered much attention. But Santorum never cited the source for this claim. Soon, his opponents and members of the media began to challenge this (and by extension, other similar claims) when they were unsuccessful in attempts to locate the source of his claim. As a result, Santorum's campaign was put on the defensive trying to defend an argument that was key to his platform.[10]

The lesson is this: Make sure you provide your audience with the sources of your statistics. Knowing that the numbers came from government entities or academic studies lends credence to your position. By the same token, numbers provided by sources with self-serving motives hurt your presentation, so watch out for hidden agendas. Numbers can be easily manipulated on each side of an issue. Make sure your sources are objective and balanced.

Examples

Examples are another type of supporting evidence. We called these stories or narratives when we used them as an attention-gaining device (see Chapter 4 for refresher on how to tell a story). But they are also powerful choices for supporting evidence. They give life to your presentation. They are powerful tools that personalize or put a "face" on your message and your ideas. They help your audience see your ideas, and they add vividness to the entire presentation. Often your message is abstract, and by using examples you make the concept more relevant to your audience. Research indicates that it's best to use a combination of narrative stories and statistics in your supporting material.[11]

For example, the 2010 earthquake that devastated Haiti gave us lots of numbers: 200,000 killed, 300,000 injured, 700,000 homeless. But while those numbers may cause us to pause, it was the stories we heard from the earthquake that truly tugged our heartstrings: the dramatic rescues from the rubble, the orphaned children wandering the streets, the hungry and thirsty victims scavenging the rubble for food and water, the injured lying in yards and waiting days for treatment.

Statistics alone cannot create a personal tie with your audience. The concept becomes more real when we hear the story of a family similar to ours struggling through such a disaster. There are three different kinds of examples that you can use to add support to your presentation, as explained next.

Brief Examples

Brief examples are used to (briefly) further illustrate a point. Think of brief examples in terms of a specific instance you might need to provide. One way to do this is to include a brief 1- to 2-sentence narrative to illustrate a point. Referring back to Elton's persuasive speech on "Hunters for the Hungry," he provides the example "Anne, a single mother of three, saves $50 a month on groceries by picking up fresh meat provided by Hunters to her local church food bank." That brief sentence provides a specific instance of someone benefiting from the program.

You might also need to provide an example of a specific claim. Returning to Elton's speech, he talks about the "nutritious game" available via the program. He then provided (brief) specific examples for his audience: "Low-fat meats such as venison and duck are available in the program." Here are two examples from student speeches:

> A new revolutionary AbioCor heart transplant system has given Robert Tools his life back. Tools was suffering from diabetes, kidney failure, and congestive heart failure. But within a month of his transplant, he could take trips outside of the hospital and was able to converse with others as he had not done in months.

or

> Some fabrics protect items from UV light better than others. For example, blue jeans provide more protection than cotton knits.

Extended Examples

Extended examples are longer stories or narratives, and they are an excellent way to generate audience interest in your topic (see Chapter 4, Narratives). Consider the following example:

> The two-story building that served as both a home for Andrea and Michael Brewer and an orphanage for 22 children lies in rubble after the January 2010 earthquake. The Brewers moved to Port-au-Prince a year ago to operate the orphanage and serve as missionaries. They managed to salvage a few mattresses and some clothes and personal items. They need a new place to live, but there is no money. So the Brewers are staying in a neighbor's home, and the children sleep outside under a huge tarp that attempts to protect them from the hot sun or the torrential rain that falls occasionally. It's the best they can do for now.

The speaker could easily have said that many orphanages in Haiti are overwhelmed after the earthquake. However, her story makes the presentation more compelling and adds a human component that the audience would not otherwise have experienced.

But, you say, you've never been to Haiti, nor do you know anyone who has. You don't have to know of the example firsthand. As mentioned in Chapter 4, many magazines and newspapers have these types of examples that you can use. As long as you cite your source, feel free to use the examples you find in the media.

Hypothetical Examples

Sometimes the examples you use will be true or factual like the ones you have just read, and sometimes they will be hypothetical or imaginary. **Hypothetical examples** allow your audience to identify with the situation you are describing. Here is an example a student used in her speech on power blackouts:

> It's 3:00 a.m., and you are sitting in front of your computer putting the finishing touches on your final paper for your English composition course. Suddenly, you hear a buzzing sound, and your power goes out. Your screen goes black. You can't remember the last time you saved your work. You start to panic as the power comes back on, and you frantically wait to see just how much work you have lost.

By using this example, the speaker is able to draw her audience into her presentation. In a classroom presentation, most of her audience members are going to be able to identify with the scenario she has depicted.

However, hypothetical examples should be used sparingly. The example would have been even more powerful if the speaker had added statistics indicating how often power blackouts occur. It's a good idea to add facts or testimony to demonstrate that a hypothetical example is realistic. Too often, student speakers want to use hypothetical examples instead of doing the research to find real examples.

Another mistake speakers make is using outrageous hypothetical examples. You cannot ask an audience of college-aged students to picture themselves as 80-year-old men who have just lost their partner of 60 years. They simply will not be able to identify. Instead, you need to find a real narrative example to share with the audience.

Tips for Using Examples

In Chapter 4, we provided tips for choosing, structuring, and delivering stories, or examples, effectively. Here is a reminder of some of those key points:

Make Examples Vivid

Detail makes examples come to life. You want to paint a mental picture for your audience. Include details that will help your audience envision the scenario you are describing. One way to enhance vividness is through the characters in your story. Make sure you mention the names of your characters. It is much easier to envision "Mary, a freshman accounting major from Springfield" than if you had just said "a female student." These small details give your examples texture and help your audience relate to them.

Make Sure Extended Examples Have a Beginning, Middle, and End

As you recall from Chapter 4, anytime you tell a story, you want to ensure it has a beginning, middle, and end. You want your examples—especially your extended examples—to be fully developed. Most of the time, you will not want to leave your audience hanging. Even if the final outcome of your story isn't essential, your audience will appreciate closure. But that does not mean you have to provide the beginning, middle, and end in one place. For example, if you provide the start of a story in your introduction, you can end it in your conclusion.

Practice Delivering Extended Examples

Not all of us are born storytellers. Some of us are naturally better at telling stories than others. So practice delivering your examples. You should never read an extended example to your audience. You should maintain good eye contact and use delivery cues that will add impact to your story. The effectiveness of a narrative ultimately depends on its delivery (see Chapter 4). Many students in this course have discovered that their extended examples did not achieve the desired effect because they read them from note cards rather than telling them with emotion.

> **You should never read an extended example to your audience.**

Practicing will also help you determine how long your story will be when it is delivered orally. Many speakers spend so much time delivering a narrative that they run out of speaking time and fail to complete the entire presentation. Don't let this happen to you. Practice your extended examples so that they achieve your desired impact.

Select the Right Example

No matter how compelling your example, it must illustrate or prove a point you are trying to make. Interesting stories that don't illustrate a point are just that—interesting stories—and your audience will be confused as to why you have included them. Make sure the point of the narrative is clear to the audience.

Select Appropriate Examples

In your eagerness to provide a compelling example, don't lose sight of how your audience might react to that example. A recent student was attempting to persuade his classmates to donate to the Society for the Prevention of Cruelty to Animals. He elected to use an extended example from a volunteer who described the upsetting conditions of the animals found in a local raid. Many students in the class became visibly sickened by the descriptions, and some even put their hands over their ears. While the example was truly compelling, it may have been too graphic to present to a lay audience. A less graphic illustration might have worked better.

Testimony

The third type of supporting evidence is testimony. **Testimony** is a quotation or paraphrase from an expert or knowledgeable source used to support an idea or point you are making in a presentation. Testimony can be very persuasive.[12] Think about the following scenario: You have a sore tooth and are talking to your friend about it. You explain that you are not from this area and so you don't have a dentist nearby. Your friend tells you that she has been seeing Dr. Browne, a local dentist, and that she finds him to be gentle, professional, and affordable. Based on your friend's recommendation, you schedule an appointment with Dr. Browne. You have been persuaded by the testimony of your friend. If you stop and think about it, many of the decisions we make in everyday life are based on the testimony of family members, friends, or co-workers.

Audiences are often swayed by the testimony of individuals they respect. Within the course of a presentation, you can use testimony to add strength to your claims. There are three types of testimony: expert testimony, peer testimony, and prestige testimony.

Expert Testimony

Expert testimony is evidence from people who have the experience or education to be recognized as authorities in their field. Since in this class you will rarely be speaking on topics about which you are an expert, expert testimony is a way to enhance your credibility. By borrowing the ethos or credibility of an expert, you add support to the claims you are making in your presentation. In trying to persuade her audience that DNA evidence is reliable, Jessie used the following testimony:

> According to Dr. Ian Findlay, a scientist involved in the human genome project at Queensland University, it is impossible to not leave behind traces of blood, semen, hair, or skin cells at crime scenes. He stated that someone would have to wear a spacesuit to avoid leaving DNA evidence at a crime scene.

Although Jessie is studying health sciences and has even worked in a crime lab, her credibility is greatly enhanced by providing the opinion of an expert.

Peer Testimony

Another type of testimony is peer testimony. **Peer testimony** consists of opinions from ordinary people, not experts, who have experience in the topic at hand. This type of evidence is compelling because it capitalizes on average experiences to which your audience can easily relate.

For some speeches, peer testimony is critical because of a lack of other types of support. You may not be able to find any statistics if you want to give a presentation on popular area hiking trails. But, you can interview fellow students who use these trails and incorporate their experiences into your presentation. Without this peer testimony, the speech might not have the impact you desire.

Prestige Testimony

Prestige testimony is a paraphrase or quotation of the opinion of a celebrity or famous individual. While these individuals are not experts on the topic, they are highly respected, and audiences often solicit their opinions. For example, millions of Americans tune in to hear Oprah Winfrey's opinions on fashion, literature, and a host of other topics. While Oprah is not much of an expert on literature, as someone who has earned a Ph.D. or written bestselling novels is, she does carry immense credibility. Millions of Americans buy books on her recommended reading list. Prestige testimony can be a strong source of evidence if you recognize the differences between it and expert testimony.

Sometimes, a source can fit into multiple categories. Robert Redford is an Academy Award–winning actor and director, and founder of the Sundance Institute, which sponsors the Sundance Film Festival each year. That gives him a lot of prestige. But he is also an active, award-winning environmentalist. This makes him an expert as well.

Redford used both of these roles in February 2012 when Congress was considering approving the Keystone XL tar sands pipeline from Canada to the United States. Many environmental groups were opposed to the pipeline. Redford used his star power to encourage his fans on Facebook and other social media to sign an online petition to Congress opposing the pipeline. When he testified about the pipeline, however, it was not only as a personality, but as an active environmentalist.

Tips for Using Testimony

Quote or Paraphrase Accurately

Make sure that you quote or paraphrase sources accurately. Individuals sometimes are misquoted, or their statements are abbreviated or taken out of context. It is your responsibility as an ethical speaker to ensure that you use their words as your sources intended.

Use Testimony from Unbiased Sources

Make sure that the testimony you are citing is from an unbiased source. Suzy, a student in this course, read an article that claimed that canned vegetables were healthier than either frozen or fresh vegetables. After further investigation, she discovered that the research presented in the article was conducted by the aluminum can industry–hardly an unbiased source. The information in the article and the conclusions of the study may have been completely accurate. However, given the biased nature of the source, these results seem a little suspicious. Your audience will likely think so as well. Make sure your testimony is from credible, competent, and objective experts.

Ethically Speaking

Just as you owe it to your audience to detail the qualifications of your experts, you also owe it to them not to misrepresent a source's expertise. This is especially true when using prestige testimony. When presenting opinions from trusted stars, make sure you don't confuse fame and expertise. Studies have shown that star power alone is not enough to create beliefs, but it can raise approval despite current beliefs.[13]

Cite the Credentials of Your Sources

When you introduce testimony, identify your source. Here are a couple of examples of how you would introduce this information within your presentation:

Beth, a freshman nursing major, had this to say about the Grand Prix on campus …

Dr. Browne, a cardiologist at MD Anderson Hospital in Houston, warns that obesity …

You owe it to audience members to inform them of the qualifications of your experts. Audience members should then be able to judge for themselves whether or not they find your experts credible.

General Tips on Using Supporting Material

Use a Variety of Types of Supporting Material

As you begin to prepare your presentation, include a variety of types of supporting materials. As discussed in Chapter 2, certain audiences are more likely to be interested in and persuaded by different types of evidence. It is important that you use a variety of materials so that you can appeal to different members of your audience.

Annie, a student in a presentational speaking course, made a mistake when she relied on a personal anecdote and peer testimony alone in a presentation to persuade her classmates that there was no need for them to get a flu shot. She shared her own personal testimony that the previous year, she had received a flu vaccine and immediately come down with the flu. She also included similar narratives from two other women she worked with who had received the vaccine but still contracted the flu. These stories were well explained and appropriate for her topic. But they weren't enough for her classmates. During a brief Q&A after her presentation, one student asked her what doctors said about the chances

It is good to use supporting materials, but not to the point where there is no new information provided or no new point of view offered by the speaker.

Michael Schiferl | Executive Vice President | Weber Shandwick

of getting the flu from the vaccine. Another asked if she had any statistics about the number of people who got the flu after receiving the vaccine. When Annie could not produce this additional support, her credibility, and thus her message, suffered.

Use a Variety of Sources for Supporting Material

Even if you use a variety of types of supporting material, your audience may question your motives or your level of research if the number of sources for your support is limited. By using different sources (newspapers, journals, interviews, etc.) and different types of material, you enhance your credibility, and at the same time increase the believability of your information.

Use Consistent and Complementary Supporting Material

Your supporting material is not a set of independent observations. All points are parts of a larger whole. They should work together to build a case or make a point. Ask yourself, "Does this evidence enhance the overall presentation?" Or, "How does this evidence or supporting material relate to other supporting material I am providing?" Often, novice speakers string together miscellaneous bits of information that do not, in totality, work together in meaningful ways.

Where to Find Supporting Material

Libraries

Students often cringe at the thought of going to the library to do research. Many of them are unfamiliar with the library and don't know where to go to get started. One of the best pieces of advice is to ask a reference librarian for help. That's what they are there for. You will find them extremely helpful, and you can find what you need in less time if you just ask for help when you need it. A Pew Research Center for the People and the Press[14] report says that college librarians have reported a decrease in the number of reference desk visits by students as campus online services have proliferated.

Most universities offer a variety of formats for those seeking assistance. Librarians are available to assist you during library hours, and many libraries will allow you to schedule a one-on-one appointment with a librarian. For those of you who might find it difficult to get to the library because of work or family or other commitments, most college libraries now offer many services that allow you to get answers to simple questions without going to the library. For example, at the University of Kentucky, you can live Web chat with a reference librarian. At Michigan State, you can instant message a librarian 24/7 or send your questions to a librarian via text message from your phone or via e-mail. Most libraries now have similar such services available.

In addition, many librarians offer online tutorials (such as Purdue's CORE, Comprehensive Online Research Education) on their websites to guide you through the research process and the confusing mass of library materials, including online access to their many databases. Some of these databases are full text; others will instruct you where to go in your library to obtain the journal or book sought. Check out your school's library page to see what services are available to you, either in person or from home.

Even if you have access to excellent libraries, you may have to go elsewhere for information. For instance, you may need to interview experts, conduct polls, go to museums, visit organizations, or use other methods to get the information and supporting material necessary for your presentation. The library is the most common source for gathering information, but not the only one.

Spotlight on Research

Students' Ability to Evaluate Online Information

Researchers' concerns about the "potentially dubious nature" of online information and college students' ability to evaluate it competently prompted two studies. The researchers were looking at students' use of Web-based information, how credible they found such information, and if they attempted to verify the information. The first study found that college students rely very heavily on the Web for information, both academic and generic. Results from the second study show that students find Web-based information more credible than do individuals from a more general adult population. As a result, students verify the information they find online significantly less often.[15]

Interviews

Sometimes the information you need is best obtained through an interview with an expert or someone who has personal experience with a topic. Luckily for you, college campuses have numerous experts (professors) and peers (students) with varied interests and experiences. And most are more than happy to be interviewed.

There are a few things to consider when planning to use this method of research.

- ◎ First, you need to decide whom to interview. Not all engineering professors study the same thing. You will need to research the correct person for your needs.
- ◎ Next, you need to arrange the interview. A word of caution: Don't wait until the last minute and assume that your subject will be available. Contact your subject well in advance of the needed meeting. Let them know what the subject of your presentation is and what information you need from them.
- ◎ You also need to prepare. Make sure you have carefully thought out and written down what questions you would like to ask. You will lose credibility if you seem unprepared.
- ◎ Please be professional during the interview. Dress appropriately, use appropriate language, and thank the person for giving up their time to help you.

Not all interviews need to be conducted in person. If you don't need a lot of information from the source, you may contact them via telephone or e-mail, or even on social media. But make sure you maintain a professional, respectful demeanor. Just because you are using e-mail does not give you the right to be casual.

Websites

Websites can be beneficial as supporting evidence, if you understand what you are dealing with. Today, government entities, news media, and for-profit and nonprofit organizations all offer their information online. You no longer have to buy a print copy of the *Washington Post;* you can access the information in that day's newspaper (and previous editions as well) online. The latest analysis of population information from the Census Bureau is located in their online newsroom for all to view.

But remember, anyone can put up a website. Although the ability to publish your own material makes the Web a powerful tool, it also means that you need to know exactly what you are dealing with when you choose to use supporting evidence from a website. By following the guidelines outlined in the "How to Evaluate the Credibility of Websites" box in this chapter, you can minimize some of these risks.

Personal Web pages carry the most danger. While they don't necessarily contain erroneous material, you should examine them critically and use them with extreme caution. In this course, it is highly recommended that you avoid personal Web pages for things like statistical support or expert testimony. However, personal web pages can be a great source for peer testimony or personal narratives. Feel free to discuss with your instructor beforehand whether material from a personal Web page is appropriate.

Weblogs

As mentioned in Chapter 3, Weblogs, or blogs, are regularly updated, self-published online information sources. While the majority of blogs are written by hobbyists,[17] about 40% are authored by experts, journalists, organizations, etc., as alternative sources of news delivery.

Blogs are often categorized by subject. For example, the *New York Times* website currently hosts 65 blogs authored by either experts or writers on topics ranging from science, to books, to healthcare. This makes it easy to search for blogs by the topic of your particular presentation on most newspapers' websites. And because by nature blog posts are shorter and more informal than regular newspaper articles, and because blogs are updated more frequently, they make excellent places for authors to share quick, interesting information that could be perfect support for your presentations. That's one reason that 89% of journalists surveyed in a study by Cision[18] said they look to blogs when researching a story.

Annie, a finance major, was asked to plan a useful information presentation on the topic of college loans to students attending a "Student Success" fair. While researching her presentation, she discovered The Learning Network on the *New York Times* website, which is billed as covering relevant issues for college-bound students. From a recent post, she discovered that the Consumer Financial Protection Bureau announced that it had opened a student loan complaint system for issues regarding student loans. Annie thought this news would make an excellent subpoint in her presentation.

Other blogs are free-standing, such as the Huffington Post, a current events blog, or the tech blog Mashable, considered by many the utmost authority on social media and technology. Blog search engines such as Google's blog search or blogsearchengine.org can help you locate blogs related to your topic. As with Web pages, it is critical here that the credentials of the blog's author be verified. Do they work in the field? Do they have degrees in the field? Have they authored articles or books in the field? Do they have any affiliations (political, employers) that might bias their judgment? These are some things to consider when judging the reliability of a blog's author.

How to Evaluate the Credibility of Websites

As previously stated, when you use Web pages as supporting evidence, you are taking a risk. Follow the guidelines[19] outlined here to minimize this risk.[20]

Examine the URL

Even sites that appear legitimate may not be, or might have a bias of which you are unaware. One such example is the National Center for Public Policy Research (http://www.nationalcenter.org/). This organization's name sounds as if it might be affiliated with the federal government. Instead, the center is a nonprofit think tank that supports the conservative viewpoint on national issues. We can look at this organization's URL or Web address for valuable information about who owns the domain, what kind of server it belongs to, and so on.

One of the most important questions you can ask is whether the URL makes sense for the claims the page is making. If the page claims to represent the U.S. Department of Agriculture, for example, and "USDA" doesn't appear anywhere in the URL, something is wrong. Also, most sites have a "Home" or "About Us" page. You can find out a lot about an organization and its affiliations by reading such pages.

The extension on a URL can reveal information as well. Most government agencies use either .gov, .mil, or .us extensions. You know you can trust information found on these websites because it comes from an official government source, such as the Department of Education or the Centers for Disease Control (CDC). Most organizations, such as the National Center for Public Policy Research, use the .org extension. That is your clue that you need to be on the lookout for possible bias in their presentation of material.

But don't dismiss all information on .org or .com websites. For example, many organizations, such as the Kaiser Family Foundation (http://www.kff.org/), and the World Health Organization (http://www.who.int/en/), provide valuable data on health issues to support statistics you might acquire from the CDC. In these cases, use the other guidelines presented here to determine if the information on the website is credible.

For more information on dissecting the URL, visit the following website at the Johns Hopkins Libraries: http://www.library.jhu.edu/researchhelp/general/evaluating/url.html.

Examine the Site's Credentials

One of the first steps in examining website credentials is examining the credentials of the authors of the websites. The Johns Hopkins University Libraries suggest that these may be the most important criteria to consider. Do the authors have the credentials necessary to make claims or give the advice they are recommending? If not, be leery of the information on the page. If the authors don't include their credentials, it is probably a sign that something is amiss.

How to Evaluate the Credibility of Websites (continued)

In addition to examining the author of specific information, you should also evaluate the publisher of the site. If the site belongs to an organization, it may not include the name of the author of each section or page. If not, who is the publishing body? Is the organization recognized in the field it represents? Does the organization presenting the information have a stake in the material presented? Does it have its own agenda? Is it affiliated with a particular political viewpoint? This could mean that the material presented on the site is biased. Is the site trying to sell something, or is it trying to get you to do something? Is it a corporate organization? Carefully examine the site, and answer all of these questions. You cannot assume that biased websites will be obvious.

All operators of websites must register their domain name, contact information, and so on, with InterNIC, the agency responsible for distributing domain names in the United States. InterNIC is currently owned by Virginia-based Network Solutions.

Various applications exist that allow you to access information about a website's operator. One example is http://alexa.com. Simply go to this site and paste in the URL in question to get some added information. This site provides information on the level of traffic the site receives, reviews, contact/ownership information for the domain name, and a list of sites that link to the page. All of this information may enable you to make a better judgment about the quality of the site. Another popular site is the WHOIS lookup at Register.com (http://www.register.com/whois.rcmx).

Examine External Links

Examine the sites that the Web page links to. These can be informative as well. Following are some questions to consider about links: Are they well-respected links, or are they suspect? Do the links work? Do the links offer other viewpoints on the subject? Do the links represent a bias?

A website found at http://www.martinlutherking.org seems legitimate, at first glance, offering information on Martin Luther King and his life. However, a quick click on the external links offers another interpretation. The site links to white supremacist groups and other sites that promote hate and racism.

Examine Citations

The evidence a particular Web page cites can be important as well. Who is cited? Are they reputable and respected sources? Can you find the material that the Web page references? Sometimes individuals fabricate sources. Check them out for yourself to examine their validity.

Examine Timeliness of Information

Check the most recent date the Web page was updated. For some topics, timeliness is extremely important.

While some blogs have single authors, many have multiple contributors. Returning to the Mashable blog, for example, each day dozens of bloggers share the duties of posting interesting information and updates on social media, technology, and business. This gives you a wider variety of expert sources for your presentation. Because bloggers frequently include their opinions on topics they are sharing, blogs can be a good source of peer and expert testimony. You don't have to personally know someone who has used the new iPad. Instead, you can find blog posts from technology experts and regular people and share their experiences in your presentation.

Spotlight on Research

Students Lack Traditional Research Skills

An October 2012 study by Project Information Literacy examined the information-seeking competencies of new college graduates in the workplace.[16] The study concluded that most of the new graduates found it difficult to solve information problems at work when they needed to use means other than the Internet. "In particular, employers expected hires to possess low-tech research competencies, such as the ability to make a phone call, to poke their heads into a co-worker's office to ask a question, to interpret results with a team member, or to scour a bound report. However, many fresh-from-college hires sorely lacked these traditional research competencies." In fact, the study concluded that young workers viewed the use of non-digitized sources as archaic and not a skill that needed to be learned.

Social Media

As outlined in the chapter opener, while many students turn to Facebook or Twitter daily, few think of social media when researching presentations. That may be because you don't think of finding anything valuable in a 140-character tweet. But many times, those tweets or those status updates are simply directing you to a full article, news release, or study that can be very useful to your research. So much information is available on social media that reporters now consider it a research staple.[21] So while you may not have time to watch the nightly television newscast or read an entire newspaper each day, following news organizations on social media allows you to in effect get a quick view of that day's headlines in micro messages.

Donita, a foods and nutrition major, knew she wanted to persuade her classmates to adopt a healthier diet. While she was not able to watch the major newscasts each night, she did follow ABC News on Facebook. A recent Facebook post by the news agency provided a link to a feature story by one of its reporters on a health study done by researchers in England. The researchers found that eating lots of fruits and veggies may not only improve our overall health, but may actually make us more attractive to others by improving our skin tone. Donita was excited that this was a subpoint many of her classmates likely would not have heard. This was new information that would have great surprise value for those listening to her presentation.

The Centers for Disease Control in Atlanta is just one example of a government agency active in sharing information via social media. For example, in addition to its main account on Twitter, @CDCgov, it has individual Twitter accounts for such research areas as cancer, HIV/AIDS, emergency preparedness, flu, global health, STDs, etc. The Twitter feeds are constantly being updated with new statistics, research, and reactions that would make excellent, credible sources of information for all types of presentations.

There are several ways to find sources on social media:

◎ You can simply check to see if an organization, company, or person has a Facebook, Twitter, or LinkedIn account by entering the name in the search boxes located on the media's main pages.

◎ On Twitter, you can also enter key words into the search box. Twitter will then find all tweets that contain those words.

◎ You can participate in "live chats" on Facebook or Twitter.

Let's return to Annie, our finance major, who wanted to give a presentation on changes to student loans. First, Annie went to Twitter and entered the key words "student loans" into the search box. Results included not only regular students' tweets commenting about various aspects of student loans but also links to news stories about student loans from such media as Inside Higher Ed, ComputerWeekly, and the Huffington Post. There were even tweets from the U.S. Department of Education, which oversees student loans, and FAFSA, the federal student loan agency, with links to news releases about recent loan news. She elected to "follow" both of these accounts so she would automatically receive any updates they sent out via Twitter.

Next, Annie stopped on Facebook and searched for the U.S. Department of Education's page. On the page's "wall," Annie noticed a status update promoting a "live chat" on Twitter hosted by FAFSA, during which students could tweet any questions they might have about financial aid and get answers. Annie made a note of this so she could participate in the live chat and use responses from the experts in her presentation. This was an opportunity for Annie to get expert testimony that she might otherwise not have had access to.

As mentioned at the start of this chapter, students often neglect social media when doing academic research. But as you can see from Annie's experience, social media can be a rich resource for finding statistics and testimony to use in your presentations.

News Releases

As mentioned in Chapter 3, news releases are communications from for-profit and nonprofit companies as well as from private and government entities. News releases can be good sources of support for your presentations, and you can access them through websites such as PR Newswire, through online newsrooms, or through links organizations provide on Twitter and Facebook. But remember, these are often from organizations that have an agenda to promote. Make sure you carefully evaluate the information in news releases for bias.

Technically Speaking

Social media can be used for more than just finding supporting evidence; it can also be used to organize it. Social bookmarking sites like Pinterest or Delicious are excellent for organizing your research. They also make it easy to share Web content you've found with other members of a group. Still, a recent study found that only 10% of students use such a site to organize academic research.[22]

Books

Books are a good place to begin your research for your presentations. They usually provide a thorough treatment of the topic that they address and therefore provide a substantial amount of material on a given topic. The primary limitation of books is that they become outdated rather quickly. It takes a good deal of time for a book to reach the shelf, from the moment it is written to the time it is published, so even books with very recent copyright dates may have dated material. This may not be important for every topic, but for those topics where information is changing quickly, such as technological or scientific advancements, books may not be the best source of supporting evidence.

Carefully examine the contents of web pages before relying on them for information.

Reference Works

Sometimes you need to check a quick fact when putting together your presentation. For example, you may need to know the date of an important historical event, the gross national product of a country, or the population of a particular geographical region. Answers to these questions can be found in a variety of common and respected reference resources, including encyclopedias, dictionaries, atlases, yearbooks, almanacs, and biographical aids, to name just a few.

Here are two Web links of commonly accessed reference works that may be beneficial to you: the CIA World Factbook (https://www.cia.gov/library/publications/the-world-factbook/index.html) and the Encyclopedia Britannica online (http://www.britannica.com/).

LexisNexis Academic, an online database, also provides excellent reference works, indexing the *World Almanac,* Roper polls, famous quotations, country profiles, state profiles, and biographical profiles. You can access LexisNexis from most university library websites. Look for the most current of the print versions; they, too, can become dated very quickly and are often updated yearly. Online versions of these publications may be the most beneficial because they are continuously updated. While reference works are good places to find quick facts, they do not provide ample material for your presentation.

Magazines, Newspapers, and Broadcast Outlets

Articles from magazines, newspapers, and broadcast outlets provide some of the best supporting materials for your presentations. These sources are published or aired often, so they usually provide current and up-to-date material. One limitation of magazines, newspapers, and broadcast outlets is that the authors are usually journalists and not experts on the topic on which they are reporting. Keep this in mind as you evaluate the material you consult for the presentation.

Most traditional media outlets have their own web pages on which their stories are indexed and archived. A simple key word search can provide you with fresh support for your presentations. Local TV and newspaper outlets are an excellent source of material to localize your presentations.

Another effective way to search these sources is an index like LexisNexis Academic. This invaluable reference for finding information indexes over 6,000 sources from all over the world. As mentioned previously, most campus libraries offer this database online. Often, you can access it from any computer on campus or even from home. All of the articles it indexes are full-text versions. This means that the entire content of every article indexed, not just the abstract, is provided within the database, so you can do some of your research from the comfort of your home.

Once you have accessed LexisNexis Academic from the database menu of your school's library, searching is simple. On the opening screen, you have several options for searching. You can simply type in your search terms on the opening page, and LexisNexis will display the results of your simple search based on the documents it judges pertinent in its database from the last two years. Or you can click on the "Advanced Options" tab to narrow your search by date or source type.

Spotlight on Research

Various Media Credibility Examined

People rate the credibility of the various media differently. If you know this, you can weigh which sources might be the most influential in your particular presentation. The Pew Research Center for the People and the Press[23] examined Americans' perceptions of news media outlets in 2012. Some interesting findings included the following:

- ◎ Local TV news was rated the most believable of all news sources.
- ◎ Local daily newspapers are more trusted than the *New York Times*.
- ◎ Partisan outlets like Fox News and MSNBC are rated the least believable.

One of the most important features of LexisNexis is its ability to search over 300 campus newspapers at https://www.lexisnexis.com/ap/academic. This can be a valuable source of information for presentations in a course like this. Learning what issues are occurring on other campuses can provide good information for persuasive presentations and even the group presentation. This provides excellent material for analogical arguments. For example, when Tammy, a student in a presentational speaking class, was arguing in support of her town making its bars smoke-free, she used LexisNexis to find several articles about the successful implementation of such a law in two other university towns in her state to bolster her argument.

LexisNexis Opening Search Screen

Use of this service is subject to Terms and Conditions

Source Directory: Find or Browse | Create Permanent Link | Help

LexisNexis® Academic

Academic Search

Search by Subject or Topic ▾

Enter Search Terms   Search

Advanced Options ▾

What's New

Video Tutorials

Research Guides

Download Content List

Academic Knowledge Center

Tools

Check out our U.S. Presidential Campaign Tracker to see candidate media coverage over time, share of voice and sentiment!

Hot Topics Links   Today's Front Page News

European Migrant Crisis	Paris Terror Attacks	2016 Presidential Election
Syria	Pope Francis	Cuba
Nobel Prize	Afghanistan	College Basketball

Search the News
U.S. and World News.

Look up a Legal Case
Federal and state cases.

Get Company Info
Over 80 million companies.

LexisNexis also offers an easy tutorial on its site. It can walk you through, step by step, any type of search in which you are interested. Use this tool to help guide more sophisticated searches; it really will be beneficial.

While traditional newspapers and magazines (both print and online editions) are an excellent source of information, don't forget that many periodicals are unique Web-only publications today. For example, *Slate* magazine (slate.com), which boasts 11 million viewers and is owned by the Washington Post company, covers science, politics, health, and other beats, yet has always existed only in an online format. In addition, many former print publications are moving online only to save costs. These range from newspapers (the *Seattle Post-Intelligencer*) to more specialized publications (*MotorBoating* magazine). So don't forget these online-only periodicals when doing research.

Newspaper Source is another database you can use to easily locate newspaper articles. This database provides abstracts and full-text articles for over 245 U.S. and international newspapers from 1994 to the present. This collection includes major newspapers such as the *New York Times,* the *Wall Street Journal,* and *USA Today,* and international papers such as the *Kyodo News International,* a Japanese publication. Visit your library's home page for information on finding these databases.

Government Documents

Federal, state, and local governments generate record-keeping documents and statistics. These materials also help keep the public informed on government activity and policy. Some good sites for governmental statistical information are the U.S. Census Bureau (http://www.census.gov/data.html), FedStats (http://fedstats.sites.usa.gov/showcase/), and the portal for the U.S. government's websites (http://www.usa.gov). For international numbers, try the UNESCO Institute for Statistics (http://www.uis.unesco.org/), which compares statistics across countries in areas such as education and technology.

You can visit your library's home page for a list of many additional websites that can facilitate the search of government documents. (The following site will give you more information on what is available to Purdue students, and it is sorted by subject: http://guides.lib.purdue.edu/govt.)

Academic Journals

Academic journals are published for scholars or individuals who do research in a particular area. They distribute original research to a particular scientific or scholarly community. They contain the latest developments in their field. Sometimes they are difficult for students to decipher because they are full of technical jargon particular to a specific subject area. However, they are highly credible sources of information.

A good place to search for academic journals is Academic Search Premier. This database indexes over 3,000 academic journals, magazines, and newspapers. ArticleFirst, another database, indexes articles from over 12,000 journals in a variety of disciplines. Proquest Research Library is a database well-suited for finding academic publications as well. This database indexes over 2,350 magazines, academic journals, and newspaper articles in many different subject areas. Some are even available in full-text versions. JSTOR, the Scholarly Journal Archive, has full-text articles from over 450 journals, including disciplines such as the social sciences, humanities, economics, and mathematics. Check to see which databases your university provides access to.

In addition, Harvard's Shorenstein Center has developed a website, "Journalist's Resource," with the goal of making scholarly research more accessible for regular people such as students, educators, and journalists. The site provides brief summaries of important scholarly studies on a wide array of topics. Links to the actual studies and other related material are provided. The site's authors say the goal is to encourage the use of high-quality scholarship by making it more accessible and understandable to the average person. The database is available from the main Web page at http://www.journalistsresource.org.

Evaluating Information Sources

Today, with a few keystrokes, we can find various types of support for any presentation we might make. But that doesn't mean it is good support. Critical evaluation of the information you find is essential. Even though web pages carry the most risk, all sources should be evaluated. With so much information available from so many different sources, you must evaluate each piece of information carefully to ensure it is the best support for your presentation.

When tasked with deciding if the information you have chosen is appropriate, each of the following areas must be evaluated. The following guidelines apply to all reference materials.[24]

Authority

This area deals with the author or creator of the information. What is his or her occupation? Education level? Experience level? Credentials? Are they sponsored or supported by a particular organization, industry, or institution? Focus and specialization can be key traits here. Make sure that a source is commenting on an area within his or her expertise.

As an ethical speaker, you owe it to your audience to find information that comes from credible sources. You might be asking your audience to make changes that affect their lives. Asking them to base their decisions on material that is less than reliable is unethical. Your supporting material should come from respected sources.

Accuracy

Obviously, we want accurate information. But how can we determine its accuracy? Well, in addition to looking at the source/creator of the information, we can also look at the explanation given. Does the source you cite provide enough evidence to support its claim or position? Were the conclusions drawn by the source appropriate based on the information presented? For example, beware of studies where people make big claims from a few number of responses.

Currency is also a form of accuracy. You want to make sure you are citing the latest material available. This is especially important when it comes to statistics. It's inaccurate to cite old statistics. An old statistic could provide an inaccurate view of the current situation.

Let's look at Dani, a student in COM114. In spring 2015, she was attempting to persuade her organization that it should add Snapchat to its social media repertoire. She cited a 2013 Pew Internet study that said Snapchat had 26 million users.[25] Dani hurt her own argument by providing an old number. According to a January 2015 businessinsider.com article, Snapchat users may be nearing 200 million.[26] This is a very big difference that might have impressed her organization more, as would have the medium's rapid adoption rate.

Objectivity

You want to watch out for bias in your information. Ask yourself if the source has given multiple viewpoints on an issue. Is the creator biased? Is the publication the information appears in published or sponsored by a special interest group? Is it possible the source is trying to persuade you to support their viewpoint or the beliefs of a certain group?

What if it is an organization you are unfamiliar with? How might you go about deciding whether it is objective? Let's examine one such organization: The National Sleep Foundation (NSF). Online, we can visit its "About Us" page to find out it is a "charitable, educational and scientific not-for-profit organization located in Washington, DC" that is "dedicated to improving health and well-being through sleep education and advocacy."[27] So we know that it is not a for-profit wanting to sell us something. Second, the organization says its membership includes "researchers and clinicians focused on sleep medicine, health professionals, patients, families affected by drowsy driving and more than 900 healthcare facilities." Here we see no mention of bed or mattress manufacturers, people who might have a financial interest in promoting sleep. The NSF also provides a link to its board of directors. Each member is an academic or a physician. Again, this lends credibility to the information it provides. Finally the organization talks about its "Sleep in America poll." It provides an extensive discussion on how the poll was conducted and analyzed for us to evaluate. We can judge, as mentioned above, whether the conclusions they made were appropriate for the information presented. And when we Google this poll, we find that every major respected news outlet (e.g., *New York Times, Washington Post, Wall Street Journal*) has used this poll. That means they respected the way it was conducted. In our evaluation then, we could use information from the National Sleep Foundation.

Relevancy

Sometimes you find fascinating material that is only tangentially related to your topic. Perhaps you have found an interesting statistic that you would like to include in your presentation just because you think your audience might find it fascinating. If it doesn't directly relate to the goal of your presentation, do not include the material. Only include information that directly helps you achieve the goal of your presentation. Doing otherwise may distract your audience and detract from your message.

Variety

Ethical speakers consult a variety of resources in hopes of validating their research in multiple places. Make sure you review a variety of types of information, ranging from scholarly journals to newspapers. Each publication has its own strengths and weaknesses. By drawing supporting materials from a variety of sources, you will compensate for any weakness a particular source may have.

Level of Information

If you don't understand the material you are presenting, chances are your audience won't either. Ask yourself who is the intended audience for the information you have found: the general public? Scholars? Professionals? Then ask yourself if the material is understandable and makes sense to you. Do you feel confident in putting this material into your own words? This is an important test. Too often, students in COM114 simply take information they do not understand and repeat it verbatim in their presentations. Support that your audience cannot understand is not strong support. If this is a test the source doesn't pass, find another source.

Citing Your Evidence during the Presentation

As discussed in Chapter 9, citing your sources within your speech will enhance your credibility as a speaker and can even make your presentation more persuasive.[28] In addition, research shows that when you provide the source for your citation first, the listener will view the cite as more credible.[29] As an ethical speaker, it is also important that you cite your sources to avoid plagiarism. The following examples demonstrate methods for citing sources orally during your presentation.

> **As an ethical speaker, it is important that you cite your sources to avoid plagiarism.**

When orally citing your material, variety is important. Don't introduce each piece of supporting evidence with, "According to …" Use variety when introducing these elements into your presentation.

Books

When citing a book, you need to cite the author, his or her credentials (if that will enhance your credibility), the title of the book, and the date the book was published. Here is an example:

> In her 2012 book, *The Top Five Regrets of the Dying,* an Australian palliative nurse said that every male patient regretted having worked too hard.

Journal or Magazine Articles

You should include the name and date of the publication. You may also want to include the name of the author or the article:

> According to a January 2016 article in *Time* magazine, Barbie represents female empowerment. "Barbie had careers at a time when women were restricted to being just housewives."

> Eliana Dockterman writes in a January 2016 article in *Time* magazine titled "Barbie's got a new body" that Barbie represents female empowerment. "Barbie had careers at a time when women were restricted to being just housewives."

> A study reported in the January 2016 issue of the *American Journal of Preventive Medicine* said that Latinos and Asians have a lower risk of coronary artery disease than whites.

> A study conducted by Dr. Jamal S. Rana of Kaiser Permanente Northern California and reported in the January 2016 issue of the *American Journal of Preventive Medicine* said that Latinos and Asians have a lower risk of coronary artery disease than whites.

Newspapers

For newspaper articles, include the name of the newspaper and the date of the article. There is no need to cite the name of the journalist:

According to a January 3, 2015, article in the *New York Times,* some hotels in New York City want to block guests from using their own wireless Internet devices to force guests to buy the wireless Internet service provided by hotels.

Interviews

To cite information from an interview that you conducted, cite the person's name, his or her credentials, and when the interview took place:

> In a November 23, 2015, interview with Professor Steven R. Wilson, Ph.D., a family violence researcher at Purdue University, he stated, "Child abuse is an interactional phenomenon; that is, parents do not strike their children at random moments, but rather at predictable times that grow out of larger daily interactions."

To cite information from an interview from another source:

> Gabriel Alcoba, a medical specialist in snakebites for Doctors Without Borders, warned in an interview with the *Washington Post* published September 18, 2015, that the world's last batch of a vital anti-venom is set to expire in June 2016, a situation that will lead to "needless death and disability."

Websites

For websites, cite the operator of the site, and if there is dated information, the date it appeared on the website. It is not always necessary to say the information was released on an organization's website:

> According to the Bureau of Labor Statistics, the January 2016 unemployment rate in the United States fell to 5%.

> The World Health Organization reported January 30, 2016 on its website that worldwide obesity has more than doubled since the 1980s.

News Releases

For news releases, cite the agency issuing the release and the date it was released. It is not always necessary to say the information was contained in a news release. It also is not necessary to cite the author of the news release:

> Teens spend about nine hours a day using media for enjoyment, according to a study released in November 2015 by Common Sense Media.

> Human-provided food is the leading cause of wild animals wandering into human habitats, according to a news release from Colorado Parks & Wildlife on January 26, 2016.

Conclusion

The use of supporting evidence is crucial to an effective presentation. Without supporting material, your information is just your opinion. You can use a variety of types of material to bolster your assertions and arguments, including statistics, examples, and testimony. Each of these types of supporting evidence has strengths and weaknesses. You should evaluate your speaking situation thoroughly to determine what evidence is best suited to your particular needs. Regardless of what you choose, using a variety of types of supporting material and citing that material effectively will help ensure that your presentation is successful.

Key Terms

Brief example	Hypothetical example	Prestige testimony
Examples	Localizing	Statistics
Expert testimony	Peer testimony	Testimony
Extended example		

Exercises

1. On Twitter, identify a topic of interest (e.g., "Should interns be paid?") that will have both supporters and detractors. In other words, the topic is debatable. Next, search for your topic using the Twitter search box. Identify three key arguments for those who favor your topic and three key arguments for those who oppose your topic.

2. On Twitter, identify a topic that you might like to give a presentation on. Search for key words on that topic (e.g., student loans, healthy eating) using the Twitter search box. From the results, identify at least three expert sources you could potentially use in your speech. Then identify three sources of peer testimony.

3. Identify a topic you might like to give a presentation on. Next, sign on to Facebook and search for the pages of three government or nonprofit organizations that are related to your topic. Monitor their wall activity. Find at least three updates that link you to useful information for your presentation. How long did it take you to find useful posts?

4. Find a live chat advertised on either Twitter or Facebook. Sit in on the chat. What types of questions are being asked and what types of answers are being provided? Did you find useful testimony you could use in a presentation?

5. Identify a topic of interest. Using at least five of the sources discussed (newspapers, Twitter, books, etc.), find possible support (statistics, testimony, etc.) for your topic.

CHAPTER 7

Outlining the Presentation

Objectives

After reading this chapter, you should be able to

- ◎ explain why outlining is important for an effective presentation;
- ◎ explain the differences between a preparation outline and a speaking outline;
- ◎ explain the differences between a framework and a preparation outline;
- ◎ construct a preparation outline following the guidelines presented in this chapter; and
- ◎ construct a speaking outline following the guidelines presented in this chapter.

Can an audience tell if a speech is well organized? Most certainly. If you haven't taken the time to plan and organize your presentation, audiences will notice. Just ask those in attendance in 2016 when former Alaska Governor Sarah Palin endorsed then presidential hopeful Donald Trump. Her endorsement speech brought comments such as "hard to understand," "bizarre improvised rant," and "rambling." So much attention was given to how unorganized her speech was–one news outlet said to call it a speech was a "stretch"–that her message–her endorsement of Trump–took a backseat in public discussion. In addition, a lack of planning resulted in what was to be a brief speech stretching out for more than 21 minutes. As the candidate himself said, "I didn't know it was going to be quite that long."[1]

You never want your lack of organization to upstage your message or cause you to run over your allotted time. One way to avoid this is to outline your presentation. The outline is a tool that speakers of all levels use to envision and critique their entire presentation. It is a fundamental error to assume that outlining is only for beginners.

An outline helps ensure that the organization of the presentation is clear and balanced, that transitions are natural and smooth, that the flow is logical and progressive, that content is supported by evidence from credible sources, that the amount of material reflects the time you have for your presentation, and that you will be able to adapt flexibly to the moment if so required.

The outlining stage of the speech preparation process is crucial. If you don't draft a blueprint, it is hard to envision the speech, which can lead to many unexpected events. As we discuss in this chapter, the outline stage determines if all the decisions you have made thus far in the presentation work together.

Why Outlining Is Important

One complaint students often make about speech preparation is the process of writing the outline. They often find this step challenging and time consuming. This chapter walks you through each of the steps of preparing both your preparation outline and your speaking outline. After reading this chapter and working through the guidelines, you will find that outlining is not as difficult as you may have initially thought.

Planning is the main function of an outline. The outline is the blueprint of your entire presentation and is the tool that ensures that your decisions in the planning process have been adequate. The outline lays the foundation for everything you want to accomplish during the speech. If something is wrong in this initial design, your presentation will likely suffer.

Once you have selected your topic, purpose, and thesis; determined your main ideas; conducted your research; and begun crafting the introduction and conclusion of your presentation, you are ready to test this plan by examining the design through a preparation outline. The outline is the initial representation of your content. It allows you the first opportunity to adapt the presentation to the audience. If you skip this step, you miss a vital opportunity to analyze your speech in terms of the audience. Through the outline, you organize what you will say in the presentation, how you will introduce the material, how you will arrange main points, how you will support those points, and how you will conclude the presentation. The outline can be best thought of as a tool to determine whether the choices you have made thus far in the planning process are effective and whether you need to resolve any problem areas.

The outline serves another important function as a mechanism for receiving feedback. In this course, your instructor or classmates will provide valuable comments on what areas of your outline are strong and what areas need improvements. By incorporating this feedback, you can strengthen the actual presentation.

Ensures Organization

One of the most important functions of the outline is to ensure clear organization. By examining how the main points and supporting material work together, you can determine whether the organizational pattern you have selected is the most appropriate for the material, the audience, and the goal of your presentation. Clear organization often characterizes a well-received presentation since audiences perceive organized speakers as more credible and become frustrated by those presentations that lack organization.[2]

Balances the Presentation

The preparation outline is a mechanism that ensures **balance.** In other words, it prompts you to make sure that all your main points are complete and that they are adequately developed. Each main point should be covered in approximately the same level of detail. For example, you

> A commonly used guideline is that introductions should comprise about 10% of the presentation time, while conclusions should comprise about 5%.

want to avoid a lengthy explanation of main point number one and cursory coverage of main point number two. Even a brief glance at a preparation outline provides basic visual clues about how balanced your presentation is. If your second main point fills up half a page and your third main point runs just two sentences, you quickly have identified a problem with balance.

From your outline, you can also measure the length of your introduction and conclusion, relative to the body of the speech.

Identifies Evidence

The outline also provides an opportunity for you to check and see whether each point has been supported with appropriate research material. If your main points do not have research supporting the claims you make, you will lose credibility and find it difficult to achieve your presentation goals. The outline also allows you to ensure that your research has been adequately cited within the presentation. A good guideline is that every point or subpoint should have at least one type of supporting evidence.

Assesses Quantity

One of the most restrictive factors of the presentational situation is the time constraint to which the speech must adhere. The outline can roughly indicate how much material you have and how long it will take you to cover it. With experience, you will be able to use the outline as a precise gauge of how long your presentation will run. It is important to note here that it is a speaker's ethical obligation to understand how much time he or she has to speak and to fill that time appropriately. Audiences place a high value on their own time and expect to get their "money's worth" when listening to a speaker. They may become resentful when speakers take advantage of the situation by speaking longer or shorter than expected.

Allows for Flexibility

One of the most important benefits of speaking from an outline rather than a manuscript or from memory is the flexibility an outline provides. When the presentation isn't committed to an exact stream of words, sentences, and paragraphs, it affords you the adaptability needed to make adjustments during the presentation. This flexible nature of an outline allows you to adapt to the specific needs of the audience and the situation.

Allows for Instructional Feedback

In the classroom situation, the outline is the only chance you will have to get feedback from your instructor before you deliver the actual graded presentation. In an English course, you can submit various versions of your actual paper and get feedback before your final draft is due. Presentations don't lend themselves to this same process. There is simply not enough time during the course of the semester for students to present "rough drafts" of their presentations. Therefore, the more detail you provide on your outline, the more feedback you can get on how to improve the content of your presentation. This means showing where you cite material, where and what you will use for a visual aid, internal summaries and previews, as well as a complete bibliography.

Now that you know the importance of the preparation outline, let's examine its format and features.

Formatting the Preparation Outline

The **preparation outline** is a detailed representation of the speech. It is carefully constructed and has a variety of features. The following sections identify each of the features that need to be included in your preparation outline.

Tip

Outlining the presentation is key. If you have a solid outline, then you are able to make adjustments on the fly for time constraints. Outlines ensure that key points get communicated.

Amy Stoehr | Founder | Real Estate Masters Guild

Full Sentences

Every aspect of the preparation outline is written in complete sentences: main points, subpoints, sub-subpoints, and transitions. This forces you to be specific about the claims you will make in your speech and ensures that your presentation will be more focused and to the point. One maxim worth heeding in this situation is, "If you can't say it, you don't know it." In other words, if you have trouble articulating your ideas in your outline, it will be impossible to do so in the presentation. If you can't outline it, you simply do not have a solid grip on your material. *One sentence per point is adequate.* The point is not to write out the entire speech word for word, but to clearly state your main ideas. Let's look at an example:

Ineffective   I. Sleeping habits

Better   I. Sleep is being widely neglected among individuals aged 18 to 35 in today's society.

The ineffective main point doesn't tell us much. What about sleeping habits? Whose sleeping habits? This main point doesn't have focus or direction. It has not been clearly articulated.

The more effective example has been expressed as a complete sentence. Notice the difference in clarity from the ineffective example. The direction of this main point is clear and more precise. The complete sentence tells us exactly what direction the main point is heading. The ineffective version would likely result in a rambling, imprecise speech. Writing your outline in complete sentences helps to alleviate this problem.

> **Do not write more than one sentence per entry in the body of the outline.**

Appropriate Symbolization

The format for the outline follows the common alphanumeric system. You designate main points with Roman numerals (I., II., III.); supporting points, called subpoints, with capital letters (A., B., C.); sub-subpoints with Arabic (regular) numbers (1., 2., 3.); and sub-subpoints with lowercase letters (a., b., c.). Further sub-subpoints will use lowercase roman numerals (i., ii., iii.). Basically, you proceed from the most important ideas to the least important. The structure for the body of the presentation looks something like this:

I. **Main Point One**
    A. Subpoint
        1. Sub-subpoint
        2. Sub-subpoint
    B. Subpoint

II. **Main Point Two**
    A. Subpoint
        1. Sub-subpoint
            a. Sub-subpoint
            b. Sub-subpoint
        2. Sub-subpoint
    B. Subpoint
    C. Subpoint
        1. Sub-subpoint
        2. Sub-subpoint

Effective Subordination

One of the primary reasons for preparing the outline is to examine and critique the relationship between your claims and your supporting evidence. This ensures that your reasoning is sound and helps the audience follow your presentation. Each claim you make should be supported by evidence.

Simply stated, the idea of **subordination** means that all of the first-level points or main points are supported by supporting points, called **subpoints.** Subpoints are supported by sub-subpoints so that each subordinate point supports the idea under which it is indented. Basically, subordination is a method of physically indenting material so that the relationship among ideas becomes clear and is visually apparent. Let's examine the following example:

I.   Childhood obesity is an epidemic in the United States (*Huffington Post,* July 27, 2014).
   A.   According to a September 12, 2014, article in the *New England Journal of Medicine,* "In developed nations, obesity is the number one health problem for children under age 17." (p. 2004).
   B.   More than a third of U.S. children are overweight (Centers for Disease Control, 2015).
   C.   Obesity in children has increased for all age, race, and sex groups since 1970.
      1.   The biggest increase in obesity, however, is among African-American and Hispanic children, up 120%.
      2.   There was a 50% increase in obesity among white children.
   D.   Not only did the number of children who were overweight increase, but the severity of the obesity increased as well.

As is demonstrated in this excerpt from a sample outline, each of the subpoints serves to support or further illuminate or explain the point above it. Take, for example, subpoint C. This statement supports and further explains the obesity epidemic for children in the United States. It provides further clarification by explaining that this is an epidemic for all age and race groups. Subpoint C is further supported by sub-subpoint 1, which states that this statistic has increased most for African-American and Hispanic children.

Subordination is also another way to ensure that we have organized our material effectively. For example, if you have a main point but can only come up with one subpoint, chances are you have chosen the wrong main point. What you have chosen simply isn't important enough (doesn't have enough support) to be a main point. You would need to go back and re-organize your presentation with different main points.

For this reason, outlining has the "**Rule of 2**" that applies to main points and subpoints. You can't have one main point; you must have at least two. Within a main point, you can't have one subpoint; you must have at least two. Within a subpoint, you can't have just one sub-subpoint; you must have at least two.

Let's check the example above to see if it applies the "Rule of 2." Main Point I does have at least two subpoints. And within those subpoints, subpoint C does have at least two sub-subpoints. The "Rule of 2" has been successfully applied to his main point. Note that not all the subpoints have to have sub-subpoints. Remember, the "Rule of 2" for sub-subpoints applies ***within*** the subpoint only. The "Rule of 2" for subpoints applies ***within*** the main point only.

Coordinated Points

In addition to subordination, your outline should follow the rules for coordination. **Coordination** means that the ideas at the same level of importance should use the same series of symbols and, therefore, be indented at the same level. Consider the main points in the following example in a speech about food safety:

I.   Wash hands and cooking surfaces often.
II.   Don't cross-contaminate various food products.
III.   Cook and store foods at proper temperatures.

This particular example outlines guidelines to follow for managing food safely, and each of these steps is as important as the next in terms of preventing food-borne illness. Each of these main points is equal in terms of importance. Violating any one of these rules for food safety could result in food poisoning. Therefore, they should all be at the same level in the outline.

The next step in preparing this outline is to add supporting material to each of these main points. For example, in the outline that follows, subpoint A under main point I ("Wash hands with soap ….") supports main point I by providing a specific example of how to wash hands properly. It is supporting material and should therefore be inserted at the appropriate spot–subordinate to main point I.

I. Wash hands and cooking surfaces often.
    A. Wash hands with soap for a minimum of 20 seconds.
    B. Use paper towels instead of kitchen towels to clean cooking surfaces.
II. Don't cross-contaminate various food products.
    A. Separate raw meat from other food in the shopping cart.
    B. Use one cutting board for meat and another for vegetables.
III. Cook and store foods at proper temperatures.
    A. Make sure there are no cold spots in cooked food where bacteria can hide.
    B. Leftovers should be refrigerated within two hours of use.

Each of the supporting details adds to the main point it follows by further elaborating on the ideas it presents.

Specific Purpose and Thesis Statements

It is important to include your specific purpose statement and your thesis statement should be at the top of your outline. After all, these are the overarching goals of your speech. Every decision that you make about what to include in the presentation should enhance these goals. So when thinking about including a point or a piece of supporting material, refer back to the specific purpose and thesis statement. If the material assists in achieving these goals, include it; if it doesn't, leave it out.

Transitions

Transitions are the elements that make your speech flow and enable your audience to follow your presentation. **Directional transitions** are used between main points to let the audience know that you are moving from one idea to another (e.g., "Now that we have discussed the causes of eating disorders, let's examine some of the treatments."). **Signposts** alert the audience to an exact location in the presentation (e.g., "The first cause …," "The most important point …," "In summary, …"). **Internal previews** are transitions used within main points that alert listeners to what lies ahead (e.g., "There are many different causes of eating disorders: media representations, concern with body image, and issues of self-esteem. Let's begin by focusing on media representations."). **Internal reviews** or summaries are also located within main points and simply restate the primary ideas of the main point (e.g., "We have examined three causes of eating disorders: media representations, concern with body image, and self-esteem"). Remember, internal previews and reviews are only necessary when a main point is extremely complex or when there are a number of ideas for the audience to keep track of.

Include all transitions, regardless of type, in your preparation outline. You are more likely to include transitions in your actual presentation when they are part of your outline.

In-text citations mark points in your outline where you are citing your reference material. Using in-text citations means you are crediting material you obtained from other sources. The APA format uses the author's last name and year of publication for the source (Natt, 2015). A complete reference that corresponds to the in-text citation should appear in your reference list. In-text citations are not the same as the oral citations (see Chapter 6) in your actual presentations. You will need both.

Reference Page

A **reference page** comprised of the sources you consulted to construct the outline completes the preparation outline. The reference page includes any books, magazine articles, newspaper articles, pamphlets and brochures, personal interviews, and Web resources. (Check with your instructor to see if Web pages are appropriate supporting material.) Use **APA style** (American Psychological Association) to format your reference list. It is important that the citations are complete and consistent. The following websites offer advice on using APA: The American Psychological Association style site (http://www.apastyle.org/) or Purdue University's Online Writing Lab (http://owl.english.purdue.edu/). A complete example of a reference page is provided at the end of this chapter.

Putting the Outline Together

The following ten steps walk you through the process of creating an outline that follows the appropriate format:

Step 1

Write your specific purpose statement and thesis statement at the top of your outline. It will look something like this:

Specific Purpose Statement   To inform my audience about the origins of photomicrography

Thesis Statement   Photomicrography is an intriguing type of photography with interesting origins in biology and photography.

Step 2

Label your introduction, body, and conclusion. This ensures that each of these components will be included in your presentation:

Introduction

Body

Conclusion

Step 3

Add Roman numerals to all of the components of the introduction, body, and conclusion:

Introduction

    I.   Attention-getter
    II. Credibility statement
    III. Relate topic to audience
    IV. Thesis statement

Body

    I.   Main point 1
    II. Main point 2
    III. Main point 3

Conclusion

    I. Restatement of thesis
    II. Clincher

Step 4

Go back and outline the body of the presentation. The body should always be constructed before the introduction or conclusion, since your introduction and conclusion will reflect the body of the presentation, once you are certain of it. Begin by adding the appropriate

> **The rule is, if you divide, you need at least two parts. Therefore, you cannot have an "a" without a "b." if you have a "1," you must also have a "2."**

subpoints to your main points, and labeling each subpoint with a capital letter. Recall that a subpoint is content that supports a main point. Sometimes, it may also be necessary to add sub-subpoints in a presentation. If you need this extra level of detail, use Arabic numbers (1., 2., 3.). It is important that you recognize that at this step you are dividing your main points into subpoints.

Step 5

Add transitions between each of your main points. If you have internal transitions, such as internal summaries or previews, mark those as well. Adding the transitions to the preparation outline increases the likelihood that you will use them during the presentation.

Step 6

Once you have arranged your main points and transitions into the standard format, go back and add your external source citations. This ensures that you cite appropriately during your presentation.

Step 7

Once the body has been finalized, write out your introduction and conclusion word for word. Simply insert the material into the appropriate place in the outline. Speakers feel the most anxious during the introduction of a presentation.[3] Therefore, it is perfectly acceptable to write out the introduction word for word. This way, if your anxiety is heightened, you won't be required to think on your feet by speaking extemporaneously. Sometimes, memorizing the introduction of the presentation can reduce anxiety.

As explained in Chapter 4, the conclusion is vital to the success of the presentation. Research has shown that the information audiences hear last can have a powerful impact on them.[4] This impact is called the recency effect. Because of the power of the recency effect, you should also write out your conclusion word for word as well. Don't leave your final comments to chance; plan an ending that will make an impact on your audience.

Step 8

Create your reference page, which completes the outline. Use a consistent style of citation, such as APA style.

Step 9

Once you have completed your outline, you are ready to finalize the entire presentation. Check for each of the following components:

- ◎ Audience analysis–relevance
- ◎ Symmetry
- ◎ Balance
- ◎ External sources/supporting material
- ◎ Requirements of the assignment

Step 10

If you need to provide a title for your presentation, do this last. (You probably won't need one for classroom presentations.) Titles are important if your presentation is to be listed in a program or announced in some way. Titles should be brief, yet encapsulate the major ideas of your presentation.

The Speaking Outline

After finalizing your preparation outline, you are ready to begin constructing the speaking outline. The **speaking outline** consists of the notes you will use to deliver your speech. It is important to remember that the speaking outline is merely a tool to jog your memory. By the time of your presentation, you will have rehearsed your speech so many times that you will know the material cold. The speaking outline functions primarily as a memory aid and as a gauge to remind you of where you are during the presentation.

At this point, you are probably wondering exactly what you should include in your speaking outline and how it should look. Speaking outlines are very idiosyncratic. Each individual likes to include some items and omit others. As you gain more experience making presentations, you will develop a style that works best for you. Until you gain this experience, here are some guidelines that will help you get started.

Guidelines for the Speaking Outline

Be Brief

To maintain extemporaneous delivery, it is important to keep the speaking outline brief. Unlike the preparation outline, the speaking outline consists of key words, phrases, and abbreviations. If your notes are too detailed, you will have trouble making eye contact and, therefore, connections with your audience. Most beginning speakers use too many notes, leaning on them as a psychological crutch that ends up interfering with the delivery of the presentation. However, if you have practiced the speech adequately, you will only need the memory cues contained in a well-written speaking outline to get you through the presentation.

Follow Structure of the Preparation Outline

The speaking outline should have the same outline style used in the preparation outline; that is, use the same symbols and indentation style as in the preparation outline. However, because the speaking outline must be brief, you will want to replicate only a brief version of the preparation outline. The example at the end of the chapter demonstrates these guidelines.

> # Checklist for a Preparation Outline
>
> ◎ Use full sentences.
> ◎ Use a consistent indentation and symbolization system.
> ◎ Include transitions.
> ◎ Include internal citations.
> ◎ Include a complete bibliography in APA style.

Include Supporting Materials

The speaking outline should include any references you need to cite during the presentation. Citing references enhances your credibility as a speaker and deters plagiarism. Also consider adding any direct quotations you plan to present. Lengthy quotations and statistics should be written out verbatim in the speaking outline so that you can cite them completely and accurately.

Be Legible

One of the most important aspects of the speaking outline is making sure it is legible and easily readable while delivering your presentation. Write or type in large letters, but only on one side of each note card. Number each card. If the stack of cards falls on the floor, you will be able to recover quickly and easily!

Provide Delivery Cues

Delivery cues are the stage directions that add emphasis to your presentation. Dramatic pauses, repetition, rate, and volume are all examples of important delivery aspects. A well-polished and effective presentation depends not only on what you say, but how you say it. Including delivery cues in your speaking outline reminds you to use these types of special features to add impact.

Delivery cues can be added to the speaking outline in a variety of ways. Some speakers use a highlighter to emphasize certain portions of the speech where their delivery is very important. Others add specific directions to themselves (e.g., "Smile") at critical points. However you choose to do it, insert your delivery cues clearly and legibly so that they do not interfere with your ability to read the outline. Here are some example cues you might add to your speaking outline:

- ◎ Slow down.
- ◎ Pause.
- ◎ Make eye contact.
- ◎ Move from the podium.
- ◎ Walk to the other side of the room.

Usually Use Note Cards

One common question that speakers often ask is whether they should write their speaking outline on note cards or sheets of paper. Most experts agree that note cards are sturdier and more adaptable. For example, note cards work with either a lectern or without one. They also tend to be less distracting and easier to rearrange. They will be less distracting than sheets of paper. Regardless of which you decide to use, it is important to write on only one side of the card or paper. Additionally, you should number each of your cards or sheets of paper.

Guidelines for an Effective Speaking Outline

- ◎ Be brief.
- ◎ Print large enough to read easily.
- ◎ Write legibly.
- ◎ Write out quotations and statistics.
- ◎ Number your note cards or pages.
- ◎ Write on only one side of the note card or paper.
- ◎ Unless you are using a lectern, use note cards.

Frameworks vs. Outlines

For some presentations in this course, you will be asked to create a framework instead of a complete preparation outline.

A **framework** lacks the formality and completeness of a preparation outline. Its main use is in planning your presentation. A framework helps you map the main ideas of your presentation but does not require that you report each element or use a rigid format.

Not everything you include in a framework will become part of your presentation. In this course, some framework elements will ask you to justify decisions you made or ask you to connect various elements of your presentation. For example, on a complete preparation outline, you would be required to note where you plan to show your visual aid during your presentation. On a framework, you might be asked to justify, in words, how this visual aid will aid in the audience's understanding of your topic. If you are unable to answer this question, you would need to re-evaluate your choice of visual aids. The answer you provide does not become a part of your presentation. It simply provides you with a way to judge the decisions you have made.

For shorter presentations you might deliver, a framework often will suffice.

Conclusion

Outlines are extremely important. Even experienced speakers cannot afford to take shortcuts at this step in the process. A great outline increases the likelihood of a successful speech, and a flawed outline translates into a flawed presentation every single time. This chapter presented several types of outlines or frameworks that play different roles during different parts of the presentation preparation.

The preparation outline is the major outline you create that enables you to see your entire presentation in a highly structured and detailed way. It affords you the opportunity to critique your presentation's organization, level of detail, use of evidence, and so on.

The speaking outline is what you actually use during the presentation. It prompts you to cover your main points, to read exact quotes, to express transitions, to gauge your timing, and to include other vital information during the presentation. However, the overall level of detail is considerably less than that of the preparation outline.

A framework on the other hand is more of a planning document and does not contain the same level of detail of a preparation outline or a speaking outline. However, going through this process helps you think critically and plan more effectively for each aspect of your presentation.

Regardless of the type, outlining can certainly make the difference between a presentation that is well planned and one that misses the mark.

Key Terms

APA style	Internal preview	Signpost
Balance	Internal review	Speaking outline
Coordination	Preparation outline	Subordination
Delivery cues	Reference page	Subpoint
Directional transitions	Rule of 2	Transitions
Framework		

Donating to Soles4Souls

General Purpose   To persuade

Specific Purpose   To persuade my audience to donate their used shoes to Soles4Souls

Thesis Statement   There is a large need for proper footwear for our more impoverished population. Your donation of a pair of gently used shoes to Soles4Souls can go a long way to solving this problem.

Introduction

Attention-Getter   One day, a son and his mother came to my dad's running store interested in purchasing a pair of shoes. My dad analyzed the boy's gait and fit him in the appropriate shoe. But the shoe was too expensive for the mother to afford. In fact, every shoe in the store was. As the heartbroken mother and son turned toward the door, my dad remembered the donations he had from an organization called Soles4Souls. Soles4Souls is an organization that accepts gently used or non-fitting shoes of all types from the local community and donates them to families and people in need.

Credibility Statement   After listening to my dad tell this story, I began researching how great the need for gently used shoes is.

Relating to the Audience   According to the Soles4Souls website, "Americans throw away more than 68 pounds of textile, including shoes, per year per person. The EPA estimates that only 15% is said to be donated or recycled" (soles4souls.org, n.d.). Why would you throw away a gently used pair of shoes if someone across the world, or even in our neighborhood, could benefit from your donation?

Thesis Statement   There is a large need for proper footwear for our more impoverished population. Your donation of a pair of gently used shoes to Soles4Souls can go a long way to solving this problem.

Transition   Before you donate a pair of shoes, I want you to understand how important your donation will be.

Body

I. **Main Point I:** More than 300 million people worldwide do not have shoes to wear and many others wear shoes that don't fit, according to Today.com in October 2015 (Today.com, 2015).

   A. **Supporting Point:** Because walking is the primary mode of transportation for millions, walking barefoot can lead to disease.

   1. **Subpoint:** Over 2 billion people have some kind of soil transmitted disease (Today.com, 2015).

   a. **Sub-subpoint:** In Africa, for example, shoes are extremely important in order to reduce trauma, like cuts that could become infected and hookworm and parasitic diseases that enter the bare foot (shoes4schools.com, n.d.).

   b. **Sub-subpoint:** In southern Ethiopia, CNN reported there's a disease called podoconiosis that's come through the soil into the pores of the feet and destroys the lymphatic system, which drains toxins from the body (CNN.com, 2009).

2. **Subpoint:** In addition, childhood obesity, especially in rural areas, is linked to children not having the proper shoes to participate in physical education activities and sports at school, just like the boy that came into my dad's store (toms.com, n.d.).

B. **Supporting Point:** A lack of shoes can also interrupt a child's education.

1. **Subpoint:** Shoes are often a requirement for children to attend school, even in other countries.

a. A delay in getting shoes will cause children to fall behind in school.

b. Many then choose to no longer continue their education (soles4souls.org, n.d.).

2. **Subpoint:** Julies Sykes, a campus representative for TOMS at the University of Georgia, saw firsthand on a spring break trip to Haiti how shoes make a difference (USAToday.com, 2014).

a. While on her trip, Sykes met a child who received a donated pair of TOMS and was now able to attend school.

b. "I believe education is the key to end poverty and I pray that day will come. Impoverished people need to be educated in order to become leaders in their communities and countries," she told USAToday in 2014.

Transition   Now that I have shown you the effects of poverty and how the lack of a good pair of shoes can affect the lives of millions, I will show you how effective your donation can be.

II. **Main Point II:** Since 2006, Soles4Souls has distributed 26 million pairs of shoes in 127 countries around the world." More than half has occurred in the U.S., according to the Soles4Souls website (soles4souls.org, n.d.).

A. **Supporting Point:** To provide disaster relief, your shoe donation will be boxed with hundreds of other donations and shipped to areas around the world with the greatest need for shoes.

1. **Subpoint:** Volunteers for Soles4Souls travel with your donation, and then distribute proper-fitting shoes to people in need.

2. **Subpoint:** Think back to your closet and all the pairs of shoes you shift through every morning.

a. Personally, I have 37 pairs of shoes and I know I only wear about seven of those.

b. Those other 60 shoes are not important to me, but could literally be the difference between life and death to someone else.

B. **Supporting Point:** It's easy to make a donation.

1. If you visit the Soles4Souls website, there is a link to make a shoe donation.

a. That page will take you to a map where you will enter your zip code.

b. That will direct you to the closest drop-off location.

2. If there's not a dropoff donation near you–sorry, there's not one in Indiana–Soles4Souls has an option for mailing in shoes.

a. On their website you can purchase a shipping label, print it out, and put that label on your box.

b. You can then mail your shoes to them through the UPS store in the basement of the Purdue Memorial Union!

c. This costs only about $5–10 depending on the size of the shoes–such a small price to pay.

Transition   Throughout this presentation I've shown you the need for your donation and how you can make a donation.

Conclusion

Restate Thesis   A lack of footwear is one of the many obstacles faced by people in poverty. Your donation of a gently used pair of shoes goes a long way to ending this.

Closing Statement   My dad found that young boy a great, like-new pair of running shoes. He said he will never forget how happy that made the boy and his mother, and how grateful they were. Go home, look in your closet, and see if you don't have a pair of shoes you can donate today.

References

Cook, S. (2009). These shoes help others get a step up. *CNN*. Retrieved from http://www.cnn.com/2009/LIVING/homestyle/03/26/blake.mycoskie.toms.shoes/

For kids in poverty, a shoe that grows with them. (n.d.) [Video] Retrieved from http://www.today.com/video/for-kids-in-poverty-a-shoe-that-grows-with-them-551518275741

Giving in the U.S. with save the children (2015, Jan. 26). Retrieved from http://www.toms.com/stories/giving/giving-in-the-u-s-with-save-the-children

Smith, S. (2014, April 16). Its TOMS really making a difference? *USA Today*. Retrieved from http://college.usatoday.com/2014/04/16/is-toms-really-making-a-difference/

Wearing out poverty. (n.d.) Retrieved Nov. 3, 2015, from soles4souls.org

Why it is extremely important to get shoes to Africa (n.d.). Retrieved Nov. 4, 2015, from https://shoes4schools.wordpress.com/2008/12/28/why-it-is-extremely-important-to-get-shoes-to-africa/

Sample Speaking Outline

The following note cards provide a speaking outline for the introduction, conclusion, and main point I for the sample outline:

Intro   Make Eye Contact !!!!!!   1

I.   Mom and son come into story. Analyze gait. Shoe too expensive. All were. Leaving heartbroken. Dad remembers.

II. After hearing

III. Soles4Souls: 68% throw away, 15% recycled. Why?

IV. Large need. Your donation helps

Transition: Before donate, understand important

                                                                              2

I. 300 mil no shoes USA Today 2015

A. Disease

 1. 2 billion soil today.com 2015

  a. Africa, hookworm, parasites shoes4schools

  b. Ethiopia podoconiosis destroys lymphatic system CNN 2014

 2. Childhood obesity

3

B. Second, interrupt education

   1. Requirement

     a. Fall behind

     b. Won't stay (soles)

   2. Julia Sykes (TOMS) Haiti

     a. Met child

     b. I believe education is the key to end poverty and I pray that day will come.
       Impoverished people need to be educated in order to become leaders in their
       communities and countries (USA Today 2014).

    Directional Transition: Now shown effects, show how donation can help

4

II. Since 2006, 26 m pairs, 127 countries, ½ US (Soles website)

   A. Boxed and shipped

     1. Volunteers distribute

     2. Your shoes

       a. I have 37

       b. Don't need 30

5

B. Easy to donate
  1. Website
    a. Map
    b. Donation centers
  2. Mail
    a. Shipping label
    b. Print off
    c. Only $5 to $10 (small price to pay)

6

Transition: Shown you need and how to help

Conclusion
  I. Lack of footwear obstacle, long way, ending
  II. Dad happy, never forget. Check your closet.

CHAPTER 8

Informative and Special Occasion Speaking

Objectives

After reading this chapter, you should be able to

- ◎ explain the differences between informatory and explanatory presentations;
- ◎ understand and explain the components of news presentations;
- ◎ understand and explain the four states of effective instructional presentations;
- ◎ understand the strategies for using elucidating explanations;
- ◎ understand the strategies for using quasi-scientific explanations; and
- ◎ understand the strategies for using transformative explanations.

It was a worldwide sensation. A photographer and lifelong vegetarian bought a McDonald's Happy Meal and placed it on her coffee table, uncovered, and took photos every day for six months. The hamburger never rotted or decomposed. The woman, Sally Davies, took to *Good Morning America,* the *Today Show,* and other news outlets to condemn the processed food produced by the fast-food giant and the dangers it presents to kids. Newspapers from England to China promoted the findings.

But J. Kenji Lopez-Alt, a blogger at "Serious Eats," was not convinced by this explanation, especially in lieu of any scientific proof.[1] He admitted the Happy Meal burger didn't rot, but he wanted to know why it didn't rot. He set up his own experiment. He used nine different burgers–both homemade and from the McDonald's menu–and recreated Davies's experiment.

So what happened? Was this a phenomenon limited to McDonald's? No. It turns out it was the size of the burger that mattered. It was only the quarter pounders–both McDonald's and ones made with fresh ground beef–that rotted. None of the skinnier burgers showed any signs of rot. "The burger doesn't rot because its small size and relatively large surface area help it to lose moisture very fast. Without moisture, there's no mold or bacterial growth," Lopez-Alt wrote in a blog post explaining his findings.

Lopez-Alt's findings mirror the official response by McDonald's. When he placed the Happy Meal burger in a plastic bag that trapped the moisture in, the burger rotted. Both Lopez-Alt and McDonald's noted that the dehydrated condition of the smaller burgers did play a role. "Of course, that the meat is pretty much sterile to begin with due to the high cooking temperature helps things along as well," Lopez-Alt wrote.

> **The two types of informative speaking are informatory speaking and explanatory speaking.**

When faced with having to explain a hard-to-understand phenomenon to an audience that already thought they understood, Lopez-Alt used a transformative explanation. He acknowledged that the McDonald's burger didn't rot, and why people might think that the processes McDonald's uses contributed to the phenomenon. But then he pointed out why that might not be the sole reason, and he provided the correct explanation instead.

Transformative explanations are just one of the options you have when tasked with explaining a topic to an audience. Our ability to explain information to an audience is extremely important. While students enrolled in this course readily see the benefits of persuasive speaking and look forward to those presentations all semester, they often overlook the importance of the informative presentation. Providing information to an audience, however, is one of the most important skills you can develop as an effective speaker. College graduates report that informational speaking is actually more common in their careers than is persuasive speaking.[2] The inability to share information effectively and increase audience understanding has consequences. Poor informative skills have been linked to military and medical disasters and unsuccessful business endeavors.

While poor informative skills can be costly, there is a good deal of research on how to present information effectively so that our audiences understand us and mistakes can be avoided. This chapter presents some of the latest theories and research to help you excel at this important communication skill.

This chapter explores the two types of informative speaking–informatory and explanatory–and speaking on those special occasions when the information you share is more ceremonial in nature. We look individually at these types of presentations, their differences, and strategies for using each effectively.

Informative Speaking

Informative speaking is the process of enhancing the understanding of your audience in relation to some important term, object, event, process, and so forth. This can be achieved through instruction, explanation, description, demonstration, clarification, or correction. Informative presentations include speeches about objects, events, or persons. They include "how to" or instructional presentations. Presentations about concepts or complex processes, academic lectures, business reports, and even analyses of events are all considered informative presentations.

The push to be able to present information to all audiences is key, no matter what discipline you are in. For example, science majors are now being told that if they can't communicate their research effectively, it will be impossible for people to support that research or apply its findings. Audiences for such scientific information are varied: the media, the general public, funding agencies, industry, and researchers from other disciplines. Each of these varied audiences will need the same information presented or explained to them in different ways.

"Our ability to fund raise and raise more dollars for research hinges on our ability to communicate to the public (our donors) about research we support and its importance," says Jennifer Campbell, assistant director of research and strategic initiatives at the Heart and Stroke Foundation of Canada.[3]

Types of Informative Speaking

Kathy Rowan, a communication professor and researcher, has described two types of informative speaking: informatory speaking and explanatory speaking.

Informatory speaking seeks to create awareness on the part of an audience regarding a specific issue. This type of speaking assumes that there is a need for new information on a topic for a specific audience. For example, we know that animals are being trained to help in the fight against terrorism. Dogs are used to detect bombs and other potentially hazardous situations. A student from a past semester took this same topic and put a spin on it, using new information. He delivered a fascinating presentation on how bees are now being trained to detect bombs. He described the program and its components. The topic was novel, and almost every audience member was interested in hearing new developments related to detecting, and thus preventing, terrorism.

In this photo, the teacher is presenting information to her students in the library. This is a good example of an informatory presentation.

Explanatory speaking, on the other hand, takes the presentation a step further. This type of speaking assumes that an audience has some knowledge of the topic but lacks sufficient understanding of the process. Therefore, the goal of this type of presentation is to deepen an audience's understanding of a specific issue.[4] Oftentimes, this explanation will answer the question of how something works or how a process occurs. For example, a student in this course gave an explanatory presentation on how a 3-D printer works. While many of us have seen objects that have been created using such a printer, we did not know the process that occurs. This presentation went beyond presenting new information and actually deepened our level of understanding of the topic.

Now that you know the differences between informatory and explanatory speaking, let's examine each in more detail.

Informatory Presentations

There are two basic types of informatory presentations: news and instructional. Each of these presentations enhances an audience's awareness of a topic. Informatory presentations are primarily delivered when an audience is interested in the latest information on a particular issue (news) or desires to know the necessary steps to complete a task (instructions).

Human beings are naturally curious. Our minds want to "bridge the gap" between the knowledge we have and current information.[5] But we have to have a certain level of confidence in order to reach a useful level of curiosity.[6] If we perceive a task to be too difficult, we are no longer curious about it. This is an important principle to keep in mind, especially in informative speaking. Your audience might tune out right away if you can't convince them early enough that they have the skills to perform the task or the ability to use the information you are providing.

In addition, you have to present just the right amount of information to the audience. If there is too small or too large a gap in our knowledge, we lose our sense of curiosity.[7] Make it challenging without appearing daunting; make it interesting without talking over their heads; make it worth their time.

News Presentations

News presentations should have relevance, surprise value, factuality, and comprehensiveness.

News presentations present interesting information to an audience on a new topic or a topic that they are already familiar with and interested in, or provide useful information to an audience. They can be presentations about objects, events, or even people. The goal of a news presentation is to create awareness of the latest information on a topic. The speaker may provide an update on some topic, introduce a new product, present a progress report, give a training or orientation session, describe an unpredictable recent event, or share information that is completely new to an audience. A news presentation can share more practical information that the audience will use in their professional lives or their personal lives, or it can simply pass along some interesting information they did not have before.

According to research in this area, news presentations should have the following components: relevance, surprise value, factuality, and comprehensiveness.[8]

Relevance

Audiences will be more receptive to your news presentations if the information is **relevant** to them. It is senseless to deliver a presentation on new technology for treating diabetes if no one in the audience has the disease or any connection to the disease. While audience members might find the topic interesting, it has little relevance to them and their everyday lives. Their attention might wane. Sometimes in a news presentation, you have to emphasize the relevancy for your audience.

Informative presentations that pass along useful information can sometimes be a bit pedestrian for both the speaker and the audience. Just think about some of the presentation topics you would need to address as a manager in an organization. Imagine having to explain to your employees the details of the new policies regarding e-mail privacy. On the face of it, this topic may not seem very exciting. This is where the relevance statement becomes particularly important (see Chapter 4). By explaining why the information is valuable and important to your employees, you can increase their motivation to listen to the information.

Surprise Value

Surprise value is the amount of novel or new information, relative to the information the audience already knows. Since the goal of the presentation is to make your audience aware of "news" in a given area, most of the information you present should be new to your audience. Surprise value is so important that even scientific journals are requiring that authors promote the surprise value in their submissions.[9] You want to spend very little time describing elements of the topic that the audience is already aware of; spend your time on the new information instead.

This is an area many students struggle with when assigned informative speeches. They have topic areas they are interested in, but they often fail to provide any surprise value in their presentations. We all know it's important to exercise or get enough sleep. We all know steps to take to avoid getting the flu. Speeches on these topics have little surprise value. But that doesn't mean you can't give a presentation on such a topic.

Rahul, a health sciences major, did a different take on the "how to avoid getting the flu" speech by giving a presentation on the top places germs breed in airplanes and how you can avoid getting sick when flying. In his thesis, he informed his classmates: "This winter, it is possible to pick up the flu bug and other germs at 30,000 feet. I'm going to identify the places germs breed most on airplanes and offer you tips on how to avoid picking up these germs when you fly."

Finding a surprise value in a topic you are interested in is not difficult. It just takes a little research on your part. Rahul was able to give a speech on a topic he was interested in, but he managed to find a surprise value by searching health sections of major news portals until he found a new take. Many students in his class were surprised to find the germiest place on an airplane could be the ice cubes in their drinks or the seatback pockets where they store their iPhones.

Comparing Informatory vs. Explanatory Presentations

Let's compare an informatory presentation and an explanatory presentation on the same topic. The first example features a partial outline of an informatory presentation; it simply tells us about a recent earthquake and its effects. We don't know how it happened, but we know what resulted. The second example shows a partial outline of an explanatory presentation. It goes beyond informing us about the event and its outcomes; instead, it explains how the earthquake occurred.

News Presentation Example

Thesis Statement   A massive 8.8 earthquake that struck Chile in February resulted in local devastation and had the far-reaching effect of actually changing Earth's rotation.

1. The earthquake devastated parts of the South American country.
   a. The Chilean government reported on March 2, 2010, that the earthquake killed more than 800 people, left thousands injured, and destroyed 500,000 homes.
   b. In the coastal regions near the quake's epicenter, additional flooding caused by the quake washed away entire towns.
      i. World Vision, an aid organization, said on its website (March 1, 2010) that entire towns have been utterly destroyed or have "totally disappeared."
      ii. According to World Vision, people are camping in the streets, in tents, and in the hills.
   c. The *New York Times* reported on March 2, 2010, that the Chilean government estimates the damages at $30 billion (Thompson & Lacey, 2010).

Transition   While the earthquake's damage was localized to Chile, the quake's effects will be felt worldwide.

2. The earthquake was so strong that it actually changed Earth's rotation.
   a. It did so by causing a slight shift in Earth's axis.
   b. As a result of this shift, the length of an Earth day has been shortened by 1.26 milliseconds.
   c. Strong earthquakes have altered Earth's days and its axis in the past.
      i. A 9.1 earthquake in Sumatra in 2004 shifted the figure axis by 2.76 inches, shortening Earth's days by 6.8 microseconds.
      ii. While the Chilean earthquake was much smaller, its effects on Earth were larger because of its location near the equator.

Comparing Informatory vs. Explanatory Presentations—Continued

Explanatory Example

Thesis Statement   A massive 8.8 earthquake that struck Chile in February was a rare megathrust quake that affected the shape of the planet and Earth's rotation.

1. A megathrust earthquake is extremely powerful and can change the shape of Earth.
    a. It is caused when one tectonic plate is shoved violently underneath another, like a spatula being thrust under a pancake, in a process called subduction. (Show visual aid.)
    b. Megathrust earthquakes cause a giant release of energy, similar to the gush of soda out of a can that has been shaken violently.
        i.   In the Chile earthquake, mass was pulled closer to the Earth's center, like metal to a magnet, as one plate was thrust under the other.
        ii. This made the planet slightly denser and more compact.
    c. According to the U.S. Geological Survey on March 1, 2010, these earthquakes are very rare.
        i.   They tend to be 7.5 magnitude or higher.
        ii. There have only been about 14 in recorded history.

Transition   These earthquakes are rare, but their effect is far reaching.

2. The change in Earth's shape affected Earth's rotation.
    a. The megathrust earthquake caused Earth to spin faster on its axis.
        i.   The planet's rotation accelerated as mass was pulled toward the center of Earth.
        ii. The accelerated rotation resembles the increased rotating speed of a spinning figure skater who brings her arms closer to her body (*Los Angeles Times*, 2010). (Show visual aid.)
    b. The increased spin shortened the length of the day on Earth.
        i.   Geophysicist Richard Gross told the *Los Angeles Times* on March 1, 2010, that he estimated that each day from now on will be 1.26 millionth of a second shorter.
        ii. You likely won't notice the difference; that's less than the time it takes to read one word.

Factuality

Factuality is the extent to which the material presented in the speech actually corresponds to the research in the given area. Here, it is important that you verify your information through several different sources and make sure that you report this information accurately to your audience. As an ethical speaker, it is your responsibility to make sure your information is accurate and presented in a straightforward manner. In addition, it is important that you have the latest information to present to your audience. A study from ten years ago might not yield the same results today. Outdated information could easily now be erroneous information. Make sure you have the latest support for your presentations.

Comprehensiveness

Comprehensiveness simply refers to the thoroughness or completeness of the information in your presentation. As an ethical speaker, you want to adequately address the information in your presentation. Given your time constraints, you may only be able to address a small portion of the latest developments thoroughly. The key here is to make sure that you present enough detail on the topic so that your audience has adequate information on which to base decisions regarding the material in your presentation. Similarly, you need to find a balance between being complete and offering too much information. Some speakers alienate their audiences by providing too much detail, especially when the material is of great personal interest. To avoid this, make sure you look at all the information you are providing in terms of what your audience needs to know. That way, you can be comprehensive while still maintaining their interest.

While all three components (surprise value, factuality, and comprehensiveness) are extremely important to an effective news presentation, the real motivation for audience involvement comes from the surprise value. So you really want to highlight this aspect of the presentation. Since this is what will be most captivating for your audience, you don't want to save the surprise value or "news" for the end of the presentation. Present this information early so you can get your audience involved right away.

Technically Speaking

Using Visual Aids

As you have read in this chapter, visual aids can be a key element in informative speeches. Visual aids add to an audience's understanding and comprehension of instructional presentations and explanatory presentations. So it is very important when making an online presentation that you take into account what you will do should your visual aids not work properly for all participants. One idea is to e-mail the participants the visual aids ahead of time, or to upload the visual aids to a common storage area, such as Dropbox. That way audience members can have them printed out, or uploaded onto their own computers, should the online meeting software fail. Make sure you number your visual aids for this purpose. That way you will easily be able to tell those who are not following along with the group what aid you are referring to.

Planning an effective news presentation requires three major skills. First, you must have a clear understanding of your audience and what types of information are likely to both surprise and be relevant to audience members. Second, you must also be a good researcher and have the skills necessary to verify the factuality of your information. Finally, you must present the information in such a way as to provide your audience with a contextual frame with which to interpret the information.[10]

What this means is that you have to present the big picture to your audience. For example, suppose you deliver new information on your organization's e-mail privacy policy. You must contextualize this new information for your audience. In other words, what does this information mean to your audience? Should audience members manage their e-mail differently? Should they limit all personal e-mails? Should e-mail only be used for specific types of communication within the organization? Answering these questions can help ensure that you achieve the goals of a news presentation.

In 2015, the World Health Organization reported that eating small amounts of processed meat–such as hot dogs, bacon or sausage–each day increased the chance of developing colorectal cancer by 18%. Meanwhile, it said red meats were "probably carcinogenic" but there was limited evidence.[11]

News media around the world correctly anticipated that after hearing this information, people would want to know what to do. Was this the end of bacon and eggs? What about hamburgers and hot dogs, the staples of American summer barbeques? Publications found numerous experts who could tell readers just that.

For example, Professor Tim Key, from the Cancer Research UK and the University of Oxford, said: "This decision doesn't mean you need to stop eating any red and processed meat, but if you eat lots of it you may want to think about cutting down."[12]

In this way, the new information was contextualized for the average person in a way they could understand and use.

What news makes a good news presentation? This confuses some students in this course. The newspaper is full of news each day. Each article is news. But not all articles would make a good news presentation. Why not? First, let's return to the surprise element. An article about the new Homecoming King and Queen at your university does contain an element of surprise; you might not have known who won and now you do. But that surprise element is low. It's not something that would make you go, "Wow, I didn't know that." Second, let's look at comprehensiveness. A news presentation needs substance. That is, the news is so important that it will take time to share all the information. Think back to the discussion in Chapter 3 about topic selection. You really don't need three to five minutes to tell me who won the Homecoming King and Queen titles. You can present that information comprehensively in less than one minute. Dragging out the topic for longer than that is a disservice to your audience.

Instructional Presentations

Instructional presentations are concerned with giving audiences directions on performing a particular task. Sometimes these types of presentations are called "how to" presentations or demonstration presentations. In this type of presentation, your goal is to move audience members from their current level of knowledge (e.g., knowing there is new software for submitting reports at work) to a desired state of knowledge (e.g., being able to use the new software to submit reports at work).

Your audience will either have no information, some information, old information or, given the propensity of people to look things up on the Web, even wrong information. It's highly likely your audience won't be homogenous; that is, you could have some people with no information and some people with some information. It is up to you to be able to relate your presentation to all these audience members.

According to the research on instructional or demonstration presentations, there are four states that must be addressed in an effective "how to" presentation.[13] First, you must explain to your audience the **desired state.** What is the goal you are hoping audience members will be able to accomplish? Perhaps it is uploading a video to YouTube from either a computer or a smartphone. In this example, you must explain to audience members exactly what you want them to be able to achieve at the end of your presentation.

> In instructional presentations, your goal is to teach your audience how to do something they couldn't do before.

Second, you must address any **prerequisite states.** What do audience members need to have or need to have completed so that they can achieve this desired goal? Continuing with our example, if you are discussing how to upload a video to YouTube, you should explain what is necessary to begin that process. First, audience members need to have a video and a computer with an Internet connection or a smartphone with the YouTube app downloaded. They also need to have a YouTube account.

Once all the prerequisites have been explained, you can begin to address the actual process of uploading a video. This is called the **interim state.** The interim state comprises all the steps you move through as you proceed toward your goal. In our example, these steps may include the following: "Locate a computer with Internet access and open up a Web browser (such as Internet Explorer). Type the following URL: http://www.youtube.com. When the page loads, enter your username and password in the upper right-hand corner of the page." Similarly you could have told your audience to locate the YouTube app on their phones, open it, and sign in at the opening screen. These directions would continue until you had walked your audience through each of the steps necessary to upload a video.

The final state that must be addressed is **unwanted states.** These are things you want the audience to avoid. In our YouTube example, these would include errors that could impede audience members' ability to effectively upload a video. People attempting to learn new skills can spend 25% to 50% of their time making and recovering from errors.[14] The best way to remedy that is to prevent those mistakes from occurring in the first place, which reduces frustration on the part of the learner. In our example, you might want to warn audience members that YouTube will not upload a video larger than 2 gigabytes or longer than 15 minutes in length. If your video is too large or too long, you will get an error message during your upload. You then have to edit the video and try again. By making audience members aware of this pitfall, you save them time.

Including each of these four states in your instructional presentation gives you a better chance of reaching audience members and ensuring that they are able to perform the task you are trying to explain.

One of the most important things you can do is make clear the rewards of engaging in the process you are explaining. Intermingling information about the rewards with the actual how-to information will increase the listener's attention.[15]

So how should you organize an instructional presentation? Historically, students have been advised to use a chronological or spatial pattern. However, simply placing your material in these types of patterns overlooks some of the important states just discussed. While you may be able to effectively use one of these two patterns, you should examine the complexity of the states you need to address and choose a pattern that will best address your informational needs.

In addition, you might want to keep in mind the idea of minimalist instruction, such as that used in technical communication. Minimalist instruction encourages an action-oriented approach.[16] That is, audience members attending instructional presentations are eager to act, to perform this new task. So don't unnecessarily delay getting to the information needed to make that happen.

Finally, in this course, you will need to keep in mind what you can likely accomplish in the time frame assigned. As mentioned at the beginning of this section, audiences want a challenge, but they won't accept a challenge seen as too daunting. You will need to decide what you can conceivably expect an audience to be able to learn to do in the three to five minute time limit assigned for your instructional presentations.

Four States of Effective Instructional Presentations

- ◎ Describe the desired state.
- ◎ Describe the interim state.
- ◎ Describe prerequisite states.
- ◎ Describe the unwanted states.

Explanatory Presentations

On the March 2, 2010 broadcast of the *CBS Evening News,* then anchor Harry K. Smith was charged with explaining a scientific phenomenon to America. The massive 8.8 earthquake that had struck Chile the previous week had actually changed Earth's rotation, resulting in shorter days. "NASA scientists say the quake may have nudged some of Earth's mass closer to its axis, speeding up its rotation, the same way figure skaters spin more rapidly when they tuck their arms in," Smith reported.

When charged with explaining a complex scientific process his audience might have struggled with, Smith used a quasi-scientific explanation. That is, he organized the information so that the audience could see relationships in the material and employed an analogy to aid their understanding. He combined this with a visual aid for additional clarity.

The *CBS Evening News* uses an analogy to explain a scientific phenomenon.

You might be asked to give a simple explanation, as *CBS News* did, in 20 seconds or you might be called upon to deliver a lengthier explanatory presentation to a group at a meeting or a conference. This section of the chapter focuses on developing strategies for explanatory speaking. As previously discussed, an explanatory presentation is a type of informative speaking that deepens the audience's understanding. It requires that you go beyond simply making the audience aware of a particular phenomenon and actually create audience understanding. For example, a speech on how to use a smartphone application creates awareness, whereas a speech on how that application works increases audience member's understanding.[17] We all know that coffee comes in styrofoam cups because styrofoam keeps liquids warm. Telling someone how that cup provides insulation is taking that understanding further. Explanatory presentations answer questions like "Why?" or "How?" or "What does that mean?"

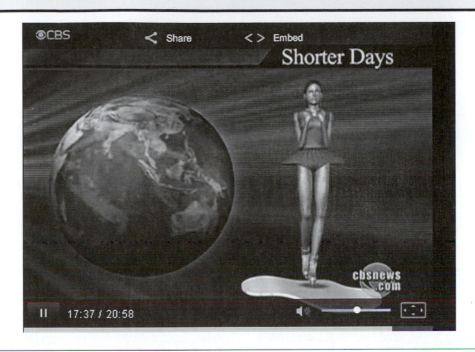

The Simple Explanation

A simple explanation takes anywhere from 15 seconds to 1–2 minutes. It must be clear and succinct. You are not just informing a colleague that you solved the problem plaguing the engineering project the two of you were working on, but you are providing a quick explanation as to how. You could be explaining the difference between impressionism and neo-impressionism to an interested, yet uninformed, museum patron. Or it could be a particular audience is only interested in an explanation of a small part of a whole process.

It may be called a simple explanation, but that doesn't mean it is simpler to give. And sometimes not knowing how to give that simple explanation can have far-reaching consequences.

When the New England Patriots were accused in the infamous "Deflate-Gate" of 2015 of letting the air out of 11 of their 12 footballs in a playoff game with the Indianapolis Colts, Coach Bill Belichick called a news conference to offer a simple explanation for what happened.[18] During the news conference, he alleged that "atmospheric conditions" rather than human subterfuge led to the footballs being deflated. According to Belichick, when players got on the field they began to rub the footballs. "It reached its equilibrium some point later on … that level was below what was set in this climatic condition." His awkward, rambling explanation quickly faced ridicule online from hundreds of people who countered Belichick's claim scientifically.

When you face a situation that requires a simple explanation, there are some things that can help determine the best response.

Coach Bill Belichick calls a news conference to explain Deflate-Gate.

Audience Knowledge Level   It's important to know what your audience knows. You don't want to talk over their heads and use lingo and technical terms they won't understand. But you don't want to talk down to them either.

You've probably heard the suggestion "You do not really understand something unless you can explain it to your grandmother" used when people are asked the best way to explain a social media application. Basically what they are doing is explaining a technology, or technology trend, to a non-user without being condescending. (But let's not use demographic audience analysis erroneously and assume that age or gender means someone is unfamiliar with technology.)

For simple explanations, one rule of thumb is to think about what confused you the first time you learned the material. Chances are, this might be confusing to your audience as well. So make sure you address this issue.

Keep It Focused   Keeping a simple explanation succinct is essential. The longer your explanation goes in a scenario where a simple explanation is needed, the better the chances you will lose your audience.

> You don't want to waste their time on explaining elements the audience already knows or that they don't need to know to understand. Avoid "the little things."

Use Stories, Examples, Definitions, Metaphors   Just because it's a simple explanation doesn't mean we can't use more advanced strategies. (See Elucidating Explanation, Quasi-Scientific Explanation, and Transformative Explanation in this section.) In fact, when we have less time for an explanation, some of these tools can help us achieve our goals more quickly.

One way to help people comprehend new knowledge is to tie it to an existing "schema," a psychology term meaning the existing patterns of knowledge we have to help us learn new knowledge.[19] So use analogies, metaphors, definitions or examples to relate the new information to information your audience already possesses. These are great, quick ways to make connections in our explanations. For example, the *New York Times* chose to use a cartoon to explain how someone would explain what a Bitcoin is and how it works to their mother. In it, they connected things a "mother" would already know (how you earn your money, where you put your money, what happens if your bank fails) to similar areas in "Bitcoinland."[20]

Make sure your comparisons are actually useful, something that everyone can relate to. Professor Brian Cox is an English physicist and professor of particle physics in the School of Physics and Astronomy at the University of Manchester in England who has created a reputation for his science programs that relate abstract theories to everyday life.[21] In his explanations, Professor Cox does a great job of using examples that can help all audience levels understand. For example, in a recent video, he went to the desert to try to help viewers understand entropy, a physics term for a gradual decline into disorder. He showed viewers abandoned houses that had fallen into disrepair and suffered structural damage (broken windows, missing doors, and roof tiles, etc.) from years of exposure to the desert's adverse weather conditions. These abandoned houses related the process of entropy to something everyday people could understand.

Also, as we learned in Chapter 6, brief examples can be used as support in a simple explanation. Stories are more likely to produce an emotional response in your audience, and according to author Daniel Willingham in his neuroscience book, such emotional reactions will make your explanation more memorable.[22]

Professor Cox uses images from the desert to illustrate examples.

How a sandcastle reveals the end of all things - Wonders o

1:29 / 5:32   YouTube

Deliver It Well   Delivery can be key to a simple explanation. You need to deliver it with confidence. During his attempt to explain "Deflate-Gate," New England coach Belichick fumbled over terms and had awkward pauses. He did not sound confident in what he was saying, nor did he say it with the authority of someone who knew what they were talking about. This contributed to his message not being viewed as credible.

Use Visual Aids   Even if you only have 30 seconds, that doesn't mean you can't pull up an image to explain something to an audience. It's easier to understand things we are not familiar with when we have both words and pictures. If available, use images, models, graphs–anything that might aid in your explanation. (See Chapter 12 for more on visual aids, including the assertion evidence model.)

In his video on entropy, Professor Cox used strong images from the desert to illustrate examples he provided to viewers. We already talked about the images of the deteriorated houses. In another portion, as the sand from a sand pile spilled through his fingers, he told listeners that "a good way to understand how is to think of objects not as single things but as being made up of many constituent parts, like the individual grains that make up this pile of sand." That image of the sand slowly filtering through his fingers stays with us, as does his explanation.

Show It in Action   If you have a process that you think your audience might find hard to understand–or even believe–walking them through it might be beneficial. Take your audience through the process step-by-step so they can understand how one step leads to the next, and ultimately the final product.

In November of 2015, 18-year-old student Ryan Chester won a $400,000 prize for his video explanation of Einstein's Principle of Relativity. Specifically he addressed the idea that places that are moving at constant speeds relative to each other are governed by the exact same laws of physics no matter how fast or slow they are moving. Key to his win were the segments that showed the theory "in action."[23]

First, in the video, Chester sits in a chair in his backyard in front of a bowl of popcorn. Nothing happens. That, he says, is because even though Earth is spinning more than 1,000 mph, so are he and the bowl. That's why it appears as if everything is staying still.

Ryan Chester's Video Explanation of Einstein's Principle of Relativity

He then moves the chair, himself and the popcorn to a minivan. At first, just as in the backyard, Ryan and the bowl of popcorn appear still because everything is moving at the same constant speed. But when the minivan speeds up suddenly and all the objects are no longer moving at the same rate, he and the popcorn go flying. Through this "show in action" video, he clearly illustrates what previously was a vague scientific concept for many people.

Ryan Chester's Video Explanation of Einstein's Principle of Relativity (continued)

Breakthrough Junior Challenge: Some Cool Ways of Looking at the Special Theory of Relativity

1:21 / 7:33

Explanatory Presentation Obstacles

In 2011, seven Italian scientists—members of Italy's National Commission for Forecasting and Predicting Great Risks—were charged with manslaughter when L'Aquila, Italy, was hit by a strong earthquake that killed 309 people, injured more than 1,500, and destroyed some 20,000 structures. According to Italian authorities, the seismologists did not accurately convey to the people of the town the threat of a large quake after the town was rocked by a series of small tremors.[24]

A fundamental task in disaster management is translating the specialized language of science into layman's terms.

"When seismologists try to talk to other seismologists, they have a way of talking to each other that can convey information very accurately," Michael K. Lindell, a professor in the Hazard Reduction & Recovery Center at Texas A&M University, told the Chronicle of Higher Education. "The problem is that the words that they use to talk to each other don't make sense to the rest of the population."

The scientists in L'Aquila overcompensated for this by oversimplifying their threat assessment when they explained it to the public, he said.

As we discussed briefly in the previous section, explanatory speaking introduces unique problems for the speaker in terms of audience analysis. We must go beyond issues of organization and support to address special challenges. As mentioned in other chapters, all good presentations require audience analysis. However, when faced with presenting difficult information, you must step back and analyze your audience in different ways.

Ask yourself:

◎   What type of educational background do these particular audience members bring to this situation that many enhance or impede their ability to process the material?

◎   What previously held ideas may interfere with this audience's ability to process this information?

◎   What are the challenges inherent in this information that might make the information difficult for an audience to understand (e.g., vocabulary terms, amount of material covered, etc.).

To provide effective explanations, you must have a thorough understanding of just what it is about the information you are presenting that may make it difficult for an audience to understand. Your goal is to anticipate what difficulties the information may present to your audience and then to design a presentation that overcomes those obstacles. By answering these questions, you will have a better insight into the needs of your audience.

Several obstacles may interfere with an audience's ability to understand a difficult presentation. These difficulties may be inherent in the material itself. Audiences experience difficulty understanding ideas or topics for three reasons:

1.   **Difficulty understanding the use of a concept or term.** For example, your audience may be unfamiliar with the idea of nanotechnology. What does this concept mean and how is it used? Other problems in understanding the use of a concept or term may surround the misuse of terminology. For example, many people outside of the world of information technology do not understand the difference between a server, an ISP, and the Internet. We often misuse these terms when describing our activities on the computer.

2.   **Difficulty understanding a phenomenon, structure, or process.** Some presentations are difficult to understand because they describe processes or structures that are hard for an audience to envision. Either the amount of the material is difficult to process or the relationship between elements in the presentation is hard for the audience to see. For example, audiences may have difficulty understanding how food is genetically engineered. This is a complicated process with many facets. Picturing and following all of the components in this process is difficult for an audience with limited understanding of genetic engineering. Therefore, laying this presentation out in such a way that the audience can follow and grasp the essential parts of the process is imperative.

3.   **Difficulty understanding particular phenomena that are hard to believe.** Sometimes information is hard to understand because the ideas surrounding the information are counterintuitive to our experience. Audiences may have trouble understanding that Earth is weightless or how forest fires could be good for a forest.[25]

Each of these three difficulties or obstacles has unique strategies that can help illuminate your ideas for an audience. The remainder of this chapter discusses each of these three difficulties in more detail, followed by a discussion of specific strategies that help increase audience understanding.

Difficulty Understanding the Use of a Concept or Term

Sometimes the difficulty in understanding information involves the concepts or definitions that surround a particular phenomenon. We often misuse certain terminology in ways that make it difficult for us to understand larger issues. A great example of this is the current debate over climate change, or specifically global warming. Global warming is the gradual heating of Earth's surface, oceans, and atmosphere. In 2014, Vox reported that a vast majority of climate change deniers point to the current weather to support their arguments. [26] "If the temperature is 10 degrees outside, how can you say global warming is occurring?" The issue becomes a distinction between the terms weather and climate.

Research has shown that for audiences to understand content in which concepts or definitions may be difficult, it is best to use an **elucidating explanation.** Elucidating explanations simply explain a concept's meaning or use. It is helpful if you can explain to the audience what is essential in the definition and what is not.

Let's continue with our climate change example. The difference between weather and climate is a measure of time. According to NASA, "weather is what conditions of the atmosphere are over a short period of time, and climate is how the atmosphere 'behaves' over relatively long periods of time.[27] When we talk about climate change, we talk about changes in long-term averages of daily weather." Weather can vary greatly from one day to the next, or even within the same day. When climate change deniers point to

Elucidating Explanations

- ◎ Provide definition of the concept
- ◎ Provide examples
- ◎ Provide nonexamples

temperatures of the current day, they are discussing the weather, not climate. Their failure to distinguish the two contributes to their inability to understand the concept of climate change. Now that you understand this obstacle, you can plan to overcome it.

Communicating Science

Science is one area that places a premium on the need to be able to share information with various audiences. Scientific findings can be hard to describe; they can be difficult to see, measure, and imagine. That's why when scientists apply for grants to support their work from government-funded research councils or private charities, in addition to the detailed scientific justification of the experiments they plan to do, they also must write a "lay summary."[28] The lay summary is a simplified version that uses plain language to explain the experiment and what researchers hope to find or discover. The thought process behind this is to "engage" the public so that the taxpayers who foot the bill for the research have some idea of how their money is being spent.

When making a presentation that uses the elucidating explanation, it is best to follow these steps:

Step 1: Provide a Definition of the Concept   Provide the audience with a definition that lists all of the essential characteristics and features of the definition. Let's examine the following example, involving cactuses: "Cactuses are a species of plants that grow in hot, dry regions. Most are stem succulents. They never have leaves and cannot remove water from cold soils, so they are dormant in the winter and grow in the summer."[29] The essential characteristics of the definition are made clear.

Sometimes, concepts have associated meanings that make a true understanding of the definition difficult. For example, audience members often consider radiation dangerous. However, not all radiation is harmful. Radiation is simply the process of emitting radiant energy in the form of waves or particles. The term *radiation* refers to the electromagnetic radiation that includes radio waves, X-rays, and even the energy from sunlight, light bulbs, and candles. By addressing the associated meaning–dangerous–along with providing a definition, you give the audience a much better understanding of the concept of radiation.[30]

Step 2: Provide Examples   While it may seem obvious to provide an example of the definition you are presenting, research on explaining information suggests that you should provide several examples. Continuing with the cactus example, you could also provide the audience with the following examples to further illuminate the definition: "The giant saguaro cactus looks like a bare tree with thick, upturned branches, while the flat prickly pear resembles a pancake."

Step 3: Provide Nonexamples   Your audience's understanding will be further enhanced if you use varied examples and nonexamples of the concepts you are explaining. Often, your audience may have difficulty deciding which examples fit the definition of your concept. By presenting examples and commonly known nonexamples, you can enhance understanding. Nonexamples resemble the concept by sharing some aspects of the criteria but fall short of having all of the criteria. By presenting some of these nonexamples, you help audience members clearly understand the difference. Continuing with the cactus example, you could use the following nonexample: "Most people commonly believe that the yucca plant is a cactus. While it may resemble cactuses, the yucca plant group has pointed, stiff, narrow leaves that grow along the stem or in clusters at the end of the stem. Remember, cactuses do not have leaves."

Sometimes, the entire goal of your presentation is to explain the definition of a concept or term. If this is the case, use a topical organizational pattern utilizing all three of the steps for elucidating explanations. For example, if the entire goal of your presentation is to explain to your audience exactly what is and what is not considered schizophrenia, you would simply use a topical pattern.

Other times, explaining a concept or definition may be a smaller part of a larger topic or purpose. Imagine that you have been asked to address your neighborhood concerning information on a halfway house being planned for your community. This program will provide transitional housing for individuals who have schizophrenia and are learning to live on their own. As you can see, understanding the disease itself is a smaller part of the overall goal. If this is the case, simply use the appropriate organizational pattern for your material, and weave in the three steps for elucidating explanations at the appropriate time.

Understanding Complex Structures or Processes

Often, what makes a particular topic difficult is the structure or the processes inherent in the topic. It is therefore difficult for an audience to picture the phenomenon in question. For example, individuals have difficulty picturing genetic mutation, understanding how global positioning systems know where we are, how bar codes are assigned to products, or even how the state's ISTEP testing works. In each of these examples, audience members struggle to envision the processes or structures that accompany these topics.

Complex structures or processes can best be explained using **quasi-scientific explanations.** Effective quasi-scientific explanations have two important characteristics. First, they help audiences attune to important features of the message. Second, they help organize the information so that audiences see relationships in the material. Simple devices you can use to achieve solid quasi-scientific explanations include organizing analogies, visual aids, repetition, and transitions.

The first tool is an analogy or metaphor, such as the ice skater example at the start of this section.[31] Analogies and metaphors are the best ways to organize the information for your audience. Organizing analogies take your material and relate it

> **Analogies and metaphors are the best ways to organize information about complex processes for your audience.**

to something with which the audience is already familiar. They re-cast one concept in terms of another that the audience member understands. Ongoing research programs in various disciplines from science to marketing have indicated that individuals understand unfamiliar concepts better when the material is presented through the use of an analogy.[32]

This tool is especially useful in communicating science and technology news. Researchers have noted that often the ideas are so new that without using metaphors it would be extremely difficult, if not impossible, to explain them.[33]

Spotlight on Research

Scientific Explanation in Mass Media

Many Americans turn to popular mass media such as television and newspapers for their science information. However, one study of 100 U.S. newspapers found that while 70% of them carried science stories, most contained little scientific explanation. In fact, 10% or less of content consisted of elucidating and/or quasi-scientific explanations. Stories in feature and science sections contained more explanation than stories in news sections. Longer stories did not contain significantly more scientific explanation, but the more time a journalist had to write the story, the more explanation he or she included. This suggests that writing explanations takes thought.[34]

Metaphor Theory tells us that a good metaphor will "lead people to think and talk productively about something that they were not previously proficient in thinking or talking about."[35] It takes the familiar (and key) aspects of the first item and exports those to the second, unfamiliar item. They can be thought of as a bridge between expert and novice understandings of materials. Metaphors allow audience members to readily use complex, new information.

In order to be effective, choose familiar objects or actions for the analogy. The audience must be able to make an immediate comparison and connection without needing additional information or explanation.[36] The analogy should be short and simple. And metaphors are most effective when they are used early in the narrative and can help listeners organize incoming information.[37]

For example, an engineer with Basic Coatings was speaking before a nontechnical audience. He explained the purpose of adding catalysts and cross-linkers to polymer resins by saying:

> To make products dry hard enough for floors, it has always been necessary to add catalysts or cross-linkers. Think of polymer resins in the solution as individual balls. If you tried to walk among the balls, you'd fall through. But if you tied string between them, you'd form a net that would hold your weight. That's what cross-linkers do: They tie the polymers together.[38]

From February 28 to March 3, 2012, an outbreak of deadly tornadoes in several Midwestern and Southern states killed more than 50 people and caused billions of dollars in damage. *ABC Evening News* reporter Ginger Zee attempted to explain to her audience on March 3 what caused this violent weather.

ABC Evening News reporter Ginger Zee uses an analogy to explain a scientific phenomenon.

Zee explained that tornadic activity occurs when a cold front is replaced by a warm front, creating a twist in which warm air is underneath cold air. In order to aid her audience's understanding, she used a simple analogy (and demonstration) that they could relate to. "It would be like you had a pencil in your hand and you twisted it one way and then another," she said, rubbing an imaginary pencil back and forth in her hands.

Here is an example that appeared in a *Popular Science* magazine article that explained how viruses such as smallpox and Ebola are filtered from blood:

Infected blood flows into the Hemopurifier through a tube extending from one artery. **The toxin filters work like a colander, allowing small viruses through but not large red and white blood cells.** The filter, which is made from biocompatible plastic called polysulfone, is coated with special plant-derived antibodies that hold fast to the pathogens, ensuring that they don't reenter the bloodstream.[39]

> **Tip**
>
> If you think your audience may not understand a concept, try to find an analogy that will help. By putting the same concept into other terms, you can make it seem a lot less mysterious.
>
> Jay Fehnel | Digital Media Executive | Redbox LLC

Members of the audience are familiar with the workings of a colander. The comparison of the Hemopurifier to this simple kitchen gadget makes the process much clearer to your audience.

Another example of an organizing analogy was used by a former student in this course, who explained the way the working memory operates by comparing it to a computer. He continued using this analogy throughout his entire presentation. Because his audience was familiar with the workings of a computer, the analogy made the explanation of the process more clear. So tailor the comparison to your audience. If your audience isn't familiar with knitting, for example, using a knitting analogy to explain a concept won't be very effective. And realize the possibility of bias in your metaphors. That's because a recent study found that metaphors influence how people collect additional information as they make decisions. So if you tell your audience that a new technology is a "beast," audience members will seek out additional information that supports your negative evaluation.[40]

While analogies might help clarify information for audience members, many presenters are unsure how to come up with them. Diagramming the process for your audience is another tool that you might find useful. Diagrams, charts, and visual representations aid audiences in processing information. Visual aids become particularly important with quasi-scientific explanations and are absolutely necessary. Whether the difficulty results from the amount of information or the relationships among the points of information, visual representations help the audience organize the material and see relationships.

Repetition is the third important device in a quasi-scientific explanation. As explained throughout this text, audiences do not have the luxury of going back to hear what you said previously, as they do when reading a text. So remind them of what you told them. They will appreciate it, and it increases the likelihood that your explanation will be effective and that your audience will retain it.

The final device is the transition. Transitions are essential in quasi-scientific explanations. Although they are important in any presentation (see Chapter 5),

Quasi-Scientific Explanations

◎ Relate the material to something the audience already understands.
◎ Use visual aids
◎ Use repetition
◎ Use numerous transitions

quasi-scientific presentations require you to use transitions more frequently. Directional transitions are the tools that link ideas and concepts together for your audience. Signposts help your audience focus on the elements that are most important to the presentation. Internal reviews and previews help with repetition. All four types of transitions should be utilized in a quasi-scientific presentation.

Research shows that when the types of devices just discussed (organizing analogies, diagrams, repetition, and transitions) are used, audience members are better able to envision the processes discussed, and their problem-solving abilities regarding the material are improved.[41] All four of these strategies are necessary in an effective quasi-scientific presentation.

Spotlight on Research

Web Misinformation

While the Web can be a valuable source of information, it can also be a source of misinformation for your audience. This is something to keep in mind when you prepare your informative speeches. A 2012 study in the *New England Journal of Medicine* found that popular Internet search engines tend to direct users to sites that provide incorrect, and even dangerous, health information.[42] The study found that more reliable sites, including sites funded by the federal government, are often overlooked by popular search engines. So chances are some member of your audience will come in with some erroneous preconceived notions based on misinformation. You will need to address the issue of possible misinformation in your presentation.

Organization of quasi-scientific presentations can take any form. Problem–solution, causal, topical, spatial, and chronological patterns are all viable options. Choose the right pattern for your information, and employ the four quasi-scientific explanation tools: organizing analogies, visual aids, repetition, and transitions.

Hard-to-Believe Phenomena

Occasionally, a topic is difficult for an audience to understand because the theories or ideas that encompass that topic are hard for an audience to believe. The difficulty with the material isn't related to any particular term or to a complex collection of information; rather, the idea itself is counterintuitive to particular audiences.

People develop lay theories around events and experiences that are familiar to them. They do not develop lay theories around phenomena that do not hold personal importance. Thus, people do not hold lay theories about new findings regarding nanotechnology or mathematical Knot Theory. They do hold lay theories about household safety, disease management, and nutrition.[43]

Lay audiences struggle to understand how Earth can be weightless or why getting a chill doesn't cause a cold. With each of these ideas, we have developed lay theories that we use to explain our world. Some of these theories are passed down from generation to generation, so they are deeply ingrained. In many cases, these lay theories are wrong. In fact, these nonscientific or lay theories are the source of our confusion and often lead to dangerous consequences. If you believe the material you are presenting to your audience is hard to understand due to some preconceived notion or lay theory the audience holds, you will want to use a **transformative explanation.**

An effective transformative explanation contains four elements: First, the explanation should contain a statement of the lay theory to which the audience currently subscribes. Second, the strengths and reasonableness of the lay theory are acknowledged in the explanation. Third, transformative presentations create dissatisfaction with the current lay theory by explaining its weaknesses. Finally, the scientific explanation is presented, and a justification is provided as to why it better explains the phenomenon in question.[44] Give audience members credit. They have no reason to give up their beliefs until another theory proves otherwise. Each of these steps in an effective transformative explanation is further explained, along with an illustrative example about cancer:

Step 1: State the Lay Theory   Present the lay theory that the audience holds or currently believes to be true. Here is an example: "It may seem reasonable to assume that if there are no people in your family who have cancer, your chances of getting cancer are low, so there's no need to undergo preventative cancer screenings."[45] You simply state what the audience currently believes regarding cancer.

Step 2: Acknowledge the Reasonableness of the Lay View   In this step, you want to show that the current view does have some merit for explaining the situation. You don't want to offend audience members by attacking their current beliefs. So explain why their current views are plausible. Continuing with our cancer example, you might say, "Family history is one source of cancer risk–a big one–in some types of cancer."

> # Transformative Explanations
>
> ◎   State the lay theory
> ◎   Acknowledge the reasonableness of the lay theory
> ◎   Show limitations with the lay theory
> ◎   Explain the scientific theory or positions

Step 3: Show Dissatisfaction with the Current View   Here you want to show audience members what is wrong with their current view. For example, you might state, "But while family history is one source of cancer risk, there are other sources. For instance, lifestyle factors such as obesity and smoking are connected to cancer." In this way, you point out problems with the nonscientific or lay view.

Step 4: Explain the Scientific Theory or Position   In this step, you lay out the true explanation for audience members and provide them with the evidence that will help them accept the less conventional notion. Continuing with the example, "According to the American Medical Association, the best tool we have for fighting cancer is to detect it early, even before it begins. Since early cancers may not cause symptoms, and since even people with no family history of cancer are at risk, you should have cancer screenings." Here you have explained why everyone needs cancer screenings. By providing audience members with this information, you may have helped them make a decision that saves their lives.

The Centers for Disease Control (CDC) has made frequent use of transformative explanations since the H1N1, or swine flu, outbreak. For example, because of its name, many rumors surfaced that the flu originated in pigs and that you could get the flu from eating pork. The CDC began a campaign to dispel this myth. It acknowledged the rumors and pointed out that the virus was originally referred to as swine flu because many of the genes in this new virus are very similar to flu viruses that normally occur in pigs in North America. It then, however, showed that there has been no reported case of transmission of the disease from livestock to humans.

One important factor related to transformative explanations is that the steps do not have to be presented in order within your presentation. As long as all four steps are present and adequate, your presentation will be effective.

Special Occasion Speaking

In 2015, when Duke won the NCAA men's basketball championship, President Barack Obama welcomed the team to the White House. As part of his presentation, he passed along his message of congratulations and recited highlights of the team's achievements on and off the court:

> But everybody knows this program is not just about winning on the hardwood. Five players made the all-conference academic squad this year. That is worth applause. This team also visited Durham elementary schools for the "Read with the Blue Devils" campaign. Coach K authored an op-ed on the importance of early childhood education. Players volunteered as mentors at the Emily Krzyzewski Center, which is named for the Coach's mother and aims to break the cycle of poverty through out-of-school programs that help young people reach college. So this is the kind of program that we hope for at any institution of higher learning. They represent their university well on and off the court. They've got a great leader in Coach K, and it's an outstanding university, an outstanding program, and they deserve our hearty congratulations. Very proud of you guys.

President Obama was speaking on a special occasion. As part of a long-standing presidential custom, he was welcoming a winning sports team to the White House to help honor their accomplishment.

At some point, you too might be called upon to deliver a special occasion speech in which you need to inform your audience about a person, an accomplishment, or a situation. Special occasion presentations should have a clear purpose: entertainment, celebration, commemoration, or inspiration.[46] You might be asked by a club you are a member of to introduce a guest speaker. You might receive an award for volunteering in your community. You might need to welcome a crowd to the dedication of your new company location. You might be asked to eulogize a friend at a funeral service. In the following paragraphs we look at four common types of special occasion speeches: the speech of introduction, the speech of acceptance, the speech of recognition, and the speech of welcome. We explore the purposes of these speeches and their structure, and offer tips for delivering these types of speeches successfully.

Speech of Introduction

One of the most common types of special occasion speeches is the **speech of introduction.** This speech introduces the audience to a speaker. These speeches are brief, often under two minutes. (In a more formal speech situation, it might be longer, about 10% of the speaker's time.) Remember, the audience came to hear the speaker, not you. Your job is simply to set the stage.

A speech of introduction has two main goals: to get the audience's attention and to establish the speaker's credibility. These goals can be accomplished by dividing our speech of introduction into three main parts: the attention-getter, background information, and identification of the speech topic.

In your attention-getter, it is your job to make the audience want to listen to the speaker. You need to start with a strong narrative, startling fact, or amusing anecdote that grabs the audience's attention. But, as with all attention-getters, we need to make sure that the story we tell or the fact we give is relevant to the speaker's reason for being there. Simply telling a funny story about the speaker will not suffice. And we don't want to embarrass the speaker with the story we choose.

Then the background information is used to establish the speaker's credibility to addressing the topic they are speaking on. A lot of speakers will have expertise in several areas. Pick and choose your background to match the occasion. For instance, if you were introducing actor and environmentalist Robert Redford to speak to the University Environmental Club, you would not provide a long list of his acting accomplishments. Instead, you would focus on his environmental work. This part of your introduction is especially important if the speaker is not well known. You want to focus on accomplishments that not only highlight the speaker's experience but also make the speaker appear competent.

Finally, you want to let the crowd know what the speaker will be talking about. You can either provide this as a general topic or give the actual title of the presentation if the speaker has provided you with one. Remember, it is your job to simply introduce the topic, not to discuss it yourself. The audience came to hear the speaker's views, not yours.

If possible, try to talk with the speaker before you prepare your introduction. There might be specific points they would like you to stress, or comments they would like you to avoid. It's also a good time to check that you know how to pronounce the speaker's name correctly and that you are using the name/title the speaker prefers.

Janet, a student at a Midwest university, was excited to welcome noted international reporter Christiane Amanpour to the regional meeting of the Society of Professional Journalists. She began her introduction with a witty anecdote, added pertinent background information about the speaker that established her credibility and identified why the audience would want to listen, and then identified the speech topic:

> Our distinguished speaker got her first job in journalism in the fourth grade; she was assigned the dangerous "cafeteria beat" for the student newspaper at Washborne Elementary. You never knew when a food fight was going to break out. Since then, her pursuit of the news has taken her to other dangerous conflict zones: reporting from the Persian Gulf, Sarajevo, Iraq, Afghanistan, and even North Korea. In her 30 years with *CNN,* and now in her role as global affairs anchor for *ABC News,* she has developed into the most recognized and respected foreign correspondent today, committed to providing us with views of newsmakers we might not otherwise have. She alone secured exclusive interviews with world leaders such as Egypt's Hosni Mubarak and Libya's Muammar Ghadafi during democratic uprisings in those countries. We are pleased to have her here today, back on U.S. soil, to speak on changes in the media that she has witnessed during her storied career. Please welcome Christiane Amanpour.

Ethically Speaking

Remember the Situation

Often we are asked to introduce a speaker or an award winner because we have a personal connection. Because we know this person, it is assumed we might have insight that would be interesting to share with the audience. But keep that audience in mind when you are picking appropriate stories to share. Sharing stories that are too personal is inappropriate. They not only might embarrass the speaker; they might also make the audience uncomfortable. In addition, watch what language you use. It is inappropriate in such instances to use curse words or words that have sexual innuendo.

Speech of Acceptance

In a **speech of acceptance,** the speaker is acknowledging receipt of an award or other honor. Many find this a difficult speech to make. While we are pleased that our efforts are being recognized, it is awkward for many of us to talk about ourselves. Remember, a well-prepared speech of acceptance does not equate to bragging. Following these guidelines will make it easier for you:

◎   Keep it brief. This is especially true in situations when others are being honored as well.

◎   Make sure the appreciation is reciprocated. Take time to thank and praise the organization that is honoring you for their hard work, as well as others who may have played a role in your success.

◎   Be yourself. People expect a genuine, sincere acceptance speech. They don't want to hear you recite your accomplishments. Rather, they want to know what really motivated you to work this hard. Tell them why the award is important to you.

While you should be yourself, that doesn't mean you shouldn't be prepared. Many people don't want to appear as if they expected an award, and thus they don't prepare. But their acceptance speech is often rambling and incoherent. Instead, take the time to prepare something. Audiences would much rather hear you articulate your feelings than hear incoherent ramblings.

Special Occasion Presentations

The Elevator Pitch

Those of you majoring in business have likely heard of the "elevator pitch" presentation. According to *BusinessWeek*, "One of the most important things a business owner can do is learn how to speak about their business to others."[47] An elevator pitch is a concise and well-practiced description of a business venture to a potential investor or a quick summation of what your company makes or does to a possible client. A variant pitch is providing a concise and professional description of your work abilities should you find yourself in an elevator with the employer of your dreams. It is so named because the length should be about the same as the average elevator ride. While in reality you likely won't be delivering this pitch in an elevator, it is still important that you be ready to inform a prospective investor or client about your business.

A couple of tips to keep in mind:

◎   Keep it fresh. Make sure you update your pitch frequently. As times change, so should the points of your pitch.

◎   Always be prepared. This means knowing your potential audience. It doesn't do any good to focus your pitch on, say, low costs, when quality is more important to a client. One pitch does not fit all needs.

Speech of Recognition

Chances are that, even if you never win an honor, you might be asked to present such an award.

A **speech of recognition** is also brief, under three minutes, though it can be longer in more formal situations. As with a speech of introduction, those in attendance are there to hear the honoree, not you.

A speech of recognition must discuss the history of the award, the requirements to win the award, and how the recipient met those requirements. Sometimes, the honor is a surprise. If this is the case, refrain from announcing the winner's name until the end of the speech of recognition. Effective speeches of recognition are sincere. Refrain from lavishing false praise on the recipient; keep it real. In addition, most recipients will receive something tangible with the honor: a plaque, a certificate, or a trophy. It will be your job to hand the recipient this award and shake their hand. Hand the recipient the award with your left hand; this will leave your right hand free to shake the recipient's hand.

Speech of Welcome

A **speech of welcome** is designed to show your audience their attendance is appreciated. These are usually very brief and highlight both the audience and the host. Imagine being asked to welcome a tour group at your local manufacturing plant, or a group of parents at a high school open house.

First, you want to gain their attention. Point out something interesting right from the start, like the new machinery they are standing next to, or the projects that students worked so hard on that line the classroom wall.

Next, you want to sincerely thank the group for coming. The spotlight is now on your audience. Then explain your organization or location to them. Let them know what your company manufactures and why it matters to them.

Finally, you express what you hope the outcome of the visit will be. Tell the parents you hope they get an idea of just what their children have been learning over the school year.

Conclusion

Informative speaking is a vital skill for you to develop. As this chapter has demonstrated, informative speaking is just as important, and can be just as challenging for the speaker, as persuasive speaking. Informative speaking consists of informatory speaking, explanatory speaking, and special occasion speeches. Each of these types of presentations contains its own set of challenges, and the chapter presented recommendations for overcoming those challenges.

Key Terms

Comprehensiveness	Instructional presentations	Speech of introduction
Desired state	Interim state	Speech of recognition
Elucidating explanation	News presentations	Speech of welcome
Explanatory speaking	Prerequisite states	Surprise value
Factuality	Quasi-scientific explanation	Transformative explanation
Informative speaking	Relevant	Unwanted states
Informatory speaking	Speech of acceptance	

Exercises

1. Pick a common myth that many people hold. Then, using a transformative explanation, debunk that myth for your classmates. Make sure you have all four parts of the explanation. If you need help looking for myths, check out websites such as the Discovery Channel's *Mythbusters*.

2. Have students choose a speech from the TED: Ideas Worth Spreading website to review (http://www.ted.com/talks). Have them identify elements such as surprise value, relevance, and comprehensiveness that speakers used effectively.

3. Show one or two clips from *Scientific American*'s "60 Second Science." Divide students into groups of 4–5. Give students 10–12 minutes to prepare a 60 Second Science presentation. Each group must use either an elucidating explanation and/or a quasi-scientific explanation.

4. Visit a website such as Science Daily, Scientific American, or the health, technology, or science pages of news portals such as Google, CNN, or Yahoo! Find two articles you think would make a good news presentation. Map out a thesis statement and main points for a speech on the topic.

CHAPTER 9

The Persuasive Process

Objectives

After reading this chapter, you should be able to

- explain the differences between informative and persuasive speaking;
- explain persuasion as a process and its implications for delivering a presentation;
- clarify the differences between beliefs, attitudes, and behaviors;
- differentiate between the types of persuasive speaking;
- understand and apply principles of the Elaboration Likelihood Model; and
- understand and apply principles of Social Judgment Theory.

In March 2016 President and Mrs. Obama were invited to speak at the popular South by Southwest, a group of music and film festivals and interactive media conferences, in Austin, Texas. As part of their speaking engagements, President Obama addressed a room of 2,100 technology executives and technology enthusiasts.[1] In his talk, the President addressed issues of security highlighted by a disagreement between Apple and the FBI regarding privacy and security. The FBI wanted cooperation from Apple to access the cell phone data of Syad Farook, an American citizen, who participated in a mass shooting rampage at the Inland Regional Center in San Bernardino, CA. Apple refused to cooperate, citing issues of privacy.

This situation raised issues between national security versus privacy for individuals and their data. This is a delicate and complicated debate with proponents on each side of the issue holding strong beliefs and attitudes. There is the need to protect national security and there is a strong need for individual freedom and privacy. The group the president was addressing felt very strongly about using encryption to protect our personal information and data so that it could not be accessed by anyone under any circumstances. The president's view is more modest on this issue. He recognized the difficulty of addressing such a potentially hostile audience about issues of security and government power when their positions differed. He did so delicately.

Here are a couple of brief excerpts of some of the comments he made:[2]

"All of us value our privacy, and this is a society that is built on a Constitution and a Bill of Rights and a healthy skepticism about overreaching government power. Before smartphones were invented and to this day, if there is probable cause to think that you have abducted a child, or that you are engaging in a terrorist plot, or you are guilty of some serious crime, law enforcement can appear at your doorstep and say we have a warrant to search your home and can go into your bedroom and into your bedroom drawers to rifle through your underwear to see if there's any evidence of wrongdoing."

"And we agree on that because we recognize that just like all of our other rights, freedom of speech, freedom of religion, etc., that there are going to be some constraints that we impose in order to ensure we are safe, secure and living in a civilized society."

"Now technology is evolving so rapidly that new questions are being asked, and I am of the view that there are very real reasons why we want to make sure the government can not just willy-nilly get into everybody's iPhones or smartphones that are full of very personal information or very personal data."

"What makes it even more complicated is the fact that we also want really strong encryption because part of us preventing terrorism or preventing people from disrupting the financial system or our air traffic control system or a whole other set of systems that are increasingly digitalized, is that hackers, state or non-state, can't get in there and mess around."

"So we have two values, both of which are important, right?

Before presenting his own arguments on the position, he acknowledged the attitudes and beliefs that many in the audience held. His talked addressed why each position was important and had merit. He began his persuasive appeal argument from a place where all agreed to establish common ground. Then he presented his own position on the issue.

President Obama recognized the difficulty in persuading hostile audiences. He picked the venue carefully, he approached areas of difference carefully, and laid an incremental plan for persuasion. This is an example of how difficult persuasion is and how it must be approached with great care. This chapter will address some of these issues.

Each day, we deliver numerous persuasive messages to our friends, family, and acquaintances. We may try to convince friends to go to the movie we want to see or eat at our favorite restaurant. We may try to convince a professor to give the class an extension on the class project. We usually have to convince a boss of the need for time off to study for an exam or to travel out of town.

All of us engage in numerous persuasive attempts like those just described each and every day. Some of these attempts at persuasion are successful, and some don't turn out as well as we might have liked. Persuasion is one of the most important skills you can develop as a communicator. To help ensure success in this arena, it is imperative that you have a firm understanding of the persuasive process and its underlying principles. Persuasion, however, is a difficult task. When crafting a persuasive message, there are many things to consider and employ. This chapter is designed to lay out some of the basic issues of the persuasion process so that this task may seem a bit more manageable.

Differences between Informative and Persuasive Presentations

Before we discuss persuasive strategies and theories, it is important that you understand the differences between informative and persuasive speaking. This will enable you to choose the best set of strategies for your speaking situation.

Persuasive Speaking Asks the Audience to Choose between Two or More Alternatives

As mentioned earlier in the text, in an informative speech, a speaker acts as a teacher. As a teacher, a presenter simply explains a particular point of view or presents information on a topic. In persuasive speaking, the task becomes more complex. In addition to illuminating the topic, the presenter must also act as a leader. You are asking audience members to do more than just learn and understand issues on a specific topic; you are also asking them to adopt a position on the issue. For example, there isn't much controversy about a speech on the history of reproductive rights in the United States. However, a speech advocating human cloning as a choice for reproduction is highly volatile. In this example, a persuasive speaker's primary goal is to convince the audience to agree with his or her position.

Persuasion asks more from an audience.

Persuasive Speaking Demands More Thorough Audience Analysis

Because persuasion relies so much on attitudes, beliefs, and behaviors, it is imperative that a persuasive speaker know as much about how a particular audience feels about an issue as possible. If you are a sales representative for Microsoft, pitching your proposal on incorporating a new computing system into an organization, you need to know what types of attitudes and beliefs the organization holds about Microsoft prior to the presentation. If the company has invested substantial time and money in a competitor's products, then the presentation should have a different focus than if the company has experience with Microsoft products. This might further be complicated by how positive or negative those experiences have been. Persuasive speakers simply must know their audience well and prepare their presentations accordingly.

Persuasive Speaking Makes More Demands of an Audience

Whereas informative presentations ask audiences to understand something, persuasive presentations go a step further. The persuasive speech asks audiences to do or change something as a function of that understanding. This is more difficult. People are often skeptical and resistant to change. They often do not see reasons to change their behavior or beliefs. Because of this, they have to process your information more carefully, evaluating the arguments and appeals in your message against the information and beliefs they hold. When it becomes apparent that your goal is to change their beliefs, they will need to take more time than they otherwise would in evaluating your message.

Persuasive Speaking Has a Higher Ethical Threshold

When asking the audience to change a behavior or to support a particular position, you are assuming an important responsibility. If you encourage your audience to vote for a particular candidate for student government, you must really know that this candidate will be the best person for the job. Another part of your responsibility is to ensure that your supporting evidence is of the highest quality. Are your experts qualified? Are your statistics up to date? Have you verified your information with more than just one source? Asking your audience to make changes or commitments based on questionable evidence is unethical. As an ethical speaker, it is your responsibility to ensure that the appeals you make are reasonable and in the best interests of your audience.

Now that you have a firm grasp of the characteristics of persuasive speaking, let's examine the process of persuasion and how you can apply it to your presentation.

What Is Persuasion?

To be successful at persuasive speaking, it is important to examine the definition of *persuasion* itself. For the purposes of this course, **persuasion** can be defined as the process of changing, creating, or reinforcing an attitude, belief, or behavior.

The Process of Persuasion

One of the most important aspects of this definition is that persuasion is a process.[3] People are rarely persuaded in one persuasive attempt. It usually takes multiple messages and multiple exposures to a message in order to persuade a particular audience. The following example illuminates this feature of the definition.

> **Persuasion can be defined as the process of changing, creating, or reinforcing an attitude, belief, or behavior.**

Imagine that you are a sales representative making a pitch to an important client. A sales rep rarely has only one chance to persuade the client. Usually, your company will make multiple presentations, send backup documents, and engage in multiple conversations with key players within that organization before a decision is reached. Each of these communication efforts with the client is a persuasive attempt. While we will focus on the persuasive presentation itself, it is important for you as a speaker to recognize that this presentation is just one of many tools you or your organization will be using to persuade the client.

In addition to having multiple opportunities to persuade a given audience, the definition also implies that persuasion is accomplished incrementally. You will have little success if you push for your ultimate goal on the first persuasive

> **Persuasion is a process.**

attempt. You have to lay the groundwork and move slowly toward your ultimate goal. Seeking too much in one persuasive attempt will backfire.

Consider how this works in real life. Imagine that you are trying to persuade your parents to buy you a new car. Simply coming down to dinner one evening and asking, "Dad, will you buy me a car?" will probably result in a less-than-successful outcome. However, if you gradually build the arguments for why you need a new car, your parents will be more likely to hear your case and think about what you are requesting.

These realizations can help you develop strategies for creating more effective presentations. Recognizing that you don't have to cover everything in one persuasive attempt ensures that the presentation can be more targeted and strategic.

Targets of Persuasion

One of the most important elements to consider when constructing a persuasive message or presentation is your **target.** Just exactly what do you want the audience to think, feel, or do? As a speaker, you must decide if your persuasive presentation will target your audience's beliefs, attitudes, or behaviors. These targets interact with each other in complex ways. Beliefs underlie attitudes, and attitudes underlie behaviors.[4] To increase the likelihood of achieving your persuasive goal, it is important to understand how these three targets relate to each other. Let's examine each of these targets in more detail.

Beliefs

> **A belief is a cognition held by an individual concerning the truth or falsity of a claim or the existence or reality of something.**

A **belief** is a cognition held by an individual concerning the truth or falsity of a claim or the existence or reality of something.[5] For example, some individuals in the medical community believe that a series of vaccinations given in early childhood is leading to an increase in autism. On the other hand, many other individuals in the medical community think this claim is false. Evidence can be presented for both sides of this claim.

One important feature about beliefs is that they cannot be proven or disproven for certain. There is always a degree of uncertainty associated with beliefs. Other points of view are possible and defendable. Consider this claim: "Violent video games are causing our country's youth to become more violent." Evidence could be presented both for and against this claim. Some experts think that the increased violence in these games affects the behavior of children and has led to events like the Columbine shootings. Other experts say that these games have a minimal effect. All of these respective experts have research to back up their claims. Audience members' beliefs concerning this claim will rest with the side they find most convincing. Here are some examples of beliefs:

◎ Climate change is caused by human activities.
◎ College education should be free.

Beliefs are usually well established and difficult to change. To change an audience's belief on any particular topic, you have to present convincing evidence.[6]

Attitudes

> **Attitudes attach a positive or negative evaluation onto a belief.**

As discussed in Chapter 2, an **attitude** is an individual's evaluation of an object, event, person, policy, and so forth.[7] Attitudes attach a positive or negative evaluation to a belief. So, our beliefs underlie our attitudes. Attitudes are learned and enduring evaluations of things that affect our behavior. People are highly motivated to act in ways that are consistent with their attitudes toward those things.[8] Because people want their attitude toward something to be consistent with their behavior, they will change their attitude to accommodate the behavior.[9]

Here are some statements that reflect attitudes; as you can see, they each attach a positive or negative evaluation to the topic:

◎ Big pharma is dangerous to healthcare.
◎ Mozart is the best composer of the classical period.

While we are ambivalent toward some attitudes, others are extremely important to us. For instance, while most people may prefer to drink either Coke or Pepsi, they will often drink the other if their favorite is unavailable. However, most people are not so lackadaisical about their attitude toward an issue such as abortion. When persuading people to change their evaluation of something, speakers need to factor in how important or strongly held an audience's existing attitudes are.[10] Also, people do not always behave in ways that are consistent with attitudes. Although they may be motivated to do so, there may be obstacles that prevent them from achieving attitude–behavior consistency. For instance, a person may hold the attitude that Mercedes automobiles are the best cars to own, yet only be able to afford a Ford Focus.

The man in this photo is speaking to a favorable audience.

Behaviors

Behaviors are observable actions. The behaviors we choose to enact are largely based on the beliefs and attitudes we hold. As mentioned previously, there is a strong link between beliefs, attitudes, and behaviors. We try not to engage in behaviors that we do not value or that are in opposition to the beliefs and attitudes we hold.[11]

Behaviors are observable actions.

Most of our persuasive attempts target behavior. We are bombarded by messages that attempt to persuade us to alter our behavior—for example, to buy a particular product or vote for a specific candidate. The daily attempts you make at persuasion are primarily targeted at behaviors. You might try to persuade your parents to contribute toward your spring break vacation or persuade your roommate to go on a blind date.

Although your primary goal may be to achieve some behavioral outcome, you may not be able to achieve this goal in a single persuasive presentation. Sometimes, we have to focus on one of the underlying beliefs or attitudes first, and incrementally build toward a behavioral change in an audience. As a speaker, you cannot underestimate the important relationship between beliefs, attitudes, and behaviors. As mentioned earlier, persuasion is a process.

Goals of Persuasion

Once you have selected a target for your persuasive presentation, you must decide on the best goal for your particular needs. There are three primary **goals** you can have in a persuasive message: You can seek to create, reinforce, or change an attitude, belief, or behavior. Let's further examine each of these goals so that you can get a better understanding of the process.

Creating

Sometimes, an audience will have no established beliefs, attitudes, or behaviors regarding a particular issue. For example, Americans had few attitudes or behaviors concerning terrorism on U.S. soil before September 11, 2001. However, after that day, President George W. Bush worked diligently to create attitudes and behaviors consistent with his plan for increased homeland security. Today, Americans' attitudes, beliefs, and behaviors toward security are much stronger and more sophisticated than in the past.

The goal of many advertising campaigns usually involves **creating** new beliefs, attitudes, and behaviors. Several years ago, Procter & Gamble introduced the Swiffer duster. Initially, I had no beliefs, attitudes, or behaviors concerning this new product. After watching commercial after commercial, being bombarded with coupons, and overhearing people in the grocery store talk about how great this new product worked, I bought a Swiffer and all of the supplies necessary to make it work. The advertisers had been successful. They capitalized on beliefs I already had, such as "My home should be clean." They convinced me that their product would help achieve a cleaner home and thus created a new behavior: buying the product.

Reinforcing

Sometimes, it is important that we **reinforce** the beliefs, attitudes, and behaviors that people already hold (see Chapter 2). Consider Sunday sermons. The purpose of these messages is usually not to change or create, but to make audience members more devout and to strengthen those beliefs, attitudes, and behaviors they already hold. You have likely heard the phrase "Preaching to the choir." Politicians are well aware of this phenomenon. Every rally and fundraising event they hold is primarily concerned with reinforcing their followers' commitment. Even though followers are already committed, they need to be reminded of why. So even when you have won over audience members, you still have to work on keeping them persuaded. This particular goal highlights the incremental nature of persuasion. Audiences are rarely persuaded in one single attempt. They must be exposed to the persuasive attempt again and again before persuasion occurs and, certainly, before the persuasion becomes enduring.

Changing

Changing a persuasive target is usually what we associate with persuasion: getting Windows computer users to switch to Apple computers, getting Republicans to vote Democrat, getting pro-lifers to become pro-choice.

Students always get excited about the persuasive assignment because they want to change the way the audience thinks or behaves. While changing persuasive targets is important, it is not always realistic. Individuals hold some beliefs and attitudes very strongly, and they are very resistant to change. After conducting a thorough audience analysis (see Chapter 2 for these methods), you will be able to determine audience members' attitudes, beliefs, and behaviors. You may even be able to discern how strongly they hold these attitudes and beliefs. Given this information, you may be able to determine how much latitude a particular audience has for movement in the direction you are advocating.

Any of the goals just discussed are appropriate for your classroom presentations. You need to be cognizant of your situation and your audience, and choose those goals that you might be able to accomplish in the amount of time allotted for your presentation. These types of situational constraints should influence the decisions you make about targets and goals.

Now that you have a better understanding of just what persuasion is, there are two persuasive theories—the Elaboration Likelihood Model and Social Judgment Theory—that can add insight as you begin to plan your persuasive presentation. Let's take a look at each of these perspectives.

The Elaboration Likelihood Model

Richard Petty and John Cacioppo, two social psychologists, have developed a way for us to better understand persuasion by examining an audience's motivation and knowledge concerning a given topic. The **Elaboration Likelihood Model (ELM)** proposes that there are two "routes" to persuasion, depending on how motivated and able the audience is to process the information in your presentation.[12]

Elaboration relates to the extent audience members will think about your message, while **likelihood** refers to the probability that they will or will not think about or elaborate on the ideas you present. So, in a nutshell, the theory's primary concern is determining how much your audience will think about the ideas you present. For this to happen, two things must be present: audience members must be motivated to process your message, and they must be able to process your message. If audience members don't understand the major tenets of nanotechnology, for example, it really doesn't matter how motivated they are by your topic. They simply won't be able to think or elaborate on your message in sophisticated ways because they don't have the knowledge necessary to do so.

According to the ELM, there are two "routes" or avenues to persuasion: the central route and the peripheral route. The **central route** is characterized by high levels of critical thinking. Messages are carefully analyzed, and your material is related to information the audience

> There are two "routes" to persuasion, depending on how motivated and able the audience is to process the information in your presentation.

already knows. Audiences engaged in the central route think about the implications of your messages and are extremely thorough in their analysis of your material.

The **peripheral route,** on the other hand, is characterized by less elaboration. Your messages are evaluated quickly, and audiences rely on simple cues or decision rules to evaluate your argument or message. **Decision rules** are mental shortcuts. When audiences lack the ability or motivation to carefully examine your ideas, they rely on decision rules. So, instead of carefully critiquing your argument or ideas, they rely on all or some of the following:

- ◎ Your credibility on the issue.
- ◎ Your likability as a speaker.
- ◎ The number of arguments you use.
- ◎ The length of your arguments.
- ◎ The perception of other audience members regarding the presentation.

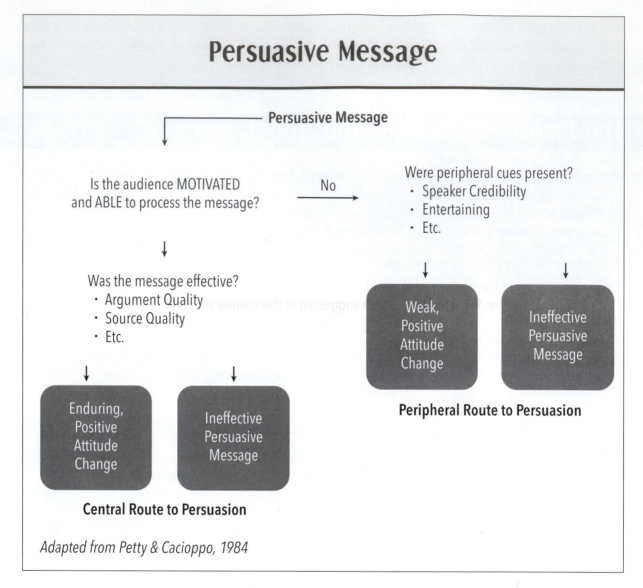

Persuasive Message

Persuasive Message

Is the audience MOTIVATED and ABLE to process the message?   No →   Were peripheral cues present?
· Speaker Credibility
· Entertaining
· Etc.

Was the message effective?
· Argument Quality
· Source Quality
· Etc.

Enduring, Positive Attitude Change

Ineffective Persuasive Message

Weak, Positive Attitude Change

Ineffective Persuasive Message

Central Route to Persuasion

Peripheral Route to Persuasion

Adapted from Petty & Cacioppo, 1984

An example used in Chapter 2 can help illustrate the ELM more clearly. Imagine that you are in an audience where the need for menu changes in the cafeteria of a local high school is being presented. The school board is recommending that all vending machines be removed from the premises. Although you attended this high school, you are now a freshman at college. You aren't highly motivated to critically think about the arguments being presented because the changes won't affect you. Because of your lack of motivation, you will likely take the peripheral route. While good logic and arguments are important, you are more likely to be persuaded by emotional appeals, the speaker's credibility, and the rest of the audience's reaction.

Your neighbor, who is a senior at the local high school, feels differently. Because the menu changes directly affect him, he is highly motivated to be critical of the messages. The speaker will want to take the central route with an audience full of involved, motivated members like your neighbor. Good logical appeals will be extremely important. The audience will be mentally questioning all of the ideas the speaker presents. If these questions aren't answered, it is unlikely that the audience will be persuaded.

Spotlight on Research

One-Sided vs. Two-Sided Messages

A one-sided message simply presents your position on a particular topic, while a two-sided message presents your position along with your opponent's position on the issue. Therefore, a two-sided message presents a balanced view of the issue. A spin on the two-sided message is the two-sided rebuttal message. It presents your position and your opponent's position, and then refutes your opponent's position.

But which of these three approaches is most effective or most persuasive? Several meta-analyses have been conducted exploring this issue. This research has determined that two-sided refuted messages are the most persuasive types of messages. That is, presenting your own arguments along with your opponent's arguments and then refuting your opponent's position is the most persuasive strategy you can employ. Therefore, the refutative pattern suggested in this chapter is optimal.

However, time constraints and other environmental factors sometimes get in the way, and it isn't always feasible to present both sides of an issue plus a rebuttal. If this is the case, simply present your own position. A one-sided message is a more persuasive strategy than a two-sided message with no rebuttal. So if you have the option, always present a two-sided message with a rebuttal. If this is not possible, simply present the one-sided message.[13]

It is important to note that persuasion that is achieved through the central route is enduring. This means that it will last. It is not as susceptible to counterpersuasive attempts. Another important factor is that persuasion achieved through the central route is highly predictive of behavior.

Persuasion achieved through the peripheral route, on the other hand, is less enduring. It is susceptible to counterpersuasion, and it is not predictive of behavior.

Applying the Principles of the ELM

One aspect of using the ELM effectively is good audience analysis. You must have a thorough understanding of audience members' motivation and their ability to think critically on the given issue. If they are both motivated and able to think critically, the central route to persuasion is the most appropriate. Good, sound logic is essential. Evidence from highly credible sources is also important. Another key factor is presenting two-sided messages with rebuttals (see the Spotlight on Research box).

If you suspect that your audience is less motivated and/or unable to process your material, take the peripheral route. Focus on building and enhancing your credibility and likability. Use emotional appeals and extended narrative examples.

If you face an audience that is mixed, meaning it is made up of both motivated and unmotivated members and those who will think critically and those who won't, identify which of these two audiences is more important, and tailor your message to them. If that is not possible, deliver a presentation that takes both the central and peripheral routes. This way, both types of audience members will get the information they need.

Another consideration when using the ELM is the goal of the presentation. Really analyze your goal, and ask yourself the following questions: Are you seeking long-term commitment from your audience? Is the target of your persuasive appeal behavioral? If you answer "yes" to both of these questions, you want to encourage your audience to use the central route when processing the information in your presentation. As mentioned earlier, this route is more predictive of long-term change and behavioral changes.[14] Utilize those strategies (i.e., quality arguments) that will encourage your audience to take that path.

Social Judgment Theory

> ## Members of an audience evaluate messages in terms of the attitudes they already hold.

Another theoretical perspective that helps us understand how persuasion works for an individual is **Social Judgment Theory.** This theory explains that members of an audience evaluate messages in terms of the attitudes they already hold and then make a decision whether to embrace a particular message or to reject it.[15] According to this perspective, our attitudes fall along a continuum. At one end is the **latitude of acceptance.** Any message that falls into this place on the continuum is accepted because it is viewed as consistent with attitudes the individual already holds. At the other end is the **latitude of rejection.** Messages that fall into this area are rejected because they are not consistent with an audience's attitudes. In addition to latitudes of acceptance and rejection is the **latitude of non-commitment.** This is that gray area that a person may not be sure about. It may be that individuals simply have not made up their mind or that they lack enough information about an issue to have a decisive attitude.

The size of these three latitudes depends on **ego-involvement,** or how committed a person is to a particular idea. The more ego-involved an individual is, the more difficult it will be to change his or her attitudes, beliefs, or behaviors. If, for example, a person is an active member of the National Rifle Association (NRA) and has firm attitudes on the right to bear arms, he or she has a large latitude of rejection regarding any argument for gun control. Additionally, the latitude of noncommitment is small. This person is not unsure or undecided on this issue. If Sarah Brady, a gun control activist, had to address an audience made up of individuals who hold these attitudes, she would have difficulty delivering any messages that would fall into their latitudes of acceptance or noncommitment. The size of these latitudes would be an important consideration when planning the presentation.

Applying Social Judgment Theory

From this discussion of Social Judgment Theory, it should be evident that a speech topic on an extremely controversial issue such as abortion would be insurmountable in a public speaking course such as the one you are taking. On a topic such as this, your audience would have very decisive areas of acceptance and rejection and very small areas of noncommitment. On average, you have roughly seven minutes to make your presentation. It is impossible to change anyone's opinion on the topic within that time frame. Because the area of noncommitment is so small, there is just nowhere for an audience member to move.

On topics that are less controversial, it is important that you understand the attitudes of your audience and present a position that is close to their attitude of acceptance. For example, if you and your audience both agree that we need more social activities on campus, but disagree on how to pay for the programs, start where you agree and slowly move to points where you disagree. Don't start right off the bat pushing for a position where you know there is disagreement. Start in the latitude of acceptance, and slowly move to areas of noncommitment.

Now that we understand all of this theory surrounding persuasion, we'll discuss how to take all of these ideas and turn them into meaningful and effective presentations.

Organizing the Persuasive Speech

This section is designed to help you organize your persuasive presentation. It presents each of the three types of persuasive speeches and discusses the appropriate way to organize each type.

Presentations Concerning Questions of Fact

If you decide to deliver a speech targeting an audience's beliefs, you will be giving a speech regarding a question of fact. Persuasive speeches regarding **questions of fact** are concerned with what is true or false, what happened or did not happen, or what exists or does not exist. If you think about it for a moment, there are very few questions for which we have

> Persuasive speeches regarding questions of fact are concerned with what is true or false, what happened or did not happen, or what exists or does not exist.

definitive answers. We know, for example, that it is 190 miles from West Lafayette, Indiana, to Louisville, Kentucky. We know that Ford makes the Explorer SUV. These are simple questions to which we have concrete answers. Everyone would agree that these are true. There are other questions of fact, however, that are not so easily answered but are often debated. Consider the following examples:

- Do other intelligent life-forms exist?
- Did Lee Harvey Oswald act alone?
- Was Princess Diana's death an accident?
- Does eating a low-calorie diet lengthen the lifespan?

We have no definitive answers to any of the preceding questions. There are many experts who believe that Lee Harvey Oswald acted alone in shooting President John F. Kennedy, and many experts who believe that he did not. We have no definitive answer to this question. We might have a definitive answer at some point in the future, but right now, we do not know for certain. Questions of fact surround a controversy. It is important to remember that if there is no controversy surrounding your claim, you are not delivering a persuasive presentation concerning a question of fact.

Organizing the Presentation

The speech regarding a question of fact can be organized in many different ways. The most common way is the topical design. Another design that is appropriate for presentations concerning questions of fact is the **causal pattern.** This particular pattern is most appropriate for those speeches where you are trying to establish a causal relationship between two variables.

Here is an example thesis statement that would follow the causal pattern of organization:

Specific Purpose   To persuade my audience that television causes attention deficit disorder in young children

Thesis Statement   Television viewing by young children affects neurological development and leads to attention deficit disorder in later years.

In this presentation, the speaker would need to argue that early exposure to television (the cause) leads to changes in brain chemistry that trigger attention deficit disorder (the effect).

Main Point One   Early exposure to television causes changes in brain chemistry.

Main Point Two   These changes in brain chemistry lead to disorders such as attention deficit disorder.

Another type of pattern to use when making a presentation regarding a question of fact is the refutative pattern. It is one of the most effective designs you can use when making a persuasive argument because it presents both sides of an argument along with a rebuttal of opposing ideas[16] (see this chapter's Spotlight on Research box for more information). While the topical and causal design patterns are appropriate for informative speaking as well, the refutative pattern is unique to persuasive speaking.

The **refutative pattern** seeks to accomplish two goals: to deflate the opposition's arguments and to bolster your own. To accomplish this task, you must point out flaws in the opponent's argument. He or she may have weak evidence or problems in reasoning, and it is important that you point those out to your audience. The key to using this design successfully is a clear understanding of the opponent's position. You must have a thorough understanding of his or her purpose, arguments, and evidence.

The refutative pattern is particularly effective when addressing an audience that is hostile or unfavorable to your position. The design works with hostile audiences because you acknowledge your opponent's arguments first and then show the weaknesses in those arguments before presenting your own position.

There are four steps in the refutative pattern:

Step 1   State the argument you are going to refute.

Step 2   State and list the errors of the opposing argument. At this step, you must present facts, figures, examples, and/or testimony to support your refutation.

Step 3   State and deliver evidence to support your alternative argument. Again, at this step, you must present evidence that the audience will find credible and persuasive in order to support your position.

Step 4   Explain how your argument or position disputes that of the opposition.

These steps can be arranged in many different ways within the body of your presentation. Let's look at one way a student organized her arguments for a classroom presentation:

Main Point One   According to the Atkins Center, high-protein diets contribute to weight loss, and therefore, to good health and disease prevention.

1. Individuals who follow these diet plans do lose weight in the short term by eating high-protein foods, which lowers their caloric intake. (Explain the basics of the diet.)
2. While individuals will lose weight in the short term, they are unlikely to continue with these diets for the long term and quickly return to unhealthy eating patterns.
3. A diet high in protein and low in fruits and carbohydrates is risky even in the short term, and recent research shows it can lead to diseases such as diabetes, heart disease, and kidney disease. (Cite some of the recent studies.)
4. When we examine the recent research on healthy eating, it becomes obvious that high-protein diets will not lead to good health or disease prevention.

Main Point Two   To reach optimum health through healthy eating, one must make lifestyle changes.

1. Lifestyle changes, not high-protein diets, lead to prolonged weight loss. (Cite some of the recent research.)
2. Fruits, vegetables, and whole grains are the optimal base for a healthy diet and have been shown to lead to a decrease in diseases such as diabetes and heart problems. (Again, cite some of the research.)
3. As you can see, adopting and maintaining a healthy lifestyle change by eating a well-balanced diet is the road to better nutrition.

In this design, the student combined steps 1 and 2 in the first main point and steps 3 and 4 in the second main point. She addressed the opposition's arguments and showed why they are flawed. There are other combinations that could have worked. You could take each of the four steps and make each a main point. There is flexibility in how you arrange the four steps. As long as all the steps are included for all of the arguments you are refuting, you will be in good shape.

Presentations Concerning Questions of Value

The persuasive presentation concerning a question of value involves the audience's attitudes on a particular topic. **Questions of value** argue that positions are good or bad, ethical or unethical, moral or immoral, or right or wrong. Here are some examples of questions of value:

- Is hunting unethical?
- Is bullfighting inhumane?
- Is solar energy the ideal form of power?
- Is the space program a good use of taxpayer money?

One important key to handling a question of value effectively is to remember that questions of value are not opinions. Simply stating, "I think solar power is wonderful," is an opinion. This is your opinion, and no one will question you

> **Questions of value argue that positions are good or bad, ethical or unethical, moral or immoral, or right or wrong.**

about it. You do not have to supply supporting evidence for your opinion. If, however, you make the claim, "Solar power is the ideal form of power," you have gone beyond stating your personal opinion and are now making a claim about a question of value.

When you go beyond personal opinion, you must justify your claim through the use of supporting evidence. You must build a case for your position. One way to build the case for your position is to set the standards for the claim you are making. For example, what makes an ideal power source? Define those standards first. Then show how solar power meets those standards.

Organizing the Presentation

Persuasive presentations on questions of value are usually organized topically. If you have a topic that requires you to set a standard against which to judge your argument, you will want to begin by laying out your standards. The second main point demonstrates how your argument measures up against the standards you have set. The following is an example of a speech positing that solar power is the ideal form of power:

Specific Purpose   To persuade my audience that solar energy is the ideal form of power.

Thesis Statement   Solar power is the ideal form of power because it is clean, cost effective, and sustainable.

Main Point One   An ideal form of power should meet the following criteria:

1. It should be clean.
2. It should be cost effective.
3. It should be sustainable.

Main Point Two   Solar energy meets all of these criteria for an ideal form of power.

1. Solar energy produces no by-products that pollute the environment, making it the cleanest form of power currently available.
2. Current advancements in solar panel construction have radically increased solar panel efficiency, making them more cost effective than they have been in the past.
3. Unlike other fuels, solar power relies on a source of energy that will not be exhausted over time and through use.

You do not always have to follow the guidelines of setting up your criteria in the first main point and using the second main point to demonstrate how your claim meets the criteria. The following is another way you might organize a speech of value:

Specific Purpose   To persuade my audience that denying Syrian refugees asylum is unethical.

Thesis Statement   Denying Syrian refugees sanctuary in the U.S. is wrong because it is both inhumane and contrary to core values established by the founding framers of the U.S.

Main Point One   Syrians face extreme physical danger due to the civil war in their country.

Main Point Two   As U.S. citizens, we are ethically bound to provide refuge to the "poor and huddled masses yearning to breathe free."

It is important to keep in mind that a speech of value may often be the catalyst that moves people to action. If someone is moved by your presentation on the unethical nature of hunting to get involved in an organization such as People for the Ethical Treatment of Animals (PETA), it is just the end result of your speech. Presentations on questions of value only argue the right and wrong of a particular issue. They do not concern themselves with what should or should not be done. Once you ask your audience to do something, you have targeted a behavior and crossed the line between questions of value and policy. Make sure that if your assignment asks you to make a persuasive presentation on a question of value, you stick to that goal. Do not make the mistake of asking your audience to take action. The action step moves you into questions of policy, which we discuss next.

Presentations Concerning Questions of Policy

The persuasive presentation concerning a **question of policy** targets behaviors, or what we should or should not be doing—as an individual, a community, or even a nation. Here are some examples of questions of policy:

⊚   Should we ban smoking in all public buildings, including restaurants and bars?

⊚   Should physical education be mandatory at every grade level in our nation's schools?

⊚   Should our community engage in curbside recycling?

⊚   Should the United States change its immigration policies?

When we think about making a persuasive presentation, most of us think about speeches on questions of policy. We usually want to persuade someone or a group of people to do something related to some policy. We might want them to vote for our candidate for homecoming court, protest a recent Purdue administration decision, or take up exercising. If you are trying to get your audience to do something, you are talking about a question of policy.

It is important to note that questions of policy almost always include questions of fact or value. While the question of policy is the primary goal of the presentation, secondary attention has to be paid to questions of fact or value. Remember, attitudes and beliefs underlie behaviors, so they may need to be addressed in order to reach a behavioral goal or policy change. Questions of policy, however, always go beyond questions of fact and value and advocate that something should or should not be done.

When making a speech concerning a question of policy, pay careful attention to the **need, plan,** and **practicality** of the proposals being presented.[17] First of all, you must demonstrate to your audience that there is a problem or a need for your proposed policy. Why should we ban smoking in all public buildings in our community? You must present evidence

> The persuasive presentation concerning a question of policy targets behaviors, or what we should or should not be doing—as an individual, a community, or even a nation.

to show that smoking in public buildings is a problem for individuals in your community. The evidence you present must be compelling enough to convince your audience that some change in policy should be adopted.

Sometimes, you are trying to change a policy, and other times, you might be arguing that a policy should remain the same. In other words, you are simply reinforcing the attitude that the current policy is adequate or reasonable. Consider the following topic: "The United States should not change its immigration policies." In this speech, you would argue that changing the current policies would cause more harm than good and advocate that the United States continue doing what it is already doing. You are still advocating a course of action.

In addition to convincing your audience that a problem or need exists, you must also demonstrate that you have a clear plan that will address the cause or causes of the problem. You must convince your audience that your solution will be able to alleviate the problem.

> **When making a speech concerning a question of policy, pay careful attention to the need, plan, and practicality of the proposals.**

Once you have established a need to change current policy and presented your plan or solution, you must demonstrate that your plan is practical. Although you may have done an incredible job of convincing audience members that there is a problem with current policy, unless you can also persuade them that your solution for alleviating the problem is feasible, you will be unsuccessful. The bottom line is that audience members want to believe your plan is workable. But they must believe that your plan will alleviate problems without causing new ones. While you may propose a wonderful plan to clean up the Wabash River, the price tag associated with your proposal might be too much for the community to absorb. The expense of the proposal could create problems in other areas for the community, such as tax increases and cutbacks in other community-funded programs.

Order of Arguments

One of the most common questions students ask is which argument should be put first and which last. Should I spring my strongest argument on my audience first (primacy effect) or wait until the very end to use my strongest evidence (recency effect)? The research at this time is inconclusive. However, one thing is for certain: Never sandwich your best or strongest piece of evidence in the middle of your presentation. It is better to end or begin with a bang.

One aspect to consider is the situation in which you are speaking. If you know that you are likely to run out of time during the presentation, do not save your best argument for the end of the presentation because you may not get to it. In a situation where time is limited and you are worried about your ability to finish the presentation, use your strongest evidence or argument first so that you can adequately explain and present that material. However, if you know that you will have plenty of time to address all of the points of your presentation, you may be able to build to your strongest piece of evidence.

You should also think about how motivated audience members are to process the arguments you will present. If they are less motivated, their attention may wane as the presentation continues, so you may want to present your strongest argument first. As with every stage in the process of developing a presentation, you must consider the situation and audience when making these types of decisions.[18]

Sometimes, when speaking on a question of policy, a speaker's only goal is to get an audience to agree that, indeed, a change in policy does need to be made. However, the speaker may not be asking anything else from the audience. In this case, the speaker is seeking passive agreement. **Passive agreement** is gaining acceptance for your position from audience members without asking them to take action. Perhaps, you persuade your audience that a change needs to be made, but you don't suggest what that change should be. Alternatively, you might seek to gain agreement from your audience, but that may be all you are seeking. You don't want audience members to take any further action. If this is the case, you are seeking passive agreement.

Sometimes, a speaker is seeking more than just passive agreement. That is, a speaker is asking for more than just an agreement that the proposed policy change should be made. The speaker seeks what we call active agreement. **Active agreement** requires both agreement and action on the part of the audience. In this case, the speaker needs the audience to get involved in order to achieve the change in policy. Perhaps the speaker asks audience members to sign a petition, buy a raffle ticket, vote for a proposition in an upcoming election, or sign a donor registration card. Regardless of the behavior the speaker advocates, the audience is being asked for more than just agreement. The audience has to become actively involved to achieve the ultimate goal of the presentation.

Organizing the Presentation

There are many ways to organize presentations concerning questions of policy. The problem-solution and the problem-cause-solution designs are organizational schemes for the presentation regarding the speech of policy. The following is an example of the **problem-solution** speech structure.

Specific Purpose   To persuade my audience that action is needed to deal with the problems created by ineffective design and placement of street and road signs in Lafayette.

Thesis Statement   Ineffective design and placement of street signs in Lafayette causes many traffic problems in our city, and there are steps we can take to improve the situation.

Main Point One   The ineffective design and placement of street and road signs in Lafayette is very dangerous. (This is the problem.)

1. It is estimated that nearly one-third to one-half of all street signs in Lafayette are missing.
2. More than one-half of the street signs in Lafayette are not clearly legible.
3. Many local accidents are a result of mistakes drivers make due to ineffective or absent signs.

Main Point Two   The problem with our road signs can be solved in a three-step process. (This is the solution.)

1. First, all of the road signs in Lafayette must be replaced with signs that meet national safety recommendations.
2. Second, the road signs must be relocated to appropriate locations within intersections.
3. Finally, missing signs must be replaced.

The **problem-cause-solution** design simply adds a third step. After outlining the problem, you add a second main point, which lays out the causes of the problem. The final or third main point in this design is the solution. The design looks like this: Main point 1, the problem; main point 2, the causes of the problem; and main point 3, the solution. I have found that when speakers use the problem-cause-solution design, their solutions are often more practical. Addressing the causes helps ensure that you propose a solution that is more feasible. This arrangement usually results in a tighter overall argument. The following is a brief example of an outline using the problem-cause-solution design:

Specific Purpose   To persuade audience members that they should recycle as a way of combating the waste disposal problem in our area.

Thesis Statement   Our landfills are overflowing, and our failure to recycle is exacerbating this issue.

Main Point One   Waste disposal is a significant problem. (This is the problem.)

Main Point Two   Why isn't our community recycling? (This is the underlying cause or causes.)

1. There is a lack of knowledge about current recycling programs.
2. Another reason has to do with the inconvenience of recycling.

Main Point Three   There is an easy two-part solution that will make recycling both easier and more convenient. (This is the solution.)

1. First, we need to implement promotional campaigns that clarify proper recycling procedures.
2. Second, city sanitation departments must be expanded to provide curbside pickup and their hours must be increased.

> **Monroe's motivated sequence provides a design to organize the entire presentation.**

In addition to these options is Monroe's motivated sequence, an adapted version of the problem-solution design. It was created at Purdue University by Professor Alan Monroe in the 1930s and is still prominently used in marketing and advertising today. **Monroe's motivated sequence** is primarily used when a speaker wants to move an audience to immediate action. While all of the other organizational patterns presented in your textbook have provided ways to organize the main points of a presentation, the motivated sequence provides a design to organize the entire presentation. There are five steps in this pattern: attention, need, satisfaction, visualization, and action.

Step 1: Attention

This step is exactly like the first step in any other presentation you make. You must gain the audience's attention. You can accomplish this through a variety of strategies.

Step 2: Need

Once you have grabbed your audience's attention, you then must convince audience members that there is a need for change. You must persuade them that the current product, policy, or candidate (for example) is problematic. You establish this need through the use of evidence. It is important that you have conducted a thorough audience analysis so that you can use the type of evidence that will convince your target audience that a need exists.

Step 3: Satisfaction

Now that you have generated a sense of need in audience members, you provide them with your solution, or satisfaction, to this need. Explain your plan. Remember, it is important at this point in the presentation that you demonstrate to your audience that the plan you are proposing is practical.

Step 4: Visualization

At this point, ask your audience to visualize your plan. You want to paint a mental picture of the solution. You want to show audience members the benefits of enacting your solution and the consequences if they do not. You must also be able to demonstrate to audience members how they will benefit directly from your proposed solution.

Step 5: Action

Once you have convinced audience members that there is a need, and you have proposed a workable solution, it is time to call them to action. Tell audience members exactly what they need to do and how to do it in order to ensure the activation of your plan. If you want them to send an e-mail to their representative, provide the e-mail address. If you want them to write a letter to the city commissioner, provide the address. If you want them to vote in the upcoming election, give details about where and when to vote. The clearer and easier you make the action step, the more likely your audience will respond to your call for action.[19] This means using a visual aid to reinforce the address, phone number, and so on. It is insufficient to deliver these types of small details without the use of a visual aid. You really need that added impact. Finally, end the speech with a resounding appeal to action that will motivate your audience to get involved.

Using Monroe's Motivated Sequence

Introduction

I.   Attention step
II. Credibility statement
III. Relevance statement
IV. Thesis statement

Transition

Body

MPI: Need step

Transition

MPII: Satisfaction step

Transition

MPIII: Visualization step

Transition

Conclusion

I.   Restate thesis
II. Action step

Here is an example of an abbreviated speech that utilizes Monroe's motivated sequence. Although it is not noted here, you must have all of the elements of the introduction and the conclusion that are required for any presentation.

Introduction

1. **Attention:** Have you ever dreamed about being a hero or heroine? Have you ever wished you could do something great, something that would really make a difference in our world? I'm here to tell you, you can, if you're willing to give just three hours a week. (Put the rest of the elements of the introduction in here.)

Body

2. **Need:** Our community needs volunteers to help take care of homeless and abandoned animals. The Humane Society of Lafayette has a program designed to care for these pets, but only volunteers can make the program work. The program needs at least 80 volunteers. At this point, we only have 58.

3. **Satisfaction:** Volunteering at the Humane Society will help to ensure that this worthwhile program continues and flourishes. Being involved in this program will also make you a hero in the eyes of some neglected animal.

4. **Visualization:** Maybe you can have an experience that will be as rewarding as mine has been. Last year I worked with a four-year-old black Labrador mix. Her name was Reba, and two afternoons each week, I bathed her and took her for a walk. She had been abandoned by her previous owners when they vacated their apartment. When I started volunteering at the shelter, she was extremely shy and nervous. But a couple of months after my visits began, she started to exhibit quite a personality. This program was remarkable. Not only was I able to help Reba adapt to her new environment and learn some important social skills, but I received the benefit of having a pet in my life. In my current situation, I can't have a pet of my own. Reba was eventually adopted by a loving family, and I have to think that some of my love and attention enabled her to make that transition more easily. But what would have happened to Reba if I had not volunteered and the program could not continue?

Conclusion

5. **Call for Action:** Won't you join me and become one of the unsung heroines or heroes at the Humane Society? You can make a difference in just one or two afternoons each week. I've got the applications with me and will be waiting for you to sign up after class. There are many animals at the shelter that need a little love and companionship while they wait for the right family. Won't you help make a difference?

Conclusion

Although persuasion is something that we engage in every day, it is a very complex process. Persuasive presentations ask the audience to choose between two or more alternatives, demand a thorough analysis of the audience, make more demands of the audience, and have a higher ethical threshold than informative speaking.

To be effective, the persuasive speech must have a strong sense of purpose. The persuasive process begins with an understanding of what you are going to target in a persuasive attempt–attitude, belief, or behavior–and what your goal is, whether changing, creating, or reinforcing that target. Once this decision has been made, you must determine whether your presentation concerns a question of fact, value, or policy and organize it accordingly. Additionally, you will want to consider other persuasive factors, such as speaker credibility and message characteristics.

Key Terms

Active agreement

Attitude

Behavior

Belief

Causal pattern

Central route

Changing

Creating

Decision rules

Ego-involvement

Elaboration

Elaboration Likelihood Model (ELM)

Goals

Latitude of acceptance

Latitude of noncommitment

Latitude of rejection

Monroe's motivated sequence

Need

Passive agreement

Peripheral route

Persuasion

Plan

Practicality

Primacy effect

Problem-cause-solution

Problem-solution

Questions of fact

Questions of policy

Questions of value

Recency effect

Refutative pattern

Reinforce

Social Judgment Theory

Target

CHAPTER 10

Strategies for Persuasive Presentations

Objectives

After reading this chapter, you should be able to

- ◎ explain the role of ethos, logos, and pathos in presentational speaking;
- ◎ define the differences between initial credibility, derived credibility, and terminal credibility;
- ◎ define reasoning from deduction, and explain tips for using it effectively;
- ◎ define reasoning from induction, and explain tips for using it effectively;
- ◎ define analogical reasoning, and explain guidelines for using it effectively;
- ◎ define causal reasoning, and explain guidelines for using it effectively; and
- ◎ discuss ethical considerations of using emotional appeals.

During the writing of this book, the U.S. was in the middle of a contentious presidential election. Businessman, Donald Trump was one of the more exciting candidates vying for the position. He was outspoken and his rhetoric was not characteristic of previous U.S. presidential candidates. After a particular challenging debate on the FOX network, Trump took aim at one of the moderators, Megyn Kelly. Trump argued that Megyn unfairly attacked him and posed unfair questions. He took his grievances to social media where he attacked Megyn. Here are a few examples of the things Trump said via Twitter:

◎ "The bimbo is back in town. I hope not for long."

◎ "She has come back looking like Nancy Grace."

◎ "Can't watch Crazy Megyn anymore."

Trump was extremely upset over the way he believes Megyn unfairly treated him in the debates. He has continued to yell insults and attack Megyn instead of focusing just on those issues that are relevant to his complaint. The name calling he has engaged in has taken away from the focus of his original complaint and made the ensuing dialog less than presidential.

Donald Trump engaged in what is called an *argument ad hominem* which is addressed in more detail later in this chapter. This is a fallacy or an error in reasoning. Trump attacked the person-in this case, Megyn Kelly-instead of keeping his criticisms to her journalistic abilities. By attacking the speaker rather than the argument, Donald Trump diverted the conversation away from the real issue to the character of the person, which was not relevant in this case. The use of an argument ad hominem typically reflects more negatively on the speaker than the person being attacked. It raises issues of credibility for the speaker. It is often viewed as a "cheap" way to make an argument. The use of such a fallacy can undermine one's potential for continued effective debate and ultimately may impede Trump's pursuit of this office.

This chapter provides you with the skills and strategies to engage in more fruitful and productive debates. If you follow the guidelines and practice these strategies, hopefully, you won't find yourself in the position of using fallacious reasoning. The chapter is designed to help you examine the various types of appeals that you have at your disposal when presenting a persuasive presentation. Often, we look for that magic bullet that will ensure our persuasive attempts are successful. But, there is no magic bullet or easy solution. Persuasion is a process. The strategies discussed in this chapter play a big part in that process. Solid reasoning, effective use of emotion, and credibility can make the difference between an effective persuasive attempt and an ineffective attempt, if you know how to implement them well. Appeals alone aren't magic bullets, but they may be the thing to push your presentation to the next level. This chapter discusses the art of using appeals and some strategies for implementing them successfully.

Ethos, Logos, and Pathos

The strategies of reasoning rely on three appeals. According to the Greek philosopher Aristotle, in his book *Rhetoric*,[1] these appeals include: appeals to ethos or credibility, logos or logic, and pathos or emotion. Although Aristotle lived in another time far removed from the society we live in today, these three appeals continue to guide the communication strategies we use in the modern world. We use these three appeals in all types of speaking, but they become even more important when delivering persuasive presentations. In this chapter, we examine each of these three types of appeals.

Using Ethos in Your Presentation

According to Aristotle, **ethos** refers to the credibility of a speaker. **Credibility** results from audience members' perceptions about the believability of a speaker. Credibility is made up of two factors: expertise and trustworthiness.[2] Speakers are judged as demonstrating **expertise** if they appear experienced, informed, trained, qualified, skilled, and intelligent. According to persuasion researcher Dan O'Keefe, all of these dimensions are concerned with one central question: Is the speaker in a position to know the truth or what is right or wrong about a particular topic? If so, we will find the speaker high in expertise.

Trustworthiness is determined by assessing a speaker's honesty, open-mindedness, sense of justice, fairness, and unselfishness.[3] Ultimately, the audience is asking the question: Is the speaker telling the truth as he or she knows it? If the audience believes so, the speaker is deemed trustworthy.

As discussed in other chapters, your credibility is in the eye of your audience. It is the perception audience members have about your credibility on a particular topic, and it can greatly affect how they react to your presentation. Will they listen attentively, or will they take what you have to say with a grain of salt? Your perceived credibility can have a profound impact on how your audience approaches your presentation.

> ## Tips For Enhancing Ethos
>
> ◎ Use strong evidence.
> ◎ Establish common ground with the audience.
> ◎ Be upfront about goals.
> ◎ Use an appropriate delivery style.

It is important to keep in mind that credibility can vary from situation to situation and from audience to audience. Credibility is the audience's perception of a speaker, and so it will vary greatly, depending on the situation. You may have great credibility with your classroom audience as a speaker on nanotechnology. After all, you are an undergraduate engineering student working in the lab of a professor involved in cutting-edge research on the topic. If you delivered a similar presentation to an audience made up of professors pursuing lines of research in the area of nanotechnology, your credibility would be questionable.

Similarly, while you may be extremely qualified and competent to deliver a presentation on one topic, you may not be qualified to deliver a presentation on another topic. For example, Anderson Cooper, a well-respected national news anchor, is well qualified to deliver a presentation to an audience on the media coverage of Iraq. We would be less likely to find Anderson Cooper competent to deliver a presentation on gracious entertaining; however, we would find Martha Stewart competent to deliver that presentation.

> ... Credibility changes from topic to topic and audience to audience, but it also changes during a presentation.

As you have seen, credibility changes from topic to topic and audience to audience, but it also changes during a presentation. There are three types of credibility that help describe the changes to a speaker's credibility during a presentation.[4] **Initial credibility** refers to the credibility a speaker has before he or she begins the presentation. This information may be publicized by posters listing a speaker's credentials. If you are introduced by someone, he or she will usually list your qualifications. You can also explain your own competence in the introduction of your presentation (see Chapter 4). So, before you even begin your presentation, your audience has already formed an attitude about how credible you will be on the topic you will address.

Derived credibility results from the actual messages you present during your presentation. Obviously, what you say or do during the presentation has a great impact on your credibility. While you may have had extremely high initial credibility, you can do things during the actual presentation that erode your credibility. Likewise, you can start a presentation with low initial credibility and, through the use of strong reasoning, effective delivery, and strong organization, achieve high credibility in the eyes of your audience.

Terminal credibility refers to the credibility of the speaker at the end of the presentation. So, if you have applied the strategies discussed in this section successfully, you may arrive at the end of your presentation with even more credibility than when you began. Don't underestimate the importance of your credibility. It can have a dramatic effect on the success of a presentation. Terminal credibility is important because it establishes the credibility you have going into future presentations. In other words, the terminal credibility in one presentation affects the initial credibility in your next presentation. So, giving a poor presentation affects your credibility as a whole.

Credibility is a big factor in persuasive speaking.

Tips for Enhancing Ethos

How can you establish credibility during your presentation? First and foremost, use strong evidence. You want to use evidence from respected sources.[5] Supporting evidence from less-than-legitimate sources won't do much to bolster your credibility. Analyze your audience and ask yourself, "What types of sources will this particular audience respect?" Use those sources. Research shows that failure to cite sources explicitly affects the credibility of the material and, potentially, the speaker.[6] You may have to vary supporting material depending on the particular audience you are addressing. You also want to ensure that your supporting evidence is timely. Outdated evidence will limit your ability to achieve your goals.

Second, you want to establish common ground with your audience. As we discussed in Chapter 2, you never want to alienate an audience. If you start off by attacking the position your audience holds, you won't get very far. Begin by showing similarities between you and your audience, and then move to areas where you may experience controversy. You want to demonstrate respect for your audience. This enhances liking for you as the speaker and is important in enhancing your character as a speaker.

Third, being upfront about your goals as a speaker goes a long way toward building your trustworthiness. It does nothing for your credibility as a speaker to have a hidden agenda.

Finally, using an appropriate delivery style will also enhance audience perception of your competence. A fluent vocal delivery is extremely important. Make sure your vocal style is free from any vocal disfluencies. Vocal pauses such as "um," "uh," and so on diminish the credibility of a speaker.[7] Wearing appropriate attire can also affect your credibility.[8] Review the guidelines on dressing appropriately in Chapter 11.

Using Logos in Your Presentation

Logos refers to logic and appeals to an individual's intelligence. You incorporate logos into your presentations by using arguments or reasoning. We build strong arguments by gathering supporting evidence, organizing solid arguments, and using reasoning to explain how that evidence supports the claims we are making. To be effective, you must ask yourself, "How does this piece of evidence support my main point?" "How can I make this connection evident to my audience?" Answering these questions is essentially reasoning.

This chapter discusses four types of reasoning: deductive reasoning, inductive reasoning, analogical reasoning, and causal reasoning. You choose the type of reasoning that best fits the evidence you have collected.

Deductive Reasoning

Deductive reasoning or a deductive argument starts with a widely accepted principle and draws a conclusion about a specific case. It moves from the general to the specific and takes the form of the syllogism. All of you have probably heard the following famous syllogism:

Major Premise   All persons are mortal.

Minor Premise   Socrates is a person.

Conclusion   Therefore, Socrates is mortal.

Syllogisms, or deductive arguments, consist of three parts: a major premise, a minor premise, and a conclusion. The **major premise** is a general statement that is widely accepted. The **minor premise** is a specific observation about a case and demonstrates that it fits within the general principle. The **conclusion** is a statement that claims that your general principle applies to your specific observation or minor premise.

Major Premise   Artificial sweeteners are unhealthy.

Minor Premise   Diet soft drinks contain artificial sweeteners.

Conclusion   Therefore, diet soft drinks are unhealthy.

Tips for Using Deductive Arguments

Deductive arguments are very powerful. If the major and minor premises are true, then the conclusion will naturally follow. Therefore, a deductive argument is an extremely strong type of argument. In order to ensure that your audience will

> **As a speaker, you have to determine how widely accepted the major and minor premises of your arguments are.**

buy your conclusion, you must ensure that your audience accepts your major and minor premises. As a speaker, you have to determine how widely accepted the major and minor premises of your argument are. Will your particular audience members accept them? If not, you will have to present evidence to persuade them. Your argument will only be successful if audience members agree with your major and minor premises. If they fail to accept them, you will not convince your audience.

Let's examine the deductive argument in the previous example. Will all audiences hold the attitude that artificial sweeteners are unhealthy? Probably not. It would take some persuasion on your part to get your audience to buy your major premise. First, you would want to examine some of the FDA-approved artificial sweeteners. Let's examine one of these: aspartame. Then you would have to present proof that aspartame poses potential health threats. You could use the following evidence: According to a 2006 article published in the journal *Environmental Health Perspectives,* aspartame has been linked to malignant tumors, lymphomas, and leukemias in mice. There are 164 studies examining the health risks of aspartame that appear in the database Medline. Ninety of these studies were independent studies, and 83% of those found aspartame to be unsafe. Seventy-four of the studies were industry-sponsored studies, meaning that the aspartame industry funded the studies, and 100% of those studies demonstrated no negative health risks. You would continue to explain what that meant to your audience.

Tips For Using Deductive Reasoning

◎ Support your major premise.
◎ Support your minor premise.
◎ Make the conclusion explicit.

You would continue to show examples such as these that link the sweetener to negative health outcomes. Then do the same for each of the other types of artificial sweeteners you decide to address. Hopefully, after presenting all of this evidence, your audience will buy or agree with your major premise.

Now you need to examine your minor premise. Quickly demonstrate for your audience that the major diet sodas contain these artificial sweeteners. Again, give examples of which sweeteners are in which sodas and in what quantities. If audience members accept your major premise and your minor premise, they will buy your conclusion as well.

> **Even though the conclusion will naturally follow in a deductive argument, explicitly state it for your audience.**

Even though the conclusion will naturally follow in a deductive argument, explicitly state it for your audience.[9] Research on persuasive messages has demonstrated again and again that persuasion is more likely when the conclusions of the argument are spelled out for the audience.[10]

Inductive Reasoning

Inductive reasoning is the opposite of deductive reasoning. Instead of starting with a widely accepted principle, you start with individual cases and draw a conclusion that applies to all of the cases you examined. For example:

◎ Horse number 1 has hooves.
◎ Horse number 2 has hooves.
◎ Horse number 3 has hooves.
◎ Horse number 10 has hooves.
◎ Conclusion: All horses have hooves.

We typically use induction when we cannot examine every case that exists, but we want to make a conclusion about an entire category. For example, while at Purdue you won't have every teaching assistant as an instructor, you may have experiences with several. Based on your experiences, you might draw a conclusion about all teaching assistants at Purdue. We make decisions based on inductive reasoning all the time. Think about how you choose the courses you take. You ask several people who have taken a course for their assessment. Based on their comments, you draw a conclusion about the course. Then you decide if you will take it or not.

Harris delivered a speech on the health benefits of coffee. He offered several examples of studies that indicated coffee was healthy. He used these examples to support his conclusion that coffee was a healthy beverage. This is an example of an inductive argument:

> Coffee has many health benefits. As noted in a 2011 article published in the journal BMC Cancer coffee drinkers have a lower associated risk of several types of cancers.[11] Coffee drinkers can also lower their risk of type 2 diabetes according to an article in a 2005 issue of JAMA.[12] And finally, coffee drinkers also lower their risks for Parkinson's disease and some liver diseases (Geriatrics & Gerontology International, 2014 & Liver International, 2014).[13, 14]

Tips for Using Induction

Inductive arguments can be persuasive if you use them well. First, you must make sure you have enough examples of specific cases to draw your conclusion. Drawing a conclusion when your sample size is too small is called a **hasty generalization.** Audiences won't be persuaded by arguments based on small sample sizes. How many samples or examples are enough? That is hard to answer. You must analyze each speaking situation and make that decision as you prepare for different audiences and occasions. Some audiences will be convinced from only a few cases, while others will want a good deal of evidence before buying your conclusion. It just depends on the knowledge and attitudes of a given audience.

Second, you must ensure that the cases you present are typical. If you have cited evidence that seems out of the ordinary, your audience will unlikely be convinced by your argument. If you feel that your cases are atypical, further support your argument by offering some statistics. This will bolster your argument and will probably be more convincing for your audience.

Audiences won't be persuaded by arguments based on small sample sizes.

Third, be careful how strong you make your conclusion. Remember, inductive reasoning is based on probability. You will never be able to examine every case in a given category. Therefore, refrain from presenting your conclusion to your audience as if it were a fact. You may want to qualify your argument. It may not be as powerful, but it is truthful.

Analogical Reasoning

Analogical reasoning is reasoning by comparison. You compare two similar cases and argue that what is true about one is also true about the other. Analogical reasoning is well suited for presentations concerning issues of policy. When advocating solutions, it is easy

Tips For Using Inductive Reasoning

- ◎ Provide multiple examples.
- ◎ Present typical examples.
- ◎ Qualify your conclusion.

to use analogical arguments to compare two policies. For example, a COM114 group presentation argued that Purdue needed an updated public transportation system. Group members described the public transportation system used at the University of Kansas and showed how that system would be a solution to the transportation problems undergraduates face at Purdue. What worked for the University of Kansas would also work for Purdue.

Tips for Using Arguments by Analogy

> **The key to using analogical reasoning well is to make sure the two things you are comparing are similar in important ways.**

The key to using analogical reasoning well is to make sure the two things you are comparing are similar in important ways. Are the University of Kansas and Purdue similar in important ways? Are they roughly the same size? Are the transportation needs of the student populations similar? Are they both state-supported universities? Answers to these and other questions are important to examine. If audience members don't consider the two things you are comparing similar, then they won't be persuaded by your argument. Making an analogical argument about two issues that are not similar in important ways is called an **invalid analogy.**

Consider the following analogical argument:

> NBC has been selling episodes of sitcoms on iTunes, a popular music downloading site. NBC's programming is receiving increased attention, and the downloads are generating large revenues. We should do the same thing with some of the programming on the Boiler Network. This would be a great way to generate revenue for Purdue.

We simply cannot assume that we would generate the same effects from downloads of our local programming or that iTunes would even be interested in disseminating our products. A local station and a national station are unlike in important ways. What works for one will more than likely not work for the other.

One important issue concerning arguments by analogy is related to medical research. Some of the research concerning health claims is conducted on animal models. It is important that you disclose this information to your audience so that they can determine if they believe that conclusion transfers to humans.

Causal Reasoning

Causal reasoning attempts to establish a relationship between two events, such that one of the events caused or led to the other event. We engage in causal reasoning every day. We try to explain what caused the football team to lose its last game, or what caused your roommate to lose his or her job. Although we use causal reasoning every day, it isn't as simple as it seems. Proving that one event caused another is difficult to do. We generally consider two events causally related if the following three conditions are met: First, the cause must precede the event in time.

Conditions For Causality

- ◎ The cause precedes the event in time.
- ◎ There is an empirical correlation between the events.
- ◎ The relationship is not caused by a third event.

Second, there is an empirical correlation between the events. This simply means that the two events move together. For example, generally, class attendance and course grade move together. As class attendance increases, so does course grade. Third, the relationship between the two events is not found to be the result of some third event.[15]

Imagine that your knee hurts before it rains, and you proclaim that your knee pain causes rain. Criterion 1 is satisfied: knee pain before rain. Every time your knee hurts, it rains. So, with criterion 2, these things move or happen together. Criterion 3 asserts the relationship between the two can't be caused by some outside variable. This example does not meet criterion 3. Your knee pain can be explained by the humidity that occurs prior to rain. The humidity associated with the incoming front causes the pain in your knee.

Tips for Using Causal Arguments

While the previous example may seem ridiculous, we often fall prey to this error in reasoning. Just because something occurs before something else doesn't mean the first event caused the second. While this is a necessary condition, it isn't sufficient. In fact, this mistake is so popular, there is even a fallacy named for it: **post hoc, ergo propter hoc** or "after this, therefore, because of this."

Another key to remember when making causal arguments is that events sometimes have more than one cause. Consider the following claim posed by a student in a presentation in this course. She argued that students in schools with music programs fared better on the ACT and SAT than students in schools with no music programs. She contended that these two events were causally related. It is obviously not that simple. Music programs are not direct causes of higher standardized test scores. Schools with music programs are usually in school districts that are well-funded. Students from higher socioeconomic groups go to well-funded schools. All of these factors (e.g., economic status, dollar per student spent, etc.) are contributors to higher standardized test scores. It isn't as simple as the student's speech suggested. Oversimplifying the relationship between two events may lead your audience to question your reasoning.

It is important to note that unless an experimental design is employed, that controls for a variety of factors, with a true control group, you cannot make a causal claim. Experimental designs with true controls groups are difficult to employ and a lot of research is unable to engage a control group. So, examine the studies that you cite and see if the methods they used were experimental before you make strong conclusions about causation.

There is no escaping causal reasoning. We engage in it every day. However, it is important for you to realize that events are rarely so simple. Acknowledging this fact in your presentation will be appreciated by your audience.

We rarely employ one type of argument in a persuasive attempt. Instead, we use them in combination. There is even evidence of this within the chapter. Take, for example, the deductive argument presented earlier in this section. The dangers of artificial sweeteners and cessation of diet soda consumption employed a deductive argument as the primary argument. However, the major and minor premises both needed additional support. In the example, induction and causal reasoning were used to support the major premise. To be persuasive, you need to use these arguments in combination.

Fallacies

Fallacies are errors in reasoning. You want to avoid fallacies in your presentation for two reasons. First, knowingly using fallacious reasoning is unethical, and second, it can hurt your credibility as a speaker. As a critical audience member, you want to be aware of fallacies when they are presented to you.

There are many types of fallacies. We have already examined some of them: hasty generalization; post hoc, ergo propter hoc; and invalid analogy. Other popular fallacies with which you should be familiar include argument ad hominem, bandwagon, slippery slope, false dilemma, straw person, and red herring.

Argument Ad Hominem

Argument ad hominem is a Latin phrase meaning "against the person." An **argument ad hominem** occurs when irrelevant personal attacks are made against a person or a group to which the person belongs instead of against the argument the person supports. Instead of attacking the argument an individual makes, a speaker attacks the person who made the claim, thereby diverting the attention of the audience from the real issue. Argument ad hominem is a popular fallacy in politics. Politicians often use this to divert attention from the real issue:

> Of course Senator Smith's proposal includes raising taxes. What else can you expect from a bleeding-heart liberal?

In this example, the speaker should address Senator Smith's proposal directly rather than call him a name. The focus has shifted from the issue to the character of the individual.

Politicians aren't the only ones who use argument ad hominems. In a recent editorial in the *Journal & Courier,* a citizen wrote "The first thing I would do is pave over illustrious Governor Give Indiana Away Mitch Daniels …." Calling former Governor Daniels names isn't going to help her win her argument. However, the writer of this editorial is obviously frustrated and has let her emotions get the best of her. When we become frustrated in an argument and allow our emotions to take over, many of us do resort to attacking someone's character, rather than their ideas. If you have a sibling, you probably have engaged in this type of fallacy during the heat of an argument!

Are issues of character ever relevant in argumentation? Is it ever ethical and/or effective to bring up an opponent's character? If the character attack is relevant to the issue at hand and it is delivered in a professional and respectful manner, it may be appropriate. Imagine the following situation: Doug, an individual in a fraternity, is running for the office of scholarship chairman. However, Doug has a GPA of 2.1. Does Doug's GPA become relevant? Probably so. How can someone with a low GPA be expected to lead the rest of the house to academic success if he himself has been unable to be successful? In this case, as long as his opponent brings this information up with respect, it is ethical. This character issue has a direct relationship to Doug's ability to do his job.

Bandwagon

The **bandwagon** fallacy assumes that because something is popular, it is right, or the best. A speaker may say that everybody else is doing it so you should too—just jump on the bandwagon. Advertisers use this fallacy all of the time. Just because one brand is more popular than another doesn't mean it is better.

Fazad used this fallacy in his presentation when he stated that AMD, the maker of a type of computer chip, had recently been shipping more of its processors to computer manufacturers than was Intel®, its competitor. Therefore, he concluded, AMD processors must be better. His conclusion was based on the fact that because AMD processors were more popular with computer manufacturers, they must be better. This isn't necessarily so; maybe they are just less expensive. Fazad needed to use additional evidence besides popularity to support this proposition of value.

You also see the bandwagon fallacy used by politicians. They use polls in a similar way. Just because 72% of the population approves of the job the mayor is doing on developing the riverfront doesn't mean the approach is correct. An evaluation of the development plan requires examination and comparison to other plans around the country. Just because something is popular doesn't make it right or wrong.

Slippery Slope

The **slippery slope** fallacy asserts that some action will inevitably lead to a chain of events that will end in a certain result. A speaker assumes that taking a step will ultimately lead to a second and third, on down the slope to an unwanted outcome. If a speaker claims that taking one step will inevitably lead to some disastrous outcome, then it is a slippery slope. For example:

> If we allow the university to build a new basketball arena, we will be increasing attention on athletics. Students will begin to study less, and they won't be as prepared for the job market. The entire reputation of the university will be at risk, and we will go down in the national rankings.

Reducing the university's ranking within public institutions is far removed from building a new basketball arena. It is highly unlikely that building a basketball arena will lead to this series of causal events.

False Dilemma

A **false dilemma,** also known as a false dichotomy, gives the audience a choice between two options when there are many more alternatives. It simplifies the situation when, in reality, the situation is rather complex. For example:

> We either raise tuition or close all computer labs on campus.

or

> We either create more community parks or juvenile delinquency rates will increase in our community.

We all know that both of these situations aren't that simple. There are a variety of ways to redistribute money on campus so that we can continue to fund the computer labs without raising tuition. Similarly, juvenile delinquency is dependent on a great many other factors than the number of recreation facilities available.

Straw Person

The **straw person** fallacy is committed when someone ignores or misrepresents a person's actual position and substitutes a weaker, distorted, or misrepresented version of that position, thereby making it easier to refute the opponent's position. For example:

> Anti-gun organizations want to revoke the Second Amendment, which allows citizens the right to bear arms.

In reality, most gun control organizations don't want to revoke the Second Amendment. They usually want to increase background checks, enforce waiting periods, and change regulations regarding gun registration. This is an overstatement of gun control advocates' actual position.

Red Herring

A **red herring** is a fallacy in which an irrelevant topic is inserted into the discussion to divert attention away from the real issue. The fallacy gets its name from English fox hunts. The farmers, in an effort to keep fox hunters and their hounds from running through their crops, would drag a smoked herring with a strong odor along the edge of their fields. This odor threw the dogs off the scent of the fox and kept them from destroying the farmers' crops. Here's an example of a red herring fallacy:

> The university wants to increase the math requirement in the freshman general education plan. How can we discuss general education requirements when parking is such an issue on this campus?

Politicians are often guilty of the red herring fallacy. To avoid controversial issues such as gun control, they often change the subject so that they will not have to answer a question on a potentially controversial issue.

Using Pathos in Your Presentation

Appeals to **pathos,** or appeals to emotion, are used to generate sadness, fear, elation, guilt, sympathy, or another emotion on the part of your audience. Emotional appeals add heart to your presentation. They can make a presentation more compelling, and they can actually enhance learning and memory.[16] Emotional appeals are especially important in speeches of policy or value. When you arouse the emotions of audience members, it is easier to build identification with them. Some common emotions aroused in presentations include fear, anger, guilt, regret, admiration, sympathy, and pride.

Notice how the speaker is clearly passionate and conveying strong emotion in this presentation. Through the use of gesturesand facial expression, the audience feels his passion.

How can you effectively incorporate emotional appeals into your presentations? Emotional appeals can be communicated through language, supporting evidence, delivery, and visual aids. Let's examine each one of these in the following sections.

Language

The use of emotion can be communicated through words that connote emotion. By choosing select words packed with emotion, you can move your audience. Consider the following excerpt from a speech delivered by Kelly, a former COM114 student:

> In March 1989, oil from the Exxon Valdez tanker spilled into the **pristine** Prince William Sound, **dumping** 11 million gallons of oil into one of Alaska's most diverse ecosystems. Because it happened in the spring, nature's **time of renewal,** the results were **tragic.** Twenty-eight hundred sea otters, three hundred harbor seals, and nine hundred bald eagles, **the symbol of American freedom,** were killed.

By choosing certain words and phrases, the horror of this tragedy becomes more real for the audience. Had Kelly chosen to deliver the opening of her presentation in the following way, the impact would not have been the same:

> In March 1989, the Exxon Valdez spilled 11 million gallons of oil into Prince William Sound, killing thousands of native species inhabiting the area.

The first opening has a much stronger impact on the audience because of the detail and the emotionally charged words that Kelly selected.

Be careful not to overdo it. A few emotionally charged words can go a long way for the audience. Overdoing it can draw the attention of the audience away from the message and onto the words themselves. Therefore, use words that pack emotion with restraint.

Supporting Evidence

The use of narratives or extended examples to support your points can have a great emotional impact on an audience. Narratives and extended examples pull audiences into your presentations and naturally grow out of the content of your presentation. The example that follows shows how Abigail involved her audience emotionally in her presentation:

> Monica Jasmin was six months pregnant with her second son, Luke. She was being very careful about the food she was eating. She avoided caffeine and stayed away from unpasteurized cheeses. She thought she was eating nutritiously when she chose a turkey sandwich from a deli tray at her office. However, the turkey sandwich that Monica ate was infested with *Listeria monocytogenes,* a bacterium that can cause the disease Listeriosis. On December 13th, she developed a fever and severe muscle pain. Her husband Tim rushed her to the hospital, but it was too late. At 6:36 a.m. she lost their baby, Luke.

By using this narrative, Abigail is able to arouse an emotional response in her audience. This story puts a face on a little known but potentially devastating illness that can occur anytime to anyone. By making us relate more to the topic, we are more involved and motivated to process her presentation on food-borne illness. Without this vivid example, her speech would not have had the impact she was hoping for.

Spotlight on Research

Using Fear and Guilt Appeals Effectively

Arousing emotions to achieve your desired effect is complicated. Let's consider a popular emotional appeal–fear appeals. **Fear appeals** are messages that communicate to an audience that they are susceptible to some negative event that will be extremely unpleasant. They are commonly used in health campaigns, and you have seen them in public service announcements. An extremely popular fear appeal used in the late 1980s was designed to stop drug usage. A TV commercial showed an egg with an announcer exclaiming, "This is your brain." The egg was then cracked and dropped into a hot frying pan, where it began to sizzle and fry. The announcer then proclaimed, "And this is your brain on drugs. Any questions?" The thought of our brain sizzling in a pan is a scary one. The ad definitely aroused fear.

Kim Witte, a professor and communication researcher, has found that three things must be present in a fear appeal for it to be persuasive. First, the appeal must arouse fear in the audience. Second, audience members must recognize that they are susceptible to the threat. Third, the appeal must be accompanied by **efficacy.** In other words, the target audience members must feel that they are able to perform the recommended response to the threat. She has found that fear appeals that provide little detail on how to avoid the threat have little success in terms of persuasive outcomes. For example, simply showing a black, shrunken, and diseased smoker's lung to an audience of smokers does little to stop the audience from smoking. But if you also explain to the audience members how they can quit smoking and repair the damage already done to their lungs, you will be more successful in your persuasive goal.

Guilt appeals are often used in our everyday lives as well. Who hasn't tried to guilt their roommate into going out when the roommate really doesn't want to or to guilt their parents into a little extra allowance? There is a good reason why we use guilt to persuade others. It works! However, in a recent meta-analysis, Dan O'Keefe, a persuasion researcher, found an interesting caveat to the guilt appeal. He found that while more explicit guilt appeals do in fact elicit greater feelings of guilt in a target audience than less explicit appeals, they are less likely to result in persuasion. So, in terms of guilt appeals, it is better to be a bit subtle than to hit your audience over the head. Remember these strategies when you are planning your persuasive presentations.[17]

Delivery

Emotion can also be communicated through the delivery of your presentation. By incorporating pauses, facial expressions, and vocal variety into your presentation, you can also move your audience. Speak from your heart, and your audience will feel your message. By demonstrating conviction and honesty, the language choices and narratives you have chosen will come alive for your audience. Remember, if you don't speak with conviction, your emotional appeals are likely to fall flat.

Visual Aids

Sometimes, the adage "a picture is worth a thousand words" is true. Imagine that you are trying to persuade your classmates to donate time or resources to the local humane society. A description of the homeless animals in the community is not nearly as compelling as pictures of these animals. Trying to describe how matted, dirty, and thin Max, a lovable mixed breed, was at the time of his rescue wouldn't do his situation justice. Only a picture of Max could adequately communicate his condition when found by the local shelter.

Although pictures can be powerful tools of persuasion, make sure they aren't too graphic for your audience. Gruesome pictures of animal cruelty or human suffering may be too much for an audience to handle. Choose pictures that convey your point, but won't overwhelm your audience.

Enhancing the Use of Pathos

Serious debate concerning the ethics of emotional appeals has ensued for many years. Some scholars advocate never using emotional appeals at all. They argue that emotional appeals have led to horrible human suffering. After all, Hitler used emotional appeals to promote hatred.

As long as emotional appeals are balanced with appeals to logic, it is perfectly acceptable to use them. Make sure that they are appropriate to the topic you are addressing. You will be unlikely to move audience members to action without involving their emotions. Just remember, all persuasive speeches should be built on evidence and sound reasoning. Emotional appeals should never be used in place of logic and good evidence.

Tips For Enhancing Pathos

- ◎ Balance emotional appeals with appeals to logic.
- ◎ Use emotionally charged words carefully.
- ◎ Use vivid narratives rich in detail.
- ◎ Use visual aids.
- ◎ Use vocal variety.

> You should refrain from using emotional appeals when addressing questions of fact.

Conclusion

Effective reasoning will have a strong impact on the success of your presentation. It is important that you learn how to use appeals to pathos, logos, and ethos well. Taking advantage of credibility by working on your competence and character will cause an audience to view your presentation more favorably. Credibility isn't enough. You must also appeal to the intellect of your audience by using logos or logic. Examine your evidence closely, and use the type of reasoning (inductive, deductive, causal, or analogical) that is most effective for your type of supporting material. Remember to avoid fallacies as you construct your arguments. They can be devastating to your presentation. Finally, don't forget the impact of pathos, or the emotional appeal. It can be quite compelling when combined with the other types of reasoning. However, your use of this appeal should be guided by good ethics.

Key Terms

Analogical reasoning	Expertise	Major premise
Argument ad hominem	Fallacy	Minor premise
Bandwagon	False dilemma	Pathos
Causal reasoning	Fear appeals	Post hoc, ergo propter hoc
Conclusion	Guilt appeals	Red herring
Credibility	Hasty generalization	Slippery slope
Deductive reasoning	Inductive reasoning	Straw person
Derived credibility	Initial credibility	Syllogism
Efficacy	Invalid analogy	Terminal credibility
Ethos	Logos	Trustworthiness

CHAPTER 11

Delivering the Presentation

Objectives

After reading this chapter, you should be able to

◎ explain the importance of good delivery to a successful presentation;

◎ explain the characteristics of good delivery;

◎ identify the four methods of delivery;

◎ explain the guidelines of successful impromptu speaking;

◎ explain the elements of vocal delivery that are vital to successful presentations; and

◎ discuss the aspects of physical delivery and their importance to presentational speaking.

In the 2015 Miss America pageant, Miss Colorado Kelley Johnson created a viral sensation when she spurned the usual talent choices and instead delivered a personal monologue. Standing in a pair of blue nursing scrubs with a stethoscope slung around her neck, her appearance was in sharp contrast to the designer gowns and sequined costumes of the other talent round performers. She spent the next two minutes telling the story of how an Alzheimer's patient had made her see how valuable nurses are. "I am a nurse" quickly became the most talked-about moment of the pageant. The clip went viral on social media, and Johnson was invited to appear on such programs as the *Today Show, Good Morning America,* and the *Ellen Degeneres Show.*

Why did her monologue touch so many people? The key was Johnson's delivery. She was praised for being "passionate" without seeming "staged or stiff." Her monologue was called "heartwarming" and "heartfelt" and "natural."[1]

Would it have been such a success had she not nailed the delivery? Probably not.

Delivery is a key to a successful presentation. A successful speaker must connect with the audience. Had Johnson read her monologue, or delivered it unconvincingly, it would not have had the impact that it did. However, good delivery takes practice and commitment. The advice offered in this chapter should get you on the right track.

The Importance of Good Delivery

It really doesn't matter how well crafted a presentation is; if the delivery is flat, the presentation will not achieve its potential. As you have been reading, a good presentation relies on solid content, effective organization, and convincing delivery. Good delivery provides three important elements to a presentation: It sets the tone for the presentation, makes the presentation more compelling, and helps illustrate the message for the audience.[2]

Spotlight on Research

Expressiveness Impacts Recall

Participants were asked to listen to a lecture that varied in terms of expressiveness on the part of the speaker. The participants were then asked to recall the information in the lecture. The study found that participants recalled more information when the presenter was expressive than when the presenter was not. Even two days later, this effect was still apparent. There was also an additional benefit in terms of motivation. Participants in the study were more motivated by the material when the presenter was expressive.

This study points out the importance of using expressive communication in your presentations. We want our audiences to remember what we have to say and be motivated to listen to us. Using expressivity in your voice, facial expression, and energy level can impact your results. This is a skill that you should work on as you progress through this course.[3]

After participating as audience members in a few presentations, students see why good delivery is important to a presentation. But they often worry about how to incorporate effective delivery techniques into their actual presentations. By the end of this chapter, which examines the characteristics of effective delivery, guidelines for delivering a speech, and ways to optimize your vocal and physical delivery, this will be clear.

Characteristics of Effective Delivery

Effective Delivery Is Conversational

Although presentations are more formal than conversations, your presentation should maintain a conversational style. You want each audience member to feel that you are speaking directly to him or her, and not to a group of people. By establishing and maintaining eye contact and responding to audience feedback (see Chapter 1), you are better able to connect with each member of the audience.

Another important feature of conversational style is expressiveness. Think about how you express your thoughts and emotions in conversations with your friends. What kinds of things do you do with your voice and face? Do you raise your eyebrows or smile? Whatever it is that you use to express yourself in everyday conversation, you should also use with an audience. Use vocal variety, facial expressions, and an upright posture that indicates you are approachable and open. We address each of these components later in the chapter and focus on skills that will help you develop a conversational style.

Effective Delivery Is Natural

One of the most important characteristics of successful delivery is to be natural. Any vocal or nonverbal feature that distracts from the message should be avoided. Think about your natural conversational style. You want to be consistent with that style. If you use a lot of gestures when you speak, use them in your presentations as well. If you are a person who uses few, if any, gestures, don't add them to your presentation; it won't seem natural for you or the audience, and the presentation may seem forced. You want your delivery to be effective and engaging but almost go unnoticed. Natural delivery does not detract from the message or presentation; it enhances it.

Effective Delivery Is Varied

Another important aspect of effective delivery is that it is varied. It becomes very monotonous to listen to a speaker whose voice does not change in volume or pitch. Sometimes, speakers develop a pattern of varied delivery that becomes predictable to the audience. For example, when they finish a final point, they move to the other side of the room. Although they are making changes and varying their delivery, it is too predictable. Effective delivery takes the audience by surprise; anything less becomes monotonous.

Effective Delivery Enhances the Message

Good delivery enhances and adds impact to the message. As part of this process, delivery should help the audience interpret the message. Increased volume can emphasize an important point; a pause helps indicate that extra attention should be paid to this point in the presentation.

Unfortunately, in too many speeches, delivery detracts from the message. Speakers who speak too softly distract from the message, forcing audience members to strain to hear them. Poor pronunciation and the use of slang words can also detract from the message. A presenter who paces from one end of the room to the other makes it very difficult for an audience to focus on the lecture's important elements.

Methods of Delivery

Stan Sigman, the former CEO of Cingular/AT&T, was invited by Steve Jobs, the CEO of Apple® Computers, to join him in his annual keynote presentation for Macworld in 2007. For those of you who don't know, Steve Jobs's presentations were legendary. He was a vibrant speaker who planned diligently for his presentations and never disappointed his audience. However, once Mr. Sigman took the stage, the presentation took a nosedive. One observer reported that as soon as Sigman hit the stage, he put his hands in his pockets and delivered his message in a monotone manner. Later, he pulled out note cards and started reading them word for word.[4] His presentation lasted only six minutes, but it generated criticism all over the blogosphere. A typical comment: CNN: "Sigman … read stiffly from a script, pausing awkwardly to consult notes."

The issue was the delivery method that Sigman chose. Those in attendance at Macworld were used to the more extemporaneous presentations that Jobs delivered. Sigman chose a more formal method that did not work well in this situation.

A better understanding of the elements of effective delivery requires knowing the different delivery methods that are available: impromptu, manuscript, memorized, and extemporaneous. Each of these methods has strengths and weaknesses. It is important that you analyze your situation and pick the method best suited for your situation.

Impromptu

The impromptu delivery method is probably the most common type of method used in presentational speaking. **Impromptu speaking** is characterized by little or no time for advanced preparation. We often call this type of speaking "off the cuff." Imagine that you are at a staff meeting and your boss asks you to report on developments in your division. Obviously, you had no advance warning that you were going to be asked to deliver this information, but now you are on the spot and must deliver a message that is both organized and effective, without having time for the usual preparation. This is impromptu speaking, and we all experience it on a fairly regular basis.

If you continue to use the strategies discussed in this book, impromptu speaking isn't any more challenging than any other type of speaking. Here are some guidelines that will help you organize and feel more confident with the impromptu method of delivery.

Guidelines for Impromptu Speaking

Step 1: Prepare to Speak   You don't have to start speaking the minute you have been asked to. Take a deep breath, rise from your chair, and walk to the front of the room to the lectern. Use this time to gather and organize your thoughts.

Step 2: Determine Your Purpose   Try to develop one or two points as you walk to the lectern to begin speaking. Think about what point or points you want to make. Because you have a very limited amount of time in which to prepare and speak, focus on one issue that you know well and can adequately address. Avoid complex issues or ideas about which you have limited **knowledge.**

Step 3: Support Your Purpose   Reinforce your purpose or points with examples, narratives, or other supporting evidence. Regardless of the type of evidence you choose, you want to provide specific details for your audience so that you justify your position or purpose.

Step 4: Prepare the Introduction   Develop an introduction. A brief sentence will suffice in an impromptu presentation. You might refer to the event at which you are speaking or to another comment that has recently been made.

Step 5: Prepare the Conclusion   Finally, conclude the presentation. One of the most common mistakes in this method of delivery is that the conclusion often rambles. Follow the guidelines in Chapter 4 for an effective ending (be brief, clear, and memorable). You want to come to a definite stop. Simply restate your point or points, and end with a memorable thought or a call to action.

Here are some additional considerations that will help you prepare for impromptu presentations:

- ◎ **Don't rush.** Take your time before you start to speak. Make sure your thoughts are clearly laid out in your mind before you begin speaking. Also, speak slowly; don't rush through the presentation.
- ◎ **Don't apologize.** Start your presentation with your introduction. Avoid statements such as, "You'll have to forgive me; I had little time to prepare today." Audience members know this, and they will not be expecting a masterpiece.
- ◎ **Focus on the topic.** Keep the focus of your presentation on the topic at hand. Remember your purpose, and don't stray from it. It is also important that you avoid any negative cognitions. Keep your mind on your subject matter, and keep negative thoughts at bay.
- ◎ **Be brief.** Remember, this is a brief presentation. Try to stay focused, and avoid rambling. You don't have to say everything that you know about a particular topic. Choose your purpose, state your point or points, provide support, and then conclude.
- ◎ **Foresee speaking situations.** If at all possible, try to anticipate those situations in which you may be called on to speak. From experience, you may know that you will have to report on your division's progress at certain staff meetings. Plan in advance what you would like to say if the situation presents itself.

Impromptu speaking has many advantages. It allows for natural delivery that aids in your ability to connect with your audience. You are free from notes and can focus on presenting your message in a conversational manner. It also affords you the ability to adapt easily to your audience's needs.

Impromptu speaking does have drawbacks, however. Individuals often feel very anxious in these situations. Additionally, many times these presentations are less than optimally organized. While these drawbacks may make impromptu speaking seem a bit daunting, following the strategies outlined in this chapter will help you be successful. With a little practice, anyone can be a good impromptu speaker.

Manuscript

The **manuscript delivery** method requires that you write out your speech word for word and deliver the presentation by reading directly from the actual manuscript.

Manuscript speaking is important when the exact wording of the presentation is paramount or when the stakes are high. For example, speeches of the president of the United States are written by professional speechwriters to address particular goals in particular situations. President George W. Bush delivered one such speech to console the American people after the events of September 11, 2001. The speechwriters spend a great deal of time choosing the right phrases and words that will evoke specific feelings and emotions in a particular audience. Therefore, the exact wording is extremely important.

Manuscript speaking is also recommended for less high profile presentations such as online tutorials when every step is important and forgetting something could result in a less than desired outcome (see Chapter 14 for more on this).

One drawback to manuscript speaking is that it is a difficult style to deliver well. As a presenter, you want to connect with your audience. For this to happen, you must maintain good eye contact and vocal variety. These are hard to maintain when reading from a document. It takes many years of practice to deliver this style of speaking effectively. In addition, manuscript speaking does not allow presenters the flexibility of adapting the presentation to the needs of their audience, which is very important to presentational speaking.

Memorized

> **The memorized presentation limits your ability to adapt to, and therefore connect with, your audience.**

Another style of delivery is to memorize the text of the speech and then simply recite it to your audience. As in the manuscript speech, the **memorized delivery** method requires that the text of the presentation is written out word for word, and the speech is then delivered from memory. This type of style has many limitations. I have seen numerous speakers who adopted this style lose their place in their speeches and become flustered. Delivery in memorized presentations also seems very stiff, and an audience can usually tell when a speech is memorized. Memorized speeches lack the vocal and physical variety normally found in other methods of delivery, such as the impromptu and extemporaneous methods. Much like the manuscript style, the memorized presentation limits your ability to adapt to, and therefore connect with, your audience. This connection is something that is important to audiences, so you should consider this constraint when choosing your method of delivery.

Sometimes, your instructor will recommend that you memorize certain elements of your presentation. For example, many instructors recommend memorizing the attention-getter and the clincher. This ensures that you are able to make adequate eye contact at these critical points in the presentation. They may also recommend that you memorize some quotations or pieces of evidence.

Unless you are delivering a very short presentation, such as a toast at a wedding or an introduction for a speaker, the memorized style is probably not your best choice. The pitfalls that accompany this type of presentation outweigh most of the benefits.

Extemporaneous

The **extemporaneous delivery** presentation is a prepared and practiced method of delivery. However, unlike with the manuscript and memorized methods, the speech is not written out word for word. You simply outline the main ideas of your

> **Extemporaneous presentations are prepared and practiced.**

presentation and use these as a memory aid as you deliver the presentation. Each time the presentation is delivered, it is a bit different because you choose the exact wording of the presentation at the time you deliver the material. By allowing the flexibility to choose the right words for the right situation, extemporaneous delivery helps the presenter to adapt to the audience. For example, imagine delivering a presentation to some colleagues within your organization. From their feedback, you notice that they are not following some of the supporting material you have provided. The extemporaneous style allows you to go over this section of the presentation again, in a different way, in hopes of reaching those individuals in your audience.

In addition to providing the flexibility to adapt to your audience, the extemporaneous presentation also allows for more dynamic delivery. Because you are not tied to your notes or relying on your memory, you have the flexibility to maintain eye contact and other delivery features that make the presentation more interesting for your audience. Extemporaneous speaking is the preferred speaking style in today's organizations, and its popularity is the reason it is stressed in this course.

In the remaining sections of this chapter, we are going to examine aspects of vocal and physical delivery, as well as give you some pointers on how to practice for your presentation.

Vocal Delivery

Sometimes, speakers underestimate the power of **vocal delivery.** They work very hard on researching, organizing, and practicing the speech, but they forget that their vocal delivery can enhance meaning and add impact to the presentation. Vocal characteristics such as volume, rate, pauses, pitch, enunciation, and pronunciation are all aspects of what we call **paralanguage,** or the nonverbal aspects of vocal delivery. These enhance the verbal message and therefore help illustrate the message for the audience. Practice using these skills to increase your effectiveness as a speaker.

Vocal Variety

The most important aspect of vocal delivery is vocal variety. **Vocal variety** is modifying the volume, rate, pitch, and use of pauses in a presentation. As a speaker, you want to emphasize vocal variety to add impact to your presentation. In the next sections, we discuss each of these issues, along with other elements of vocal delivery. The key to remember is to vary the use of all of these components.

Volume

Volume is the loudness of a speaker's voice and is one of the most important aspects in terms of intelligibility. In some speaking situations, you will use an electronic device, such as a microphone, that will enhance your own voice and enable the audience to hear you, no matter how softly you speak. However, many presentations you make will be delivered without the aid of electronics. Therefore, it is important for you to get a feel for how loudly to speak.

If you speak a little louder than you think is necessary, you are probably speaking at the right level. Look around the room once you begin your presentation. Does the audience seem to be straining to hear you? Do the people sitting in the back of the room seem to be leaning forward in their chairs? If so, raise your volume.

Most of the time, speakers err on the side of speaking too softly rather than too loudly. However, some of us do have rather strong and booming voices. Check audience feedback to make sure people are comfortable with the level at which you are speaking. If they seem to be straining forward in their seats, you are probably speaking too softly. If they seem uncomfortable and are leaning back, lower your voice.

> **Most of the time, speakers err on the side of speaking too softly rather than too loudly.**

When you practice, friends and family members can give you feedback on how effective your volume level is. Try to remember, however, that each speaking situation is unique. The size of the audience, along with the acoustics of the room, will make a difference in the volume you need to project. Attuning to audience feedback is probably the safest way to assure that you are speaking at a volume that is effective.

Rate

Rate is the speed at which we speak. The typical native English speaker speaks approximately 165 to 180 words per minute.[5] This range varies greatly throughout the United States. People in the South generally speak more slowly than people on the East Coast. Although we can process language much faster than this, this seems to be the rate most of us are used to and comfortable with in presentational situations. Therefore, you want to strive to fall somewhere around this figure. If you speak too fast, audience members may have a hard time following you. If you speak too slowly, audience members may find themselves wanting to finish your words and phrases for you, rather than focusing on your message. Again, look for audience feedback; if members of the audience seem to be straining to hear you, you may be speaking too quickly.

Pitch

Pitch refers to the placement of your voice on the musical scale. Some of us have very low-pitched voices, and some have rather high-pitched voices. The important aspect of pitch is that you vary the pitch of your voice. Otherwise, your speech will become very monotonous for your audience. You also want to be careful that you do not fall into a pattern of using pitch in the same way over and over again. For example, some people's voices rise in pitch at the end of a statement, turning every statement into a question. This can be very irritating to an audience.

One good way to examine the range of your natural pitch is to record yourself speaking. By listening to yourself, you can get a good idea of your vocal habits and the natural characteristics of your speaking voice. From this examination, you will gain a much better idea of how to vary the pitch of your speaking voice.

Pauses

Pauses are brief silences between words, phrases, or sentences. Pauses are another tool you can use to add dramatic impact to your delivery. After delivering an important point, pause for a second and let the audience think about what you have just said. The planned use of incorporating pauses into a presentation can have a big impact on the presentation's effectiveness.

Consider the impact of the following statement: "According to data from the Centers for Disease Control in 2015, 48 million cases of foodborne disease occur in the U.S. each year, sending about 105,000 people to the hospital and resulting in 2,000 deaths. That's about one in seven people in the country getting sick from food every year." These are powerful statistics, so let the audience absorb them. Pause between the two sentences so that the audience can really think about the power of these numbers. Often, speakers rattle through their statistics too quickly, thereby limiting the statistics' effectiveness. Use pauses to highlight important material and to add impact to certain aspects of your message. You will be surprised how much they can add to a presentation.

Vocal Nonfluencies

Sometimes, we are uncomfortable with silences, and so we fill them with vocal nonfluencies or vocal fillers. **Vocal fillers** or **vocal nonfluencies** are vocalized pauses ("uh") or sounds ("um") that fill breaks or pauses between meaningful words or sentences. They are used when a speaker is trying to decide what to say next. These usually occur in the middle of a sentence or thought. We use them to fill in that "dead time" while we are mentally composing what comes next.

Some common vocal fillers are "um," "like," "you know," and "you know what I mean?" Vocal fillers can be extremely distracting, taking away focus from the intended message. While a few vocal fillers are acceptable, overuse can have a negative impact on the presentation. In fact, several investigations have found that as vocal nonfluencies increase, perceptions of speaker credibility decrease.[6] Your ability to persuade your audience is also impacted by nonfluencies.[7] With practice, you can learn to limit your use of vocal fillers.[8]

Enunciation

Enunciation is the act of articulating words clearly and precisely. Enunciation is yet another important aspect of good vocal delivery. You want to make sure that you deliver words clearly and distinctly so that the audience understands you. Many times in casual conversation, we cut off the endings or beginnings of words. This is very common. We often say *'cause* instead of *because, goin'* instead of *going*. Although this is acceptable in casual conversation, in a formal presentation, it may cause an audience to question your competence and credibility.

Pronunciation

Mispronunciation of a word during your speech can ruin your credibility.

Pronunciation is the articulation of a word in accordance with the accepted standards of the language. Mispronunciation of a word during your speech can ruin your credibility. Why should an audience consider you an expert in the field if you are mispronouncing key words related to your topic? It is imperative that you are certain of the pronunciation of unfamiliar or difficult words. If you are unsure, consult a dictionary.

It is easy to mispronounce even common words. Again, while acceptable in casual conversation, mispronunciation of everyday words is unacceptable in front of an audience. This type of mistake will not only call your competence into question but can also confuse your audience. For example, many people say "affect" when they mean "effect." This difference in words can muddle an important point for an audience.

Physical Delivery

Another aspect of your presentation is the **physical delivery,** or how you present your body. How you carry yourself, gesture, move, and make eye contact are all essential features of the presentation. Let's examine each of these so that you can incorporate them effectively into your presentation.

Gestures

Humans have extremely expressive hands, and they are used quite often in communication.[9] Although we commonly use our hands in one-on-one interactions, people never seem to know what to do with their hands during a presentation. The use of **gestures** is one of those areas that cause speakers much concern. Often, speakers put their hands in their pockets and start playing with their change. Other times, speakers tuck their hair behind their ears again and again. Sometimes, speakers clinch their hands behind their back. Not only are these gestures ineffective, they also distract from the message. Remember, one of the goals of delivery is to enhance the verbal message. If your gestures detract from rather than complement the message, they will be ineffective.

To use gestures effectively in presentations, you need to understand that there are three different types of gestures: adaptors, emblems, and illustrators.[10]

Adaptors are nonverbal behaviors that reveal things about our internal state, and they tend to provide comfort when we are in stressful situations. As previously mentioned, many speakers tend to tuck their hair behind their ear again and again during a presentation. This tucking behavior is an adaptor and communicates to audiences that speakers are anxious or feeling unsure of themselves. Other examples of adaptors include constantly moving your feet and crossing your arms. Adaptors should be avoided in

The use of gestures in a presentation is appropriate as long as they do not detract from the message.

presentations. They can affect your credibility because they communicate apprehension. Often, however, we are unaware of our use of adaptors. It is important that you watch yourself on video to determine if you are engaging in these types of gesture. You can also practice in front of an audience and ask audience members to watch for any sign of adaptors.

Emblems are gestures that can be directly translated into verbal language. Examples include the OK sign, the thumbs-up sign, and the peace sign. They are unique to a given culture. So, if you do use an emblem in your presentation, you need to make sure that it is universally understood by your audience.

Illustrators are the most common type of gesture, and they are hand or arm gestures that accompany and enhance the verbal message you are delivering. Unlike emblems, they cannot be substituted for words. They may include movements that emphasize words, movements that demonstrate size (e.g., "about this big"), or even movements that emphasize relationships.[11] For example, Peter raised one hand and lowered the other as he said to his audience, "As education levels rise, the number of televisions in the home declines." His gesture simply illustrated his message for his audience.

To illustrate or complement your verbal message, your gestures must appear natural. If you are a person who uses few gestures in natural conversation, then use few in your presentations. Gestures can add a great deal of impact to the presentation, if used appropriately. As you become an accomplished speaker, you will develop a style that works for you. One guideline to follow is this: If the gesture distracts from the message, do not use it.

Movement

Common questions beginning students ask in this course are: "Where do I stand?" "Should I walk around or stand still?" "Should I use the podium or not?" Your instructor will provide guidelines for using the podium or lectern in your classroom. Outside of the classroom, it depends on the situation and the type of presentation.

Regardless of the speaking situation, there are a few guidelines that apply. Much like gestures, **movement** can add a good deal of impact to your presentation. However, it can also be very distracting. You must move with purpose to be effective. Many times, novice speakers start to pace in front of their audience. You have probably seen professors use this same strategy. They walk from one side of the room to the other with no purpose. It is very distracting. We start concentrating on when they will cross the room, rather than the verbal message itself.

Movement during your presentation can be very effective if you do it with purpose. Move to add impact to a particular or compelling point within the presentation. If you are standing behind a lectern, you might walk to the side of it to make an important point. You can also move during transitions to signal to the audience that you are moving from one point to another. No matter when you decide to move, it must be done with purpose.

Eye Contact

Eye contact is probably the most important component of physical delivery. It allows us to connect with our audience. Eye contact ensures that our presentation remains conversational and that members of the audience feel that we are addressing each of them individually.

Eye contact with an entire audience can be a bit uncomfortable at first. It may seem a bit strange to focus on members of the audience by looking directly

When using speaking notes, maintain eye contact with the audience.

at them. Therefore, many speakers avoid eye contact. Other speakers tend to favor one side of the room over the other. You may notice this phenomenon with some of your professors. They lecture to only one side of the room. If you are lucky enough to be sitting on their preferred side of the classroom or lecture hall, you feel that you have connected with them. If you are sitting on the side that received little or no eye contact, however, you will feel disconnected from the speaker. Favoring one side of the room is a very common mistake. If you think you are guilty of this common nonverbal delivery mistake, have friends watch your practice session and give you feedback, or videotape yourself to see. In American culture, presenters who do not maintain eye contact with the audience are perceived as less trustworthy, competent, and concerned than those who maintain adequate eye contact. Therefore, when addressing your audience, it is important that you develop and implement this delivery strategy effectively.

You also want to make sure that your eye contact is effective. You need to look directly at audience members. A popular myth about presentational speaking is that a speaker should look over the heads of the audience to a spot on the wall. This is not effective, and your audience will not perceive that you have made adequate eye contact. You must look directly into the faces of your audience members.

The importance of eye contact cannot be overstated. Not only is it a tool for connecting with audience members, it also allows you to get feedback from them. Are they interested? Do they seem confused? With effective eye contact, you can gauge audience feedback and make necessary adaptations as the presentation progresses.

> **Tip**
>
> When you must read from notes, create no more than three or four large-font bullet points on one note card or sheet of paper.
>
> Carmine Gallo | CEO of Gallo Communications

Facial Expression

Your **facial expressions** during your presentation are a very important source of emotional information.[12] As this text has mentioned again and again, you have to identify and connect with your audience in order to reach them. Your facial expressions are a valuable tool in this process. Communicate through your facial expressions (e.g., smiling, squinting, scowling) the emotions you want your audience to feel.

Too many times, speakers stand at the podium like wooden statues and stare blankly out into the audience. This is hardly going to influence or engage your audience. You want to motivate the audience to listen and get excited about your ideas. One key way to do so is through facial expressiveness. Expressiveness can actually motivate an audience. Don't restrict yourself in front of your audience—it is a good thing to show a little emotion through facial expressions.

Appearance

A common question students ask is, "What should I wear?" There is no simple answer. Some research indicates that a professional **appearance** adds to your credibility.[13] However, simply putting on a suit, regardless of the speaking situation, is not a surefire way to increase your credibility. In fact, in some situations, this type of attire may actually hurt you. For example, suppose that you have been hired by the county outreach program to provide lectures to area farmers on new developments in pesticides. Showing up to one of these sessions dressed in a suit may hurt your credibility with this particular audience. Farmers will be dressed in work clothes, and in order to feel that you have credibility, they need to be able to relate to you and feel that you are similar to them. Appearance is an important part of this process.

You will want to dress professionally for the particular audience that you are addressing. What is professional attire for an accountant is not the same for a computer programmer. Research indicates that being radically over- or

> **Being radically over- or under-dressed for an occasion can lead to negative perceptions.**

under-dressed for an occasion can lead the audience to have negative perceptions of the speaker.[14] Thus, a good guideline is to dress slightly better than you anticipate your audience to be dressed.

Much like all the other aspects of nonverbal delivery, it is important that your appearance does not distract from your message. You want to present a comprehensive picture of competence. A professional appearance that takes into account the context can help you achieve this goal.

Speaking with a Translator

One speaking situation that can really impact delivery is speaking with a translator. Speaking with a translator is a difficult task to perform well. However, in our global world, more and more of us are being faced with complex speaking situations such as this. Many of you will work for companies with global offices and interact with colleagues who speak different languages. It is not uncommon to make a presentation to an entire audience of individuals who speak another language than you do. Therefore, it is important that you learn some tips for facing this type of speaking situation.

There are primarily two ways in which translation can work. The most formal method is called **simultaneous translation.** It requires audience members to wear earphones, and your presentation is presented in another language as you speak. Many times, you will need to prepare a manuscript speech if this method of translation is used. This allows the speech to be translated ahead of time.

The second method is more interactive. It is called **delayed translation,** and it allows you to speak and then wait while your presentation is presented in small pieces to your audience. This method allows the translator to ask questions of clarification as you deliver your material and also allows the audience to listen to both you and the translator.

The best situation is to know and have an established relationship with your translator in advance. It is also best if the translator is an expert in your topic area. So the best possible situation would be for you to present your presentation while your business colleague performed the delayed translation. Your colleague would know you and your conversational style, as well as be familiar with the content area. This would be the easiest situation to face, as it reduces the chance for confusion and misunderstanding as you make your presentation.

Even if you don't know your translator in advance of the presentation, ask for a meeting prior to the presentation. Practice your presentation with the translator, and give the translator an opportunity to ask questions and clarify any confusion that may arise. Avoid meeting your translator for the first time at the presentation.

During the practice session, it is important to determine a couple of things. First, how fast can you talk? Will the translator be able to keep up with you? Work this out in advance. It will probably require you to speak a little more slowly than you usually do. Second, don't get carried away. It is easier for a translator to deliver your ideas more accurately if you break them down into small ideas. Always complete an idea before you stop to wait for the translation. Third, it is more important than ever that you use transitions, especially signposts, to help the translator keep up with your material and organize it for the audience.

One odd artifact of the delayed translation process is what to do when the translator is speaking. After all, you are still out there, front and center. The most important thing is for you to stay engaged. Don't look down at your notes. Continue to watch the translator and look interested. Try to refrain from distracting nonverbal behaviors during this time as well.

While you might think that speaking with a translator is a rare situation, it is becoming more and more common. During this past year, one of the authors of this book presented with a translator on three different occasions. Be prepared. There is nothing worse than having a presentation flop because you or your translator were not prepared for the challenge.

Practicing the Presentation

You can plan, organize, and research an incredible presentation, but if your delivery is flat, all that planning will have been in vain. You simply have to practice your speech in order for it all to come together. Menzel and Carrell[15] emphasize that more preparation leads to more effective speeches.

As mentioned previously in the chapter, Steve Jobs, the CEO of Apple, was a phenomenal presenter. However, presentations like Jobs' don't come easily. According to those close to him, Jobs put in hours of grueling practice.[16] He put in at least two full days of rehearsal before the actual presentation.[17] This does not include the time he took to prepare the message or construct the slides. This was just rehearsal time. The bottom line is this: If you want your presentation to have real impact, you have to put in the time for rehearsal.

For you to have enough time to rehearse thoroughly, you should complete your full-sentence outline or preparation outline three days before you plan to deliver your presentation.

Here are some step-by-step guidelines to help you with your practice sessions.

Step 1   Practice aloud with your preparation or full-sentence outline. Check the outline for the following items: Is it too long or too short? Is it organized appropriately? Do you have adequate support for each idea? Once you have answered these questions and fixed any deficiencies, it is time to write the speaking outline (check the guidelines in Chapter 7).

Rueff describes how he prepares and practices for a presentation: "For large speaking engagements that I know about in advance, it can take months of preparation. Regardless of the presentation type, I always spend time practicing. It's important."

Rusty Rueff | Former Executive VP Communications | Electronic Arts

Spotlight on Research

Practice Impacts Performance

Over one hundred students enrolled in a public speaking course were videotaped delivering speeches. The students also filled out questionnaires regarding preparation time, speaking experience, and other variables, such as GPA. Researchers then rated the effectiveness of the students' delivery. As it turns out, speeches with the best delivery were given by students who had practiced in front of a live audience. Practice with an audience was a better predictor of effective delivery than speaking experience or student GPA.

As you can see, practicing in front of a live audience can have a big impact on your overall delivery. Find a couple of friends or family members to act as your audience. Run through the presentation in front of them several times. Practice is essential to good speaking, so don't underestimate it.[18]

Step 2   Practice delivering your speech from your speaking outline. Rehearse the presentation several times until you are comfortable with the outline you have prepared. Go through the speech from beginning to end. Make sure you rehearse all aspects of the presentation. If you use a narrative as the attention-getter, make sure you practice the entire narrative. If you are using visual aids, they should be completed at this point and incorporated into the practice sessions. Remember, you should not be memorizing the speech, but becoming comfortable with the ideas of the presentation.

Step 3   Add delivery cues. Once the verbal message seems solid, start adding some of the aspects of delivery that will create impact in your presentation. Don't forget to mark delivery cues on your speaking outline so that you will be sure to incorporate them into your presentation. You might also try videotaping yourself or speaking into a recorder. All of these methods will help you get a good idea of what the speech will sound like to other people. However, the best way to determine how your presentation will be received is to present it to others. Ask your friends and family to act as audience members and to provide feedback. This will help you tweak those last-minute details.

Step 4   Put it all together. Try to replicate the actual speaking situation as closely as possible. If you are giving a classroom presentation, see if you can get access to your classroom and practice there. If you are giving a presentation to your organization, try to gain access to the conference room and have a quick run-through. Practicing in the actual circumstances where you will be delivering the presentation is an excellent way to ensure that you are prepared.

The most important aspect of preparing for your presentation is to start early. If you don't leave yourself enough time to work through all of the little details of your presentation, your audience will know it. Lack of preparation time can also affect your confidence. So give yourself plenty of time to rehearse for your presentation.

Conclusion

The verbal content of your presentation is only one aspect of the message you are trying to convey to your audience. You simply cannot overestimate the impact that the nonverbal aspects of communication can have on your presentation. It is important that you pay close attention to both your vocal delivery (volume, rate, pitch, pauses, enunciation, and pronunciation) and physical delivery (gestures, movement, eye contact, appearance). To put all of the aspects of your presentation together, you must leave yourself plenty of time to rehearse. Guidelines for practicing your presentation include delivering your speech from the speaking outline, adding vocal and physical delivery cues, and practicing in circumstances similar to those of the actual presentation. In general, you should strive to take the delivery of your message as seriously as you do the construction of the presentation.

Key Terms

Adaptors	Illustrators	Pronunciation
Appearance	Impromptu speaking	Rate
Delayed translation	Manuscript delivery	Simultaneous translation
Emblems	Memorized delivery	Vocal delivery
Enunciation	Movement	Vocal fillers
Extemporaneous delivery	Paralanguage	Vocal nonfluencies
Eye contact	Pauses	Vocal variety
Facial expression	Physical delivery	Volume
Gestures	Pitch	

CHAPTER 12

Presentation Aids

Objectives

After reading this chapter, you should be able to

- ◎ explain the major advantages of using visual aids in a speech;
- ◎ understand how to use a numerical chart effectively;
- ◎ understand how to display presentation aids effectively;
- ◎ understand guidelines for creating effective multimedia presentations; and
- ◎ understand the guidelines for delivering a speech with presentation aids.

According to a 2016 article in *Forbes,* the standard for public speaking has increased because of the rise of Internet video, especially the massively popular and influential TED talk series.[1]

This new standard extends to visual aids as well. As noted, the TED presenters keep their slides simple: one main idea per slide and no excessive bullet points, relatively simple graphs, or an image that conveys an emotional message. And the visual aids do what they are supposed to do: aid the presentation, not control it.

"The graphics support a story that the presenter is telling. Often presenters talk for 30 or 60 seconds with no graphic on the screen, a graphic appears when needed to illustrate a point, and then back to speech mode. The presenter paces the talk, not the graphics [i.e., there are no pauses for "next slide, please"]. Contrast this to what happens too often in business presentations: the charts tell the story, and the person is there to explain the charts."[2]

Because of the pervasiveness of computers, it is rare to see presentations in a professional context that do not make some use of presentation aids. In fact, most people think that they have to have some sort of presentation aid, such as a slick set of PowerPoint, Keynote, or Prezi slides, or their presentation will be perceived as ineffective. Because computers make the creation of presentation aids very easy, they are often misused. Many people do not spend the time necessary to make good decisions about how to integrate these aids into their presentations; instead, they rely solely on the templates provided in the software package.

A **presentation aid** is defined as any item used to enhance the presentation itself. Examples of presentation aids include physical objects, charts, graphs, maps, models, diagrams, audio/video material, sounds, photographs, and so on. Aids can also be presented through a variety of mediums, such as overhead projectors, computers, and televisions. Regardless of the presentation aid's medium or type of content, the key to using aids is that they must enhance understanding. Presentation aids cease to facilitate presentations when they detract from the presentation itself. It is easy to use presentation aids inappropriately. This chapter helps you understand the different types of common presentation aids and how to integrate them successfully into presentations.

Functions of Presentation Aids

Visual aids can make a difference in a presentation if they are used well. According to consultants from EMS Communications, one element that stood out in Rio de Janeiro's successful pitch to host the 2016 Summer Olympic Games was the presenters' effective use of visual aids during their presentation. One slide in particular delivered a big impact. It was a map that showed the locations of all the modern Olympic Games. The argument Brazil was trying to make was that the games have taken place in Asia, Europe, North America, and even Australia. However, the games have never been held in South America. While the presenters could have communicated this message orally, it became much more effective when the audience could see the disparity visually. Additionally, they used better video to capture the essence of their city than other teams. These things, in conjunction with a solid presentation, gave the Rio de Janeiro team the edge. Presentation aids can function in a variety of ways. When used properly, they can have a significant impact on the presentation and the audience.

Increase Clarity and Retention

Presentation aids are used to enhance audience understanding. They can achieve this goal in three specific ways. First, they can clarify complex information. Large amounts of statistics and numerical information are difficult for an audience to process. By providing this information in a more concise manner—for example, in a chart—the audience's ability to process the information and understand your material is greatly enhanced.[3]

Second, presentation aids help to illustrate abstract information. How could audience members be expected to understand the differences between Neoclassical and Gothic architecture if they didn't see examples of these styles? The two photos featured in this section clearly show the differences between these two styles. It is hard to imagine explaining these different styles to an audience with words alone. The pictures are necessary in explaining your point to your audience.

Esztergom Basilica in Hungary,
an example of Neoclassical architecture.

Façade of Duomo in Florence, Italy,
an example of Gothic architecture.

Finally, presentation aids actually improve the ability of the audience to remember the information in the presentation. Studies have shown that audiences retain only 20% of what they hear. However, when an audience hears and sees the information a speaker presents, that number jumps to 50%.[4]

Increase Presentation Effectiveness

Presentations that incorporate aids have also been shown to be more effective.[5] Visual aids can actually increase the persuasiveness of a presentation. A study conducted by the University of Minnesota's School of Management and the 3M Corporation found that the use of visual aids can increase the persuasiveness of a presentation by up to 40%.[6]

Increase Speaker Effectiveness

Using presentation aids can affect the audience's perceptions of the speaker. Research has indicated that an average speaker who uses presentation aids will be perceived by the audience as better prepared, more credible, more professional, and more dynamic than an average speaker who does not use presentation aids. Research has also indicated that communication apprehension is decreased for those speakers who use presentation aids.[7] The speaker can relax because the focus of the audience is directed toward the visual aid as well as toward the speaker.

Types of Presentation Aids

Numerical Charts

Charts play a critical role in many presentations. Often, much of the information we need to illustrate is numerical in nature. Numerical data, especially tabular data, is very difficult to communicate verbally. "The primary purpose of any chart is to demonstrate relationships more quickly and more clearly than is possible using a tabular form."[8]

This makes charts a perfect choice for oral presentations during which audiences are limited in their ability to study complex sets of information. We are usually interested in displaying relative differences among numbers, rather than the details of the specific numbers themselves. This is where charts can be very helpful.

Charts graphically illustrate complex information so that the meaning of the numbers is clearer to the audience. In the context of an oral presentation, it is difficult for an audience member to carefully study a large table of rows and numbers. Not only is tabular information difficult to see, it is time consuming to process. To illustrate this, compare the following two ways of presenting the same information. Figure 1 shows the data in tabular form, while the Figure 2 shows the same information in a chart. Though both are useful, the chart is easier to process and understand. In fact, you do not need to even know the exact numbers to see the general pattern of milk production in the United States. According to both the table and the chart, more milk was being produced in 2011 than in 2007. However, it is much easier for your audience to identify the trend, and they can do so more quickly, using the chart rather than the table.

Milk production increased significantly from 2002–2011.

Million Pounds	Year
170,000	2002
171,000	2003
172,000	2004
176,000	2005
182,000	2006
186,000	2007
190,000	2008
189,000	2009
193,000	2010
196,000	2011

Figure 1. U.S. milk production in pounds. Source: USDA.

The key to using charts effectively is to know what type of chart to use, based on the type of information you are trying to communicate. In this section, we cover three types of numerical charts: pie, bar, and line/column. All of these charts allow you to make different types of comparisons between and among numbers. Depending on the types of comparisons you need to make, you need to use different types of charts. Pie charts allow you to make comparisons between the relative sizes of different parts of a larger whole. Bar charts allow you to compare how different things rank in size. Line and column charts allow you to make comparisons of data over time, or to make comparisons about the frequency at which certain items are distributed. Though there are many additional types of charts, these three types are very popular, and mastery of them will allow you to communicate many different types of numerical data clearly and succinctly. The following sections describe each type of numerical chart in more detail and provide tips on using them effectively.

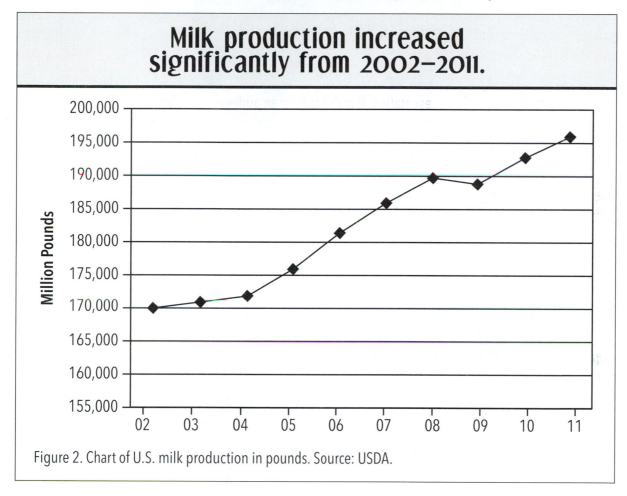

Figure 2. Chart of U.S. milk production in pounds. Source: USDA.

Parts of a Whole

Pie charts are one of the most popular types of charts. They are used when you are comparing parts of a whole. If you are interested in showing how different parts of something go together to make up a whole, then a pie chart is the right choice. Any time we are talking about parts of a whole, we are talking about percentages of the total. For instance, a pie chart might represent the percentage of student credit hours offered by instructor position or the percentage of sales accounted for by certain geographical regions, as seen in the example shown in Figure 3.

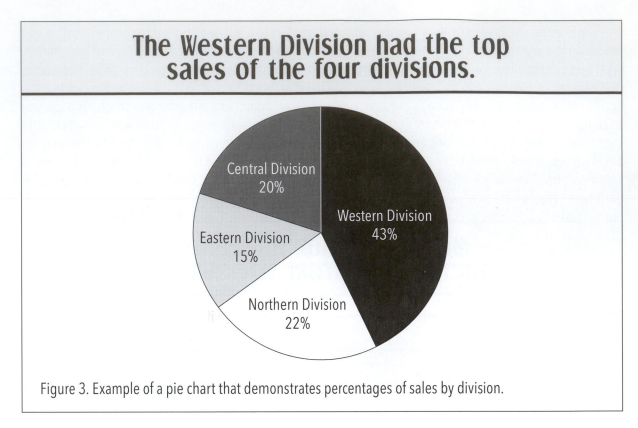

The Western Division had the top sales of the four divisions.

Central Division 20%

Eastern Division 15%

Northern Division 22%

Western Division 43%

Figure 3. Example of a pie chart that demonstrates percentages of sales by division.

When using a pie chart, you should usually only use six segments. If you have more than six segments or "pieces of pie," consider collapsing some of the smaller segments into an "other" category. Because of the way our eyes have been "trained" to read an analog clock, we read pie charts in a clockwise fashion. So put the most important segment at the 12 o'clock position.[9]

Because pie charts are extremely popular and easy to use, they are often misused. A common mistake is using pie charts to make comparisons. Pie charts shouldn't be used to make comparisons across years, divisions, and so on. They are not well suited for examining trends. They simply take a snapshot in time. For example, if we want to examine the percentages of majors in the School of Liberal Arts for 2015–2016, a pie chart is the answer. However, if we want to compare percentages of majors in liberal arts in 2015–2016 with those in 2014–2015, then a column chart is a better choice. Another common mistake made with pie charts is the three-dimensional effect. These effects are extremely difficult for your audience to interpret and should be avoided in oral presentations. For clarity reasons, two-dimensional pie charts are best.[10]

Item Comparison

Bar charts are the chart of choice when making comparisons among different types of items. These types of charts allow for easy visual ranking across items in a category. Like the pie chart, the bar chart is a snapshot in time. It should not indicate changes over time.[11] For instance, if I wanted to compare sales calls made by various salespersons in my division, I might use a bar chart like the one shown in Figure 4. In this example, it is easy for your audience to recognize at a quick glance which salesperson has made the most calls in the last month.

When using bar charts, keep in mind that the vertical dimension is not a scale; it is not used for measuring—just labeling. In our example, it is labeled with names of salespersons, but this could easily be company names, industries, geographical regions, and so on.[12]

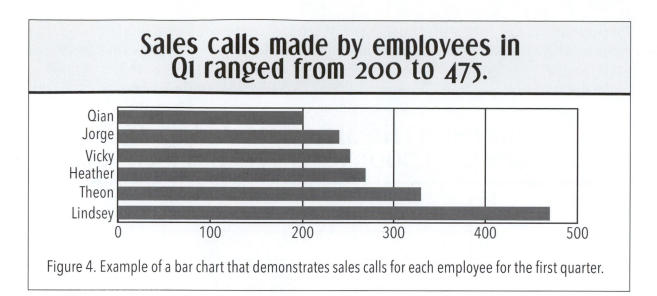

Figure 4. Example of a bar chart that demonstrates sales calls for each employee for the first quarter.

Research on the clarity of bar charts finds that understanding is enhanced if bar charts are two-dimensional.[13] Three-dimensional effects impair our ability to interpret spatially, thus leading to misinterpretation.[14] Researchers also recommend using backgrounds that contrast with graph colors; in addition, cool colors have been found to be more attractive to audiences than warm colors.[15]

Ethically Speaking

Graphs should be presented in a straightforward manner that actually improves understanding of the data. This means that you should not include effects that are unnecessary. For example, many of the graphing functions in presentation software automatically provide a 3-D effect. This effect has actually been shown to interfere with the audience's ability to process and understand the graph. As an ethical speaker, you want to present your information in a manner that avoids confusing or misleading your audience. Leave the special effects off. Sometimes the more simply you can construct a chart or graph, the better.

Time Series Comparisons

Column and **line charts** are most appropriate for comparing changes over time in a set of data. They are not well suited for snapshots, but they are useful in examining trends. If the chart has few data points, fewer than six or seven, a column chart is usually preferred. Column charts are better suited for data that occur within a set time period. So, if you want to trace changes over several years, each column would represent one year.[16] As with the other types of charts previously discussed, keep the chart simple and two-dimensional so that audiences can easily interpret its meaning. An example of a column chart is shown in Figure 5.

In a chart with many data points, line charts usually work best. They are most effective for data that have no set beginning and ending date.[17] When using line charts, make the line bolder than the base line. This will ensure that your chart stands out and can be read easily. See Figure 2 in this chapter for an example of a line chart.

The process in choosing the right chart type is easy. First, you must determine what you want to convey to your audience. What is the specific point you are trying to communicate? Once you have identified this, ask yourself what type of comparison your goal implies. Is it a component comparison or percentage, an item comparison, or a time series comparison? Finally, the answer to this question will lead you to choose the correct chart type.

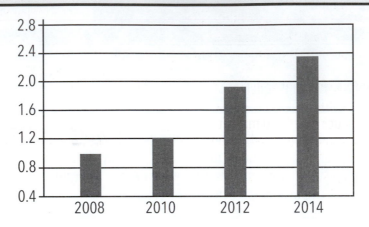

Figure 5. An example of a column chart demonstrating the number of firearms found in passenger carry-ons during a six-year span is easily visualized in this graph.

Text Charts

Text charts list key ideas or phrases under a heading. Usually, this is the type of chart you see on text PowerPoint or Keynote slides. These charts often use bullets and list items such as goals, functions, guidelines, and so on. Often, people misuse text charts by listing too much information on the slide. Read the guidelines in the section on using presentation software effectively for more advice on using text charts well.

Tips for Using Numerical Charts

- ◎ Visually try to signify the most important numerical information by ranking (highest to lowest or lowest to highest) the information in the chart or by otherwise visually distinguishing important information.
- ◎ Use high-contrast colors.
- ◎ Keep the number of segments in a pie chart to six or fewer. If you need more segments, you can often combine many smaller components into an "others" category.
- ◎ Avoid creating a separate legend; instead, put the labels in the appropriate positions in the chart.
- ◎ Avoid using special effects, such as tilting to show perspective. This interferes with the ability to see proportions accurately.

Maps

Maps organize information spatially. If you have arranged your main points in a spatial pattern, chances are you will need to use a map as a presentation aid. Maps are particularly helpful when you are trying to discuss geographically oriented topics. They are also useful anytime you want to break information down by regions. Perhaps you are delivering a presentation on a recent flu outbreak and you want to demonstrate how the flu has spread across a particular state. Maps can also be used to provide directions within a speech.

The map in the example that follows shows the Ho Chi Minh Trail very clearly. Clarity is a key issue here. Maps often provide too much detail and make it hard for an audience to see the actual idea you are trying to communicate. Make sure your maps are easy to read, like the one in the example.

This is a map of the Ho Chi Minh Trail. Notice how the trail is clearly marked and visually easy to distinguish for the audience.

Diagrams

A **diagram** is a simple illustration that demonstrates the key ideas and how they relate to each other. Diagrams are especially helpful in demonstrating steps in a process. Flow charts are another type of diagram commonly used in presentations. Additional examples of diagrams include organizational charts, diagrams that illustrate steps in a process, and cycle diagrams.

The diagram to the right illustrates the emergency exits on a commercial airliner. This type of diagram drastically increases a person's ability to understand exactly where the exits are located. It provides a visual representation that could not be communicated as clearly with words alone. As you can see, the diagram highlights the exits in a contrasting color so that they are readily apparent to the audience. It is simple in design so that the important aspects of the diagram stand out.

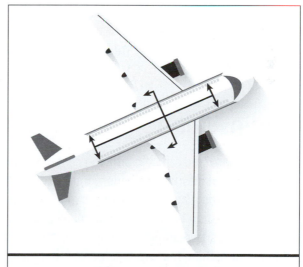

Aviation safety diagram identifying emergency exits.

Photographs

Photographs can also be effective presentation aids. They illustrate events, people, or other objects more effectively than a speaker can with words alone. Imagine trying to explain the architecture of Frank Lloyd Wright without showing some of his masterpieces. Oral spoken descriptions cannot do his work justice. Unless an audience can see these beautiful works of art, they will not understand his genius. The photo to the right shows his design for the Guggenheim Museum in New York. A mere description could not adequately convey the beauty in this piece of art. Your audience has to see it to appreciate it.

Photos are easy to locate. They are all over the Internet. If you are going to use photographs, make sure they are very large and easy to see. The best way to display photos is to project them through a presentation software program, such as Keynote, PowerPoint, SlideRocket, and so on. Your audience has to be very close to you to see an actual photograph of any size. To achieve maximum impact with a photo, make sure it can be seen from the back row and that all necessary details are clear.

If you do use a photo from the Internet, make sure you cite the source from which it was retrieved. Like all material that you use for your presentations, you must give proper credit when you use someone else's material.

Example of Frank Lloyd Wright's architecture.

Audio/Video

Audio and/or video can help bring presentations alive in ways that make your presentations very memorable. Some types of information benefit from audio/video information. We live in such a media-saturated world that not including audio/video information often seems like an oversight to many audiences. Because audio/video information is so compelling, many people prefer getting news and entertainment from television or on their iPads to reading newspapers or other sources of print information. Whether or not this is a good thing is something that is often debated, but the point is that you can often use this source of information to succinctly make points that are difficult to make with words. The primary difficulty with audio and video is that they entail using additional equipment, such as DVD players. If you have to use this type of equipment, you should be sure that your videos are queued to the right spot prior to your presentation. You should also avoid trying to fast forward or rewind to locate material during the presentation. The ideal solution is to capture this information digitally and play it using presentation software. Embed your video and audio clips into your slide presentation for a more seamless presentation. This way you can completely control what your audience sees and hears. There are additional guidelines for using audiovisual equipment in Chapter 4.

Creating Multimedia Presentations

Most professional presentations today make use of "presentation software" that utilizes computers and display devices, such as liquid crystal display (LCD) projectors. The most common software on the market today that creates these types of presentations is Microsoft PowerPoint, although other packages offer similar functionality, such as Apple's Keynote, Prezi, and others. This type of software lets you create "slides" that can contain text, images, audio, video, and animations to help guide users through your presentation.

Because presentation software is relatively easy to learn, it is often overused or used ineffectively.[18] The following sections will help you identify when and how you should use this type of tool so that you may avoid common pitfalls.

Advantages to Using Presentation Software

There are several reasons to use presentation software. First, because presentation software provides you with visual information to support your presentation, you provide your audience with another exposure to your material that helps them retain and understand important information.[19] Second, presentation software breaks up the monotony of your presentation and adds visual interest to your information. Third, by using this type of software, you can integrate different types of information into one standard format that you can easily manipulate during your presentation. For instance, if you need to use charts, sounds, and text to display different types of supporting information, you can do so entirely within a single set of slides, minimizing the need for multiple pieces of equipment. Fourth, presentation software often provides tools for creating speaking notes, outlines, and other types of materials, such as handouts. Fifth, most presentation software allows you to save your notes in a form that can be uploaded to the Internet or some other sharing software for those who could not attend an event. Finally, because of its usefulness and popularity, audiences often expect speakers to use presentation software.

Types of Presentation Slides

We can usefully classify our PowerPoint slides into three types: text-only slides, pictorial-only slides (which can include figures and graphics in addition to actual photos), and mixed slides that incorporate both of these previous types. The topic of your presentation will often determine the makeup of your presentation. For example, economics presentations are almost 50% text only. Compare that to the natural sciences, where nearly two-thirds of slides contain pictorial information.

Don't be fooled by the names. Text slides in presentations, especially more scientific presentations, are more than just words on a screen. The creator also has to consider the spatial arrangements of the information, or "visual text." Some things to consider in the visual text include the hierarchal relationship of the information (i.e., most important to least important) or a relevance structure (this must come first, etc.).

Text slides can be either static (all the text is revealed at once), or dynamic, which fade in information incrementally. And research shows us that audience members respond differently to these two types. As a result, you will need two different strategies for integrating them into your presentations.

For static slides, audience members will focus on the slide and "overhear" the speaker. On the other hand, with dynamic slides, audience members will divide their attention back and forth between the slide and the speaker. Because of this, dynamic slides work better in more complex situations where the integration of what the speaker is saying and the slides is more critical to understanding.

Pictorial-only slides include drawings, photographs, photo collages, maps, charts, etc. They function to demonstrate, visualize, illustrate or back up information being presented. With both pictorial-only and mixed slides, the audience is attracted immediately when the slide is displayed, but subsequently returns their focus to the speaker, before finally, but briefly, re-fixating on the slide. Presenters can use this time to point out elements of the pictorial element that audience members might not have noticed or focus on in their initial look.[20-22]

Using Presentation Software Effectively

Slides Are Not Designed to Tell the Entire Story

As you may have heard or read, there has been substantial criticism over the last few years regarding the effective use of PowerPoint and similar slide presentation programs.[23] These criticisms relate to the amount of text on a slide and the overall organization of the slides themselves. The following section identifies three areas that limit the effectiveness of speakers and offers solutions for addressing each limitation:

Too Much Text

Many people do not use PowerPoint and other presentational tools to maximum advantage. One common mistake people make is to include way too much information on one slide. They often use PowerPoint as a way to outline the whole presentation and then show that outline on their slides as they go. In this type of presentation, every point and subpoint in the presentation is represented on slides, and speakers simply advance through all of these points as they move through the presentation. This creates a boring, text-heavy, and largely useless set of slides that does more to distract attention away from the speaker than anything else. The slides actually compete with the speaker for attention. When you flash a text-laden slide in front of your audience, they have to make a choice. Will they read the slide or listen to you?[24] Remember, you are the presentation, not the slides. You want the focus of the presentation to be on you. Otherwise, there is no point in your being there. Just post the slides to a website and let the audience read them.

When developing slides, it is important to keep in mind that they are merely the background. You are the main event, so to speak. While slides should make sense on their own, they should not provide all the details an audience needs to hear in order to understand the point you are making. You are the presentation; you are the expert. You bring something to the audience that a slide simply cannot replicate. Slides should help explain the ideas you are presenting, but they should not contain all of the information.[25]

Phrase Headlines

Another area of criticism relates to the organization of the slide itself. Typically, slides are constructed using a phrase as a headline along with a list of bullet points.[26] Phrase headlines and bulleted lists are problematic for audiences. Critics have argued that this layout limits the way we think about the presented information and can actually interfere with normal cognitive processes. One critic in particular, Edward Tufte, a Yale professor who studies the visual display of quantitative information, has been especially vocal. He argues that the slide layout templates, which come standard in popular software packages, oversimplify and fragment subject matter in ways that can prevent audiences from getting the "big picture."[27] Others have argued that the listing style of PowerPoint actually limits the connections people can make between ideas.[28]

One concrete suggestion that has been offered by experts to increase the effectiveness of slide presentation software templates is to use a full sentence rather than just a phrase as the title for a slide.[29] The full-sentence headline has three advantages over the phrase headline. First, it introduces the audience to the purpose of the slide more effectively. Consider the phrase *Color in Diamonds* as a title, versus the full-sentence headline *In diamonds, colors (which are rare) come from impurities, defects, and irradiation.*[30] With the full-sentence headline we know exactly what the slide is conveying. Second, a full-sentence headline can focus the attention of the audience on the most important aspect of the slide. Finally, a full-sentence headline can orient the audience to the key arguments and assumptions of the presentation.[31] It is similar to a thesis statement for your presentation. Think of it as a statement of purpose for the slide.

Using Full-Sentence Headlines Effectively

- ◎   Headlines should be succinct.
- ◎   Headlines should be declarative, not interrogative.
- ◎   Headlines should appear at the top of the slide.
- ◎   Headlines should not exceed two lines.
- ◎   Headlines should be left justified.
- ◎   Headlines should use bold 28 point type.
- ◎   Avoid using all capitals.

In addition to conveying information succinctly, full-sentence headlines have been demonstrated to increase audiences' retention of the material presented on slides.[32] Some researchers in the area also argue that full-sentence headlines are also more persuasive. So there is an added bonus over clarity alone.[33]

In order to implement full-sentence headlines effectively, there are a couple of tips to keep in mind. First, make sure your sentence headline appears at the top of the slide and is left justified. This helps the audience read the slide more quickly.[34] Normally use 28 point type and bold for the headline. This provides easily readable text and reserves room for important graphics.[35] Avoid using all capital letters in headlines–they are harder for audiences to read. Headlines should not extend past two lines of text.[36] Finally, full-sentence headlines should be written in the form of a declarative sentence and not phrased as a question.

Ineffective vs. Improved Slide

Ineffective Slide

Uniform Resource Locators (URLS)

- Uniform Resource Locators
  - Example
    - http://www.bigsercersomewhere.com/process.html
- 3 Main Parts
  - Hyper-text Transfer Protocol
  - Server Name
  - HTML Files

Improved Slide

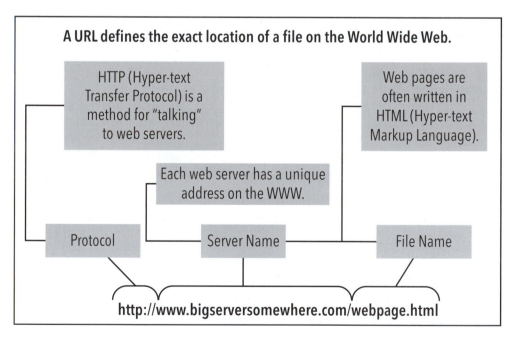

Figure 6. The ineffective or traditional slide on top has a headline phrase that doesn't tell the audience much about the purpose of the slide. The improved slide uses a full-sentence headline that tells the audience the purpose of the slide. The improved slide demonstrates the relationship between the bulleted points referenced on the first slide so that the audience can see how the parts are related. The relationship between elements becomes clear upon presentation of the slide to the audience.

Reliance on Bulleted Lists

As mentioned previously, another criticism of presentation software program templates relates to the use of bullet points. Experts in slide design have been critical of the bulleted list used in many slideshow presentations.[37] The key concern is the inability of a bulleted list to demonstrate a relationship between all of the material presented on the slide. When there is a relationship between the items in your bulleted list, it is better to demonstrate that relationship visually for your audience rather than just listing the items. When you just list points, the relationship can be harder for your audience to see. So if your points demonstrate part of a process, for example, show visually how those points connect to one another. Flow charts, models, graphics, and diagrams are much more useful in communicating relationships than mere lists.

Although bullet points should not be your default selection when developing a slide, they can be effective if used in moderation. The following guidelines should help you use bullet points more effectively and avoid some of their inherent defects. First, make sure your slide is clearly limited to one idea. Your sentence headline should make that point clear. All of your bullets should relate to that main idea. Second, bullet points are not designed to demonstrate the sequence of ideas. They are best used to present inductive reasoning and not deductive reasoning (see Chapter 11). Third, do not use more than two levels of bullets. Too many bullets complicate things for an audience. Finally, use complete sentences for first-level categories.[38] Before using a bulleted list, stop and ask yourself if this is the best way to represent your material. If so, keep in mind the guidelines suggested above and you should be just fine.

When bullet points won't work, use images, graphics, or charts instead. In many instances, images and graphics can overcome the limitations of the bulleted list. Images can often orient the audience to the topic and show how subcomponents are related or fit together. We know that audiences learn more effectively from words when they are accompanied by representative images rather than by words alone.[39] Images should be explanatory, not merely decorative.[40] Thus, an effective slide will contain a sentence headline that makes a claim, accompanied by visual support and, when necessary, accompanied by text. This format is known as the **assertion-evidence model,** and research shows it to be extremely effective, especially in scientific and technical presentations.[41] The assertion-evidence structure assumes that visual aids are necessary to help the audience understand and remember the content. When compared to text alone, this approach has been found to make presenters more focused and better understood.[42] Figure 6 demonstrates this principle. Notice how the use of the full-sentence headline along with the graphic demonstrates better slide construction. We can now visualize and understand how the steps in this model/process are related. We use the assertion-evidence model not to inform but to prove our claim made in the headline with visual evidence. Research shows us that this format not only makes communication more efficient and memorable, but also more persuasive.[43]

Some presentation software programs rely less on bulleted lists and may make it easier to follow the suggested guidelines. There are numerous software packages, both proprietary and free, that can help you achieve these goals (e.g., Keynote, Prezi, etc.). Many of these programs are less linear in their approach to slide development and may make it easier for you to get out of the bullet rut.

Guidelines for Assertion-Evidence Slides

Style

1. Begin each body slide with a sentence-assertion headline that is left justified and no more than two lines.
2. Support the assertion headline with visual evidence: photographs, drawings, graphs, or words and equations arranged visually.

Typography

1. Use a bold sans serif typeface such as Arial or Calibri.
2. Use 28 point type for the headline, 18–24 point type for the body text, and reference listings in 14 point.
3. Avoid setting text in all capital letters, in italics, or in underline.

Layout

1. Keep blocks of text, including headlines, to one or two lines.
2. Keep lists to two, three, or four items.
3. Be generous with white space, especially between text blocks and graphic elements within the slide.[44]

Take Advantage of the Build Feature

Most software presentation programs allow you to use "builds" when you present your material. Builds allow only so much text to appear on a slide at a time. In this way, you control what your audience sees when. Instead of revealing all of your material at once, the speaker has control over when it appears. This keeps your audience from reading ahead. It is a great feature, but unfortunately, speakers don't take advantage of it as they should.

Keep the Slides Simple

Keep the number of slides to a minimum. Only put genuinely useful information that actually supports your points on slides. In a ten-minute presentation, you should have no more than four or five slides. If you have more than that, you may be including nonvital information on slides, which has been shown to reduce learning in audiences.[45] Too many slides also complicate what you have to keep up with during the presentation (working the slides instead of focusing on the audience), constantly shifting audience attention away from you.

Slides should not serve as a memory device for the speaker. Instead, they are used to increase understanding and clarity in the audience. Use them toward that end. This means the amount of material on any one particular slide should be limited. The more text there is on a slide, the more likely it is for a speaker to read the slide.[46] Research has indicated "that reading and hearing identical verbal information simultaneously can significantly reduce the comprehension by audience members" because they have to split their attention.[47] It is more effective to limit the material on each slide and to explain it rather than read it to the audience.

Use Slides Only When Needed

Only show slides when you are specifically addressing them. This keeps the presentation focused on you, rather than on your presentation aid. Presentation software programs let you "blank" the screen with a simple keyboard command when you are not using the slide. Projectors often have "black out" buttons on their remotes as well. Presenters do not use this feature enough.

Use Effective Design Principles

When preparing your presentation slides, use high-contrast colors, large font sizes, and consistent typefaces. Nothing is worse than a PowerPoint presentation with so much small text that the audience cannot read it easily. Also, people find it easier to see large, bright text (yellows and whites) on dark backgrounds (black and blues) than dark text on light backgrounds when it is projected onto a screen. The reverse is true for printed material. Finally, try to keep the number of fonts you use to a minimum. Choose one or two, and use them consistently across all slides.

Avoid Special Effects

Keep special effects, such as slide transitions, sound effects, and animations, to a minimum. Many amateur PowerPoint users load their presentations with so many prebuilt special effects that their presentations become goofy and annoying. These features should always be used very sparingly. Other than the occasional subtle slide transition, these features do more harm than good and should be avoided.

Avoid Standing in the Shadows

Remember, you are the presentation, not your slides. If the presentation slides could speak for themselves, you could simply put your presentation up on the Web and allow your audience to read it for themselves. Because you are the focus of the presentation, avoid standing off to the side of the screen in the shadows.[48] Because the lights are dimmed, the area to the side of the screen is usually very dark. It becomes easy for you, the presenter, to get lost. Don't let that happen. Make sure the room is well lit before you begin your presentation so that the audience can see you. This way they can identify with you before you dim the lights. Make sure that you continue to connect with the audience even though the room is dark. Stay in the most well lit area and use a remote control slide advancer if possible. This tool will allow you to stay out in front of your audience rather than behind a computer. If the presentation contains a question-and-answer session, turn up the lights for that segment. Never forget, you–not the presentation aids–are the presentation.

Tips for Designing Presentation Aids

Prepare Presentation Aids Carefully

Your presentation aids are a part of the overall effect of the presentation and deserve as much attention as all of the other parts of the planning process. Spend time carefully proofreading your presentation aids. Check spelling and grammar closely. Nothing can ruin your credibility more quickly than a typo. Create your presentation aids in advance so that you have ample time to catch mistakes. Get a friend to read over them for you. Another trick that may be helpful is to read visual aids backwards. Sometimes we just can't find those mistakes because we know what should be there, and we see what we expect to see. Reading them backwards can help catch some of those small oversights such as double words or missing articles. You can never check too closely.

Choose Fonts Carefully

Most of us don't think about fonts and just use the default the software program suggests.[49] Be proactive about the font. You want to think about what you are trying to convey; choose a font that is not only easy to read but also communicates the appropriate tone of your message. Fonts that automatically "pop up" with templates aren't always the best choice. So think about them and be deliberate in your choice.

There are basically two types of fonts: serif and sans serif. Serif typefaces have curls at the ends of the letters. Sans serif fonts do not have these curls and are plain at the ends of the letters (see Figure 7). In a recent study comparing serif and sans serif fonts, audiences found no significant differences in the readability, professionalism, interest, or attractiveness characteristics of the two font types.[50]

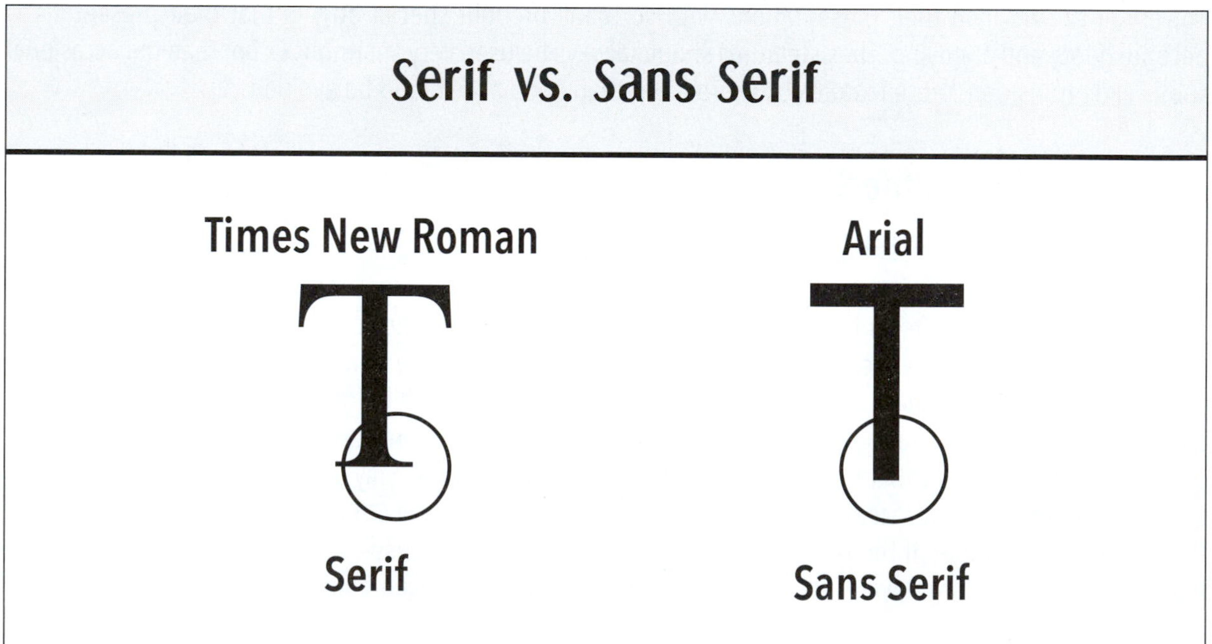

Serif vs. Sans Serif

Times New Roman — Serif

Arial — Sans Serif

Figure 7.

Fonts are important and can communicate more to an audience than you might think. Studies have shown that fonts convey a personality to an audience.[51] Fonts with heavier strokes are typically rated as strong, aggressive, and masculine. Some fonts like **Comic Sans** are rated as funny, happy, and creative, while **Courier New** is rated as dull, plain, unimaginative, and conforming.[52] The bottom line is that the font you choose is important. It communicates a tone for the whole presentation. Make sure you choose a font appropriate to the material that you are presenting to your audience.

Spotlight on Research

Your Font Matters

Jo Mackiewicz, professor and author of *Visual Composing: Document Design for Print and Digital Media*, has conducted several studies examining perceptions of fonts in PowerPoint presentations. In one study she examined ten of the most popular fonts and asked audiences to rate them on the following dimensions: comfortable to read, professional, interesting, and attractive. Gill Sans was rated as the most comfortable to read, the most interesting, and the most attractive. Times New Roman was perceived as the most professional by audience members. Consider this study when choosing your font. It is important to be active about the selection of your font. Don't let the software program choose for you. It might not be the best choice for your audience or your situation.[58]

Regardless of what font you choose, it needs to be consistent from slide to slide. The headline of a slide should use 28 point type. Font within the body text of a slide should be 18–24 points.[53]

Regardless of which font you decide to select, stick to just one. You can use features such as bold, color, and size to add impact. Font size should stay between 18 and 24 points. Anything larger than 24 points is overwhelming. However, audiences have trouble reading fonts smaller than 18 points.

Serif Fonts	
◎ Century Schoolbook	◎ Garamond
◎ Times New Roman	◎ Palatino
	◎ Bookman Old Style

Sans Serif Fonts	
◎ Arial	◎ Tahoma
◎ Century Gothic	◎ Gill Sans
◎ Verdana	◎ Futura

Use Color

Color can be a very effective tool in a presentation. According to research, color can increase motivation and participation of an audience by up to 80%.[54] Color also enhances learning and improves retention by more than 75%.[55] Color advertisements out-sell black-and-white advertisements by 88%.[56] Color can also help an audience focus attention.[57] This gives you some idea of how important color can be. However, more color isn't necessarily better. As noted in the color and culture box, color can have unwanted implications, so it is important to follow some guidelines when implementing color in your slides.

Color and Culture

It is important to note that color does have cultural implications. So, do some research if you are addressing a global audience about what colors might mean in a particular context. For example, white in Asian cultures is associated with death and mourning. Black is associated with fear and anger in Slavic countries.[61] Yellow represents warmth in the U.S. but infidelity in France.[62] Blue denotes high quality, trustworthiness, and dependability in the U.S., Japan, Korea, and China.[63] In fact, researchers have noticed a preference for blue across a variety of cultures. This is actually called the "Blue Phenomenon."[64] Think about the color of your slides and presentation aids and what they might communicate to a particular audience. You wouldn't want to lose your audience just because you chose the wrong color for a visual aid. Do some investigating on the front end so you don't end up making an audience uncomfortable. For more on this, see Chapter 14 "Presenting to a Global Audience."

While color can have a dramatic impact on a presentation, it is still important to use it with caution. Audiences find cool colors such as blue and green more attractive than warm colors such as red, orange, or yellow.[59] Certain color combinations are not advisable, due to deficiencies in color perception (color blindness): red/green, brown/green, blue/black, and blue/purple. These color combinations should always be avoided.[60]

As with any other element, color can be overdone. Be careful about overwhelming the audience with too much color. Color should be used to highlight certain key aspects to which you want to draw attention.

Keep Presentation Aids Simple

Avoid putting too much information on a presentation aid. Each aid should contain only one idea or illustrate only one concept. If you need to use two different charts that have no relation to each other, use separate presentation aids. Oftentimes, students will put three different presentation aids on one slide. Don't fall into this trap—it only confuses audiences. Rather than focusing on your message, they will wonder why three unrelated pictures are on the same slide.

When using text on a presentation aid, a good guideline to follow is to use only six lines of text per aid. Each line should be limited to six or seven words. This will keep your visual from overwhelming the audience.

Tips for Using Presentation Aids

Using presentation aids takes practice. They take time to prepare properly. However, if you invest time in creating them, and make good choices about what to use, then your presentation will benefit from their inclusion. The following tips will help ensure that your use of presentation aids is as effective as possible.

Avoid Using the Chalkboard

By preparing your aids beforehand, the need for you to use items such as a chalkboard to illustrate points is eliminated. Chalkboards or other tools for rapidly displaying information have their place, especially in regard to answering questions from the audience. However, they are not appropriate presentation aids. It is hard to write neatly when time is an issue. Turning your back to the audience so that you can draw on the board only interferes with your ability to connect to the audience. Even if you were able to prepare the drawing on the chalkboard ahead of time, it would lack the professionalism you are trying to achieve.

Practice, Practice, Practice

Use your presentation aids during practice sessions for your presentation. You should know exactly when to show them and when you should remove them from view. This is easy if you keep your aids to a minimum. Having many presentation aids complicates your presentation and can be a source of confusion for you during the presentation.

Have a Backup Plan

Presentation aids that use technology are always prone to possible failure. You should have a backup plan in case of technical difficulties. You should construct your presentation so that if the technology doesn't work, you can still go on. Also, you can always bring an alternative version of your presentation aid. For instance, if you hope to use a computer to project PowerPoint slides, you might bring a backup set of transparencies to use as an alternative. If worse comes to worst, be prepared to deliver the presentation without your presentation aids. As a speaker, you should always be prepared for this possibility.

Stay Focused on Your Audience

Many novice speakers get so caught up in making sure their presentation aids are working correctly that they end up speaking to their aids rather than to the audience. This is very common in PowerPoint presentations. By keeping your presentation aids simple, and by practicing, you can use your aids successfully and still focus on your audience.

Avoid Passing out Presentation Aids

Handouts are very tempting to create, and it is OK to use them. However, the mistake comes when you pass them out before or, worse, during your presentation. All this serves to do is distract your audience from what you are saying. If at all possible, provide handouts at the end of your presentation if you want your audience to have something to refer to later.[65] Also, avoid passing objects around. This often causes more confusion because audience members are seeing your objects at different times. Handouts and objects that are passed out usually cause more harm than good. You don't want them competing for your attention.

Display Presentation Aids Only When Explaining Them

Presentation aids are designed to attract the attention of your audience, and that is exactly what they do. If you display an aid when you are not discussing it, some members of the audience will focus on the aid rather than on the message you are delivering. So a good rule to follow is this: Present the aid only when you are discussing it. After you have completed your explanation, remove the presentation aid. If it is a transparency, turn off the overhead projector; if it is a PowerPoint slide, "blank" the screen.

Explain Your Presentation Aids

No matter how professional and clear your visual aids are, they cannot speak for themselves. You need to explain them to your audience. The audience doesn't know what to look for when examining your presentation aid. What is important about the presentation aid? Point that out to the audience. Even though it may be tempting, don't rush through the explanation of your presentation aid. You selected this material for a reason. Take the time to give your audience a thorough explanation.

"Referring actions"–both verbal and gestural–are important when explaining your presentation aids. They help indicate what is important to the audience, what you as the presenter want them to focus on. "In combination with speech, it (i.e., the gesture) even succeeds quite regularly in creating new meanings that are not represented either in the words spoken or on the slide pointed at.[66]"

A presenter has several options when explaining aids:

Tip

Don't give out presentation aids ahead of time–it is human nature to jump ahead and look at what is going to be said, losing audience interest.

Michael Schiferl |
Executive Vice President |
Weber Shandwick

◎ **Verbal References:** At the bottom of the slide, here, etc.
◎ **Gestures:** Pointing, waving, etc.
◎ **Technology-Based References:** Arrows on the slide, laser pointers, etc.

Your audience will also dictate just how extensively you need to explain your PowerPoint slides. The most important determinant is the audience's prior knowledge of your presentation subject. The higher knowledge an audience has, the fewer gestures or technology-based references are needed. The higher level of knowledge allows the audience members who interpret spoken references to the slides in the way the presenter intended. To more novice audiences, however, the lack of gestures and technology-based references is "highly problematic." The audience simply does not have enough knowledge to understand just where to look, or what they are looking for exactly, from spoken references alone.

Keep these fundamentals in mind as you explain your presentation aids:

1. **Timing:** Make sure your words and slides are synchronized properly.
2. **Wording and Language:** The same key words should be used on the slide and in the speech. Resist the urge to refer to something by different names in your speech and on your slide.
3. **Sequence:** Actions on a slide should appear in a successive order.
4. **Accuracy:** You need to make sure that you are pointing to the exact area on the slide. A general wave in the direction will not suffice.[67]

Conclusion

Presentation aids, if used effectively, can significantly help an audience in understanding your message. Certain types of information, such as numerical information, can drastically benefit from the use of presentation aids. The important thing is to use the appropriate chart or graph at the appropriate time. When using presentation software, make sure that you avoid the common mistakes related to both design and to presentation. The key is to make sure that whatever you use actually adds meaning to your message. Gratuitous or ill-prepared visual aids will detract from your message, not enhance it. Every aspect of the design process should be considered carefully, from medium, to color, to font, to how the aid will be displayed. A well-prepared visual aid can add real value to your presentation. If you follow the guidelines in this chapter, you will be successful in implementing these tools.

Key Terms

Assertion-evidence model

Bar charts

Charts

Diagrams

Line/column charts

Pie charts

Presentation aid

CHAPTER 13

Presenting as a Group

Objectives

After reading this chapter, you should be able to

- ◎ structure an effective group presentation;
- ◎ understand the importance of practicing as a group;
- ◎ understand how conflict can affect group presentations; and
- ◎ work successfully in multicultural groups.

How much is a successful group presentation worth? Well in the case of Japan, about $40 billion. The International Olympic Committee awarded Tokyo the 2020 Summer Olympics after a group presentation that "wowed" the committee.[1]

The biggest challenge for the Japanese group was to make a more "western style" presentation.[2] Making a strong emotional appeal wasn't entirely comfortable for all of the speakers, according to Nick Varley, founder and CEO of Seven46, the London-based consultant involved in the Tokyo event. But he encouraged each member to step out of their comfort zones and to appeal to the I.O.C on a personal, heartfelt level. Group members were encouraged to use their time to tell personal stories, to smile, and to demonstrate passion. The result was a 45-minute presentation that was more direct and emotional than the I.O.C members were expecting, he said, which likely made a larger impact on committee members and resulted in them awarding Tokyo the Games–which some experts estimate could be worth $40 billion to the region.

Preparing and Delivering the Group Presentation

In Chapter 1, you learned that the number one skill employers seek in employees is communication skills. But in that same survey, employers ranked teamwork skills as the third most sought after skill. Many tasks that were performed by individuals even ten years ago are now done in small and large groups.[3]

Whether you are preparing an individual presentation or a group presentation, much of the presentation process is identical. Good group and individual presentations share many commonalities: There must be a clear goal, thorough audience analysis, adequate research to support your claims, and clear organizational structure. The difference is that these activities must be coordinated throughout the group, which does present some unique challenges and opportunities for conflict. There is also added difficulty in just how you make a uniform presentation when you have several speakers rather than just one.

The following guidelines will help you overcome some of the challenges associated with coordinating and delivering effective group presentations. The guidelines are presented in two ways: First, each section presents the fundamentals that apply to a particular concept, regardless of speaking context. Second, when appropriate, the concepts are applied to your actual group project in this course so that you can see how to incorporate them more effectively.

Group Conflict

Working in groups is not always easy. In some instances, conflict will result. You can categorize conflict in work groups into three types: relationship, task, and process conflict.[4] Being aware of such conflicts can help you avoid these barriers to group work. Knowing how to work through such conflict is important. Many groups you will work with, both in college and out, will not be self-assigned; that is, you won't have the opportunity to choose your group members. Learning to work through conflict will be key to having a successful group experience.

Relationship conflict is an awareness of interpersonal incompatibility. You simply may dislike one of your group members. This can lead you to feel annoyed or irritated when you are around that person. In this situation, it is key that the group leader promotes respect and attempts to keep the work environment friendly.

Spotlight on Research

Importance of Group Goals

It's possible you have been assigned group work at some point in your academic career and wondered why you couldn't just do the work yourself. If that's the case, your instructor did not do a good job of pointing out the benefits of group work. Research in England found that for group work to be effective, members of the group must understand why they were asked to work together. The authors examined pairings of workers from the health-care and social work industries. Researchers found that simply placing practitioners in a team did not foster team spirit. Instead, organizations need to make it a priority to develop team relationships. This includes everything from pointing out the benefits of working together to making sure that teams have both the time to meet and places to meet.[5]

Task conflict refers to differing opinions relating to a group task. This could be disagreement over your group topic. Such conflict can lead to passionate differences of opinion among group members, but not negative feelings toward individual group members. In actuality, some task conflict has been shown to be beneficial to group performance.[6] Teams actually benefit from some differences of opinion. Conflict, when constructive, helps groups make better decisions and avoid "groupthink," which promotes the need for group consensus over good decision-making skills.[7] It is important, however, that you construct your criticism in such a way as to attack the idea you don't like, not the source of the idea.[8] You want to make it very clear that you dislike Jane's idea for a topic, not Jane herself. So don't be afraid to offer your opinions on what your group assignment should look like.

A third type of conflict is **process conflict.** This is when your group may disagree about how to proceed to accomplish your task. You might disagree over who should do what or whose responsibility it is to see that a task is done. This conflict is the most dangerous to your COM114 group project. Research has shown that groups who continually disagree about task assignments perform poorly.[9] More specifically, the sooner your group can agree on who is responsible for what, the more successful your group will be.[10] Poor-performing groups have more process conflict at the start of a project.

The Preparation Stage

Choose a Leader or Point Person

All group presentations and group projects will go more smoothly if one person acts as the liaison between the client and the other group members. This individual is responsible for knowing who is doing what and making sure the group has the resources it needs to accomplish the task at hand. The leader is also responsible for coordinating group meeting times, sharing contact information, and establishing group practice sessions. In short, the group leader is not an autocratic dictator demanding that his or her ideas and goals are carried out; rather, this individual helps the group stay on task and works to make sure that information is exchanged by all group members. The leader really serves as a group organizer or project manager.

Types of Group Decision Making

Not all groups arrive at a final decision in the same way. In some business situations, it's better for a leader to be the decision maker for the group. In others, it's best for the group to have some input or even make the decision. Here are some common types of decision making:

Authoritarian   In this method, decisions are made by the group leader, with or without discussion.

Democratic   Also known as majority rule. You take a vote; the option receiving the largest number of votes wins.

Consensus   All members of the group agree. This is the most desired course.

Rush to Judgment   Here, group members make a quick decision in order to get it out of the way. Watch out for this in your COM114 group discussions. Too often, students who aren't sure what to do simply "pick something" without adequately weighing the pros and cons of the idea.

In your group project for this class, the group leader will make sure all team members have exchanged phone numbers and e-mail addresses. The leader will also be the point person with your instructor. Although the entire group is responsible for ensuring that the group's project is consistent with the instructor's assignment, the team leader is responsible for setting up meetings and for follow-up e-mails between the group and the instructor. The leader is also responsible for arranging meeting locations and practice sessions. He or she also ensures that the group has the resources it needs, such as a computer, visual aids, and so on. Although there are many other tasks that the group leader may undertake, these are the most common.

Establish the Goal

Once the group has decided on a leader, it can move toward establishing its goal. The concept of group efficacy, or how effectively a group functions, is very relevant to establishing the goal for your group work in COM114. **Group efficacy** is defined as a group's consensual belief about its ability to perform a particular task.[11] This belief will influence which tasks groups choose to perform, how much effort they expend, and how they respond if problems arise. A group has some idea of its capabilities, and the goal is evaluated in the context of those beliefs.[12] In other words, it is important that you set a goal for your group project that all members think can be achieved.

> **Remember to establish this goal in light of time constraints and other environmental constraints.**

As with individual presentations, the goal for any group presentation must be very clear. Specific goals lead to better performances.[13] Just what is it that you want your audience to do, think, or feel as a result of your presentation? Remember to establish this goal in light of time constraints and other environmental constraints. Will you really be able to accomplish your goals, given the budget constraints and other concerns? In addition, make sure your goal is not too simple. The goal affects individual task performance; if you don't ask much of your group members, you won't get much!

You also need to make sure that everyone is committed to that goal and what they need to do to achieve it. The work of your group will be influenced by the personal style and individual behavior of every member of the group.[14] If group members don't believe the group can pull off this presentation on this topic, they won't put forth the necessary effort.[15] By the same token, if group members perceive the job as too easy, they might not feel the need to be committed to achieve it.[16] In other words, they might think that they can slack off a little and that it won't hurt the presentation as a whole.

Once your group has decided on its goal, it becomes important that you think about who your audience is and how you can best achieve the goal. With regard to the project in this course, you should think very carefully about your goal. Just what type of problem do you want to solve, or what kind of problem can you realistically solve with about four weeks of preparation? This is a small amount of time to put together a presentation. You need to think about what you can realistically accomplish, given your time and resource constraints. You will not be able to solve the university's parking problem, day-care issue, or transportation issue in this limited amount of time and with the budget constraints you have been given.

Reflective Thinking Method

A well-known problem-solving approach is the reflective thinking method developed more than 80 years ago by American philosopher John Dewey. The process involves these steps:

Define the Problem   If a group can't understand the problem, it won't be able to find a solution. The best way to define the problem is to phrase it in the form of a question of policy (see Chapter 9).

Analyze the Problem   The group tries to discover the causes and extent of the problem. This will require extensive research. The best decisions are made by having the best and most up-to-date information available.

Establish Criteria for a Solution   Identify the characteristics of a good solution. For instance, if you were trying to solve the problem of how to make up a budget shortfall, one criterion could be that the solution could not result in any layoffs of personnel.

Consider Possible Solutions to the Problem   Generate many ideas before judging any of them. Here, you can use the brainstorming technique discussed in Chapter 3. Each member of the group should contribute ideas to avoid one or two dominating the discussion. In this way, your group will generate many ideas before judging any of them.

Decide on a Solution   Once the group has considered all possible solutions, it can now find the best answer to the problem. It is best for the group to come to a consensus.

Your group can now implement your solution–put your plan into action. Then, you can follow up to see if any adjustments need to be made.[17]

Your goal should be to tackle a problem that the university could actually implement. Several of the group presentations in this course have resulted in projects that Purdue has actually funded. One such project sought to strengthen international and domestic student relationships through university-sponsored social activities.

The group received funding to form the Purdue Cultural Awareness Committee to coordinate and organize the activities. The goal of these social and educational activities was to increase cultural awareness and to promote student interaction through social gatherings.

Conduct Research

Once a group has a clearly established goal, it can begin to discuss research. In a 2005 episode of the NBC reality series *The Apprentice,* the group Net Worth lost a challenge due to poor research on the part of the group. Their goal was to design a tech-friendly clothing line designed for clothing manufacturer American Eagle. Unlike their challengers, Magna Corporation, who went out and surveyed individuals in the target market about what technological needs they had, Net Worth just guessed. In the end, the executives from American Eagle said that their lack of research, and therefore, knowledge of the market, hurt them considerably. In any type of presentation you make, you cannot underestimate the importance of solid research.

The nature of the group presentation in this course rests on good, solid research. Therefore, research is an issue for the entire group. Everybody should take an active role in the research process. Although you don't want to waste time replicating each other's work, you do want to make sure that you thoroughly research each aspect of the presentation. By having two or more individuals researching the same area, you lessen the chance of missing some vital piece of evidence.

Once the general research has been completed, you can ask certain individuals to go back and strengthen specific sections. For example, the Purdue Cultural Awareness Committee decided once their research was collected that they needed to interview students about diversity on campus.

Assign Tasks

It's important that each member of your group be assigned a role. That will result in stronger individual performances, in part by raising group members' belief that they can do the job they've been given.[18] It is important that everyone in the group feel they are contributing something important. Group participation can be tied to how much power or prestige individual group members think they have.[19] If group members feel they have been given an unimportant task, a response might be to lower participation in all group matters.

Everybody in the group has strengths: use them to your advantage.

Your group project is dependent on all group members doing their parts. Your group can be defined as being **resource interdependent.**[20] All group members can complete their part of the project individually, but they share research and other resources, and the whole task is not complete until all members have completed their parts. It is very important that each member of your group understand that the project as a whole depends on the individual parts being completed both on schedule and competently. Your group project will suffer if one task is not performed at the level of the others. A common complaint at this stage is that less motivated members of the group avoid doing their share of the work and leave the bulk of the effort to those individuals willing to step in and pick up the slack. To try to avoid this, assign tasks early in the planning stages of the project, giving more reluctant members time to do their share and the group time to wait them out.

At this point the group needs to think about who has certain strengths on the team. In this course, you have an advantage. You have seen each other present several times over the course of the semester, so you have a very good idea who on your team is strong in what area. Perhaps one of your team members is very strong in delivery skills; give this individual the most visible parts of the presentation to deliver. You will want to open and close the presentation with the strongest speaker in the group, so make sure that the group identifies that individual early. Maybe someone else is really good at organizational structure; have this individual coordinate and finalize the group outline. If someone is technically oriented, have this individual prepare the PowerPoint template and incorporate the visuals. Everybody in the group has strengths; use them to your advantage.

What you want to avoid, however, is a group presentation that looks like a series of individual presentations, made one after another, rather than a group presentation. The presentation should draw on the group and its collective strengths. A team can deliver a much more powerful presentation than an individual. So take advantage of this aspect of working on a team.

To achieve a more cohesive presentation, you will want to be careful how you divide the workload. Don't divide the project in the following manner: One person conducts the research, one person constructs the PowerPoint presentation, one person writes the introduction, one person writes the conclusion, and, finally, someone puts it all together. This will result in disaster. First of all, the introduction and conclusion should be written last, once the body is finalized.

Here is an example of how a group might proceed in assigning tasks. For the first group meeting, each group member should be responsible for coming up with at least two ideas for the group project. The group should then meet face-to-face and discuss the pros and cons of each group member's proposals. Finally, at this meeting, the group should choose an idea for the project.

Everyone should be involved in conducting preliminary research.

At this point, research becomes an important aspect. Everyone should be involved in conducting preliminary research. Have at least two group members cover each area of research to make sure that the group doesn't miss important details. Once the research has been conducted and you can answer important questions, then you can fine-tune. You can determine what holes you have in your arguments and evidence and then decide how to fill those in. Filling in holes is usually a less daunting task. As mentioned before, it won't take the entire group to go out and interview key figures. At this point, that part of the research can be divided up among members.

Next, the group should begin writing the body of the presentation. At least two team members should develop each main point. Then go back and put the body together. The entire group should examine the body and provide input for improvement. Next, two individuals should develop the introduction and at least two individuals should develop the conclusion. The entire group should critique these elements before they are finalized.

The last step in the presentation is developing the visual components. Once the group has decided on the design of the visuals and overall plan, one person on your team can develop the visual aids. However, the entire group should review the final product, looking for typographical errors.

Stay on Task

It is important throughout this process that the group stays on task. In this class, because the group presentation isn't until the last week of classes, the temptation is there to delay work on the project. This usually results in poorly researched and poorly performed presentations. Such projects often take longer than we expect. Build in time for unforeseen problems that inevitably pop up. Procrastination can undermine the efforts of the group.[21]

Instead, the group needs to have a schedule that sets various deadlines for parts of the project as the semester progresses. Even artificial deadlines can create a need to get something done. It is important to keep everyone on task the whole time. In this course, another way to ensure your group is on task is the two scheduled status update reports you are required to present. You will be asked to have certain tasks completed by set dates, and to report on these completions, or any stumbling blocks you encountered that have delayed completion, to your instructor and classmates. These reports can help ensure steady progress on your presentation and allow for feedback on the process from your instructor and classmates.

Group members need to be aware that some people have different pacing preferences: Some people prefer to spread out parts of the assignment over time; others say they work best under deadline pressures and like to leave tasks until the last minute. Group members need to remind each other of deadlines and urge each other to stick to the schedule.[22] Such reminders keep group members focused. If group members miss deadlines or submit sub-par work, the group leader should intervene and offer suggestions and encouragement to get them back on task.[23]

In a college setting, it is often difficult to find a time when all group members can meet face-to-face. But in-person meetings aren't always necessary. For example, your group can exchange ideas or drafts of outline sections via e-mail. In addition, technologies such as Dropbox or Google Docs allow groups to set up file-sharing portals that all group members can access from any computer. Communication platforms like Google Hangouts or Skype allow groups to meet virtually and save the time of having to travel to one location for a group meeting. This is where the careful assignment of tasks will benefit your group; if all group members understand their roles, there is less need for communication.

Group meetings should be about the project, not Boilermaker basketball or the latest hot movie or television show. Too much communication not focused on the group project itself actually hurts your ability to accomplish your goal.[24]

Develop the Presentation Template

As this chapter has stressed, a group should look like a group when it presents. One element that will help you achieve this goal is a PowerPoint template. You can have one person design all the slides for the presentation, or each individual can design his or her own, and one person can implement the design. Regardless of how the presentation is put together, you will want it to appear as if one person designed the entire thing. Make sure that the group has designed a template that everyone can follow so that the presentation takes on a more uniform appearance. You will also want to make sure that font type and size are the same from slide to slide as well. If you prepare a template with enough detail, this step should already be done for you. Also, pay attention to the vocabulary used on each slide. Make sure each team member is using consistent language and abbreviations.

You can use one of the templates Microsoft® supplies with its product, or you can create your own. Creating your own template is relatively simple and makes the PowerPoint look customized, and therefore professional. However, if you don't have the skills to customize the templates, don't try it. You will probably be better off with one of the Microsoft templates.

Design Presentation Format

Introductions

As with any other type of presentation, the group presentation will also have an introduction. Within the introduction, you must accomplish all of the tasks emphasized throughout this text: gain attention, establish credibility and relevance, introduce the topic (thesis), preview the main points, and so on. However, you have an additional component when presenting as a group: You also have to introduce individual group members and state their roles in the presentation and/or organization. The audience will want to know who all of the group members are and their roles. So simply saying, "This is Mary from marketing, and she will discuss marketing," isn't good enough. Be specific about the point of Mary's segment. To achieve this goal, ask all group members to write one sentence that encapsulates the most important idea in their section of the presentation. Use this material to help structure the introductions of each group member.

Speaker Transitions

Transitions are an important element in any presentation. They become increasingly important in group presentations because they are the element that bridges one speaker to another. Good transitions can help unify the presentation, while poor ones can make it seem like one individual presentation after another. According to Peter Giuliano, chairman of the Executive Communications Group, "Each presenter should wrap up his or her own segment, then establish a link to the next presenter."[25]

Here is an example: "You have seen from my examples and testimony that there is a lack of cohesiveness among students in our department. I will now turn the podium over to Ken, who will discuss how we may be able to bridge some of these differences between students by employing some unique strategies."

In this example, the speaker has summed up the main point of his or her portion of the presentation and has previewed the main point of the following speaker. It is simply a directional transition with the addition of the name of the next speaker.

The 10-Minute Rule

Researchers have found that our minds begin to wander after 10 minutes. It's a good idea to insert "soft breaks" every 10 minutes or so in a group presentation to give the audience's minds a rest and to keep them engaged.[26] The audience should not hear from one voice for longer than 10 minutes. Moving on to another speaker is considered a soft break. So are video clips, images, or stories. Seeking audience participation by conducting a poll or by asking for questions are other examples. Remember to give your audience that much-needed mental break.

Question-and-Answer Session

The question-and-answer (Q&A) session is a vital part of the presentation. Make sure the group has a plan for how this section will be handled. There is nothing worse than ending with a Q&A session that is disorganized. Chapter 15 provides greater detail on this issue.

Practice the Presentation

No matter how much individuals practice their individual sections, you cannot overestimate the importance of the group practice session. At the bare minimum, a group should run through its presentation at least once at full dress rehearsal level. This means a run-through from start to finish with no stops. This way, you can tell how the group is doing on time, identify rough spots, and determine if there are any oversights or replications in terms of material. It allows you to identify where each group member will stand so it is easy to move unobtrusively. All visual aids should be employed during the dress rehearsal and should be scrutinized one more time for typographical errors. It is also essential to ensure that all of your technology is working seamlessly. If possible, practice the presentation in the room where it will actually take place.

Absolutely nothing substitutes for actually giving your presentation in front of a live audience. Perhaps you could gather a group of friends to watch your presentation and offer input. Or, you could videotape your group practice and review it together to identify areas for improvement.

Don't leave your practice session to the last minute. The group needs to leave enough time to make adjustments if necessary. Remember, practice makes perfect. Although these group practice sessions may be difficult to coordinate, they will pay off!

Tip

The more you practice as a group, the better the presentation will be. It's important that presenters subjugate their egos to the content. If you have one presenter who decides to "wing it," this can step on the toes of all the other presenters.

Amy Stoehr | Founder and CEO | Real Estate Masters Guild

Make Contingency Plans

It is important to make contingency plans for your group presentation. Inevitably, situations arise that could affect your presentation. What will you do if a group member suddenly becomes ill and cannot be there on the day of your presentation? Who will be responsible for that role? How will that material be presented?

Planning for technological miscues is a must. What will you do if your PowerPoint doesn't work or your video won't play? How will your audience get the information contained there? Knowing ahead of time how you will handle such interruptions can make your response seem more professional to your audience.

The Actual Presentation

During the actual presentation, it is essential that all group members stay involved.[27] After all, if group members aren't interested in their presentation, why should the audience be interested? And believe it or not, the audience will be watching all members of the group, not just the person speaking, so it is essential that you show interest. Be very aware of your nonverbals; it is easy to send negative messages to the audience with a sigh or a yawn.

Staying alert and interested during your group presentation is vital to its success. If you aren't interested or engaged, why should your audience be?

In addition to appearing interested, you must also pay attention to the audience. Observing audience reaction can help in two ways. First, it can help you adapt to the needs of the audience during the presentation. For example, if during a team member's portion, you notice that the team member is losing the audience's attention, then modify your part of the presentation to compensate. Refer back to Chapter 2 for guidelines on how to adapt to the audience during the presentation. Second, it also helps to watch the audience's reaction to various parts of the presentation. How are various messages being received by the audience?[28] For example, when your group presents information on cost, how do audience members react? Do they seem shocked or pleasantly surprised? This information can be very valuable to the group or organization later.

Unless it is absolutely necessary, resist leaning over and whispering to a team member. This shifts the attention and can call professionalism into question. And as Giuliano,[29] from the Executive Communication Group, warns, "The worst thing any team member can do, of course, is to show disagreement with what another presenter is saying."

To appear as a group, it is also important that group members dress in a consistent manner. This does not mean that anyone in the group should have to purchase new clothing, but it is important to be cohesive. Imagine an entire group showing up to make a presentation wearing business casual except one member, who wears a suit and tie. It becomes obvious to the audience that the group does not have good communication. Discuss wardrobe as one of the final steps in preparing for the presentation.

The Business Presentation

Perhaps the most common place that informative presentations occur are at work. And many of these business presentations are group presentations. The National Association of Colleges and Employers (NACE), a non-profit group that links college career placement offices with employers, in the fall of 2014 surveyed hiring managers about what skills they plan to prioritize when they recruit from the class of 2015 at colleges and graduate schools. Large companies such as Chevron, IBM, and Seagate Technology responded that one of the top two skills they seek is the ability to communicate verbally with people inside and outside an organization.[30]

The business presentation is defined as "prepared speeches delivered in a professional business context."[31] It could be an engineer updating a client about a project. It could be a manager updating the office staff on quarterly sales. Or it could be the group charged with picking out the office's new furniture presenting their findings to co-workers.

Here are some tips that will help ensure your business presentation is successful:

1. Determine what your purpose is and stick to it.
2. Determine your audience. Will you be speaking to bosses, co-workers, subordinates, or customers? Are you speaking to an audience of native English speakers or clients in another country? Each of these audiences will necessitate an adaption of your presentation to their previous knowledge levels.
3. Determine your organizational pattern. This will be affected by steps 1 and 2. Think you might have trouble convincing customers of a need? Monroe's Motivated Sequence, with its visualization step, will work well. Think your boss might be resistant to adopting a new system? Why not use the refutative pattern to alleviate his concerns.
4. Determine the best supporting material for your presentation.
5. Determine the best presentation aids to complement your presentation. (See Chapter 12 for more on presentation aids.)
6. Adapt to your communication channel. As you will read in Chapter 14, you have many options for delivering presentations in today's business world. Will you be presenting face-to-face or via an online meeting technology such as WebEx™? Will it be a text-based meeting, or will you have video? Will it be a rich or a lean presentation? (See Chapter 14.)
7. Finally, if possible, rehearse and revise. For example, do you need to eliminate some information due to time constraints?

The Status Report

Before you are called upon to give that final presentation, it's quite likely you will be asked to provide updates on your project through its various stages. These updates are commonly called **status reports.** The request could come from a boss, a client, or even another member of your team. Being able to give an effective status report is a skill that is underrated in the workplace.

Three Components of Status Reports

Project statuses should be organized from the highest level of details to the lowest levels. These levels comprise the three major components of a project status: overall, milestones, and issues.[32] That's why you start with the overall report. If everything is fine and on schedule, it could be there is no need to discuss the other components. If everything is not OK, it's likely because a milestone was missed. That could be because of an issue that arose. Or issues could have arisen that could but as of yet have not endangered a milestone. This allows for an audience to see a clear connection in your report.

Status Update

Regional | posted: 1/28/2015 3:06 AM

Community meetings to give updates on Detroit rail project

Associated Press

DETROIT -- Residents and businesses in Detroit's Midtown and downtown areas can receive updates on construction of a $140 million light rail project.

Some lanes of Woodward Avenue along the streetcar's 6.6-mile roundtrip route are closed for work on the project.

Overall

This is the overall status of a project. You will not be discussing individual elements but the project as a whole. If you are simply stating how well the project is going–its overall health–status report points might include

- the project name or description;
- the overall project status;
- how much of the project you planned to have completed by this time;
- how much of the project you have actually completed by this time;
- how far behind, or ahead, you are; or
- any major or minor issues you face;

These elements should provide a sound overview of how the project is progressing for an audience that does not need more details and is not going to be getting more involved in your project.

Milestones

Milestones are the major accomplishments or parts of your project that must be completed by specific dates. You could provide which ones are complete, which are in progress, and which are upcoming. The purpose of this is to scrutinize the schedule. Have you accomplished enough in the amount of time? Will there be enough time to accomplish what is left? Some milestones are more difficult or time consuming than others. This needs to be taken into account when reporting.

When reporting on milestones, be sure to include

- ◎ the milestone name;
- ◎ the percent complete of the milestone;
- ◎ the planned start;
- ◎ the planned finish;
- ◎ the actual start; and
- ◎ the actual finish;

For your group project in COM114, you will have milestones set by your instructor, such as picking your group's topic or turning in your group outline. You will also have milestones set by your group leader that will ensure your project keeps moving forward.

Issues

These are the obstacles that have emerged or that could emerge that threaten the success of your project. Providing details of these allows your superiors or your project partners to decide if they should step in and help.

There are two types of issues: blocking issues and normal issues.[33] Blocking issues are major. The issue can literally "block" your project from moving forward. This could lead to your project not being completed on time. A normal issue is a smaller, more minor problem that you anticipate being solved relatively quickly. It likely will not delay the project's timely completion. For example, let's say you volunteered to take photos for your COM114 final group project and discover your camera batteries are dead. This is a small issue that will take little time to fix and will not hold you up significantly from obtaining the pictures your group needs. However, let's say the building you wish to photograph does not allow cameras inside; now you have a larger issue that could delay your project. You might have to seek a meeting with a manager to explain your project and ask for special permission to take photographs. You might have to then file a formal, written request. That request might have to be reviewed by a board. This is a larger issue that could delay you obtaining the photographs you need.

Important information that you should share on your issues:

- ◎ **Issue Name:** This is where you give a brief description of what the issue is.
- ◎ **Date Reported:** The older an issue is, the more likely it is that somebody else needs to become involved in resolving the issue.
- ◎ **Priority or Severity of the Issue:** Is this a blocking issue or a normal issue?
- ◎ **Who:** Who is currently working to resolve the issue?
- ◎ **Expected Resolution Date:** Provide a time and date for when the issue will be resolved. If this is not possible, provide some date specifics. For example, you plan to try A to resolve the issue for two days. If that does not work, you will move to B.
- ◎ **Current Activity:** What is currently being done to resolve this issue?

It is very important when working in a group to report any issues that develop promptly to the entire group or to a designated group leader. This will allow the group to make adjustments in a timely manner. In your COM114 final group project, be sure to let your group leader know immediately if an issue arises. Suppose you are tasked with finding narratives to support a main point, yet your research has turned up none. Don't wait to let your group know. This could be indicative of a larger issue. For example, it could mean that the main point chosen is not strong, and the group needs to choose new main points. This is not something you want to wait to do until the last minute.

It is critical when giving a status report to be honest. If you are behind in your project, or if you didn't do the work, it is best to tell your group members or manager when asked. They might be able to offer suggestions, or help. And you most certainly will be found out eventually. You don't want it to be during the final presentation to an important client.[34]

Technically, any update you provide on a project, any questions you answer, can be labeled a status report. The key is to provide that update at the level equivalent to the way you were asked.[35] So, if your boss asks you unexpectedly to give a quick update at a meeting, give just that, a quick update. Don't stand there for 5 minutes going into too much detail. If he or she wants more information, they can ask.

Before you even begin, think about the way the request for an update was worded. Did your boss ask for an update on the overall project, or on just one element? You want to make sure that you not only answer the question but that you devote the time you have to that question alone. You do not want to bring in tangential information that is not really related to the question posed.

And be proactive if possible: If someone has assigned you a task, it's a good idea to let them know the status even before they ask. This doesn't mean you need to provide daily updates. But when you've reached a milestone, or encountered a problem, go ahead and let your superiors or your team members know.

Working in Multicultural Groups

Multicultural groups or teams are a way of life in business today.[36] Research has found that diverse groups are more creative problem-solvers.[37] Now attention is being focused on training students to be effective members of such teams.[38]

Here at Purdue, we are blessed to have a very diverse student population. In fact, a report released by the Institute of International Education in 2015 ranked Purdue third among U.S. public institutions for international student enrollment.

However, research shows that cultural differences among group members can lead to misperceptions and increased conflict, which in turn can negatively affect performance.[39] One problem is that different cultures may view "progress" in different ways; what might be "slow going" in one culture is "too slow" in another.[40]

For diverse groups to be successful, you need to be aware of the differences that exist between cultures.[41] You also need to be aware that you might have some stereotypes about certain cultures. The group should adapt by acknowledging these cultural gaps and working around them.[42] Once your group recognizes diversity for the positive contribution it can make to group performance, diversity actually can become a source of group cohesiveness.[43] It is necessary for each group member to assume responsibility for figuring out how to work with the differences.

Here are four barriers your group might have to overcome: direct versus indirect communication, trouble with accents and fluency, differing attitudes toward authority and hierarchy, and conflicting norms for decision making:[44]

◎   Americans use direct communication. However, in some cultures, it is inappropriate to ask, or answer, a direct question, such as, "Do you want to do this or that?" Make sure your decision making doesn't put group members on the spot.

◎ Accents and problems with translation may affect communication between members. A non-native English speaker might be struggling to find the exact words needed to offer input in your COM114 group project. This pause often leads to some misunderstandings. Some could equate a lack of fluency with a lack of competency.[45] Or sometimes, that silence is mistaken for agreement. Don't assume anything. Instead, make the extra effort to encourage all group members to participate. Acknowledge the language barriers, and move on from them.

◎ In some cultures, group members expect to be treated differently based on their status in a group or organization. A perceived hierarchy within your COM114 group could affect participation. It is important that obvious subgroups don't form in your group. Attempt to make your group egalitarian.

◎ Cultures can differ enormously when it comes to decision making, particularly how quickly decisions should be made and how much analysis is needed ahead of time. Americans like to make decisions very quickly, compared to other countries. Group members from other cultures might be hesitant to move so quickly. What does this mean for your group project? Well, for example, an international group member might not immediately offer suggestions for a possible topic. Instead, build in time for members to research possible topics before asking for ideas from group members.

A key factor to success in a multicultural group is learning to actively value diversity and use it as a resource.[46] What is it that each member brings to your group? What perspectives and knowledge can members from other cultures provide? Use these to benefit your presentation.

Conclusion

This chapter is a guide to successful group presentations. As long as the group prepares thoroughly by choosing a leader, establishing a clear goal, conducting good research, staying on task, and utilizing each member's strengths, the group presentation can be effective. To achieve success, it is important that the group function as a team, rather than as a collection of individuals. To do this, the group must take steps to avoid any conflict that might result. The group must also welcome diversity. Using design templates, effective introductions, adequate transitions, and group practice sessions are the means through which groups can achieve the necessary uniformity to be successful.

Key Terms

Group efficacy	Relationship conflict	Task conflict
Milestones	Resource interdependent	10-minute rule
Process conflict	Status report	

CHAPTER 14

Presenting Online

Objectives

After reading this chapter, you should be able to

◎ explain the benefits of online presentations;

◎ understand the challenges of online presentations;

◎ adapt to the challenges of online presentations;

◎ explain the differences between asynchronous and synchronous presentations; and

◎ use best practices to create and deliver online slide and video presentations.

When a massive snowstorm shut down Washington, DC, in 2016, Jessica Wandless, coordinator for the Military Extension Internship Program and Purdue alumna, turned to an online conference and collaboration tool to conduct a scheduled week-long orientation for new interns.[1] Wandless said the tool allowed the interns, who could not get to the nation's capital because of closed roads and airports, to go through orientation remotely.

Wandless also uses the tool, WebEx, to conduct monthly meetings with interns in places as dispersed as Japan, Italy, Spain and Cuba. "It helps them stay connected to each other throughout the internship." It also allows the program to conduct a capstone project where each intern makes a final virtual presentation to a group of fellow interns as well as the program's leaders.

For a variety of reasons, more and more presentations are moving online.

In 2009, when a recession prompted companies to trim budgets, many began to replace face-to-face meetings with virtual presentations and web conferences as a means to save money. But a recent survey shows that while reducing travel is still a key benefit, improved efficiency is the reason that most business executives continue to conduct business virtually when possible.

The survey found that 94% of more than 4,700 business executives worldwide cited improved efficiency and productivity as the main reason for communicating virtually. A majority also said it allowed them to get to know co-workers and customers that they might otherwise have never communicated with personally.[2]

Still many executives prefer face-to-face meetings.[3] *Forbes* found the top reasons cited were the ability to "read" another person, greater social interaction, and the building of stronger relationships. They also thought face-to-face meetings were more persuasive and engaging. Even so, virtual and online presentations are increasingly common and represent a core skill for contemporary presenters. So, it is essential that you develop these skills as well as those required in face-to-face presentations. This chapter will overview different types of online presentations and offer some tips for being effective and engaging in the virtual context.

Presenting Online

Increasingly, we work, communicate, and interact with people who live in other cities, states, and even countries. And that's being reflected in the job market. Job descriptions no longer ask for proficiency with Word or Excel. Instead, they seek applicants with knowledge of remote presentations, demonstrations, and webinars in general.[4] Videoconferencing is especially prevalent when companies present to international markets. For example, a Global IP survey found that 80% of business people surveyed in China and 60% in South Korea had participated in a video presentation.[5]

Students who understand the role that digital technologies play in facilitating and transforming interaction with **distributed audiences** have substantial advantages over those who do not. "Distributed" means that the audience is geographically dispersed. Making presentations that are distributed live through videoconferencing software or placed online for viewers to access at their leisure is increasingly common. A Weber Shandwick survey found that 56% of conferences now offer some type of live videoconferencing. "We see the future of the conference industry migrating toward more intimate, peer-to-peer forums where companies can create their own channels for discussion in an effort to drive business," said Jennifer Risi, Executive Vice President of Weber Shandwick's Global Strategic Media Group.[6]

Although you probably have many questions and concerns about online, or virtual, presentations, one of the most common is, "Are they effective?" New studies suggest that you can learn just as much from a mediated presentation as you can from a face-to-face presentation.[7]

Much of what is known about online presentations comes from the research being conducted in the area of distance education. This research has indicated that online lectures and presentations can be as effective as traditional learning environments, if you choose the right technology for the message you want to deliver.[8]

All presentations, whether online or traditional, should share certain things in common. As stressed throughout this text, all presentations should be goal-driven, ethical, and audience-centered or responsive to feedback. However, the ways in which these things are accomplished can look very different, depending on the type of online presentation you are creating. Different types of online presentations have different characteristics that will force you to carefully evaluate your goals in terms of what you are trying to accomplish, evaluate the needs and abilities of your audience, and determine how you will respond to audience feedback.

This chapter introduces you to some of the benefits and challenges of online presentations as well as the various tools used to present online. It also provides some strategies for making such presentations effective.

Ethically Speaking

Preparing for an Online Presentation

Adequately preparing for your presentation is not only a practical requirement, it is an ethical one as well.[9] Your audience expects a lot from you and your presentation. They gave up their valuable time (and in many instances, money) to attend your presentation. But a recent poll of 600 business executives found that nearly half of the respondents spent more time preparing in-person or traditional presentations than online presentations.[10] Just remember, with any presentation, the more you put in to it, the greater the benefit to all involved. If an audience can tell that you did not put 100% effort into your online presentation, they won't respond positively to your message.

Benefits of Online Presentations

Corporations have already realized the importance of using online presentations to reach distributed audiences. A great example is BDO Seidman, a professional services firm that serves clients through 35 offices in the United States and an international global network of alliance firms in 105 countries. MaryEm Musser, Assistant Director of BDO Seidman's Center for Professional Development, said the company began using online presentations to provide live and on-demand training to a large number of people within the shortest possible time frame. Such a solution "has allowed us to remove time and geographic barriers," she said. "We no longer consider ourselves a distributed organization." During the first eight months of implementing an online approach, BDO delivered training on five new technologies to more than two thousand people.

"It's given us the ability to meet face-to-face more frequently," Musser said. "If faced with the costs to fly everyone in for live meetings, plus the time away from the office, the travel wear and tear, and other expenses, we probably would not be engaging in these projects. That's a huge shift in how we conduct business."[11]

Many refer to such presentations as **webinars.** A webinar is short for Web-based seminar. It can be a presentation, lecture, class or workshop that is transmitted over the Web. Business executives responding to a study said the main reason they attended or conducted webinars was to save travel costs.[12]

But there are many more benefits to delivering presentations online than saving money. In addition, online presentations also facilitate environmental efficiency, labor efficiency, decision-making, and coordination, and because of this, online presentations are becoming pervasive forms of communication.[13]

Cost Savings

As discussed, the economic advantages of presenting online are relatively easy to understand. Distributed organizations, and organizations trying to reach a distributed audience, find much of their expenses consumed by travel. A company may have offices in many locations, or even more common, its clients are distributed around the state, nation, or world. Airfares, hotel accommodations, and scheduling of facilities are expensive for both the companies and their clients. The possibility of eliminating or drastically limiting those expenses can save companies substantial amounts of money over time for both internal and external communication. Instead of spending money on these factors, companies are increasingly investing in online technologies that maximize profitability in the long term.[14]

When Oscar Koenders, General Manager of Toshiba Computer Systems marketing division, went looking for ways to save money, he zeroed in on the high cost of business travel associated with training and meetings. Typically, during these presentations, trainers present marketing ideas and budgets, and then get live feedback. The company decided to give videoconferencing applications a try. Since then, the company has cut travel costs by 75%.[15]

Time Savings

In addition to costs associated with travel, traditional presentations are also seen as a less efficient use of employee time. Lost productivity due to traditional presentations that involve travel is also a factor driving investments in online alternatives. Additionally, one online presentation can reach many more people over a span of time than a series of traditional presentations in small venues. Reducing unnecessary redundancy of effort through the presentation of material online can maximize profit.

In our previously noted example, Toshiba estimates that by eliminating the time spent traveling, it saved 866 worker hours in the first year. That translates into an additional 115 full working days. Toshiba said that, in turn, translates into a 25% increase in employee productivity.

Green

The need to reduce travel has become more acute in the business world, and one of those reasons is environmental concerns.[16] SunGard®, one of the world's leading software and information technology (IT) services companies, signed up for online services as part of its plan to reduce carbon emissions. The service allowed SunGard to eliminate an estimated 22,000 nonessential business trips. "Customers simply expect you to be an environmentally responsible company. By reducing our emissions, we've taken another step toward embracing corporate practices that are not only better for our bottom line, but better for the environment, too," said Jennifer Sweet, senior manager for corporate responsibility for SunGard.[17]

Faster Decision-Making

Spotlight on Research

Trust in Distributed Groups

As you have seen in this chapter, making a presentation to a distributed group brings a lot of added challenges. An additional challenge that needs to be discussed is the issue of trust. Research shows that members of distributed work groups are more likely to distrust each other and that it takes longer to build up trust among members in such situations. What does that mean for your online presentation? Obviously, the issue of credibility, as discussed in Chapter 10, is key here. You know your initial credibility could be adversely affected because of the distributed setting. That means that you will need to make sure that you derive credibility during your actual presentation, resulting in a stronger terminal credibility that will carry over to the next online presentation before the group.[18]

Many decisions in today's business environment are made by groups. Virtual presentations that eliminate the need for travel make it easier for people to meet sooner, and thus, make decisions sooner. One study found that decision-making cycles could be reduced by months using virtual presentations.[19]

Effective Coordination

Coordination between presenter and audience is another factor driving online presentations. Depending on your circumstances, it is often very difficult to find common times for meetings and presentations. Additionally, people are often involved in meetings and presentations that are not directly relevant to their work. By presenting online, companies have the ability to target participants who need the information, and participants have the ability to participate in presentations that they know will be beneficial.

Types of Online Presentations

All online presentations are not the same. There is a vast array of possibilities for creating presentations for online delivery. These can range from simple tasks such as uploading a PowerPoint presentation to the Web, to streaming audio and video, to fully interactive Web conferences. Each of these types of online presentations has different characteristics, as well as advantages and disadvantages.

Synchronous, or *live* presentations, occur when the audience accesses the presentation while you are delivering it. When we say that things are **synchronous,** or "in sync," we simply mean they are occurring at the same time. Face-to-face interaction is synchronous, as is Internet chat. When you deliver your presentation to your classroom audience, it is synchronous because your audience receives your message as you present it. Online, synchronous communication occurs during phone presentations where people dial in to a phone conference to hear a presentation; through videoconferencing technology, where audio and video are delivered to remote points through phone or satellite technology; or through contemporary Web conferencing systems, where audio, video, and other data are presented live on the screen while the audience views the presentation. In most cases, synchronous presentations have more in common with traditional presentations than asynchronous presentations do.

Asynchronous communication does not occur simultaneously. The message you present is not received by your audience as you deliver it, but at some later time. E-mail is an example of asynchronous communication. When we look at the Web, asynchronous presentations are the most common type of presentation out there. These presentations can take the form of web pages, streaming audio or video, and multimedia presentations that combine text, graphics, audio, video, animations, and so on. We often call asynchronous presentations **on-demand presentations** because audiences can access this type of presentation at any time. You've probably watched many on-demand presentations for instructional purposes, such as those that illustrate step-by-step how to download a song on iTunes or how to use new social media tools, such as Twitter.

Let's examine each of these types of communication in more detail.

Synchronous Presentations

Just a few years ago, an online meeting was a novelty. Now, online meetings, courses, webinars, video lectures, and other forms of online presentations are becoming the norm. A *Harvard Business Review* survey found that 41% of respondents attend a virtual presentation once a month; 30% attend more than three a month. That same survey found that 30% were presenting online at least once a month.[20]

Just because a presentation is online doesn't mean it's easier to construct or present. Online presentations have similarities to in-person presentations but also present some new challenges.

Planning the Synchronous Presentation

Some of the rules that govern in-person presentations transfer to the virtual environment. But there are also a new set of skills you will need to develop to ensure professional, beneficial virtual presentations.

Many presenters who are very effective with live audiences can struggle when they present virtually. The virtual environment makes special demands on a presenter. The level of scrutiny an audience has toward an in-person presenter

> **Many presenters who are very effective with live audiences can struggle when they present virtually.**

is mitigated by the distance from audience member to speaker. Chances are that your virtual presentation will be either a medium or close-range shot. That's like having your whole audience 2–4 feet from your face, which makes a video presentation more intimate. And yet, in many instances, you might not be able to see your audience, or your whole audience. This is a difficult adjustment for some presenters.

Being able to present before a live audience well does not mean that you can automatically do the same virtually. By following the suggestions below, you will increase the chances of a successful virtual presentation.

Tips for Synchronous Presentations

- Practice using the technology prior to the presentation to ensure you are comfortable. The first time you use the technology should not be during your presentation. Practice with a remote audience ahead of time.

- Have a moderator help you monitor audience questions and deal with technical issues so you can focus on the presentation.

- Record questions that are asked if your session has a chat function. Make sure you get back to everyone with complete answers, even if it's after the meeting.

- Make sure that audience members have a chance to configure their computers correctly and test their connections prior to the start of the meeting.

- Have a backup plan ready in case there are technical difficulties.

- If you need notes or other materials, avoid paper shuffling. Have everything clearly laid out in a logical order.

- If your audience is following your presentation in written form, announce your place often, such as when you change to a new page or slide.

- When referencing visual aids, remember that you cannot draw audience members' attention to specific points in your slides by using a laser pointer, for example. Pointing should be built into the presentation by using animated arrows, circles, or other symbols.

- Keep tuned in to the participants. Don't let the session be a passive experience for participants. Prompt some form of interaction every few minutes. Keep the presentation interactive.[65]

Setting

When presenting in-person, you have little choice over your environment. You are scheduled in a particular room, at a particular time of day, provided with a stage or podium. But the setting is a key element you can manipulate when presenting online.

Lighting

Make sure your office window or other source of natural light is not behind you. You should always face your light source. Your computer monitor is one source of light.

For best results, you should not rely on natural light alone.[21] It's best if you control the lighting. The average person can accomplish the look of professional lighting at your desk or even standing in front of your office (or dorm or apartment) wall with just two lights: the key light and the fill light. Just a little effort can make a big difference. The key is to get enough light in front of your face so your audience can see you. This is accomplished with the key light.

The key light illuminates your face. It doesn't have to cost much to produce a quality looking image from your webcam. A book lamp makes a great key light. Tip it to a 45-degree angle to your left or right. It should be higher than your face and aimed directly at your face.

The fill light is not as bright as the key light. Place it on the opposite side from the key light and slightly lower than the camera. The role of the fill light is to light the other side of your face.

Once you have your lighting in place, you need to play with the exposure, brightness, contrast, and other settings on your webcam software to get the effect you want.

Obviously professional lighting is available for purchase. But you don't have to spend a lot of money to get professional-looking results for your virtual presentations.

Camera Angles

Unless you are recording a professional online presentation in a studio, it's likely you will find yourself in front of a computer screen delivering your presentation via either a portable webcam or the webcam built into your computer. You've likely not given much thought to where you should position yourself in relation to the camera other than making sure your whole head or upper body is visible. But the positioning of the camera in relation to the presenter can influence the way your viewers perceive you.[22]

Research shows us that the positioning of the presenter in relation to the camera can affect audience attitude.[23] If you have a portable webcam or you can manipulate the position of your laptop's webcam, you should keep the following options in mind.

- ◎ **Eye Level:** This allows you to avoid looking up or down at your audience. This is the way most people interact in casual situations and will put the viewer at ease. To achieve this, you have to look at the webcam not the screen. This gives your audience eye contact. With practice, you will be more comfortable doing this. Also, avoid leaning in toward the camera. This could distort your image.
- ◎ **High Angle:** You want to avoid a situation where the camera looks down on you. Looking up to the camera is awkward and psychologically conveys to the viewer that you are weaker.[24]

- ◎ **Low Angle:** By contrast, a low angle shot–where the camera looks up at you–can make you appear more powerful. CEOs and public officials often film from an angle positioned slightly below their eye level. But the danger of this angle is it can appear that you are looking down, or talking down, to your audience. It also can be unflattering to some body types.

Framing

Framing is what we decide to include, or not include, in our image. For the purpose of virtual presentations, think of it as what your audience will see on their computer screen. Everything in your frame is important, even the background (discussed below).

Most likely for virtual presentations you will have either a medium or a close-up shot. If you are going to film yourself standing up, the medium shot is actually recommended. In some instances you might want to record a full shot (if you are recording a live presentation for archival purposes, for instance).

Headroom is the amount of space between the top of your head and the top of your frame. Ideally you don't want to cut off the top of your head. That can be very distracting to your viewers and can convey a claustrophobic feel.

Rather than placing yourself in the exact middle of frame, position yourself slightly off center. This is known in photography circles as the rule of thirds.

Rather than placing yourself in the exact middle of frame, position yourself slightly off center. This is known in photography circles as the rule of thirds. To apply the rule of thirds, imagine a 3 by 3 grid overlaid on your computer screen. You want to position yourself where the grids intersect not in the exact middle. Images have been found to be more interesting if the important elements lie on one of the grid lines or at their intersections.[25]

Backgrounds

A poor background choice can detract from you and the message you are presenting. You don't want your viewers distracted by your messy desk! Make sure you choose an uncluttered setting or a simple wall for your backdrop.

Colors and Wardrobe

Just as you think carefully about your wardrobe for an in-person presentation, so should you for a virtual presentation. Everything a viewer sees, including your clothes, can influence their opinion of you and your message. It's best to stick with a classic wardrobe that won't "date" you or your presentation.

Colors to Avoid

- ◎ Bright reds, oranges and yellows tend to "glow" on screen.
- ◎ Black absorbs light and can be too dark on most videos.
- ◎ White reflects light. If you have a paler skintone, it can make you appear washed out.
- ◎ High-contrast patterns, like stripes, polka dots, and checks all create a wavy, moving pattern on screen.

- It's true that a camera can add 5–10 pounds. So you want to avoid loose clothing that will make you look much larger on camera than you are.
- Avoid any fabric that wrinkles easily. Wrinkles are enlarged on camera. And viewers do no equate wrinkles with credibility.
- Certain fabrics, like silk, can make a rustling noise that your microphone will pick up.
- And certain fabrics, again like silk, will show perspiration stains more clearly.

Solid colors work best on screen. Rich earth tones (browns and grays) and pastels work best on camera. But if you are in to bright colors, many brighter shades of blue and purple look good on screen. Also check to make sure that your colors work well with your background. You don't want your clothes to either blend in to or clash with your background.

And avoid wearing anything large or flashy. Necklaces, pendants, bracelets, and dangling earrings can make noise and distract viewers with movement.[26]

Content

Follow these steps to ensure that the content of your virtual presentation is strong:

1. **Clarify what you are trying to do.** What is the purpose of this presentation? Are you trying to educate staffers about a new initiative? Are you making a sales pitch? Are you updating committee members on a project? Decide what the purpose is and stick to it.

2. **Engage your audience.** One of the challenges of online presentations is that you can't always see your audience. You can't see if people are bored, or confused, or even enjoying your presentation. Plan ahead of time how you will keep your virtual audience engaged. For example, schedule an online poll to see if everyone understands. Solicit questions. Or have everyone take 15 seconds and type in a specific thing they have learned in the presentation. Give mini quizzes at points during the presentation. It also helps to use images in your presentation as this can break up the monotony.

   It is important that you take the time to frame specific questions. Don't say: "What do you think?" Ask specific questions. "Do you agree with the changes?" Once you have the answer to your key question, you can ask viewers to expound on their answers.

   In addition, you have to maintain a high energy level. You don't want it to appear that you are simply reading your presentation.

3. **Frame the issue.** Highlight the key points and refer to them often. Make sure that you have something to say in your meeting and you are focusing on it. It's easy to lose an online audience to other things on their computers or phones.

4. **Manage your own anxiety.** Just as with in-person presentations, the best way to manage anxiety is to prepare. Have alternatives available should technical issues develop. And just as polls can be used to engage your audience, they can also be used to manage your anxiety. If you see from a poll that your audience is paying attention and understanding your materials, this will alleviate some of your anxiety about whether your message is being received.

5. **Know your audience.** Frequently, online presentations are attended by people in different time zones, even different countries. A 10:00 a.m. meeting for you could be a 6 a.m. meeting for other participants. Not everyone might have your energy level. What can you do to adjust for these differences?

Delivering the Synchronous Presentation ——————

You will definitely still need to practice. You may feel silly at first but "presenting" to a computer screen or camera presents a whole new set of challenges.[27]

Eye Contact

Eye contact is a harder issue to manage online. But it is just as critical. You want to look at your audience, just as you would in a real world presentation, but you don't want to appear to stare at them. That would seem awkward and uncomfortable. This is difficult to remember, however, because instead of a group of faces to scan, you are staring at a computer screen.

Use these tips to connect to your virtual audience.[28]

◎ Attempt to visualize an audience in front of you instead of a computer screen. (See Chapter 1.)

◎ It won't appear natural if you continuously stare directly into the camera. Glance down at your notes occasionally. If you are about to show a slide, glance to the side as if you are watching it appear. Mixing it up will make you seem less ominous.

◎ While you don't want to stare directly at the camera the whole time, you also don't want to spend too much time looking down or off to the side. Looking down at your notes–just like an in-person presentation–will make you seem unprepared. Glancing off the side will make you seem less confident or uninterested.

◎ Finally, if you have both a live and virtual audience at the same time, ignore the cameras. Limit your eye contact to your live audience.[29]

Movement

Just like in an in-person presentation, you will want to use natural gestures for emphasis at various points of a virtual presentation. But a camera can magnify these. If your hands get too close to the camera, they will appear larger than they are in proportion to the rest of your image. So keep your hands close to your body.

In addition:

◎ You want to make sure that your hand movements are not flashing in and out of the frame. When configuring your frame, you want to leave enough room to make natural hand gestures. But be warned that big, broad gestures can come off as artificial on camera.

◎ You will also need in some instances to move your hand gestures higher than you normally would, at about the chest level. Think of that presentation you're making on Skype that shows you from the chest up. This may seem unnatural, but if you leave them at waist level–which is more natural for us–they likely will be out of view of the camera.[30]

◎ You also want to avoid fidgeting. Just like you don't want to play with your note cards while you are giving a speech in class, you don't want to click your pen on and off during a virtual presentation. To avoid such fidgeting, make sure your hands are empty.

◎ You also want to avoid any distracting gestures, such pushing your hair back or itching your face. These gestures are magnified on camera and become much more obvious–and distracting.

◎ Finally, if you are seated, remember to keep your chair still. Any on screen movement will really catch the viewer's eye.

Voice

Just like in person, you want the audience to feel your passion for your topic. One way to do this is you make sure you sound excited about your material vocally. Make sure you are varying your pitch, volume, and inflection to avoid a monotonous sounding virtual presentation that might drive viewers to check their Facebook pages. You also want to continue to use pauses frequently to separate your important points, especially when you are delivering complex information.

But you also don't want to seem to shout at your audience. This can be tricky to judge when on camera. A good rule of thumb is to speak as if your viewer was four feet away from you and let your microphone do the rest.

Posture

Keep your head and chin level. You may have to remind yourself of this. You will negatively impact your onscreen appearance if you begin to slouch down in your chair or relax your posture too much.

Behavior

Always assume that people can see and hear you. You may think you have logged off Skype, or that attention is focused on someone else during a WebEx presentation, but mistakes happen. So never say, or do, anything that could be embarrassing or taken out of context. You should always be on.

Presenting to a Global Audience

Technology now allows our presentations to reach global audiences. Different cultures can have an impact on the content and delivery of your online presentation. To be effective when presenting to a global audience, speakers need to be sensitive to cultural differences. You need to recognize the preferred communication styles of your diverse audience and adapt your own style accordingly.

As a result, it is even more important that you conduct a thorough audience analysis before you present to a global audience (see Chapter 2). In addition to standard demographic, psychological and environmental analysis, you also need to familiarize yourself with the culture of the audience and be aware of any stereotypes you might have of your audience that might offend diverse audience members and hurt your credibility.

> **To be effective when presenting to a global audience, speakers need to be sensitive to cultural differences.**

One determination you will need to make is if the audience you are presenting to comes from either a low-context or high-context culture. Anthropologist Edward Hall said messages are influenced "by the amount of information implied by the setting or the context of the communication itself, regardless of the specific words spoken.[31]" **Low-context cultures** prefer messages where the actual words determine the message, not the context. Exact meaning is conveyed through precise and specific language. You mean exactly what you say. In contrast, **high-context cultures** prefer messages where the meaning is implicit in the context in which the words are spoken. Nonverbal expressions take on more importance.

People from high-context cultures might find people from low-context cultures too straightforward and abrupt, while people from low-context cultures often wish people from high-context cultures would get to the point quicker.

There are certain things you can do when addressing an audience of a different culture to ensure the success of your presentation. In this section we discuss some of these.

Selecting Supporting Material

In Chapter 6, we discussed the various supporting materials available to you. Culture can play in role in what materials you choose for your global presentation.

In many cultures, narratives enjoy high credibility as supporting materials. One study found that in Africa, for example, the success of a persuasive message can depend on how many personal stories and anecdotes are employed.[32] Asian cultures also tend to rely on stories to convey the main messages of presentations.[33]

But many European audiences will find facts and statistics as the most compelling support.[34] As you can see, supporting materials for global presentations are culturally dependent. Make sure you employ a mix of supporting materials so you can enhance your message to a diverse audience.

Constructing Your Presentation

Too often, we focus our word choice on the **denotative meaning.** This is the definition found in most dictionaries. Most people will agree that this is what a word means. But many words also have a **connotative meaning.** This is the "definition" you must be aware of when employing language in a global context. Connotative is the meaning attached to the word over time, based on personal experiences and associations. Take, for example, the word immigrant. Its denotative meaning is a "person who comes to a country to take up permanent residence." But given your personal experience with immigrants, you might have developed either a positive or negative view. This will affect your reaction when you hear this word.

You need to choose words that are inclusive but avoid those that might have connotative meanings for your audience. You also should avoid any sexist, racist, or ageist language. Again you must be culturally sensitive in your word choice. For example, some Asian cultures highly value the elderly. Any ageist language that does not afford them respect would not be received well.

You also want to be avoid using any *slang* terms in your presentation. Most in the audience will not understand slang terms. They will either need to interrupt to ask about the term or lose that portion of your message. Remember, common expressions may not translate into other cultures. Or, it's possible they have a whole different meaning. For instance, in England, saying, "I'm stuffed," actually means you are pregnant.

Delivering Your Presentation

If you need to address an audience from a different culture, you need to be aware of how your delivery and dress will affect your credibility.

This list was developed by experts:

Connect with Your Audience   It's helpful when addressing an audience in another country to start with a few words in their own language. Greeting them with "hello" or "welcome" in their native language is a nice way to start the presentation.

Speak Slowly   Audience members need more time to take in what you have said and then translate that into their own language. Or, sometimes, a translator will be used so everyone can understand a presenter. Listeners need a bit longer to process the information when it's being translated. Talk more slowly than usual and build in additional pauses to allow the translator and your listeners to catch up.

Articulate Well   In addition to slowing down, make sure you take the time to enunciate clearly. This will help audience members if they are struggling to identify the words you have said.

Adjust Speech Length   If you are using a translator, cut the length of your planned speech. The translator will need time to take in what you have said and then interpret that in another language. This will add time to your presentation.

Avoid Humor   Jokes and humorous stories often don't translate well. That makes for an awkward moment in your presentation. Avoid using humor.

Smile   It will put your audience at ease and make you appear approachable.

Gestures   Much of nonverbal communication is learned and can vary from culture to culture. The "OK" symbol in the United States actually means money in Japan. They can be just as connotative as language.

Some cultures find gestures distracting and distasteful. In those instances, try to limit your use of gestures, or make sure you use them to illustrate something you have said. Other cultures, such as those from South America, tend to use hand gestures liberally and will expect you to illustrate your presentation accordingly.

Remember when verbal and nonverbal messages conflict, receivers tend to believe the nonverbal cues.

Visual Aids   The more diverse your audience, the greater the need for visual aids to help get your message across.[35] Studies show that well-chosen visual aids can help overcome language differences in presentations to diverse audiences.[36]

Again, your research will help you decide what visual aids will work best with your audience.

Research shows that low-context cultures will prefer more text heavy visual aids with a set color scheme and structure.[37] High-context cultures, however, prefer visually heavy supporting aids that follow a more diverse color scheme and structure.

In addition, the color schemes you select for your visual aids can have an impact globally. Colors have different connotations in different cultures. For example, in Venezuela, yellow often has a negative meaning. In China, white is associated with funerals or mourning. Do some research, and use "culture friendly" colors on your slides.

Dress   In Chapter 10 we learned that what you wear can have impact on your initial credibility. This is just as true with a global audience. You want to be sure to respect the local business dress culture. For example, some Middle Eastern and Asian countries have very conservative dress codes, especially for women. In these countries, dressing norms in the U.S. are interpreted as discourteous and provocative.[38] We also want to respect the local culture when it comes to choosing colors. As with our visual aids, when we choose our attire, we must keep in mind the cultural significance of colors. Blacks, beiges, and whites are the norm in the Middle East, while Latin America encourages bright colors in work clothes. Be sure you research the business dress culture for the audience you will address.

Asynchronous Presentations

Aware of the major shifts in the way people communicate, many companies are turning to asynchronous presentations on platforms such as YouTube and Facebook to talk with not only customers but employees as well.[39] Zurich Financial Services CEO James Schiro began uploading one- to two-minute videos of his presentations to employees as he crisscrossed the world to ensure them of the company's health during the recent financial industries recession.

Schiro said that more people are interested in watching a video than reading another e-mail. He also felt like the video format would get across a different message. He said video "humanizes" people and provides more emotional engagement than text.[40]

At Cisco, more and more employee-to-employee communication is taking place via video. The company has an internal employee video-sharing platform called C-Vision. Between three and four hundred videos are uploaded a month. About 38% are team and organizational updates that last under ten minutes, and 24% are for product and sales updates.[41]

Think about how many times you have googled how to do something. Or used the words "how does" or "what is" in a search field. Often, the results returned were short, explanatory videos or narrated PowerPoints. That's because such asynchronous presentations are extremely effective at introducing and explaining visual concepts or simulating a process.

Thanks to inexpensive programs like PowerPoint and Prezi, it is fairly easy to create professional, asynchronous presentations for Web use. Most of these involve some form of multimedia or narration. People learn better when words are presented as narration rather than text.[42] This is called the Modality Principle and is one of the reasons that all those explanatory and how-to presentations on the Internet are so effective.

As was stated previously, asynchronous presentations also are an excellent way to provide information that supplements an event. Think of a callout for a college club. What about all those people who couldn't be there in person? Having an asynchronous presentation that hits the highlights of the callout and lets people know how to join is a natural companion to an in-person presentation.

Asynchronous presentations alone are not the best way to share more technically complex, scientific materials. In these instances, asynchronous presentations are best used for short presentations of 5 to 15 minutes that expand upon or supplement a topic, or highlight just one element of the topic.[43] That's because the compacted nature of the slides lead to generalizations and acronyms rather than specific, technical description and because PowerPoint is very limited in its ability to display scientific symbols and measurements.[44] Also, the Modality Principle is not likely to apply in situations in which the text is long and complex, or has technical terms or symbols.[45]

One of the benefits of using PowerPoint in an online environment is that it allows the instructional designer more time to focus on the narration as opposed to the live presenter, who has one shot at it. And unlike with a live presentation, the message in the narration can be repeated and controlled by the end user.[46] Just hit pause or replay. This is especially useful for a presentation that is attempting to instruct and has many different steps.

Planning the Asynchronous Presentation

While you won't be doing a traditional, full-sentence outline for an asynchronous presentation, that doesn't mean you don't need to plan. Remember, the permanency of such presentations means we need to plan even more. Think of the following suggestions as the outline stage of an asynchronous presentation.[47]

◎ **Draft the narrative.** Don't start by opening PowerPoint. Think about the narrative first. What's your title? Does the content lend itself to a list? What stories are you going to tell? What are the key messages? Answer these questions before you open up the software.

◎ **Good PowerPoint presentations include stories.** The easiest way to explain more complicated ideas or processes is through examples or sharing stories that underscore the point. Stories also are easier for your audience to remember. This is true both for in-person and online presentations.

◎ **Compile photos and images.** Interesting PowerPoint presentations have more images than words (see Assertion Evidence Model, Chapter 12). PowerPoint is not the best option for delivering content that is mostly text. Think visually. Compile the photos that you will use to support the narrative. Stay away from clip-art and keep to high-quality images that you take or that your use from professional photo sites.

   Remember though, these images must aid your presentation in some way. You should not use a photo simply to have a photo.

◎ **Create video clips.** Include multimedia video clips in. It breaks up the slides. While you're creating the content in step one, think about existing videos you can insert or develop your own.

◎ **Storyboard the slides.** In this step, begin to visualize your presentation. Use a notebook, sketchpad or whiteboard. It doesn't matter if you're good at drawing. What will go on each slide? Consider using the 1:1 concept. For every slide with a key point there should be a visual slide.

◎ **Write a script.** Don't think that you can just "wing it" when narrating your slides. While storyboarding helped to determine the sequence of your slides and the best way to present the information, a script will allow you to see holes in your presentation. (See below for more specific tips on writing a script.)

◎ **Create the presentation.** Now you can open PowerPoint and begin transferring the narrative, content, video, images, and sketches to the actual slides.

◎ **Rehearse the audio portion of the presentation.** Remember slides complement the story but you are the storyteller. Before you begin recording a narrated asynchronous presentation, rehearse. One rule of thumb is to deliver the audio 10 times before actually attempting a recording.[48]

Writing the Script

Remember as you are writing your script that since this is a less formal presentation style, your narration should sound less formal than an in-person presentation.[49] Narration scripts should sound friendly and conversational. For example, you can use contractions, or sentence fragments, just as you might in a conversation with a friend. Your tone should be friendly.

One way to achieve this is to use less complex sentences. Sentences that contain conjunctions such as and or but, or compound predicates (multiple verbs) can be confusing to follow. Remember, your audience is listening to your narration. We don't want them to have to pause and rewind to get what you just said.

One way to identify such areas that need rewriting is to read the script aloud before you actually narrate the slides. It is likely that you will find phrases or even sections that need to be rewritten. It's also where you might notice any text-heavy slides that might need to be broken up between two or more slides.

And while an in-person presentation relies on a key word outline that encourages more extemporaneous delivery, you want to strictly follow your narration script. You don't want to ad-lib. This might throw off the timing of your presentation. Any humorous or other asides should actually be written into the script, even though you might "deliver" them as more off-the-cuff.

That even applies to any pauses you might need to plan. If you have a lot of narration on one slide, plan where you will stop and take a breath. And write that into the script "wait," or "pause," or "take a breath." But just as you don't want your slides to be too text-heavy, you also don't want to talk too long on one slide. Consider how you can spread the narration over more slides.

Recording the Asynchronous Presentation ——————

Recording the audio narration is the final step to prepare it for online delivery. Use the following tips to ensure a quality presentation:

- Choose a recording space that is quiet. You do not want to be interrupted or have your narration ruined by background noise.
- Record the PowerPoint presentation using the "Slide Show" option in PowerPoint so that the recorded result will be full screen.
- Recording works best if you have a headset microphone instead of the microphone on your computer.
- Close all other applications on your computer that might make noise.
- Have your script, or at least notes, to highlight key talking points. And print out your slides so you will know which slide is coming up. This lowers the chances for awkward pauses or vocal fillers as you are speaking. Organization and preparation are key to a seamless delivery.
- Make sure your presentation doesn't sound like you are reading it. It should sound extemporaneous.
- Before you record narration for the entire presentation, do a test with your introduction slide. This could find sound issues right away and save you some time.
- One attempt might not be enough. If you notice quality issues, or errors, or poor delivery, you should record the presentation again.
- You don't have to complete your narration in one sitting. You can do it slide by slide and return at a later time to finish.
- Sit back and view your entire presentation as if you were the audience. Was anything unclear? Did you noticeably stumble in delivery? Did you spend too much time on a slide? If yes, record these slides over and insert into your presentation.

The Format of the Asynchronous Presentation ——————

Just as you followed a prescribed organizational pattern for your in-person presentations, so, too, should you spend time organizing your asynchronous presentations. The exact organization of your presentation will depend on its purpose. Is it an informative or instructional presentation? The following format is a general format that is a good base for you to begin with:

Opening

- Your first slide should be your title slide.
- Optional: Welcome viewers to your presentation.
- Briefly state the topic/purpose of the presentation.
- Briefly summarize the highlights of the presentation.

Slides

- ◎ Don't put your entire script on slides. The narration should be more than just you reading the slides. Also, if you put too much text on the slides, viewers will read the slides instead of listening to your narration.
- ◎ Don't use too much text (see Chapter 12). It makes the presentation boring. Images, video, and charts provide more memorable content.
- ◎ Use standard fonts and limit the number, size, and color of fonts you use (see Chapter 12). Too many fonts can be distracting to a viewer.
- ◎ Use only quality images and graphics. Charts should be clean and clear. Images should have a purpose and enhance understanding.
- ◎ Allot 1–2 minutes maximum per slide. Lingering longer on a slide can bore an audience.
- ◎ Proofread everything. Mistakes can affect the credibility of the presentation.
- ◎ Avoid sound effects and transition effects. These can be distracting and are viewed as amateur.
- ◎ Avoid animation for animation's sake. It can be annoying and give your presentation an amateur feel. When done tastefully, it can be an effective way to demonstrate a change. (As a rule of thumb, avoid animation with noise!)
- ◎ Make sure you have high contrast between text and background.

Speaking

- ◎ Relax.
- ◎ Talk at a moderate rate of speech.
- ◎ Speak clearly and distinctly.
- ◎ Speak naturally. Use extemporaneous delivery even if using a script.
- ◎ Be personable yet professional.
- ◎ Be enthusiastic. You want people to be just as enthusiastic about your topic as they would be seeing you deliver the presentation in person.
- ◎ Use devices such as arrows or highlighting to direct attention to important parts of graphics.
- ◎ When you say something important, pause for a few seconds. Allow the information to be absorbed by the viewer.
- ◎ Provide examples or narratives that illustrate the points on your slides.
- ◎ Engage the viewer. For example, ask a question and allow time for the viewer to "answer."
- ◎ Don't read the slide text word for word. Viewers can read faster than you can talk.
- ◎ Your narration must match up to your slides. Learning will be adversely affected if the narration and slides are out of sync.[50]

Conclusion

- ◎ Concisely summarize your key points and main ideas.
- ◎ Resist the temptation to add new material or to ad-lib a few last words.[51]

It's always a good idea to make your presentation available in a downloadable print form. Viewers can take notes on slides during the presentation, or have a convenient way to revisit information without having to rewatch your entire presentation.

> **It's always a good idea to make your presentation available in a downloadable print form.**

The issue of synchronicity can have a huge effect on your presentation and will have strong implications for the decisions you make when planning your presentation. The important thing to remember is that both synchronous and asynchronous presentations can be very effective. You just have to choose the right method for your message.

Working Together

Often, synchronous and asynchronous presentations can work in concert with each other. It is not uncommon for speakers to deliver a live presentation via a videoconferencing tool that is simultaneously recorded and distributed for on-demand access at a later time. Karen Bingham, the vice president of e-Business at Toshiba CSG, said the use of videoconferencing has resulted in the company being able to provide more training programs with fewer resources.[52] Its synchronous online training sessions are recorded and then made available to be replayed at any time.

One survey found that 97% of people who failed to attend a webinar for which they were registered were still interested in the topic.[53] For that reason, a majority of the companies surveyed had previously made an on-demand version of a live event available, with more than half saying they always provide a replay of a synchronous event. Similarly, a presenter may distribute an on-demand presentation but schedule a live question-and-answer session to be presented through a Web chat once the audience has viewed the presentation.

The nature of your presentation content will often determine which type of presentation you will want to use. If you have timely information that will be quickly outdated, synchronous presentations may be more effective than asynchronous presentations. One of the complaints about the Web is that much of the content is never maintained. It quickly becomes outdated, and hence irrelevant or inaccurate. However, if your material will not be obsolete very quickly, then asynchronous presentations may be more effective.

One important caveat is that not all presentations are well suited for delivery in an online context. Regardless of how they are presented, certain sorts of announcements or situations that are highly emotional are simply not effective when presented online. Because of the emotionality involved with particular situations or topics, there is a high reliance on nonverbal aspects of the message. Both the sender and the receiver need to be face-to-face so that they both can observe the nonverbal communication that transpires. No matter how carefully crafted, your narrated PowerPoint will not do a good job communicating the need for necessary layoffs. In this case, it is better to find a way to present the message in person, or the presentation will appear insensitive.

Now that you know about the different types of online presentations, let's examine some of the benefits and challenges the online environment poses.

Challenges of Online Presentations

While online presentations promise many potential rewards, as we have discussed, they are not without their own set of challenges. The next section outlines some of the difficulties or obstacles that online presentations may present along with some practical solutions for addressing these obstacles.

Challenges of Synchronous Presentations

Synchronous online presentations present their own set of challenges. Some of these are related to the technology itself. The next section details some of the more common challenges.

Technical Difficulties

First, research shows that the technical quality of the videoconferencing system can play a role in how effective the presentation is perceived by the audience.[54] Poor quality means that speakers have to work harder to get their message across. There are several ways technical quality can compromise the effectiveness of a presentation. Most commonly, lack of sufficient bandwidth to share information can result in dropped audio, pixelated images, and jerky video. These problems can be intermittent or sustained through out the whole presentation. They can also affect some participants but not others, based on the quality of their individual connections. Either way, they can be distracting and encourage people to drop out of the presentation or create distractions for those unaffected while time is expended trying to address the participants who are having problems. Furthermore, technical problems, though usually not the speaker's fault, compromise the speaker's credibility since they are often the easiest target to blame for problems.

Technical Expertise and Extra Planning

As a speaker, you are expected to be an expert in both your content and the medium through which you are communicating. If you do not fully understand the capabilities and limitations of the systems you are using to deliver an online presentation, you should expect the worse to happen during the presentation. There are several things you can do to make sure you understand the environment.

First, you need to have realistic practice sessions if you are using a technology for the first time, if at all possible. Plan several run-throughs until you feel completely comfortable with the system. Ideally, you will try to simulate key components of your presentation. For instance, if you expect audience members to be logging into the web conferencing system from different locations, try to have a practice run where people are logging in from different locations. If you expect to be answering questions through a text chat system, you should practice answering questions through chat. Additionally, Web conferencing platforms will alter your presentation slides for viewing through a browser to make the file sizes as small as possible. As a result, slides that look great on your computer can look blurry and unprofessional during the conference. The best way to avoid this problem is to make sure you view your slides in the platform you are using. Do so several days before the planned Web conference to allow time to make modifications to the slides if necessary.

Professionally Speaking

Web Conferencing for Presentations

Stephanie Grebe, Assistant Director, Global Internships, University of Iowa

Former Recruiting Coordinator

Consortium for Universities for International Studies, CIMBA

CIMBA is an Italian study abroad program that is comprised of students from over 30 universities from around the United States. As the Recruiting Coordinator, it was Grebe's responsibility to communicate with these students about their questions and concerns as they prepare for their study abroad. Because of the distance, it was challenging to reach all of these students personally and ease their concerns, she said.

Using a program called Elluminate, they held several "CIMBA Live Q&A Sessions" online leading up to their departures. This program offers various features that make for an interactive and personalized presentation. During the presentation, two former CIMBA participants were on camera and available to answer any questions students had about packing, traveling, classes, and more. They utilized the video feature to physically show students recommendations for travel backpacks, adapters, converters, and electronic devices. They were welcome to voice in their questions if they had a microphone on their computer, or they could type them into a chat field. Elluminate also allowed them to have a PowerPoint presentation or announcements running throughout the chat.

A challenge experienced was presenting on a camera. "While many of our presenters are used to making live presentations, the camera is a different experience. We have had to stage our presentations with a background that is professional and not distracting. We have also had to adjust the lighting to ensure the participants could see us clearly. We also have had to adjust our technique for presenting. On camera, it is very noticeable when you are not animated and smiling, so we have found it important to remain extremely positive while on camera, so not to appear bored. Another thing that is very noticeable on camera is movement. When presenters would adjust their hair and clothing, or rock back and forth, it was very distracting on camera."

"My advice for someone using this type of technology is to practice several times. This allows you to become familiar with the program features and how to fluidly use them in a presentation. I'd recommend having several participants in your trial run, to practice microphone techniques and technology troubleshooting. I would also recommend recording these trial runs and watching them back. This will allow you to see your performance and decide what techniques may not be suitable for online presenting on camera."

Second, it is good to have a moderator or assistant help you with audience questions and/or technical difficulties. Having this additional support will allow you to focus all of your energy on your message. Speakers have enough to focus on. Monitoring a busy chat system for questions while moving through a presentation is just too much for one speaker to handle. However, an assistant who is focusing on questions can perhaps answer some of them for you and also prompt you when important questions come in. Likewise, having someone specifically working to address technical problems for the audience can allow you to focus on the presentation and training.

Even if you have practiced, arrive early and make sure all aspects of the technology are working smoothly on the day of the presentation. Even though everything may have worked the afternoon before, it is essential that you ensure all components will be ready to go when you are. As with any technology, there is always the potential for failure. So, have a backup plan. What will you do if one of the components of your presentation simply will not work? If your technology does fail, don't get flustered. Use this opportunity to demonstrate how polished and competent you are in the situation. Quickly revert to plan B, and deliver the presentation with confidence. This will go a long way in building your credibility as a speaker. For instance,

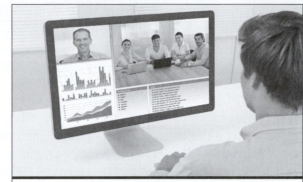

Even if you have practiced, arrive early and make sure all aspects of the technology are working smoothly on the day of the presentation.

if you are using a Web conferencing system, you might schedule a backup phone conference line just in case there are network problems. In addition, it's a good idea to preposition materials for the audience to download in case you have to make do without video.[55] Remember, the more technology you use, the more likely the chance of a technical glitch. Use simultaneous video or Web with audio only if the presentation requires it.

Delivery Challenges

While delivery is always important in presentational speaking, it is extremely important in online presentations. You need to make sure you speak clearly. You might be unaware of some competing noise at the listener's location.[56] In addition, you are competing with distractions listeners in a face-to-face presentation won't have: e-mail, computer games, and so on. More than 80% of people in a recent survey admitted to multi-tasking while a webinar was on.[57] You need to be dynamic in your delivery to combat these things competing for your audience's attention. Other research shows that your credibility might be judged more by how well you communicate your mediated message than what you said.[58] People use different information to form impressions of video presenters than they do with those of face-to-face presenters. Finally, without an audience in front of you, you might be tempted to look down at your notes more or read your presentation. This will result in a flat presentation that neither an online nor a live audience will want to see.

Interactivity

One assumption that is often made is that online presentations suffer from limited amounts of speaker/audience interactivity. Presenters report that they can't gauge audience reaction to materials.[59] In addition, audience members are often unaware of each other and cannot gauge each other's reactions. In most presentational speaking courses, one of the key requirements for most speakers is to be extemporaneous. Speakers are expected to adapt to audience needs during their delivery, answer questions, and engage the audience in a variety of ways. How can online presenters hope to accomplish this? Doesn't the technology itself get in the way of interaction? The short answer is "yes." Online presentations typically provide fewer traditional ways of responding immediately and effectively to diverse and changing audience needs. However, a better question for communicators to think about is "How do I leverage appropriate technologies to provide for audience interaction and adaptation?"

In live or synchronous presentations, the situation is different. Like traditional presentations, there are ways to receive feedback immediately, as well as ways to respond immediately. Audiences can ask questions through audio and video, or through social media, such as Twitter. Some research indicates that it is better to have questions and answers throughout a synchronous online presentation, instead of at the end.[60] This way audience members stay engaged. Avoid providing answers that are brief or abrupt. This may be interpreted as anger on the presenter's part for the interruption of the presentation.

It is likely that you will not be able to see your audience. Therefore, you will not have access to the visual cues an audience provides. Are they bored? Are you moving too fast? Are they confused? How will you know and how will you be able to adapt in this situation? This is where the different tools, such as chat rooms and polls, become important. You can pose questions through polling that can indicate just how well your audience is following the information you are presenting. Additionally, an audience that is engaged in some type of activity, such as polling, is more likely to remember your information than a passive audience simply listening to your presentation.[61] You can also keep audiences involved by keeping the presentation changing visually. By giving audiences something new to look at they will be more likely to stay engaged with the presentation.[62]

Environmental Constraints

Timing is also key in synchronous presentations. Just like we learned in Chapter 2 that environmental factors such as time of day might influence your face-to-face presentation, time also impacts your online presentation. A synchronous presentation can span several time zones. You need to take this into consideration when scheduling the presentation. A 10:00 a.m. meeting time for you could be before dawn somewhere else. If possible, schedule the presentation during normal business hours for everyone involved, keeping in mind when audience members at remote locations might need to break for lunch and so forth. It is important to the success of your presentation that you find a time that is convenient for the most audience members. Another option if you have a regularly scheduled online presentation time that includes people from several time zones is to rotate the starting time. That way, no one person has to get up early or stay after hours every time.[63] In addition, it's likely that some dispersed participants will join the presentation a little late. Not everyone can arrive at the exact same time. It's OK to plan to start the presentation a few minutes later to accommodate late arrivals, but make sure you end on time.[64]

Professionally Speaking

Virtual Presentations

Human resources units are adopting virtual presentations at a rapid pace. For example, when The Bostonian Group, a leading insurance adviser to businesses, needed a better way to communicate its benefit platforms to employees of its customers, it turned to virtual presentations. Key executives of customer companies narrated the presentations. That way, the presentations took on the fabric of the actual organization. Employees could share the presentations with spouses so that "nothing was lost in translation." And clients with multiple locations had a simple method to share information. In fact, communicating benefit changes or options, or explaining new programs to employees, is one of the most popular current uses of online presentations.[66]

Infrastructure

An additional limitation that needs to be specifically addressed is that new technologies and new techniques for communicating require both a sufficient technology infrastructure to support the presentation and the technical skill to take advantage of that infrastructure. For instance, if you want to build a Web presentation, do you have a website to host it? If you want to record audio and video, is there recording and digitizing equipment or computers available? If you want to participate in an online presentation or event, do you have appropriate Web browsers, or plugins, or network connections that allow you to participate? These are the types of things meant by infrastructure. Online presentations require appropriate online environments. Be sure to research what resources your current organization or university has before making commitments that may be difficult to implement.

Challenges of Asynchronous Presentations ─────

Asynchronous presentations come with their own set of obstacles or challenges. Some of the more common are discussed in the following section.

Permanency

First, the on-demand, and therefore permanent, nature of the media requires more formality on the part of the speaker. This means that you should use a manuscript style when delivering this type of presentation. Part of the benefit of an extemporaneous presentation is flexibility, which allows a speaker the ability to adapt to the needs of the audience. Since adaptability is not possible in an asynchronous presentation, the added formality of a manuscript presentation has more benefits in this context. As mentioned in Chapter 8, manuscript speeches are difficult to deliver well. You don't want them sounding canned or monotonous. Therefore, this type of presentation needs to be carefully rehearsed to achieve the desired impact.

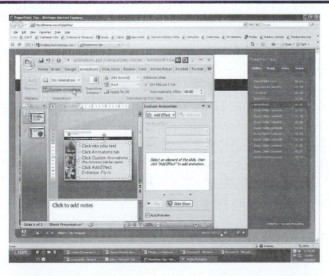

This instructional on-demand video on how to animate your PowerPoint slides makes use of voice-over narration.

Carmine Gallo, a noted presentational speaking expert, has said that asynchronous presentations require certain delivery modifications.[67] First, because facial expressions or hand gestures can't be used for added emphasis, you need to punctuate key words with your voice. Gallo advises presenters to go through their script and underline the most important words prior to recording the presentation. Next, people tend to speak faster or slower than normal when they record their voice. Keep that in mind as you record your narration. Finally, that soda or juice you have to drink right before your recording session can affect the quality of your voice. That's because drinks that contain caffeine or sugar can give you dry mouth—stick with water.

Accessibility

Online content should also be checked for accessibility to ensure that people with vision or hearing impairments can access the information. With large distributed audiences, the various needs of audience members can be great. One of the benefits of an on-demand presentation is its ability to reach a wide audience. You do not want to artificially limit this audience by failing to adapt to potential impairments. For example, some individuals use screen-reading software to vocally narrate textual material. If you have a lot of images, you need to be sure alternative labels describe the image.

Technically Speaking

Synchronous and Asynchronous Simultaneously

Suppose you deliver a synchronous presentation that is recorded or archived for asynchronous distribution at a later point in time. How could you adapt to both of these environmental constraints simultaneously? While this is an extremely challenging speaking situation, there are small adaptations that you can make that will help to ensure your presentation will be effective in both of these environments. Focus on the synchronous challenges and then make your adaptations. First, if using presentation slides such as PowerPoint, make sure that the video captures both the speaker and the slides. You might want to have two cameras, one to focus on the speaker and one to focus on the video. This method of recording would necessitate some editing on the back end, but would ensure both the speaker and the visuals were captured adequately. Alternatively, you could use one camera that zoomed in on the slides when they were essential to understanding the point you were trying to make. A second consideration is the timeliness of your examples and materials. Asynchronous presentations can live for years on the Web. Your material can become quickly outdated so use examples that will remain timely so they will continue to resonate with audiences for some time to come. Finally, if you engage in a question-and-answer session with your live audience, make sure you repeat their questions so that asynchronous audience members can actually hear their questions. These are a few ideas for helping you to manage both of these environments simultaneously.

Interactivity

In an asynchronous environment, how can an audience provide feedback? While the type of feedback won't be immediate as it is in a traditional presentation or even a synchronous presentation, presenters can make adaptations so that some interaction with the audience is possible. For example, speakers often use technologies such as online discussion forums, e-mail, feedback forms, and other Web technologies as a way of answering audience questions and responding to feedback. While these may seem limited on the surface, they do have their own advantages. First, when feedback to online presentations is provided electronically, there is then an archive of audience questions and responses to those questions. Second, this type of feedback can be used by the presenter to actually adjust portions of the presentation to clarify any problems. So the presentation is being adapted for future audiences based on feedback from past audiences. While adjusting with feedback isn't necessarily always used, it still can occur. Finally, by having this type of asynchronous dialogue between a presenter and an audience, we can begin to see how online presentations persist as a part of a larger conversation between presenter and audience. That is not possible in a traditional environment.

Presentational Aids

Presentational aids can be more detailed in an asynchronous presentation. Audiences will have the ability to read your PowerPoint slides at their leisure, so the slides can contain more detail than they might in more traditional presentations. Charts and figures may have more detail because audience members can more closely scrutinize them. However, remember the contiguity principle.[68] Comprehension is best when you place text near, or insert it into, corresponding pictures. You don't want to make the viewer have to work to match text and pictures. Also, research indicates that the use of voice-over narration adds both interest in and instructional value to asynchronous presentations.[69]

Common Tools for Online Presentations

Presenters often think that delivering presentations online requires that they be extremely technically sophisticated or learn a whole new set of tools. These presumptions are only partly true. Many of the technologies you currently use to support traditional face-to-face presentations are also useful in delivering online presentations. Additionally, you may already be using other technologies for other situations besides giving presentations that can also be used to facilitate online presentations.

In this section, we will discuss two technologies that you are probably already aware of, and possibly, experienced using: slide creation tools, like Microsoft's PowerPoint, and online audio/video and chat software, such as Microsoft's Skype. With these two technologies alone, presenters can create and deliver a variety of common types of online presentations.

Using Slide Presentation Software in Online Presentations

Because of the benefits that corporations realize from them, online presentations will continue to grow in popularity. New programs are being developed every day to aid this process. Some are made just for Web presentations; others, such as Microsoft PowerPoint, can be modified to be uploaded to the Web. As an employee, you will be expected to understand how to present in traditional mediums, but you will also be expected to have the skills to create a variety of Web-based presentations.

The most popular technology accompanying contemporary presentations is the use of presentation software that creates "slides," such as Microsoft PowerPoint, and alternatives, such as Apple Keynote, Prezi, and many others. Most students are familiar with this type of software and learn to use it early in their academic careers; if they do not already know how to use it. In addition, a simple Google search will uncover numerous web pages and asynchronous presentations outlining how to use various presentation software packages. The most typical use of these packages is to create slides in support of a live, in person, presentation. These tools often anticipate the need to share presentations online and often have special features to support these activities. There are several benefits to this because these features allow you to

◎ provide people who could not attend the opportunity to see your presentation;

◎ provide people with the ability to review information in your presentation at a later date; and

◎ provide an alternative way to present to audiences when it is not possible to provide a live presentation.

Tip

The biggest benefit of online webinars is obviously the savings in travel cost and time. But even an hour in someone's office is precious. Make sure you prepare as if you are standing in front of two hundred people in an auditorium, because, virtually, you are.

Professionally Speaking | David Goad | Senior Marketing Manager | Cisco

On the surface, this may seem like a simple task. It is not uncommon for people to e-mail, burn to CD, or publish to the Web standard PowerPoint (.ppt) files for others to view. However, this is problematic for a couple of reasons. First, it assumes that viewers of the presentation have PowerPoint software, or a PowerPoint viewer, installed on their computers. This is often not the case. Second, file sizes of standard PowerPoint presentations are often very large and thus are difficult to distribute electronically. Because of this, you also need to become familiar with alternative ways of working with PowerPoint to provide more effective presentations for Web and electronic delivery that will make it easier for your audiences to access your presentation. Among the options are converting the PowerPoint slides to HTML, creating HTML-based narrated PowerPoint presentations for online delivery, and creating a streaming video presentation of your narrated PowerPoint presentation.

Before you begin creating your asynchronous Web presentation, remember that the actual act of creating the PowerPoint presentation is only a part of the process. In fact, a majority of your time should be spent on collecting your ideas, organizing them, sketching out your presentation, and rehearsing your narration. Even the most professional PowerPoint presentation can't overcome issues such as missing information or a lack of organization.

Creating Slides for Online Use

As you learned in Chapter 12, slides can have a major impact on an audience. Use the tips and guidelines discussed there for creating impactful and effective slides. Once you have an effective set of slides prepared, you can share them with your online audience. The primary limitation of simply sharing your slides is that slides are usually meant to compliment an oral presentation, not replace it. So, sharing only the slides is likely to cause more confusion if they have not been designed to stand on their own without narration. Therefore, if you anticipate providing slides online, you might need to consider narrating them as well. This is easy in synchronous web conferences, because you are typically delivering your audio while you show your slides through web conferencing software. However, for on-demand or asynchronous presentations, you have several choices.

1. Tools like Microsoft PowerPoint and Apple Keynote have built-in features that let you record audio for slides and save them as a part of the presentation. Though this makes the presentation very large, these tools provide ways of exporting the presentation that will compress the presentation into another format that can be shared on the Web, or through video sharing sites like YouTube.

2. Third-party tools are often available that can help. For instance, Adobe Presenter is a plugin for Power-Point that lets you export a narrated presentation in Flash so it can stream more easily over the Web. You can also use screen capture software (e.g., Techsmith's Camtasia, Adobe's Captivate, Jing, etc.) that allows you to record your computer screen and audio to a movie format that can be uploaded to sites like YouTube for distribution to your audience.

3. The final option is to not use audio at all. Ask yourself if you really need audio or would text provide sufficient explanation? Instead, could you use embedded text on some slides to provide sufficient instruction and understanding?[73] If this is the case, you could add slides and additional content to compensate for the missing audio and upload the slides to sites such as SlideShare (slideshare.net) for distribution to others.

Take the time to review the software you use to determine the options you have at your disposal and test how well it works for you. Increasingly, new features are added to slide creation software specifically to make developing online presentations easier.

Spotlight on Research

Knowledge Transference in Online Presentations

Whether in-person or online, the main objective of many presentations is to share knowledge. The question then becomes, is an online presentation as effective at achieving this goal as an in-person presentation? Researchers attempted to determine this using 95 senior medical students in a primary care medicine clerkship based at a university and distant clinic sites. Half attended lectures in person, while the others received their lectures online. Researchers found that the students in the online lecture group had equal post-lecture knowledge of the lecture material as those attending class in person.[72]

If you do need to add an audio narration, you should be sure to approach its addition with the same care you do the creation of the slides in the first place. Your audio should complement and enhance the slides, not distract from them. Make sure you have a script that allows the narration to flow smoothly. There is no reason to read text word for word as it appears on the screen. Chances are your audience will have already read the words before you even speak them. Known as the split attention principle, we read and hear at different speeds.[74] This makes the narration redundant and slows the presentation. In addition, make sure you have access to a quality microphone. If your narration is muffled or unclear, it will detract from, instead of add to, the effectiveness of the presentation.

Technology Options

Conducting Synchronous Online Presentations

Depending on the organization you belong to, and your access to resources, you may have several choices for conducting live online presentations.

◎ **Video Conferencing Systems:** Many companies use expensive video conferencing systems to connect distributed offices. These usually have dedicated video cameras and television monitors that can connect one room to one or more other rooms to facilitate meetings. Companies include Polycom and Tandberg.

◎ **Web Conferencing Systems:** Web conferencing systems allow a wide variety of capabilities, including, audio, video, slides, whiteboards, and chat rooms to facilitate interaction with standard computers, webcams, and an Internet connection. Popular systems include WebEx, Adobe Connect, and Go To Meeting.

◎ **Skype:** This alternative to the telephone is a popular way for presenters to share their web camera and desktop with remote participants. It also has a free version that can make it attractive to organizations. Currently, it is also being used to interview candidates for positions in organizations.[70]

◎ **Google+:** Google+'s "hangout" feature allows small groups of individuals to have live discussions through webcams and microphones.

Sharing Asynchronous Presentation Material

Depending on the type of media you are creating, you may have one or more options for making your on-demand content available. Here are some currently popular choices.

◎ **YouTube (youtube.com):** YouTube is the most popular video-streaming site, and many professionals create YouTube channels for uploading their presentations. These can then be linked to, or embedded in, other sites, discussed through the comment section, and tracked over time to assess popularity.

◎ **Podcasts (www.apple.com/itunes/podcasts/):** Podcasts are audio or video files, usually managed through Apple iTunes, to allow files to automatically download to computers and sync with iPods, iPhones, and similar devices so people can access presentations through mobile devices, even when not online.

◎ **Slideshare (slideshare.net):** Slideshare is a social media system for uploading and sharing PowerPoint slides, PDFs, videos, and other resources. You can also sync your slides with MP3 audio files to create on-demand webinars.

Using Audio/Video/Chat Software for Live Presentations

Increasingly, organizations are using web-based alternatives to video conferencing systems to facilitate live presentations. Some of these are familiar to Internet users, such as AOL's Instant Messenger, Google+'s Hangouts, Google Video Chat, and Skype. Most of these tools were initially designed to facilitate quick "chats" with friends and co-workers as an alternative to e-mail. However, over time these tools often began to integrate more functionality to allow for richer interactions that also included audio and video. These enhancements became viable because users had increasing access to more bandwidth than when the tools were initially developed.

There are many commercial tools that corporations and educational institutions sometimes use that support advanced features. WebEx, Elluminate and Adobe Acrobat Connect Pro, for example, allow for multiple presenters presenting to many users logged in at many different locations, and support additional tools such as online whiteboards and polling tools. However, commercial tools are not necessary for high quality live presentations.

Using Skype for Live Presentations

One tool that has recently taken off for facilitating remote presentations is Microsoft's Skype program. Originally developed as a Voice over Internet Protocol (VoIP) service to provide telephone-like functionality to Internet users, Skype now supports a wider range of functionality, including the ability to chat, share video, and share computer screens. Skype is often used by television networks and shows as an inexpensive way to do remote interviews with guests as an alternative to expensive satellite video systems.

Basic use of Skype is free with the creation of a login account on their site for point-to-point interaction with another location. There are several things you should consider if you plan to use Skype as a way of making an online presentation.

- ◎ Consider your bandwidth. Sharing audio and video over the web requires more bandwidth than audio alone. Having a wired Ethernet connection will usually provide better results than using a wireless access point.
- ◎ Use a good microphone or, preferably, a headset microphone. The built-in microphone in many laptops is low-quality and easily picks up background noise and static. Also, external microphones can pick up noise from the computer speakers and create feedback.
- ◎ Develop a strategy for monitoring and handling audience questions. Are they going to speak directly to you through the microphone or send them through text over chat? Having a moderator to help organize questions from the audience can be helpful.
- ◎ Test your connection prior to the presentation to make sure everything works on both ends. The quality of your presentation requires that the technology is working at both locations. Waiting to the last minute to test things out is a recipe for disaster and looks unprofessional to audience members.
- ◎ Get comfortable toggling between your video and your slides. Skype allows you to use both, but not at the same time. However, your audience probably wants to see both you and your slides. So identify points ahead of time where you can shift from one to the other.

Skype is relatively easy to learn to use, but using it well requires practice. Additionally, many of the techniques you develop on a tool like Skype will translate well to other tools, even though there may be slight technical differences in how you use alternatives. Regardless, you should approach the use of any system with the same care you use in developing the content of your presentation. If you do not appear to know what you are doing, it reflects on your overall credibility as a speaker and distracts from your message.

Conclusion

Online presentations are increasingly popular in today's global marketplace. Understanding the online environment and possessing the skills to make an effective presentation online are real assets for anyone entering the workforce. Although online presentations have much in common with traditional presentations, they also involve developing new skills. Synchronous and asynchronous presentations present many challenges that you must be able to address if your presentation is going to be effective. Fundamental issues, such as understanding your goal and adapting to your audience, are still present when presenting online. However, the way you meet your goals and adapt to your audience may be different. Synchronicity and interactivity are all important items to consider as you develop your online presentation.

Key Terms

Asynchronous

Connotative meaning

Distributed audience

Denotative meaning

High-context cultures

Interactivity

Low-context cultures

On-demand presentations

Synchronous

Webinar

Exercises

1. Here are a few links to examples of narrated PowerPoints created by individuals and organizations. Watch a few of these presentations and critique them using the guidelines discussed in this chapter. http://www.youtube.com/watch?v=hffuxPorvMo; http://www.youtube.com/watch?v=dAQEBgb6yzo; http://www. youtube.com/watch?v=RN2Mh22Mqn8.

2. TED is a nonprofit organization that is dedicated to "ideas worth spreading." They have two annual conferences where they bring together innovators from a wide variety of disciplines, such as technology, science, education, design, entertainment, etc. to share ideas. The best of these presentations are taped and distributed on their website and YouTube channel. These speeches or talks that are posted to their website are excellent examples of asynchronous presentations. Visit presentations posted on this site to get a sense of how speakers adapt to this challenging speaking environment.

3. Find out what systems your university or college uses to facilitate online presentations. Try to experiment with one of those systems to evaluate how easy it is to use. Report your findings back to the class.

4. Create a narrated PowerPoint presentation and upload it to the Web.

5. Practice recording audio with your computer.

6. Practice delivering your presentation via Skype to a family member or friend. How is this presentation different from the ones you have delivered face-to-face in class? What were the challenges you faced?

CHAPTER 15

The Question-and-Answer Session

Objectives

After reading this chapter, you should be able to

◎   conduct effective question-and-answer (Q&A) sessions; and

◎   understand the influence of social media on question-and-answer sessions.

When global public relations firm Weber Shandwick polled the top conference organizers about trends in conference programs, several interesting trends emerged. Among them, 72% of conference organizers reported they are planning more time for question-and-answer sessions versus just three years ago. In addition, 70% plan more interactive sessions between speaker and audience.[1]

> **The question-and-answer session is the last thing an audience hears, so it leaves a strong impression.**

The question-and-answer (Q&A) session is as important as the presentation itself. It is the last thing the audience hears (recency effect), so it leaves a strong impression. Although most speakers consider the Q&A an afterthought, it should be at the forefront of your preparation. Many decisions are made and perceptions formed during the Q&A. Accounts are won and lost over this often-neglected component. A speaker or group member who is unable to answer questions effectively can undermine the impact of a well-prepared presentation. On the other hand, a speaker or group member who answers questions well can strengthen the impact of the presentation and enhance credibility.

It is important to a successful presentation that you prepare thoroughly for the Q&A and that you put as much thought and energy into this component as any other. View the Q&A as another avenue to reach your audience. You will be able to clarify positions or data, and explain details that you may have forgotten to include during the formal part of the presentation. When available, recognize how social media can be used to enhance your interaction with the audience, especially during a Q&A. Some guidelines for achieving a successful Q&A are discussed in the following section.

Guidelines for an Effective Q&A

Prepare for the Q&A

Many times, speakers ask, "How can someone actually plan for a Q&A? After all, anything could happen, right?" Actually, it may seem overwhelming at first, but you can do many things to prepare for the Q&A. It is much more predictable than you might first imagine. By anticipating questions and developing a plan, you have more control over the Q&A than you first thought.

Prepare for your Q&A. You can anticipate tough questions and should never look shocked or unsettled.

Anticipate Questions

Try to put yourself in the place of audience members. Really try to understand their position and perspective. From this vantage point, what questions do you think they could have about the material you presented? For example, sometimes a presentation is so limited by a time constraint that you may have to leave out important details. In this case, it is easy to anticipate possible questions audience members might have. Obviously, they would ask follow-up questions requesting more detail. Another example is the hostile audience. With this type of audience, it is also easy to predict where you and the audience differ in terms of attitudes, beliefs, and behaviors. Once again, it is easy to predict their objections and potential questions. Anticipate as many questions as you can, and plan in advance how you will deal with these questions and concerns should they arise.

In the two scenarios just discussed, it is relatively easy to predict what an audience might ask; other times, it isn't as apparent. We are often so engrossed in our own material that it becomes difficult to imagine what an audience might find difficult or where further elaboration may be needed. Get feedback from others to help you with this aspect of your presentation. If you can't think of questions a possible audience may have, ask friends and family to sit in on a practice session and then solicit their questions. It is always a good idea to get as much practice on each aspect of the presentation as you can. Therefore, a trial run-through with an audience can achieve three goals: It can provide you with an additional practice session for the presentation itself, it can generate possible audience questions, and it can give you the experience of participating in a Q&A before the real thing.

Carmine Gallo, a noted communication skills coach and author of *The Presentation Secrets of Steve Jobs: How to Be Insanely Great in Front of Any Audience,* says that to reduce the number of actual questions you have to prepare for, you should organize potential questions into categories, which he calls "buckets".[2] "Well-prepared speakers do not memorize answers to hundreds of potential questions. Instead, they prepare answers to categories of questions." During the Q&A, presenters listen for "trigger" words that identify from which "bucket" to pull their answers. For instance, all questions that contain words such as "costs," or "resources," or "expenses" would fall into the same bucket and elicit the same prepared response. The key, Gallo said, is for the answer to each category trigger to make sense, no matter how the question is phrased.

Have a Plan

If you are in a group situation, developing a plan for how you will handle the Q&A is essential. Will one person take all questions and divert them to the appropriate member of the team, or will all questions be directed at and answered by the team leader? Whichever way you decide to run the Q&A is fine. There is no prescribed plan that is best in all situations. However, it is essential that you have a plan. It looks completely unprofessional for several team members to stare at each other before someone finally answers. It also looks unprofessional for several team members to jump in to answer the same question or to contradict one another. Make sure the session is as organized as possible.

Answering Questions

Now that you know how to get prepared for the questions, you need some strategies for delivering the answers to the questions. Follow the guidelines outlined next, and your Q&A should be effective.

Keep Answers Concise and Direct

Answer each question as directly and as concisely as possible. Audiences appreciate a clear and direct response. If the answer is as simple as a "yes" or "no," simply say so and move on to the next question. If you spend too much time on any one question, you may run short on time during the Q&A, and some audience members may not have the opportunity to ask their questions.

Repeat Each Question

After each question is asked, repeat or rephrase the question for the entire audience. First, it is difficult for other audience members to hear questions. There is nothing more frustrating than listening to a speaker answer a question that you didn't hear. Second, it is also frustrating to have to sit through a long answer to a question the speaker misunderstood. You want to interrupt, "That's not what I asked." Finally, rephrasing or repeating a question also gives you some additional time to formulate your answer and allows you to make sure that you understood the question.

Listen to the Entire Question

Listen to each audience member's entire question. Don't start formulating your response mentally while he or she is still speaking. You may miss some important details of the question. Wait to answer until you know exactly what was asked. Make sure you fully understand the question. If you don't, ask for clarification.[3]

What If I Don't Know the Answer?

If you don't know the answer to a question, be honest. It is better to admit that you do not know than to talk around the issue, use fallacious reasoning, or answer as if you are certain when you are not. Imagine the credibility issues for you as a speaker if you answer a question incorrectly and someone in the audience knows the answer. This can be devastating.

Here are a few strategies that can help in these situations. First, you can always ask audience members if they know the answer to the question. Let's imagine that you are delivering a presentation on "The Benefits of Alzheimer's Support Groups." The audience is made up of family members of Alzheimer's patients and local aging administrators and social workers who work with families who are experiencing this disease. Maybe someone asks you the question, "How many families in our county are currently using support groups?" Given that you are not from their particular county, you may not know the answer to this question. It would be perfectly acceptable to say, "I am not familiar with the numbers in this county. Does anyone in the audience have that information?" If not, say, "I will try to locate that information and get back to you." It is important to remember, however, that if you promise to get back to an audience member, you must do so. Your credibility can be called into question if you make empty promises.

What If No One Asks a Question?

It is possible that audience members will not have any questions. Audience members suffer from communication apprehension just like speakers do. They often have questions; they just don't want to be the first to ask them. If after you open the floor for questions, there are none, simply say, "A question I am often asked is …" and go ahead and answer the question. This usually loosens up an audience, and the questions will come streaming in.

If audience members still fail to ask a few questions, ask them what they think of the issue at hand. This strategy may get them talking. You can also inform the audience that you will be available for questions after the presentation if anyone wants to engage in a one-on-one dialogue.

What If I Can't Understand the Questioner?

If you are having trouble understanding a question because of a language barrier or environmental factors, such as noise in the room, politely ask the audience member to repeat. If you still can't understand him or her, say that you are having difficulty hearing and that you'd be happy to wait around after the presentation and talk with the individual one-on-one.

What If a Group Member Provides Wrong Information?

As noted previously, it looks unprofessional for group members to contradict one another. However, audience members will notice if a group member provides a blatantly wrong answer about a critical part of your proposal. If this happens, you must find a way to correct the information immediately. There are ways to phrase the correction in a professional manner. You could say something like, "I think Jane misunderstood your question …" or "Mark actually just provided you with preliminary numbers. The final cost actually is …" Resist the urge, however, to make additional comments on others' answers. Correcting a group member during a Q&A or adding on to an answer given should be done in only the most extreme circumstances.

What If Someone Asks a Question Clearly Answered by the Presentation?

If someone asks a question already answered in the presentation, try explaining the information differently. Chances are the person simply didn't understand the point the first time around. It's also possible that others in the audience didn't as well. Refrain from embarrassing the questioner. You don't want to tell the audience member that the information was already covered. Simply answer the question again without pointing out that the information was missed the first time.

With Whom Should I Make Eye Contact?

Make eye contact with the audience member asking a question during the time he or she is actually asking the question, but speak to the entire audience when giving the reply. Also, avoid moving closer to the individual who asked the question as you give your response. These two strategies will keep the entire audience involved while you answer the question, and therefore keep everyone interested.

> **Make eye contact with the entire audience when giving a reply.**

Dealing with Difficult Audience Members

Most audience members are polite, ask their question, and are happy to go on their way. Sometimes, however, you will be confronted by audience members who are intent on monopolizing the entire session by engaging you in a debate or some other inappropriate behavior. The most important thing to remember here is to never lose your cool. Handle these situations as delicately as possible. However, it is important to remember that you are in control. Don't be afraid to assert yourself and redirect negative behavior and energy.

It is a mistake to engage disruptive audience members in a one-on-one dialogue. Allow audience members one question and one follow-up question. It is up to you to maintain control of the session. If, after answering a difficult individual's second question, it becomes clear that he or she is going to ask another one, simply look out to the entire audience and ask: "Does anyone else have a question?"

Another option is to simply tell the difficult audience member that you find this discussion interesting and that perhaps you could talk after the presentation is over. Explain that you want to ensure that everyone in the audience has a chance to have their questions answered, and simply move to the next question.

Often, an audience member will respond with a loaded question. These are questions that are worded so that any response will appear negative. For example, "What are you doing with all the money you are making from our tuition hikes?" Stephen D. Boyd, Ph.D., a noted communication consultant, says, "Don't answer a loaded question; defuse it before you answer" (Boyd, 2004). He uses the following example as an illustration: Suppose an audience member asks the following question, "What are you doing with all the money you are making from increased prices?" Simply reply, "I understand your frustration with the recent rate increase. I believe what you are asking is, 'Why such a sudden increase in rates?'" Then go on to answer that question. By answering a loaded question, you just set yourself up for conflict.

Stay Confident

Many times, individuals find the Q&A threatening. Whereas you have control over the formal aspect of the presentation, you have less control over questions the audience may ask. It is true that audience members may ask difficult questions and try to challenge you or your ideas; however, if you have thought about the Q&A and planned in advance, you can handle these issues effectively and with confidence.

Don't dread the Q&A session. Remember, this is a great opportunity for you to sell yourself, your ideas, your product, or even your company. Stand up straight. Look audience members directly in the eye and exude the confidence that you have demonstrated throughout your presentation.

Communications expert Chris Brogan speaks as the backchannel is displayed behind him (source: Mykl Roventine/CC BY 2.0/ https://www.flickr.com/photos/myklroventine-events/4361200097/in/photostream).

The New Backchannel

Audience comments, questions, and concerns are no longer limited to the post-presentation Q&A. You need to be aware that audience members are now using social media via their smartphones and computers to have conversations in real time about the presentation you are giving. And it doesn't stop there. Previously, the only participants in a presentation were the people in the room at the time. However, Twitter and other social media tools allow that presentation, and the audience's reaction to that presentation, to extend beyond the physical room.[5] People can now follow the presentation on the **backchannel** both in and out of the room. And those people outside the presentation can interact with those in the audience, sharing resources, questions, and so forth.

Notes

Social Times lists numerous benefits to using the backchannel for your Q&A, including the following:

- ◎ It allows people who would normally be too shy to ask questions via the backchannel.
- ◎ People can ask their questions when they occur to them, and your Twitter moderator can bookmark them for the Q&A session.
- ◎ If there are too many questions for the time available, your Twitter moderator can prioritize them. Audience members can play a role in this by re-tweeting the questions that they would most like asked.
- ◎ Project the backchannel during the Q&A, and point out the questions you're answering. That will make sure that people who aren't following the backchannel don't feel excluded (and of course, do take questions the traditional way too!).[4]

Cliff Atkinson, communications expert and author of the book *The Backchannel,* has updated the definition of *backchannel* to include the influence of social media: The backchannel, he says, is a "line of communication created by people in an audience to connect with others inside or outside the room, with or without the knowledge of the speaker at the front of the room. Usually facilitated by Internet technologies, it is spontaneous, self-directed, and limited in time to the duration of a live event."[6]

And it's here to stay, experts say. The Weber Shandwick survey found that business leadership conferences are featuring more blogging and Twittering during events (58%). Conference-provided chat rooms are the norm.[7] Smart presenters anticipate that audience members will be using the backchannel, Atkinson[8] notes.

The backchannel can either be a good or bad thing. It can hurt a presentation when audience members post negative feedback online for all to see. It can also drastically change the atmosphere in the room. It can be a positive influence if the presenter uses it to engage or respond to the audience or to keep a conversation going once the presentation has ended.

There are several ways presenters can use the backchannel to their advantage. It is important that presenters show the audience they understand and welcome the conversations taking place on the backchannel. Many display the backchannel in real time on large screens during their presentation. The most common channel being used by participants is Twitter. One thing presenters can do to reinforce this is to set up a Twitter hashtag ahead of their presentations and let attendees know it's been created. The **hashtag** is a word or phrase prefaced by the #tag. A hashtag added to a tweet acts as way to create categories for tweets that others can use as well. This way, tweets can easily be grouped together using the search.twitter.com feature. For example, if everyone at your presentation adds a pre-set hashtag to their tweets (e.g., #speakertalk), everyone's comments can be grouped together and found more easily.

A new set of tools is cropping up that allow presenters to participate in the backchannel conversation even while they are presenting.[9] Two examples are Keynote Tweet for Mac and PowerPoint Twitter Tools for Windows, which is actually a suite of eight free tools. These are presentation add-ons that allow speakers to embed tweets into their presentations and automatically have those tweets pushed live when the slide is revealed. It makes it really easy for the audience to re-tweet parts of your presentation. In addition, PowerPoint Twitter Tools for Windows allows participants to do things such as vote or take a poll and have the poll results pushed live to the slide on the screen.

The Online Question-and-Answer Session

Just because your presentation is online does not mean you can't involve the participants in a Q&A session. Presentations are more beneficial if participants can be involved. Adding this element to your online presentation also provides the added benefit of helping you get to know your audience better.[10]

Most online presentation software allows for limited verbal Q&A between presenter and audience or a larger text-based exchange similar to a chat function. Some come with a "hand up" function to let the presenter know that an audience member has a question. It's very important that you familiarize yourself with this function before your presentation.

You will also have to decide if you are going to allow/answer questions during the presentation or if you will handle all questions at the end of the presentation. Even if you are using something as simple as Skype you can hear and answer audience questions at the conclusion of a presentation.

While some elements of preparing for a Q&A are the same as an in-person presentation, the online Q&A can present another unique situation. Specifically, research has found that normally reticent colleagues feel more comfortable voicing their opinions and asking questions during online meetings. This means questions asked could be more direct or difficult to answer. So you must prepare carefully for an online Q&A.[11]

Here are some steps you can take to ensure that your online Q&A is successful:

1. Include an announcement that there will be a Q&A session in any material distributed before the presentation. Knowing they can ask questions either during or after the presentation will allow participants to keep track of the questions they have.

2. Rehearse answers to possible questions. Just as you do in your in-person presentations, think of the online Q&A as part of your presentation and rehearse it. Think of questions you might get and rehearse how you would answer them. With a text-based option, you can have some answers pre-prepared.

3. If using a text-based Q&A, make sure you doublecheck your answer before you hit send. An embarrassing typo can derail a presentation.

4. If you will have a large audience, it's a good idea to have someone to aid the presenter to keep track of question during the Q&A. It would be very distracting for a single presenter to try and read all the questions themselves.

5. Decide and let your audience know how you will answer submitted questions that you did not have time to get to.

6. Use a polling option during your presentation to get an idea what you might need to address in the Q&A since the audience's nonverbal feedback will not be available to you.

7. Record or save the text-based Q&A and make it available online for those who might have had to leave the presentation early.

A successful online Q&A can have the same positive effects on a presentation that a well-conducted in-person session does. Your audience will leave on a positive note with their questions answered.

Notes

Olivia Mitchell, author of the e-book "How to Present with Twitter (and Other Backchannels)," lists common feedback that people may offer via the backchannel:

- Having problems with your delivery (e.g., talking too quietly, talking too fast)
- Not familiar with the language you're using, such as acronyms or terminology
- Getting confused or lost
- Wanting you to go deeper on a particular issue
- Disagreeing with your point of view
- Finding the content level either too easy or too hard
- Not interested in the topic
- Poor visual aids[12]

If you are concerned about your ability to present *and* keep track of the backchannel, ask a colleague to be your Twitter moderator.[13] Ask the moderator to alert you to feedback from the backchannel—but only those issues that you can do something about. If people tweet they are having trouble hearing you, you can speak up. But don't respond to issues you aren't prepared to defend or discuss properly at that moment just because they are being raised on the backchannel.[14]

As a presenter, make sure you learn from the backchannel.[15] After your presentation, look at the Twitterstream. You'll get to see the real-time audience reaction. Look for places in your presentation where people appeared confused. What ideas generated the most excitement? What ideas were the most re-tweetable? This kind of feedback will prove invaluable when you prepare for your next presentation.

Provide Closure

Take the opportunity to leave the audience on a positive note.

Just as your presentation comes to a clear ending, so also should your Q&A. You want to maintain control as much as possible. If you run out of time for additional questions, tell the audience that you are out of time and close the session.

If it seems that all questions have been answered, simply respond by saying, "If there are no more questions, I would like to thank you for your time and participation." Regardless of whether you run short or long, always thank audience members for their participation and thoughtful questions. Then provide a very short one-or two-sentence wrap-up statement that sums up your thoughts or the conclusion of your presentation. You want to have the final word. Take the opportunity to leave the audience on a positive note.[16]

Conclusion

In this chapter, you learned that question-and-answer sessions are extremely important to the presentation. Though often overlooked, they are a great opportunity for you to clarify your position and strengthen your connection to your audience. To be successful, you need to plan ahead for the Q&A and then maintain control of the session. You also need to keep in mind how new modes of communication can affect your Q&A. By managing questions effectively and having the last word, you may find that the Q&A enhances your speaker credibility.

Key Terms

Backchannel

Hashtag

REFERENCES R

Chapter 1

[1] Cohen, B. (2015, September 10). Why Michigan State practices public speaking. *Wall Street Journal.* Retrieved from http://www.wsj.com

[2] National Association of Colleges and Employers. (2014, November 18). The skills/qualities employers want in new college graduate hires. Retrieved April 15, 2015, from https://www.naceweb.org/about-us/press/class-2015-skills-qualities-employers-want.aspx

[3] Mantell, R. (2012, November 18). Must-have job skills in 2013. *Wall Street Journal.* Retrieved from http://www.wsj.com/articles/SB10001424127887324735104578118902763095818

[4] Mantell, R. (2012, November 18). Must-have job skills in 2013. *Wall Street Journal.* Retrieved from http://www.wsj.com/articles/SB10001424127887324735104578118902763095818

[5] Mantell, R. (2012, November 18). Must-have job skills in 2013. *Wall Street Journal.* Retrieved from http://www.wsj.com/articles/SB10001424127887324735104578118902763095818

[6] Ligos, M. (2001, June 20). Getting over the fear-of-speaking hump. *New York Times,* p. G1.

7 McKay, J. (2005, February 6). Employers complain about communication skills. *Pittsburgh Post-Gazette*. Retrieved November 2, 2005, from http://www.post-gazette.com

8 McCabe, D. (2005). Center for academic integrity assessment project. Retrieved March 24, 2006, from http://www.academicintegrity.org/cai_research.asp.

9 Smith, S. (2014, July 23). 10 high-profile plagiarism cases. Retrieved from http://www.politico.com/gallery/2014/07/10-high-profile-plagiarism-cases-001770?slide=0#ixzz3wwzUxpSz

10 Karp, J. (2006, May 4). Raytheon penalizes CEO financially after plagiarism. *Wall Street Journal*. Retrieved from http://www.wsj.com

11 Weisman, A. (2015, January 26). Singer Sam Smith has to pay Tom Petty royalties over the song "Stay with Me." Retrieved April 15, 2015, from http://www.businessinsider.com/sam-smith-pays-tom-petty-royalties-over-stay-with-me-2015-1

12 Grow, K. (2015, March 10). Robin Thicke, Pharrell lose multi-million dollar "Blurred Lines" lawsuit. Retrieved April 15, 2015, from http://www.rollingstone.com/music/news/robin-thicke-and-pharrell-lose-blurred-lines-lawsuit-20150310

13 The plagiarism spectrum: Tagging 10 types of unoriginal work. (n.d.). Retrieved from http://turnitin.com/assets/en_us/media/plagiarism_spectrum.php

14 Akst, J. (2010, September 9). When is self-plagiarism ok? *The Scientist Magazine*®. Retrieved from http://www.the-scientist.com/?articles.view/articleNo/29245/title/When-is-self-plagiarism-ok-/

15 Text recycling. (2013). Retrieved March 5, 2014, from http://ori.hhs.gov/plagiarism-19

16 Akst, J. (2010, September 9). When is self-plagiarism ok? *The Scientist Magazine*®. Retrieved from http://www.the-scientist.com/?articles.view/articleNo/29245/title/When-is-self-plagiarism-ok-/

17 Bailey, J. (2012, August 1). Self plagiarism: 5 scenarios to discuss. *Plagiarism Today*. Retrieved from http://www.plagiarismtoday.com/2012/08/01/self-plagiarism-5-scenarios-to-discuss/

18 Markel, M. (2010). *Technical Communication* (9th ed.). Boston, MA: Bedford/St.Martin's.

19 Bongard, S., al'Absie, M., & Lovallo, W. R. (1998). Interactive effects of trait hostility and anger expression on cardiovascular reactivity in young men. *International Journal of Psychophysiology, 28,* 88–92.

20 McCroskey, J. C. (1977). Oral communication apprehension. A summary of recent theory and research. *Human Communication Research, 4,* 78–96.

21 Booth-Butterfield, S., & Gould, M. (1986). The communication anxiety inventory: Validation of state-and context-communication apprehension. *Communication Quarterly, 34,* 194–205.

22 Kelley, L. (1984). Social skills training as a mode of treatment of social communication problems. In J. Daly & J. McCroskey (Eds.), *Avoiding communication: Shyness, reticence, and communication apprehension* (pp. 189–208). Beverly Hills, CA: Sage.

23 Richmond, V. P., & McCroskey, J. C. (1998). *Communication apprehension, avoidance, and effectiveness* (5th ed.). Boston, MA: Allyn and Bacon.

24 Hoffman, J., & Sprague, J. (1982). A survey of reticence and communication apprehension treatment programs at U. S. colleges and universities. *Communication Education, 31,* 185–193.

25 Bodie, G. (2009). A racing heart, rattling knees, and ruminative thoughts: Defining, explaining, and treating public speaking anxiety. *Communication Education, 59,* 70–105.

26 Richmond, V. P., & McCroskey, J. C. (1998). *Communication apprehension, avoidance, and effectiveness* (5th ed.). Boston, MA: Allyn and Bacon.

27 Richmond, V. P., & McCroskey, J. C. (1998). *Communication apprehension, avoidance, and effectiveness* (5th ed.). Boston, MA: Allyn and Bacon.

28 McCroskey, J. C. (1970). Measures of communication-bound anxiety. *Speech Monographs, 37,* 269–277.

29 Richmond, V. P., & McCroskey, J. C. (1998). *Communication apprehension, avoidance, and effectiveness* (5th ed.). Boston, MA: Allyn and Bacon.

30 Fremouw, W. (1984). Cognitive-behavioral therapies for modification of communication apprehension. In J. Daly & J. McCroskey (Eds.), *Avoiding communication: Shyness, reticence, and communication apprehension* (pp. 209–218). Beverly Hills, CA: Sage.

31 Richmond, V. P., & McCroskey, J. C. (1998). *Communication apprehension, avoidance, and effectiveness* (5th ed.). Boston, MA: Allyn and Bacon.

32 Allen, M., Hunter, J., & Donohue, W. (1989). Meta-analysis of self-report data on the effectiveness of public speaking anxiety treatment techniques. *Communication Education, 38,* 54–76.

33 Ayres, J., & Hopf, T. S. (1992). Visualization: Is it more than extra-attention? *Communication Education, 38,* 1–5.

34 Bodie, G. (2009). A racing heart, rattling knees, and ruminative thoughts: Defining, explaining, and treating public speaking anxiety. *Communication Education, 59,* 70–105.

35 Ayres, J., & Hopf, T. S. (1992). Visualization: Is it more than extra-attention? *Communication Education, 38,* 1–5.

36 Ayres, J., & Hopf, T. S. (1992). Visualization: Is it more than extra-attention? *Communication Education, 38,* 1–5.

37 Ayres, J., & Hopf, T. S. (1992). Visualization: Is it more than extra-attention? *Communication Education, 38,* 1–5.

38 Ayres, J., Hopf, T., & Ayres, D. M. (1994). An examination of whether imaging ability enhances the effectiveness of an intervention designed to reduce speech anxiety. *Communication Education, 73,* 252–258.

39 Anderson, P. L., Zimand, E., Hodges, L. F., & Rothbaum, B. O. (2005). Cognitive behavioral therapy for public-speaking anxiety using virtual reality for exposure. *Depression and Anxiety, 22,* 156–158. Heuett, B. & Heuett, K. (2011). Virtual reality therapy: A means of reducing public speaking anxiety. *International Journal of Humanities and Social Science, 1*(16), 1–6. Wallach, H. S., Safir, M. P., & Bar-Zvi, M. (2009). Virtual reality cognitive behavior therapy for public speaking anxiety: A randomized clinical trial. *Behavior Modification, 33,* 314–338.

Chapter 2

[1] Burke, K. (1950) *Rhetoric of motives.* Los Angeles, CA: University of California Press.

[2,2] Ivy, D. K., & Backlund, P. (1994). *Exploring gender speak: Personal effectiveness in gender communication.* New York: McGraw-Hill.
Wood, J. (2009). *Gendered lives: Communication, gender and culture* (8th ed.). Boston: Wadsworth.

[3] Kotz, D, (2011, July 12). Rise in STD in older women, sexless trend in 20-somethings [Web log post]. Retrieved from http://www.boston.com/Boston/dailydose/2011/07/rise-std-older-women-sexless-trend-somethings/WEbtr2ZhLARZWwqJ6LnGQJ/index.html
Sharples, T. (2008, July). More midlife (and older) STDs. Time. Retrieved from http://www.time.com/time/health/article/0,8599,1819633,00.html

[4] The Journal of Consumer Affairs. (2011). Older women lack important information about sexual health [Press release]. Retrieved from http://www.wiley.com/WileyCDA/PressRelease/pressReleaseId-100943.html

[5] Fishbein, M., & Ajzen, I. (1975). *Belief, attitude, intention and behavior.* Reading, MA: Addison-Wesley.
O'Keefe, D. (2002). *Persuasion: Theory and research* (2nd ed.). Thousand Oaks, CA: Sage.

[6] Rokeach, M. (1973). *The nature of human values.* New York: Free Press.

[7] Perloff, R. M (2010). The dynamics of persuasion: Communication and attitudes in the 21st century (4th ed.). New York: Taylor & Francis.

[8] Festinger, L. (1957). *A theory of cognitive dissonance.* Stanford, CA: Stanford University Press. Harmon-Jones, E. (2009). *Cognitive dissonance theory.* In S. W. Littlejohn & K. A. Foss (Eds.), *Encyclopedia of Communication Theory* (pp. 109–111). Thousand Oaks, CA: Sage Publications.

[9] Kim, M-S., & Hunter, J. E. (1993). Attitude-behavior relations: A meta-analysis of attitudinal relevance and topic. *Journal of Communication, 43,* 101–142.

[10] Banas, J. A. & Rains, S. A. (2010). A meta-analysis of research on inoculation theory. *Communication Monographs, 77,* 281–311.
McGuire, W. J., & Papageorgis, D. (1961). The relative efficacy of various types of prior belief-defense in producing immunity against persuasion. *Journal of Abnormal and Social Psychology, 62,* 327–337.

[11] McGuire, W. J., & Papageorgis, D. (1961). The relative efficacy of various types of prior belief-defense in producing immunity against persuasion. *Journal of Abnormal and Social Psychology, 62,* 327–337.

[12] Banas, J. A. & Rains, S. A. (2010). A meta-analysis of research on inoculation theory. *Communication Monographs, 77,* 281–311.

[13] Butler, J. L., & Baumeister, R. F. (1998). The trouble with friendly faces: Skilled performance with a supportive audience. *Journal of Personality and Social Psychology, 75*(5), 1213–1230.

[14] Sherif, M., & Sherif, C. W. (1967). Attitude as the individual's own categories: The social judgment-involvement approach to attitude and attitude change. In C. W. Sherif & M. Sherif (Eds.), *Attitude, ego-involvement and change* (pp. 105–139). New York: Wiley.

15 Petty, R. E., & Cacioppo, J. T. (1986). The elaboration likelihood model of persuasion. In L. Berkowitz (Ed.), *Advances in Experimental Social Psychology 19,* 123–205. New York: Academic Press.
   Reynolds, R. A., & Reynolds, J. L. (2002). Evidence. In J. P. Dillard & M. Pfau (Eds.), *The persuasion handbook: Developments in theory and practice* (pp. 427–444). Thousand Oaks, CA: Sage.

16 Petty, R. E., & Cacioppo, J. T. (1986). The elaboration likelihood model of persuasion. In L. Berkowitz (Ed.), *Advances in Experimental Social Psychology 19,* 123–205. New York: Academic Press.

17 Petty, R. E., & Cacioppo, J. T. (1986). The elaboration likelihood model of persuasion. In L. Berkowitz (Ed.), Advances in Experimental Social Psychology 19, 123–205. New York: Academic Press.

18 Wood, W., & Kallgren, C. A. (1988). Communicator attributes and persuasion: Recipients' access to attitude-relevant information in memory. *Personality and Social Psychology Bulletin,* 14, 172–182.

19 Dribben, E. & Brabender, V. (1979). The effective mood inducement upon audience receptiveness. *Journal of Social Psychology, 107*(1), 135–136.

20 Anghelcev, G., & Sar, S. (2011). The influence of pre-existing audience mood and message relevance on the effectiveness of health PSAs: Differential effects by message type. *Journalism & Mass Communication Quarterly, 88*(3), 481–501.

21 Dribben, E & Brabender, V. (1979). The effect of mood inducement upon audience receptiveness. *Journal of Social Psychology, 107*(1), 135–136.

Chapter 3

1 Taylor, J. (2016, January 18). Citing 'Two Corinthians,' Trump struggles to make the sale to evangelicals. National Public Radio. Retrieved from http://www.npr.org/2016/01/18/463528847/citing-two-corinthians-trump-struggles-to-make-the-sale-to-evangelicals

2 Taylor, J. (2016, January 18). Citing 'Two Corinthians,' Trump struggles to make the sale to evangelicals. National Public Radio. Retrieved from http://www.npr.org/2016/01/18/463528847/citing-two-corinthians-trump-struggles-to-make-the-sale-to-evangelicals

3 Ball, M. (2016, January 18). The religious rights Donald Trump dilemma. Retrieved from http://www.theatlantic.com

4 Petty, R. E., & Cacioppo, T. J. (1984). The effects of involvement on responses to argument quantity and quality: Central and peripheral routes to persuasion. *Journal of Personality and Social Psychology, 46,* 69–81.

5 Keller, J. M. (1987). Development and use of the ARCS model of motivational design. *Journal of Instructional Development, 10*(3), 2–10.

6 Shaw, D. E. (1996). Information search process model: How freshmen begin research. *Proceedings of the 1996 Annual Conference of the American Society for Information Science.* October 19–24, 1996. Baltimore, MD. Retrieved from http://www.asis.org/annual-96/ElectronicProceedings/swain.html.

7 Bullas, J. (2012). Blogging statistics, facts and figures in 2012: Infographic. Retrieved from http://www.jeffbullas.com/2012/08/02/blogging-statistics-facts-and-figures-in-2012-infographic/#aK8DmLcp5wqijt8I.99

8   Bullas, J. (2012). Blogging statistics, facts and figures in 2012: Infographic. Retrieved from http://www. jeffbullas.com/2012/08/02/blogging-statistics-facts-and-figures-in-2012-infographic/#aK8DmLcp5w qijt8I.99

9   Outing, S. (2002, July 18). The basic weblog. Retrieved from http://www.poynter.org/content/ content_print,asp?id=6620&custom

10 Brodeur Partners. (2008, May 21). Brodeur survey tracks beat reporter views on social media. *Market Wired.*

11 Gaudin, S. (2010, January 26). Twitter now has 75M users; most asleep at the mouse. *Computerworld.* Retrieved from http://www.computerworld.com/s/article/9148878/Twitter_now_has_75M_users_ most_asleep_at_the_mouse?taxonomyId=1

12 https://twitter.com/search?q=LifeAtPurdue

13 https://www.facebook.com/PurdueUniversity

14 Miller, G. R. (1972). Persuasion. In C. R. Berger & S. H. Chaffee (Eds.), *Handbook of communication sciences* (pp. 446–483). Newbury Park, CA: Sage.

Chapter 4

1   Nishi, D. (November 9, 2013). To persuade people, tell them a story. *Wall Street Journal.* Retrieved from http://www.wsj.com

2   Nishi, D. (November 9, 2013). To persuade people, tell them a story. *Wall Street Journal.* Retrieved from http://www.wsj.com

3   Booth, A. (2007). Using evidence in practice. *Health Information and Libraries Journal, 24,* 145–149.

4   Petty, R. E., & Cacioppo, J. T. (1986). The elaboration likelihood model of persuasion. In L. Berkowitz (Ed.), *Advances in experimental social psychology, 19* 123–205. New York: Academic Press.

5   Ellis, R., Levs, J. & Hamasaki, S. (2015, January 5). Outbreak of 51 measles cases linked to Disneyland. *CNN.* Retrieved from http://www.cnn.com/2015/01/21/health/disneyland-measles/

6   Hedges, K. (2013, December 11). How to tell a good story. *Forbes.* Retrieved from http://www.forbes. com/sites/work-in-progress/2013/12/11/how-to-tell-a-good-story/print/

7   Hedges, K. (2013, December 11). How to tell a good story. *Forbes.* Retrieved from http://www.forbes. com/sites/work-in-progress/2013/12/11/how-to-tell-a-good-story/print/

8   Widrich, L. (2012). The science of storytelling: Why telling a story is the most powerful way to activate our brains. *Lifehacker.* Retrieved from http://lifehacker.com/5965703/the-science-of-storytelling-why-telling-a-story-is-the-most-powerful-way-to-activate-our-brains

9   Paul, A. (2012, March 17). The neuroscience of your brain on fiction. *New York Times.* Retrieved from http://www.nytimes.com/2012/03/18/opinion/sunday/the-neuroscience-of-your-brain-on-fiction. html?pagewanted=all&_r=1&

10 Paul, A. (2012, March 17). The neuroscience of your brain on fiction. *New York Times*. Retrieved from http://www.nytimes.com/2012/03/18/opinion/sunday/the-neuroscience-of-your-brain-on-fiction.html?pagewanted=all&_r=1&

11 Widrich, L. (2012). The science of storytelling: What storytelling does to our brains. *Buffersocial.* Retrieved from https://blog.bufferapp.com/science-of-storytelling-why-telling-a-story-is-the-most-powerful-way-to-activate-our-brains

12 Nielsen (2012). Global trust in advertising and brand messages. Retrieved from http://www.nielsen.com/us/en/insights/reports/2012/global-trust-in-advertising-and-brand-messages.html?_hstc=124833621.34f5db81d32cd2200b0b9248 6fc08886.1390609123818.1390609123818.1390609123818.1&_hssc=124833621.1.1390609123818&_hsfp=3104465416

13 Stanton, A. (2012, February). The clues to a great story. [Video file]. Retrieved from http://www.ted.com/talks/andrew_stanton_the_clues_to_a_great_story

14 Hsu, J. (2008). The secrets of storytelling: Our love for telling tales reveals the workings of the mind. *Scientific American Mind, 19*(4), 46–51.

15 Green, M.C. (2004). Transportation into narrative worlds: The role of prior knowledge and perceived realism. *Discourse Processes, 38*(2), 247–266.

16 Green, M.C. (2004). Transportation into narrative worlds: The role of prior knowledge and perceived realism. *Discourse Processes, 38*(2), 247–266.

17 Hsu, J. (2008). The secrets of storytelling: Our love for telling tales reveals the workings of the mind. *Scientific American Mind, 19*(4), 46–51.

18 What is insula? (2013, May). Retrieved from http://www.neuroscientificallychallenged.com/blog/2013/05/what-is-insula

19 Widrich, L. (2012). The science of storytelling: Why telling a story is the most powerful way to activate our brains. *Lifehacker.* Retrieved from http://lifehacker.com/5965703/the-science-of-storytelling-why-telling-a-story-is-the-most-powerful-way-to-activate-our-brains

20 Widrich, L. (2012). The science of storytelling: Why telling a story is the most powerful way to activate our brains. *Lifehacker.* Retrieved from http://lifehacker.com/5965703/the-science-of-storytelling-why-telling-a-story-is-the-most-powerful-way-to-activate-our-brains

21 Hsu, J. (2008). The secrets of storytelling: Our love for telling tales reveals the workings of the mind. *Scientific American Mind*, *19*(4), 46–51.

22 Gillet, R. (2014, June 4). Why our brains crave storytelling in marketing. Retrieved from http://www.fastcompany.com/3031419/hit-the-ground-running/why-our-brains-crave-storytelling-in-marketing?partner=rss

23 van den Brock, P., & Lorch, R. F. (1993). Network representations of causal relations in memory of narrative texts: Evidence from prime recognition. *Discourse Processes, 16,* 75–98.

24 What is it about storytelling that helps bring a presentation alive? (2005). *Total Communicator. III*(4). Retrieved from http://totalcommunicator.com/vol3_4/storypresent.html

25 Hsu, J. (2008). The secrets of storytelling: Our love for telling tales reveals the workings of the mind. *Scientific American Mind, 19*(4), 46–51.

26 Gonzalez, J., Barros-Loscertales, A. , Pulvermuller, F., Meseguer, V., Sanjuan, A., Belloch, V., & Avila, C. (2006). Reading cinnamon activates olfactory brain regions. *Neuroimage, 32*(2), 906–912.

27 Hersman, D. A. P. (2012). We are our brother's and our sisters' keepers. *Vital Speeches of the Day, 78*(2), 54–58.

28 Gerard, C. (2012). We need to remind ourselves why we entered this profession. *Vital Speeches of the Day, 78*(1), 15–17.

29 van den Brock, P., & Lorch, R. F. (1993). Network representations of causal relations in memory of narrative texts: Evidence from prime recognition. *Discourse Processes, 16,* 75–98.

30 Haq, H. (2011, April 18). Greg Mortenson's "Three cups of tea"–A "beautiful story" but also "a lie"? Retrieved from http://www.csmonitor.com/Books/chapter-and-verse/2011/0418/Greg-Mortenson-s-Three-Cups-of-Tea-a-beautiful-story-but-also-a-lie

31 Lechleiter, J. C. (2011). The return on innovation. *Vital Speeches of the Day, 77*(1), 13–18.

32 Burke, K. (1950). *Rhetoric of motives.* Los Angeles, CA: University of California Press.

33 Hewgill, M. A., & Miller, G. R. (1965). Source credibility and response to fear-arousing communication. *Speech Monographs, 32,* 95–101.
    Hurwitz, S. D., Miron, M. S., & Johnson, B. T. (1992). Source credibility and the language of expert testimony. *Journal of Applied Social Psychology, 24,* 1909–1939.

34 Starks, C. J. (2010). How to write a speech. *Vital Speeches of the Day, 76*(4), 153–156.

35 Frymier, A. B., & Shulman, G. M. (1995). "What's in it for me?" Increasing content relevance to enhance students' motivation. *Communication Education, 44,* 40–50.

36 Daly, J., & Vangelisti, A. (2003). Skillfully instructing learners: How communicators effectively convey messages. In J. O. Greene & B. R. Burleson (Eds.), *Handbook of communication and social interaction skills* (pp. 871–908). Mahwah, NJ: Lawrence Erlbaum Associates.

37 Cordova, D. I., & Lepper, M. R. (1996). Intrinsic motivation and the process of learning: Beneficial effects of contextualization, personalization, and choice. *Journal of Educational Psychology, 88,* 714–730.

38 Neuman, S., Burden, D., & Holden, E. (1990). Enhancing children's comprehension of a televised story through previewing. *Journal of Educational Research, 83,* 258–265.

39 Cruickshank, D. R. (1985). Applying research on teacher clarity. *Journal of Teacher Education, 26,* 44–48.

40 Dixon, F. A., & Glover, J. A. (1990). Another look at number signals and preview sentences. Bulletin of the *Psychonomic Society, 28,* 287–288.
    Kardash, C. M., & Noel, L. K. (2000). How organizational signals, need for cognition, and verbal ability affect text recall and recognition. *Contemporary Educational Psychology, 25,* 317–331.

41 Insko, C. A. (1967). *Theories of attitude change.* New York: Appleton-Century-Crofts.

42 Daly, J., & Vangelisti, A. (2003). Skillfully instructing learners: How communicators effectively convey messages. In J. O. Greene & B. R. Burleson (Eds.), *Handbook of communication and social interaction skills* (pp. 871–908). Mahwah, NJ: Lawrence Erlbaum Associates.

43 Davis, S. (2011). The rough road to an export economy. *Vital Speeches of the Day, 77*(1), 11–13.

44 Starks, C. J. (2010). How to write a speech. *Vital Speeches of the Day, 76*(4), 153–156.

45 O'Keefe, D. J. (2002). *Persuasion: Theory and research* (2nd ed.). Thousand Oaks, CA: Sage.

46 Gendelman, J. (2010). *Virtual presentations that work.* New York: McGraw-Hill.

Chapter 5

1 Meyer, B. J. F., & Poon, L. W. (2001). Effects of structure strategy training and signaling on recall of text. *Journal of Educational Psychology, 93,* 141–159.
Rickards, P., Fajen, B. R., Sullivan, J. F., & Gillespie, G. (1997). Signaling, notetaking and field independence-dependence in text comprehension and recall. *Journal of Educational Psychology, 89,* 508–517.
Towler, A. J., & Dipboye, R. L. (2001). Effects of trainer expressiveness, organization and trainee goal orientation on training outcomes. *Journal of Applied Psychology, 86,* 664–673.

2 Mayer, R. E., Bove, W., Bryman, A., Mars, R., & Tapangco, L. (1996). When less is more: Meaningful learning from visual and verbal summaries of science textbook lessons. *Journal of Educational Psychology, 88,* 64–73.

3 Sharp, H. J., & McClung, T. (1966). Effects of the organization on the speaker's ethos. *Speech Monographs, 33,* 182–183.
Thompson, E. C. (1960). An experimental investigation of the relative effectiveness of organizational structure in oral communication. *Southern Speech Journal, 26,* 59–69.

4 Gabriel, R. F. & Mayzner, M. S. (1963). Information "chunking" and short-term retention. *Journal of Psychology: Interdisciplinary and Applied, 56,* 161–164.

5 Miller, G. A. (1956). The magical number seven, plus or minus two: Some limits on our capacity for processing information. *Psychological Review, 63,* 81–97.

6 Bodie, G., & Powers, W. & Fitch-Hauser, M. (2006). Learning: Toward an innovative and blended approach to teaching communication-related skills. *Interactive Learning Environments, 14*(2), 119–135.

7 Meyer, B. J. F., & Poon, L. W. (2001). Effects of structure strategy training and signaling on recall of text. *Journal of Educational Psychology, 93,* 141–159.
Rowan, K. E. (2003). Informing and explaining skills: Theory and research on informative communication. In J. O. Greene & B. R. Burleson (Eds.), *The handbook of communication and social interaction skills* (pp. 403–438). Mahwah, NJ: Erlbaum.

8 Lorch, R. F., & Lorch, E. P. (1996). Effects of organizational signals on free recall of expository text. *Journal of Educational Psychology, 88,* 38–48.

9 DeKay, S. (2012). Where is the research on negative messages. *Business Communication Quarterly, 75.* Retrieved from http://bcq.sagepub.com/content/75/2/173.full.pdf+html

10 Rickards, J. P., Fajen, B. R., Sullivan, J. F., & Gillespie, G. (1997). Signaling, notetaking and field independence-dependence in text comprehension and recall. *Journal of Educational Psychology, 89,* 508–517.

Chapter 6

1 Head, A., & Eisenberg, M. (2010, November 1). How college students evaluate and use information in the digital age. Retrieved from http://projectinfolit.org/pdfs/PIL_Fall2010_Survey_FullReport1.pdf

2 *Seattle Times.* (2011, June 3). Retrieved from http://seattletimes.nwsource.com/html/opinion/2015227485_guest05head.html

3 O'Keefe, D. J. (1998). Justification explicitness and persuasive effect: A meta-analytic review of the effects of varying support articulation in persuasive messages. *Argumentation and Advocacy, 35,* 61–75. Reinard, J. C. (1988). The empirical study of the persuasive effects of evidence: The status after fifty years of research. *Human Communication Research, 15,* 3–59.

4 O'Keefe, D. J. (1998). Justification explicitness and persuasive effect: A meta-analytic review of the effects of varying support articulation in persuasive messages. *Argumentation and Advocacy, 35,* 61–75.

5 Head, A. (2016). Staying Smart: How today's graduates continue learning once they complete college. Retrieved from Project Information Literacy website: Agency name website: http://projectinfolit.org/component/k2/item/73-latest-research

6 Allen, M., & Preiss, R. W. (1997). Comparing the persuasiveness of narrative and statistical evidence using meta-analysis. *Communication Research Reports, 14,* 125–131.

7 Sullivan, C., & Smith, C. M. (2006). Five tips for writing popular science. *Writer, 119,* 23–25.

8 Clausen, L. (2004). Localizing the global: "Domestication" processes in international news production. *Media Culture & Society, 26*(1), 25–44.

9 Lagnado, D., & Harvey, N. (2008). The impact of discredited evidence. *Psychonomic Bulletin and Review, 15,* 1166–1173.

10 Hill, J. (2012, March 11). Parsing Santorums statistic on God and college: Looks as if it's wrong. Retrieved from http://chronicle.com/article/Parsing-Santorums-Statistic/131113/

11 Allen, M., Bruflat, R., Fucilla, R., Kramer, M., McKellips, S., Ryan, D. J., & Spiegelhoff, M. (2000). Testing the persuasiveness of evidence: Combining narrative and statistical forms. *Communication Research Reports, 17,* 331–336.

12 Reinard, J. C. (1998). The persuasive effects of testimonial assertion evidence. In M. Allen & R. W. Preiss (Eds.), *Persuasion: Advances through meta-analysis* (pp. 69–86). Cresskil, NJ: Hampton.

13 Jackson, D., & Darrow, (2005). The influence of celebrity endorsements on young adults' political opinions. *International Journal of Press/Politics, 10*(3), 80–98.

14 Pew Research Center for the People and the Press. (2002). The Internet goes to college: How students are living in the future with today's technology. Retrieved from http://www.pewinternet.org

15 Metzger, M., Flanagin A., & Zwarun, L. (2003). College student Web use, perceptions of information credibility, and verification behavior. *Computers and Education, 41*, 271–290.

16 Head, A. (2012). How college graduates solve information problems once they join the workplace. Retrieved from http://jrnetsolserver.shorensteincente.netdnacdn.com/wp-content/uploads/2013/01/PIL_fall2012_workplaceStudy_FullReport.pdf

17 State of the Blogosphere. (2011). Retrieved from http://technorati.com/social-media/article/state-of-the-blogosphere-2011-introduction/

18 Cision. (2010). Retrieved from http://us.cision.com/news_room/press_releases/2010/2010-1-20_gwu_survey.asp

19 Barker, J. (2005). Evaluating Web pages: Techniques to apply and questions to ask. Retrieved from http://www.lib.berkeley.edu/TeachingLib/Guides/Internet/Evaluate.html

20 Katz, I., & Macklin, A. (2007). Information and communication technology (ICT) literacy: Integration and assessment in higher education. *Journal of Systemics, Cybernetics and Informatics, 5*(4), 50–55.

21 Grier, T. (2010). Most print and online journalists use social media for story research. Retrieved from http://www.poynter.org/how-tos/digital-strategies/e-media-tidbits/100373/most-print-and-online-journalists-use-social-media-for-story-research/

22 Head, A., & Eisenberg, M. (2010, November 1). How college students evaluate and use information in the digital age. Retrieved from http://projectinfolit.org/pdfs/PIL_Fall2010_Survey_FullReport1.pdf

23 Pew Research Center. (August 16, 2012). Further decline in credibility ratings for most news organizations. Retrieved from http://www.people-press.org/2012/08/16/further-decline-in-credibility-ratings-for-most-news-organizations/

24 Purdue libraries. Evaluating information sources. (n.d.) Retrieved from http://lgdata.s3-website-us-east-1.amazonaws.com/docs/1272/329981/evaluatingsources.pdf

25 Colao, J.J. (2013, October 28). Pew study suggests Snapchat has 26 million US users. Forbes. Retrieved from http://www.forbes.com/sites/jjcolao/2013/10/28/ pew-study-suggests-snapchat-has-26-million-u-s-users/

26 Shontell, A. (2015, January 3). Snapchats monthly active users may be nearing 200 million. Business Insider. Retrieved from http://www.businessinsider.com/snapchats-monthly-active-users-may-be-nearing-200-million-2014-12

27 National Sleep Foundation (n.d.) Retrieved from http://sleepfoundation.org/

28 O'Keefe, D. J. (1998). Justification explicitness and persuasive effect: A meta-analytic review of the effects of varying support articulation in persuasive messages. *Argumentation and Advocacy, 35*, 61–75.

29 Sternthal, B., Dholakia, R., & Leavitt, C. (1978). The persuasive effect of source credibility: Tests of cognitive response. *Journal of Consumer Research, 4*, 252–260.

Chapter 7

1   Johnson, J. (January 21, 2016). Trump didn't expect Palin's endorsement speech to be 'quite that long'. Retrieved from https://www.washingtonpost.com/news/post-politics/wp/2016/01/21/trump-didnt-expect-palins-endorsement-speech-to-be-quite-that-long/

2   Sharp, H. Jr., & McClung, T. (1966). Effects of organization on the speaker's ethos. *Speech Monographs, 33,* 182ff.

3   Behnke, R. R., & Sawyer, C. R. (2001). Patterns of psychological state anxiety in public speaking as a function of anxiety sensitivity. *Communication Quarterly, 49,* 84–94.
    Finn, A. N., Sawyer, C. R., & Behnke, R. R. (2003). Audience-perceived anxiety patterns of public speakers. *Communication Quarterly, 51,* 470–481.
    Freeman, T., Sawyer, C. R., & Behnke, R. R. (1997). Behavioral inhibition and the attribution of public speaking state anxiety. *Communication Education, 46,* 175–187.

4   Kahana, M. J., & Howard, M. W. (2005). Spacing and lag effects in free recall of pure lists. *Psychonomic Bulletin & Review, 12*(1), 159–164.

Chapter 8

1   The truth behind burgers the everlasting happy meal: burgers that size don't rot. (2010). *Gizmodo.* Retrieved from http://gizmodo.com/5682815/the-truth-behind-the-everlasting-happy-meal-no-burgers-that-size-rot?skyline=true&s=i

2   Johnson, J. R., & Szczupakiewicz, N. (1987). The public speaking course: Is it preparing students with work-related public speaking skills? *Communication Education, 36,* 131–137.

3   Linte, C. (2010) Communicating your research in lay language. *Engineering in Medicine and Biology Magazine,* 5–7.

4   Rowan, K. (2003). Informing and explaining skills: Theory and research on informative communication. In J. Greene & B. R. Burleson (Eds.), *The handbook of communication and social interaction skills.* Mahwah, NJ: Erlbaum.

5   Loewenstein, J. (1994). The psychology of curiosity: A review and reinterpretation. *Psychological Bulletin, 116,* 75–98.

6   Loewenstein, J. (1994). The psychology of curiosity: A review and reinterpretation. *Psychological Bulletin, 116,* 75–98.

7   Loewenstein, J. (1994). The psychology of curiosity: A review and reinterpretation. *Psychological Bulletin, 116,* 75–98.

8   Rowan, K. (2003). Informing and explaining skills: Theory and research on informative communication. In J. Greene & B. R. Burleson (Eds.), *The handbook of communication and social interaction skills.* Mahwah, NJ: Erlbaum.

9   Huckin, T. N. (1987, March). Surprise value in scientific discourse. Paper presented at the annual meeting of the Conference on College Composition and Communication. Atlanta, GA.

10   Rowan, K. (2003). Informing and explaining skills: Theory and research on informative communication. In J. Greene & B. R. Burleson (Eds.), *The handbook of communication and social interaction skills.* Mahwah, NJ: Erlbaum.

11   Gallagher, J. (October 26, 2015). Processed meats do cause cancer–WHO. BBC News. Retrieved from http://www.bbc.com/news/health-34615621

12   Gallagher, J. (October 26, 2015). Processed meats do cause cancer–WHO. BBC News. Retrieved from http://www.bbc.com/news/health-34615621

13   Farkas, D. K. (1999). The logic and rhetorical construction of procedural discourse. *Technical Communication, 46,* 42–54.

14   van der Meij, H. (1995). Principles and heuristics for designing minimalist instruction. *Technical Communication, 42,* 243–261.

15   Blackwell, A. F. and Burnett, M. (2002). Applying attention investment to end-user programming. In *Proceedings of the IEEE Symposia on Human-Centric Computing Languages and Environments* (pp. 28–30).

16   van der Meij, H. (1995). Principles and heuristics for designing minimalist instruction. *Technical Communication, 42,* 243–261.

17   Rowan, K. E. (1990). The speech to explain difficult ideas. *Speech Communication Teacher, 4,* 69–71.

18   Wilson, R. (2015, January 24). Bill Belichick uses science, 'My Cousin Vinny,' to explain Deflategate. CBS Sports. Retrieved from http://www.cbssports.com/nfl/eye-on-football/24989032/bill-belichick-uses-science-my-cousin-vinny-to-explain-deflategate

19   Explanations: Top ten teaching tips. (2013). Retrieved from http://www.huntingenglish.com/2013/05/11/explanations-top-ten-teaching-tips/

20   Abrams, R. & Niemi, R. (2014, April 2). How to explain bitcoin to your mother. *New York Times.* Retrieved from http://www.nytimes.com/interactive/2014/04/02/business/dealbook/How-to-explain-bitcoin-to-your-mom.html?smid=tw-nytimes%E2%80%8B

21   Sherrington, T. (2013). *Great lessons 6: Explaining.* Retrieved from http://headguruteacher.com/2013/02/13/great-lessons-6-explaining/

22   Willingham, D. (2010). *Why don't students like school?: A cognitive scientist answers questions about how the mind works and what it means for the classroom.* San Francisco: Jossey-Bass.

23   Retrieved from http://www.sciencealert.com/watch-this-video-explaining-einstein-s-special-theory-of-relativity-won-a-teenager-400k

24   Rocca, F. (October 4, 2011). Scientists on trial for what they said. *Chronicle of Higher Education.* Retrieved from http://chronicle.com/article/When-Explaining-Science-Is-a/129274

25   Rowan, K. E. (1992). Strategies for enhancing the comprehension of science. In B. V. Lewenstein (Ed.), *When science meets the public* (pp. 131–143). Washington, DC: American Association for the Advancement of Science.

26 Matthews, D. (May 12, 2014). John Oliver shows how to debate climate deniers. Retrieved from http://www.vox.com/2014/5/12/5710538/john-oliver-shows-how-to-debate-climate-deniers

27 NASA–What's the difference between weather and climate? (February 1, 2005). Retrieved from http://www.nasa.gov/mission_pages/noaa-n/climate/climate_weather.html

28 Curry, S. (2008). Run that by me again? Retrieved from http://www.lablit.com/article/435

29 Cactus. (n.d.). Retrieved from http://eduscapes.com/nature/cactus/index3.htm

30 Rowan, K. E. (1990). The speech to explain difficult ideas. *Speech Communication Teacher, 4,* 69–71.

31 Sullivan, C., & Smith, C. M. (2006). 5 tips for writing popular science. *Writer, 119,* 23–25. Rowan, K. (2003). Informing and explaining skills: Theory and research on informative communication. In J. Greene & B. R. Burleson (Eds.), *The handbook of communication and social interaction skills.* Mahwah, NJ: Erlbaum.

32 Thagard, P. (1992). Analogy, explanation, and education. *Journal of Research in Science Teaching, 29,* 537–544.

33 Pitcher R. (n.d.) The use of metaphors in science and technology. Retrieved from http://teachingtomtom.com/2012/11/29/the-use-of-metaphors-in-science-and-technology/

34 Long, M. (1995). Scientific explanation in U.S. newspaper science stories. *Public Understanding of Science, 4,* 119–130. Retrieved from http://pus.sagepub.com/cgi/content/abstract/4/2/119

35 Bransford, JD & Johnson, MK (1972). Contextual prerequisites for understanding: Some investigations of comprehension and recall. *Journal of Verbal Learning and Verbal Behavior 11,* 717–726.

36 D'Arcy, J. (1999, July). Bridging the knowledge gap. *Security Management, 43,* 31–34.

37 Bransford, JD & Johnson, MK (1972). Contextual prerequisites for understanding: Some investigations of comprehension and recall. *Journal of Verbal Learning and Verbal Behavior 11,* 717–726.

38 Thibodeau, P. H., & Boroditsky, L. (2011). Metaphors we think with: The role of metaphor in reasoning. *PLOS One.* Retrieved from DOI: 10.1371/journal.pone.0016782

39 Kohn, D. (2006, April). The blood cleaner. *Popular Science,* 36–37.

40 Sullivan, C., & Smith, C. M. (2006). 5 tips for writing popular science. *Writer, 119,* 23–25. Rowan, K. (2003). Informing and explaining skills: Theory and research on informative communication. In J. Greene & B. R. Burleson (Eds.), *The handbook of communication and social interaction skills.* Mahwah, NJ: Erlbaum.

41 Rowan, K. E. (1992). Strategies for enhancing the comprehension of science. In B. V. Lewenstein (Ed.), *When science meets the public* (pp. 131–143). Washington, DC: American Association for the Advancement of Science.

42 Emery, G. (2012, August 8). Drug Websites provide wrong information. ABC News.com. Retrieved from http://abcnews.go.com/Health/story?id=117290&page=

43 Rowan, K. (2003). Informing and explaining skills: Theory and research on informative communication. In J. Greene & B. R. Burleson (Eds.), *The handbook of communication and social interaction skills*. Mahwah, NJ: Erlbaum.

44 Emery, G. (2012, August 8). Drug Websites provide wrong information. ABC News.com. Retrieved from http://abcnews.go.com/Health/story?id=117290&page=.

45 Rowan, K., & Botan, C. (2006, May). Communicating proteomic science to lay audiences, Part II. Presentation for the BIO IT Coalition at George Mason University, Fairfax, VA.

46 American Communication Association (n.d.). Retrieved from http://textcommons.org/node/92

47 Pincus, A. (2007, June 18). The perfect (elevator) pitch. *Businessweek*. Retrieved from http://www.businessweek.com/careers/content/jun2007/ca20070618_134959.htm

Chapter 9

1 Elmer-DeWitt (2016). Here's what Obama said at SXSW about Apple vs. FBI. *Fortune*. Retrieved from: http://fortune.com/2016/03/12/obama-sxsw-apple-vs-fbi/

2 Shear, M.D. (2016). Obama, at South by Southwest, calls for law enforcement access in encryption fight. *New York Times*. Retrieved from: http://www.nytimes.com/2016/03/12/us/politics/obama-heads-to-south-by-southwest-festival-to-talk-about-technology.html

3 Miller, G. R. (1972). Persuasion. In C. R. Berger & S. H. Chaffee (Eds.), *Handbook of communication science* (pp. 446–483). Newbury Park, CA: Sage.

4 Fishbein, M. (1967). A consideration of beliefs, and their role in attitude measurement. In M. Fishbein (Ed.), *Readings in attitude theory and measurement* (pp. 257–266). New York: John Wiley.
Kim, M. S., & Hunter, J. E. (1993). Attitude-behavior relations: A meta-analysis of attitudinal relevance and topic. *Journal of Communication, 43*, 101–142.

5 Perloff, R. M. (2003). *The dynamics of persuasion*. Hillsdale, NJ: Lawrence Erlbaum.

6 Fishbein, M. (1967). A consideration of beliefs, and their role in attitude measurement. In M. Fishbein (Ed.), *Readings in attitude theory and measurement* (pp. 257–266). New York: John Wiley.

7 Fishbein, M., & Ajzen, I. (1975). *Belief, attitude, intention and behavior: An introduction to theory and research*. Reading, MA: Addison-Wesley.

8 Festinger, L. (1957). *A theory of cognitive dissonance*. Stanford, CA: Stanford University Press.

9 Eagly, A. H., & Chaiken, S. (1993). *The psychology of attitudes*. Orlando, FL: Harcourt.

10 Sherif, M., & Sherif, C. W. (1967). Attitude as the individual's own categories: The social judgment-involvement approach to attitude and attitude change. In C. W. Sherif & M. Sherif (Eds.), *Attitude ego-involvement, and change* (pp. 105–139). New York: Wiley.

11 Festinger, L. (1957). *A theory of cognitive dissonance*. Stanford, CA: Stanford University Press.

12 Petty, R. E., & Cacioppo, J. T. (1984). The effects of involvement on responses to argument quantity and quality: Central and peripheral routes to persuasion. *Journal of Personality and Social Psychology, 46,* 69–81.

13 Allen, M. (1991). Meta-analysis comparing the persuasiveness of one-sided and two-sided messages. *Western Journal of Speech Communication, 55,* 390–404. O'Keefe, D. J. (1999). How to handle opposing arguments in persuasive messages: A meta-analytic review of the effects of one-sided and two-sided messages. *Communication Yearbook, 22,* 209–249.

14 O'Keefe, D. J. (2002). *Persuasion: Theory and research.* Thousand Oaks, CA: Sage.

15 Sherif, M., & Sherif, C. W. (1967). Attitude as the individual's own categories: The social judgment-involvement approach to attitude and attitude change. In C. W. Sherif & M. Sherif (Eds.), *Attitude ego-involvement, and change* (pp. 105–139). New York: Wiley.

16 Allen, M. (1991). Meta-analysis comparing the persuasiveness of one-sided and two-sided messages. *Western Journal of Speech Communication, 55,* 390–404.
O'Keefe, D. J. (1999). How to handle opposing arguments in persuasive messages: A meta-analytic review of the effects of one-sided and two-sided messages. *Communication Yearbook, 22,* 209–249.

17 Lucas, S. (2006). *The art of public speaking.* New York: McGraw-Hill.

18 O'Keefe, D. J. (2002). *Persuasion: Theory and research.* Thousand Oaks, CA: Sage.

19 O'Keefe, D. J. (1997). Standpoint explicitness and persuasive effect: A meta-analytic review of the effects of varying conclusion articulation in persuasive messages. *Argumentation and Advocacy, 34,* 1–12.

Chapter 10

1 Aristotle. (1954). *Rhetoric.* (W. R. Roberts, Trans.). New York: Modern Library.

2 O'Keefe, D. J. (2002). *Persuasion: Theory and research.* Thousand Oaks, CA: Sage.

3 Bradley, P. H. (1981). The folk-linguistics of women's speech: An empirical examination. *Communication Monographs, 48,* 73–90; Falcione, R. L. (1974). The factor structure of source credibility scales for immediate superiors in the organizational context. *Central States Speech Journal, 25,* 63–66.
O'Keefe, D. J. (2002). *Persuasion: Theory and research.* Thousand Oaks, CA: Sage.

4 McCroskey, J. C. (2000). *An introduction to rhetorical communication.* Boston, MA: Allyn & Bacon.

5 O'Keefe, D. J. (2002). *Persuasion: Theory and research.* Thousand Oaks, CA: Sage.

6 Pjesivac, I., & Rui, R. (2014). Anonymous sources hurt credibility of news stories across cultures: A comparative experiment in America and China. *International Communication Gazette, 76*(8), 641–660.

7 Greene, J. (1984). Speech preparation processes and verbal fluency. *Human Communication Research, 11,* 61–84.
Street, R. L., Jr., & Brady, R. M. (1982). Speech rate acceptance ranges as a function of evaluative domain, listener speech rate and communication context. *Communication Monographs, 49,* 290–308.

8 Carpenter, C. J. (2012). A meta-analysis and an experiment investigating the effects of speaker disfluency on persuasion. *Western Journal of Communication, 76*(5), 552–569.

9   O'Keefe, D. J. (2002). *Persuasion: Theory and research.* Thousand Oaks, CA: Sage; Struckman-Johnson, D., & Struckman-Johnson, C. (1996). Can you say condom? It makes a difference in fear-arousing AIDS prevention public service announcements. *Journal of Applied Social Psychology, 26,* 1068–1083.

10 O'Keefe, D. J. (2002). *Persuasion: Theory and research.* Thousand Oaks, CA: Sage.

11 Yu, X., Bao, Z., Zou, J., & Dong, J. (2011). Coffee consumption and risk of cancers: A meta-analysis of cohort studies. *BMC cancer, 11*(1), 96.

12 van Dam, R. M., & Hu, F. B. (2005). Coffee consumption and risk of type 2 diabetes: A systematic review. *Jama, 294*(1), 97–104.

13 Qi, H., & Li, S. (2014). Dose–response meta-analysis on coffee, tea and caffeine consumption with risk of Parkinson's disease. *Geriatrics & gerontology international, 14*(2), 430–439.

14 Saab, S., Mallam, D., Cox, G. A., & Tong, M. J. (2014). Impact of coffee on liver diseases: A systematic review. *Liver international, 34*(4), 495–504.

15 Babbie, E. (2001). *The practice of social research.* Belmont, CA: Wadsworth.

16 Doerksen, S., & Shimamura, A. P. (2001). Source memory enhancement for emotional words. *Emotion, 1,* 5–11; *Journal & Courier.* (2007, April 1). Road improvement: What roads need improved and why?, p. A11.

17 O'Keefe, D. J. (2000). Guilt and social influence. In M. E. Roloff (Ed.), *Communication Yearbook 21* (pp. 1–33). Thousand Oaks, CA: Sage.
    Witte, K., & Allen, M. (2000). A meta-analysis of fear appeals: Implication for effective public health campaigns. *Health Education and Behavior, 27,* 591–615.

Chapter 11

1   Stump, S. (Sept. 22, 2015). Watch Miss America contestant's heartwarming monologue about being a nurse. Retrieved from http://www.today.com/style/watch-miss-america-contestants-heartwarming-monologue-about-being-nurse-t43571

2   Ekman, P., & Friesen, W. (1969). The repertoire of nonverbal behavior: Categories, origins, usage, and coding. *Semiotica, 1,* 49–98.

3   Towler, A. J., & Dipboye, R. L. (2001). Effects of trainer expressiveness, organization and trainee goal orientation on training outcomes. *Journal of Applied Psychology, 86,* 664–673.

4   Gallo, C. (2010). *The presentation secrets of Steve Jobs: How to be insanely great in front of any audience.* New York: McGraw-Hill.

5   Engstrom, E. (1994). Effects of nonfluencies on speaker's credibility in newscast settings. *Perceptual and Motor Skills, 78,* 739–743.
    Rubin, J. (1994). A review of second language listening comprehension research. *The Modern Language Journal, 78,* 199–221.

6   Burgoon, J. K., Birk, T., & Pfau, M. (1990). Nonverbal behaviors, persuasion, and credibility. *Human Communication Research, 17,* 140–169.

7   Carpenter, C. J. (2012). A meta-analysis and an experiment investigating the effects of speaker disfluency on persuasion. *Western Journal of Communication, 76*(5), 552–569.

8   Greene, J. O. (1984). Speech preparation processes and verbal fluency. *Human Communication Research, 11,* 61–84.

9   Anderson, P. A. (1999). *Nonverbal communication: Forms and Functions.* Mountain View, CA: Mayfield Publishing Company.

10 Ekman, P., & Friesen, W. (1969). The repertoire of nonverbal behavior: Categories, origins, usage, and coding. *Semiotica, 1,* 49–98.

11 Anderson, P. A. (1999). *Nonverbal communication: Forms and Functions.* Mountain View, CA: Mayfield Publishing Company.

12 Anderson, P. A. (1999). Nonverbal communication, forms and functions. Mountain View, CA: Mayfield Publishing Company.

13 Morris, T. L., Gorham, J., Cohen, S. H., & Huffman, D. (1996). Fashion in the classroom: Effects of attire on student perceptions of instructors in college classes. *Communication Education, 45,* 135–148.

14 Roach, K. D. (1997). Effects of graduate teaching assistant attire on student learning, misbehaviors, and ratings of instruction. *Communication Quarterly, 45(3),* 125–141.

15 Menzel, K. E., & Carrell, L. J. (1994). The relationship between preparation and performance in public speaking. *Communication Education, 43,* 17–26.

16 Gallo, C. (2010). *The presentation secrets of Steve Jobs: How to be insanely great in front of any audience.* New York: McGraw-Hill.

17 Evangelist, M. (2006, January 5). Behind the magic curtain. *Guardian.* Retrieved from http://www.guardian.co.uk.

18 Menzel, K. E., & Carrell, L. J. (1994). The relationship between preparation and performance in public speaking. *Communication Education, 43,* 17–26.

Chapter 12

1   Hixon, T. (March 21, 2016). What entrepreneurs can learn about public speaking from TED talks. Retrieved from http://www.forbes.com/sites/toddhixon/2016/03/01/entrepreneurs-time-to-tune-up-your-public-speaking/#527426f72e69

2   Hixon, T. (March 21, 2016). What entrepreneurs can learn about public speaking from TED talks. Retrieved from http://www.forbes.com/sites/toddhixon/2016/03/01/entrepreneurs-time-to-tune-up-your-public-speaking/#527426f72e69

3   Garner, J. K., Alley, M., Gaudelli, A. F., & Zappe, S. E. (2009). Common use of PowerPoint versus the assertion-evidence structure: A cognitive psychology perspective. *Technical Communication, 56*(4), 331–345.
    Mayer, R. (2001). *Mutlimedia learning.* New York: Cambridge University Press.

4   Pike, R. W. (1992). *Creative training techniques handbook*. Minneapolis, MN: Lakewood Books.

5   Christe, B., & Collyer, J. (2005). Audiences' judgments of speakers who use multi-media as a presentation aid: A contribution to training and assessment. *British Journal of Educational Technology, 36,* 477–499.

6   3M Corporation. (1995). The power of color in presentations. Retrieved April 10, 2004, from http:// www.3m.com/mettinnetwork/readingroom/meetingguide_power_color.html
     Vogel, R. D., Dickson, G. W., & Lehman, J. A. (1986). P*ersuasion and the role of visual support: The UM/3M Study.* Minneapolis, MN: University of Minnesota School of Management.

7   Ayres, J. (1991). Using visual aids to reduce speech anxiety. *Communication Research Reports, 72,* 73–79.

8   Zelazny, G. (2001). *Say it with charts* (4th ed.). New York: McGraw-Hill.

9   Zelazny, G. (2001). *Say it with charts* (4th ed.). New York: McGraw-Hill.

10 Robbins, N. B. (2005). *Creating more effective graphs*. Hoboken, NJ: John Wiley & Sons, Inc.

11 Zelazny, G. (2001). *Say it with charts* (4th ed.). New York: McGraw-Hill.

12 Zelazny, G. (2001). *Say it with charts* (4th ed.). New York: McGraw-Hill.

13 Mackiewicz, J. (2007). Perceptions of clarity and attractiveness in PowerPoint graph slides. *Technical Communication, 54,* 145–156.

14 Robbins, N. B. (2005). *Creating more effective graphs*. Hoboken, New Jersey NJ: John Wiley & Sons, Inc.

15 Mackiewicz, J. (2006). Perceptions of clarity and attractiveness in PowerPoint graph slides. *Technical Communication, 54,* 145–156.

16 Zelazny, G. (2001). *Say it with charts* (4th ed.). New York: McGraw-Hill.

17 Zelazny, G. (2001). *Say it with charts* (4th ed.). New York: McGraw-Hill.

18 Tufte, E. R. (2006). *The cognitive style of PowerPoint: Pitching out corrupts within.* Cheshire, CT: Graphics Press.

19 Alley, M., Schreiber, M., Ramsdell, K., & Muffo, J. (2005). How the design of headlines in presentation slides affects audience retention. *Technical Communication, 53*(2), 225–234.

20 Bucher, H., & Schumacher, P. (2006). The relevance of attention for selecting news content. An eye-track-ing study on attention patterns in the reception of print and online media. *European Journal of Communication Research, 31*(3), 347–68. Retrieved from DOI:10.1515/COMMUN.2006.022

21 Bucher, H., & Schumacher, P. (2006). The relevance of attention for selecting news content. An eye-track-ing study on attention patterns in the reception of print and online media. *European Journal of Communication Research, 31*(3), 347–68. Retrieved from DOI:10.1515/COMMUN.2006.022

22 Bucher, H., & Schumacher, P. (2006). The relevance of attention for selecting news content. An eye-track-ing study on attention patterns in the reception of print and online media. *European Journal of Communication Research, 31*(3), 347–68. Retrieved from DOI:10.1515/COMMUN.2006.022

23   Keller, J. (2003, January 22). Is PowerPoint the devil? *Chicago Tribune*. Markel, M. (2009). Exploiting verbal-visual synergy in presentation slides. *Technical Communication, 56*(2), 122–131.
     Parker, I. (2001, May 28). Absolute PowerPoint. *The New Yorker*, p. 76.
     Thompson, C. (2003). PowerPoint makes you dumb. *New York Times*. Retrieved from http:// www. nytimes.com
     Tufte, E. R. (2003). PowerPoint is evil. *Wired*. Retrieved from http://www.wired.com/wired/archive/11.09/ ppt.html

24   Doumont, J. L. (2004). The cognitive style of PowerPoint: Slides are not all evil. *Technical Communication, 52,* 64–70.

25   Doumont, J. L. (2004). The cognitive style of PowerPoint: Slides are not all evil. *Technical Communication, 52,* 64–70

26   Alley, M., & Neely, K. A. (2005). Rethinking the design of presentation slides: A case for sentence headlines and visual evidence. *Technical Communication, 52,* 417–426.

27   Tufte, E. R. (2006). *The cognitive style of PowerPoint: Pitching out corrupts within.* Cheshire, CT: Graphics Press.

28   Alley, M., & Neely, K. A. (2005). Rethinking the design of presentation slides: A case for sentence headlines and visual evidence. *Technical Communication, 52,* 417–426.

29   Jennings, A. (2009). Creating marketing slides for engineering presentations. *Technical Communication, 56,* 14–27.
     Markel, M. (2009). Exploiting verbal-visual synergy in presentation slides. *Technical Communication, 56,* 122–131.
     Doumont, J. L. (2004). The cognitive style of PowerPoint: Slides are not all evil. *Technical Communication, 52,* 64–70
     Alley, M., Schreiber, M., Ramsdell, K., & Muffo, J. (2005). How the design of headlines in presentation slides affects audience retention. *Technical Communication, 53*(2), 225–234.

30   Alley, M., Schreiber, M., Ramsdell, K., & Muffo, J. (2005). How the design of headlines in presentation slides affects audience retention. *Technical Communication, 53*(2), 225–234.

31   Alley, M., Schreiber, M., Ramsdell, K. & Muffo, J. (2005). How the design of headlines in presentation slides affects audience retention. *Technical Communication, 53*(2), 225–234.

32   Alley, M., Schreiber, M., Ramsdell, K. & Muffo, J. (2005). How the design of headlines in presentation slides affects audience retention. *Technical Communication, 53*(2), 225–234.

33   Alley, M., Schreiber, M., Ramsdell, K., Muffo, J. (2006). How the design of headlines in presentation slides affects audience retention. *Technical Communication, 53,* 225–234.

34   Jennings, A. (2009). Creating marketing slides for engineering presentations. *Technical Communication, 56,* 14–27.

35   Garner, J. K., Alley, M. Gaudelli, A. F., & Zappe, S. E. (2009). Common use of PowerPoint versus assertion-evidence slide structure: A cognitive psychology perspective. *Technical Communication, 56,* 331–345.

36 Alley, M., & Neely, K. A. (2005). Rethinking the design of presentation slides: A case for sentence headlines and visual evidence. *Technical Communication, 52,* 417–426.

37 Jennings, A. (2009). Creating marketing slides for engineering presentations. *Technical Communication, 56,* 14–27.
Alley, M., & Neely, K. A. (2005). Rethinking the design of presentation slides: A case for sentence headlines and visual evidence. *Technical Communication, 52,* 417–426.
Alley, M., Schreiber, M. M., Ramsdell, K., & Muffo, J. (2006). How the design of headlines in presentation slides affects audience retention. *Technical Communication, 53,* 225–234.
Doumont, J. L. (2005). The cognitive style of PowerPoint: Slides are not all evil. *Technical Communication, 52,* 64–70.

38 Shwom, B. L., & Keller, K. P. (2003). The great man has spoken. Now what do I do? A response to Edward R. Tufte's "The cognitive style of PowerPoint." Retrieved from http://www.communipartners.com/articles_presentations.html

39 Mayer, R. E. (2001). *Multimedia learning.* New York: Cambridge University Press.

40 Garner, J. K., Alley, M., Gaudelli, A. F., & Zappe, S. E. (2009). Common use of PowerPoint versus the assertion-evidence structure: A cognitive psychology perspective. *Technical Communication, 56*(4), 331–345.

41 Alley, M. (n.d.) Rethinking presentation slides: The assertion-evidence approach. Retrieved from http://www.writing.engr.psu.edu/slides.html

42 Garner, J. & Alley, M. (2013). How the design of presentation slides affects audience comprehension: A case for the assertion-evidence approach. *International Journal of Engineering Education, 29*(6), 1564–1579.

43 Alley, M. & Neely, K. (2005). Rethinking the design of presentation slides: A case for sentence headlines and visual evidence. *Technical Communication, 52(4),* 417–426.

44 Effective presentations in engineering and science: Guidelines and video examples. (n.d.) Retrieved from http://www.engr.psu.edu/speaking/Visual-Aids.html

45 Mayer, R. E. (2001). *Multimedia learning.* New York: Cambridge University Press.

46 Garner, J. K., Alley, M., Gaudelli, A. F., & Zappe, S. E. (2009). Common use of PowerPoint versus the assertion-evidence structure: A cognitive psychology perspective. *Technical Communication, 56*(4), 331–345.

47 Garner, J. K., Alley, M., Gaudelli, A. F., & Zappe, S. E. (2009). Common use of PowerPoint versus the Assertion-Evidence Structure: A cognitive psychology perspective. *Technical Communication, 56*(4), 331–345.

48 Blokzijl, W., & Naeff, R. (2004). The instructor as stagehand: Dutch student responses to PowerPoint. *Business Communication Quarterly, 67,* 70–77.

49 Fox, D. (2010). Free will for typeface selection: Myth or reality? *Usability News, 12*(1). Retrieved from http://www.surl.org/usabilitynews/132/

50 Mackiewicz, J. (2006). Audience perceptions of fonts in projected PowerPoint text slides. *Technical Communication, 54,* 295–307.

51 Brumberger, E. R. (2003). The rhetoric of typography: The persona of typeface and text. *Technical Communication, 50,* 206–223.

Fox, D. (2010). Free will for typeface selection: Myth or reality? *Usability News, 12*(1). Retrieved from http://www.surl.org/usabilitynews/132/

Fox D., Shaikh, A. D., & Chaparro, B. S. (2007). The effect of typeface appropriateness on the perception of documents. *Proceedings of the Human Factors & Ergonomics Society 51st Annual Meeting,* pp. 464–468. Baltimore, MD.

52 Shaikh, A. D., Chaparro, B. S., & Fox, D. (2006). Perception of fonts: Perceived personality traits and uses. *Usability News, 8*(1). Retrieved from http://www.surl.org/usabilitynews/81/PersonalityofFonts.asp

53 Alley, M., & Neely, K. A. (2005). Rethinking the design of presentation slides: A case for sentence headlines and visual evidence. *Technical Communication, 52,* 417–426.

54 Zelazny, G. (2001). *Say it with charts* (4th ed.). New York: McGraw-Hill.

55 InFocus Corporation. (2004). Using fonts effectively in your multimedia presentation. Retrieved April 10, 2004 from http://www.presentersuniversity.com/coursesarchivesfonts.php

56 Green, R. E. (1984, October). The persuasive properties of color. *Marketing Communications.*

57 Mackiewicz, J. (2006). Perceptions of clarity and attractiveness in PowerPoint graph slides. *Technical Communication, 54,* 145–156.

58 Mackiewicz, J. (2006). Perceptions of clarity and attractiveness in PowerPoint graph slides. *Technical Communication, 54,* 145–156.

59 Mackiewicz, J. (2009). Color: The newest tool for technical communicators-Redux. *Technical Communication, 56,* 3–13.

60 Mucciolo, T., & Mucciolo, R. (1994). *Purpose movement color: A strategy for effective presentations.* New York: MediaNet, Inc.

61 Aslam, M. M. (2006). Are you selling the right colour? A cross-cultural review of colour as a marketing cue. *Journal of Marketing Communications, 12,* 15–30.

62 Neal, C. M., Quester, P. G., & Hawkins, D. I. (2002). *Consumer behaviour: Implications for marketing strategy* (3rd ed). Sydney: McGraw-Hill.

63 Jacobs, L. Keown, C., Worthley, R., & Ghymn, K. (1991). Cross-cultural colour comparisons: Global marketers beware? *International Marketing Review, 8,* 113–138.

64 Mackiewicz, J. (2009). Color: The newest tool for technical communicators–Redux. *Technical Communication, 56,* 3–13.

65 Doumont, J. L. (2004). The cognitive style of PowerPoint: Slides are not all evil. *Technical Communication, 52,* 64–70.

66 Bucher, H.-J. & Niemann, P. (2012). Visualizing science: The reception of PowerPoint presentations. *Visual Communication, 11*(3), 283–306.

67 Knoblauch H. (2008). The Performance of Knowledge: Pointing and Knowledge in PowerPoint Presentations. *Cultural Sociology, 2,* 75–97.

Chapter 13

[1] Gallo, C. (September 26, 2013). 7 proven presentation principles that Tokyo used to win the 2020 Olympics. Retrieved from http://www.forbes.com/sites/carminegallo/2013/09/26/7-proven-presentation-principles-that-tokyo-used-to-win-the-2020-olympics/#1bf1f01e115d

[2] Gallo, C. (September 26, 2013). 7 proven presentation principles that Tokyo used to win the 2020 Olympics. Retrieved from http://www.forbes.com/sites/carminegallo/2013/09/26/7-proven-presentation-principles-that-tokyo-used-to-win-the-2020-olympics/#1bf1f01e115d

[3] Canfora, G., Cimitile, A., Garcia, F., Piattini, M., & Visaggio, C. A. (2006). Evaluating performances of pair designing in industry. *Journal of Systems and Software, 80,* 1317–1327.

[4] Jehn, K., & Mannix, E. (2001). The dynamic nature of conflict: A longitudinal study of intragroup conflict and group performance. *Academy of Management Journal, 44,* 238–251. Retrieved from http://www.jstor.org/stable/3069453

[5] Jelphs, K., & Dickinson, H. (2008). *Working in teams.* United Kingdom: Policy Press.

[6] Jehn, K., & Shah, P. (1997). Interpersonal relationships and task performance: An examination of mediating processes in friendship and acquaintance groups. *Journal of Personality and Social Psychology, 72,* 775–790.

[7] Janis, I. (1972). *Victims of groupthink: A psychological study of foreign-policy decisions and fiascoes.* Boston: Houghton, Mifflin.

[8] Troyer, L., & Youngreen, R. (2009). Conflict and creativity in groups. *Journal of Social Issues, 65,* 409–427. Doi: 10.111/j.1540-4560.2009.01606.x

[9] Jehn, K., Northcraft, G., & Neal, M. (1999). Why differences make a difference: A field study of diversity, conflict, and performance in workgroups. *Administrative Science Quarterly, 44,* 741–763.

[10] Jehn, K., & Mannix, E. (2001). The dynamic nature of conflict: A longitudinal study of intragroup conflict and group performance. *Academy of Management Journal, 44,* 238–251. Retrieved from http://www.jstor.org/stable/3069453

[11] Bandura, A. (1982). Self-efficacy mechanism in human agency. *American Psychologist, 37,* 122–147.

[12] Podsakoff, P. M., & Farh, J. (1989). Effects of feedback sign and credibility on goal setting and task performance. *Organizational Behavior and Human Decision Processes, 44,* 45–67.

[13] Locke, E. A., & Latham, G. P. (1990). A theory of goal setting and task performance. In I. L. Janis (Ed.), *Victims of groupthink: A psychological study of foreign-policy decisions and fiascoes* (p. 277). Oxford, England: Houghton Mifflin.

[14] Guerrero, L., Alarcon, R., Collazos, C., Pino, J., & Fuller, D. (2000). *Evaluating cooperation in group work.* Paper presented at the sixth annual meeting of the Collaboration Researchers' International Workshop on Groupware. Retrieved from http://ieeexplore.ieee.org/xpls/abs_all.jsp?arnumber=885148&tag=1

[15] Whitney, K. (1994). Improving group task performance: The role of group goals and group efficacy. *Human Performance, 7,* 55–78. Doi: 10.1207/s15327043hup0701_5

16 Klein, H. J., & Mulvey, P. W. (1990). The setting of goals in groups: An examination of processes and performance. Unpublished manuscript, Ohio State University, Columbus, Ohio.

17 Poole, M., & Hollingshead, A. (Eds.). (2005). *Theories of small groups: Interdisciplinary perspectives.* Thousand Oaks, CA: Sage.

18 Earley, P. C., & Lituchy, T. R. (1991). Delineating goal and efficacy effects: A test of three models. *Journal of Applied Psychology, 76,* 81–98.

19 Shelly, R. K., & Webster, M. A., Jr. (1997). Status orders in discussion groups. In S. R. Thye, E. J. Lawler, M. W. Macy, & H. A. Walker (Eds.), *Advances in group processes, 16,* 199–218. Stamford, CT: Jai Press.

20 Johnson, D. W., & Johnson, R. T. (1989). *Cooperation and competition: Theory and research.* Edina, MN: Interaction Book Company.

21 Gevers, J., Rutte, C., & Van Eerde, W. (2006). Meeting deadlines in work groups: Implicit and explicit mechanisms. *Applied Psychology: An International Review, 55,* 52–72. Retrieved from http://web. ebscohost. com/ehost/pdf?vid=2&hid=108&sid=5556c5f4-4ffa-4c9b-8478-5d1ddf697341%40sessionmgr111

22 Pychyl, T. (2008, January 8). Meeting deadlines in work groups: Implications for the workplace [Web log message]. Retrieved from http://www.psychologytoday.com/blog/dont-delay/200806/meeting-deadlines-in-work-groups-implications-the-workplace

23 Shelly, R., & Shelly, A. (2009). Speech content and the emergence of inequality in task groups. *Journal of Social Issues, 65,* 307–333.

24 Guerrero, L., Alarcon, R., Collazos, C., Pino, J., & Fuller, D. (2000). *Evaluating cooperation in group work.* Paper presented at the sixth annual meeting of the Collaboration Researchers' International Workshop on Groupware. Retrieved from http://ieeexplore.ieee.org/xpls/abs_all.jsp?arnumber=885148&tag=1

25 Giuliano, P. (2005). Ask the expert: Team or group presentations. *The Total Communicator, 3.* Retrieved from http://totalcommunicator.com/vol3_1/expert2.html

26 Gallo, C. (April 30. 2013). Delivering a PowerPoint? Your audience will tune out after 10 minutes. Retrieved from http://www.forbes.com/sites/carminegallo/2013/04/30/delivering-a-powerpoint-your-audience-will-tune-out-after-10-minutes/#3138182979ab

27 Newborne, E. (2002). Tag-team pitches: Group presentations are a different ball game: Here's how to play. *Sales and Marketing Management, 3,* 154.

28 Giuliano,P.(2005).Ask the expert: Team or group presentations. *The Total Communicator, 3.* Retrieved from http://totalcommunicator.com/vol3_1/expert2.html.

29 Giuliano, P. (2005). Ask the expert: Team or group presentations. *The Total Communicator, 3.* Retrieved from http://totalcommunicator.com/vol3_1/expert2.html.

30 Adams, S. (2014, November 12). The 10 skills employers most want in 2015 graduates. *Forbes.* Retrieved from http://www.forbes.com/sites/susanadams/2014/11/12/the-10-skills-employers-most-want-in-2015-graduates/

31 Floyd, K. (2014). *Public speaking matters.* New York, NY: McGraw Hill.

32 Redmond, R. (n.d.) How to report status on a project. Retrieved from http://www.projectsmart.co.uk/how-to-report-status-on-a-project.php

33 Redmond, R. (n.d.) How to report status on a project. Retrieved from http://www.projectsmart.co.uk/how-to-report-status-on-a-project.php

34 How to give a good status report. (2011, November 2). Retrieved from http://www.completeitprofessional.com/how-to-give-a-good-status-report/

35 How to give a good status report. (2011, November 2). Retrieved from http://www.completeitprofessional.com/how-to-give-a-good-status-report/

36 Tirmizi, S. (2008). Towards understanding multicultural teams. In C. Halverson & Tirmizi (Eds.), *Effective multicultural teams: Theory and practice* (pp. 18–19). New York: Springer.

37 King, E. B., Hebl, M. R., & Beal, D. J. (2009). Conflict and cooperation in diverse workgroups. *Journal of Social Issues, 65,* 261–285.

38 Matveev, A., & Miller, R. (2004). The value of intercultural competence for performance of multicultural teams. *Team Performance Management, 10,* 104–111. Retrieved from http://www.emeraldinsight.com/Insight/ViewContentServlet?Filename=Published/EmeraldFullTextArticle/Articles/1350100502.html

39 Iles, P. (1995). Learning to work with difference. *Personnel Review, 24,* 44–60.

40 Halverson, C. & Tirmizi, S. (2008). *Effective multicultural teams: Theory and practice.* USA: Springer

41 Iles, P. (1995). Learning to work with difference. *Personnel Review, 24,* 44–60.

42 Brett, J., Behfar, K., & Kern, M. C. (2006). Managing multicultural teams. *Harvard Business Review, 84,* 84–91.

43 King, E. B., Hebl, M. R., & Beal, D. J. (2009). Conflict and cooperation in diverse workgroups. *Journal of Social Issues, 65,* 261–285.

44 Brett, J., Behfar, K., & Kern, M. C. (2006). Managing multicultural teams. *Harvard Business Review, 84,* 84–91.

45 Iles, P. (1995). Learning to work with difference. *Personnel Review, 24,* 44–60.

46 Iles, P. (1995). Learning to work with difference. *Personnel Review, 24,* 44–60.

Chapter 14

1 Stephens, D. (March 4, 2016). Global collaboration topic of next WebEx Users group meeting. Retrieved from http://www.itap.purdue.edu/newsroom/news/160222_WebEx_Users_Group_TLT.html

2 Weinstein, I. & Nilsson, A. (Febuary, 2013). End user survey: The "real" benefits of video. Retrieved from http://www.gbh.com/wp-content/uploads/2015/12/wainhouse-the-real-benefits-of-video-wp-enus-2.pdf

3 Forbes. (2009). Business meetings: The case for face-to-face. Retrieved from http://images.forbes.com/forbesinsights/StudyPDFs/Business_Meetings_FaceToFace.pdf

⁴ Webinar presentation skills as a job requirement? (2010, March 4). Article posted to http://www.thevirtualpresenter.com/2010-appearances-public-only/webinar-presentation-skills-as-a-job-requirement/

⁵ Burt, J. (2010). Video conferencing on the rise, survey shows. *Eweek.* Retrieved from http://www.eweek.com/c/a/VOIP-and-Telephony/Video-Conferencing-on-the-Rise-Survey-Shows-137811/#sthash.pkqmyCRK.dpuf

⁶ Weber Shandwick. (2009). Business leadership conferences still in demand and growing despite economic recession. Retrieved from http://www.webershandwick.com/Default.aspx/AboutUs/PressReleases/2009/BusinessLeadershipConferencesStillInDemandandGrowingDespiteEconomicRecessionAccordingtoNewWeberShandwickStudy

⁷ Anderson, A. H. (2006). Achieving understanding in face-to-face and video-mediated multiparty interactions. *Discourse Processes, 41,* 251–287.

⁸ Moore, M. G., & Thompson, M. M. (1990). *The effects of distance learning: A summary of literature.* University Park, PA: American Center for the Study of Distance Education.; Tallent-Runnels, M. K., Thomas, J. A., Lan, W. Y., Cooper, S., Ahern, T. C., Shaw, S. M., & Liu, X. (2006). Teaching courses online: A review of the research. *Review of Educational Research, 76,* 93–135.

⁹ Boyd, S. (n/d). Ethics in Public Speaking. Retrieved from http://www.sideroad.com/Public_Speaking/ethics-in-public-speaking.html

¹⁰ 1080 Group (2009). Engage! How to avoid the seven sins of live, online presentations: A 1080 paper prepared for Citrix online. Retrieved from http://www.workshifting.com/downloads/downloads/G2MC_1080Group_SevenSinsofOnlinePresentations-1.pdf

¹¹ WebEx Communications, Inc. (2006). BDO Seidman saves millions with WebEx enterprise edition. Retrieved from http://static.webex.com/fileadmin/webex/**documents**/enterprise/pdf/casestudy_cs_bdo_seidman.pdf

¹² 1080 Group (2009). Engage! How to avoid the seven sins of live, online presnetations: a 1080 paper prepared for Citrix online. Retrieved from http://www.workshifting.com/downloads/downloads/G2MC_1080Group_SevenSinsofOnlinePresentations-1.pdf

¹³ Koleva, B., Schnädelbach, H., Benford, S., Greenhalgh, C. (2001). Experiencing a presentation through a mixed reality boundary, *Proceedings of the 2001 International ACM SIGGROUP Conference on Supporting Group Work.* Boulder, Colorado, USA.

¹⁴ Lindstron, R. L. (2002). Being visual. Presenters University. Retrieved from http://presentersuniversity.com/visuals_visuals_being_visual01.php

¹⁵ Toshiba. (2005). Toshiba computer systems increases marketing efficiency with WebEx. Retrieved from http://static.webex.com/fileadmin/webex/documents/enterprise/pdf/high_tech/casestudy_toshiba.pdf

¹⁶ Koleva, B., Schnädelbach, H., Benford, S., Greenhalgh, C. (2001). Experiencing a presentation through a mixed reality boundary, *Proceedings of the 2001 International ACM SIGGROUP Conference on Supporting Group Work.* Boulder, Colorado, USA.

17   WebEx Communications, Inc. (2009). Software company reaps the benefits of online meetings. Retrieved from http://static.webex.com/fileadmin/webex09/ files_en_us/pdf/casestudies/SunGard_CS_D3.pdf

18   Bos, N., Olson, J., Gergle, D., Olson, G., & Wright, Z. (2002). Effects of four computer-mediated communications channels on trust development. Panel conducted at the 2002 Computer Human Interaction (CHI) conference of ACM, Minneapolis, MN.

19   Frost & Sullivan. Measuring the True Benefits of Web Collaboration: Demystifying the Productivity Paradox. While paper sponsored by WebEx Communications, October 2005. Retrieved from http://www.immagic.com/eLibrary/ARCHIVES/GENERAL/GENREF/F050930F.pdf

20   Browne, N. (2014, April 24). Presentation tools that go beyond next slide please. Retrieved from https://hbr.org/2014/04/presentation-tools-that-go-beyond-next-slide-please

21   Studio lighting tips for your video presentations. (n.d.) Retrieved from http://stebian.com/2012/08/studio-lighting-tips-for-your-video-presentations/

22   The lowdown on camera angles for filming your online videos. (n.d.) Retrieved from http://stebian.com/2011/03/video-presentations-get-the-lowdown-on-camera-angles-for-filming-your-online-videos/

23   The lowdown on camera angles for filming your online videos. (n.d.) Retrieved from http://stebian.com/2011/03/video-presentations-get-the-lowdown-on-camera-angles-for-filming-your-online-videos/

24   The lowdown on camera angles for filming your online videos. (n.d.) Retrieved from http://stebian.com/2011/03/video-presentations-get-the-lowdown-on-camera-angles-for-filming-your-online-videos/

25   How to use the rule of thirds. (n.d.) Retrieved from http://www.imore.com/how-to-rule-thirds-photos-iphone

26   How to dress for success in your video presentations. (n.d.) Retrieved from http://stebian.com/2011/12/how-to-dress-for-success-in-your-video-presentations/

27   Ways to master your fear of speaking on video. (n.d.) Retrieved from http://stebian.com/2014/03/3-ways-to-master-your-fear-of-speaking-on-video/

28   Presenting to camera avoid these common eye contact pitfalls. (n.d.) Retrieved from http://stebian.com/2011/05/presenting-to-camera-avoid-these-common-eye-contact-pitfalls/

29   Usershoff, R. (2011, December 16). *Virtual presentations.* Retrieved from https://remarkableleader.wordpress.com/category/virtual-presentations/

30   On camera cheating techniques to look great on video. (n.d.) Retrieved from http://stebian.com/2012/07/common-cheating-techniques-to-look-good-on-video/

31   Hall, E. T. (1976). *Beyond culture.* Garden City, NY: Anchor Press

32   Miller, A.N. (2002). An exploration of Kenyan public speaking patterns with implications for the American introductory public speaking course. *Communication Education, 51,* 168–182.

33   Xiao, X. (1996). From the hierarchical Ren to egalitarianism: A case of cross-cultural rhetorical mediation. *Quarterly Journal of Speech, 82,* 38–54.

34 Lustig, M.W. & Koester, J. (2010). Intercultural competence: Interpersonal communication across cultures (6th ed.). Boston, MA: Allyn & Bacon.

35 Gamble, T.K. & Gamble, M.W. (1998). Public speaking in the age of diversity (2nd ed.). Needham Heights, MA: Allyn & Bacon.

36 Gamble, T.K. & Gamble, M.W. (1998). Public speaking in the age of diversity (2nd ed.). Needham Heights, MA: Allyn & Bacon.

37 Usunier, J-C., & Roulin, N. (2010). The influence of high- and low-context communication styles on the design, content, and language of business-to-business web sites. *Journal of Business Communication, 47* (2), 189–227.

38 Tulshyan, R. (March 18, 2010). Quirkiest cultural practices from around the world. Forbes. Retrieved from http://www.forbes.com/2010/03/18/business-travel-etiquette-forbes-woman-leadership-global.html

39 Gallo, C. (2010). Record voice for your next presentation. Retrieved from http://www.businessweek.com/smallbiz/content/jan2010/sb2010016_891182.htm

40 Gallo, C. (2010). Record voice for your next presentation. Retrieved from http://www.businessweek.com/smallbiz/content/jan2010/sb2010016_891182.htm

41 Cisco Systems. (2008). Communication and collaboration: Cisco on Cisco. Retrieved from http://www.ciscosystems.lt/en/US/solutions/collateral/ns340/ns856/ns870/CiscoonCiscoCollaboration.pdf

42 Cognitive Theory of Multimedia Learning. (n.d.) Retrieved from https://sites.google.com/site/cognitivetheorymmlearning/modality-principle

43 PowerPoint does rocket science—and better techniques for technical reports. (n.d.) Retrieved from http://www.edwardtufte.com/bboard/q-and-a-fetch-msg?msg_id=0001yB&topic_id=1

44 PowerPoint does rocket science—and better techniques for technical reports. (n.d.) Retrieved from http://www.edwardtufte.com/bboard/q-and-a-fetch-msg?msg_id=0001yB&topic_id=1

45 Clark, R., & Mayer, R. (2011). E-Learning and the science of instruction: Proven guidelines for consumers and designers of multimedia learning (3rd ed.). San Francisco, CA: John Wiley & Sons.

46 Are narrated PowerPoint presentations really training? (2013, April 15). Retrieved from http://training-force.com/are-narrated-powerpoint-presentations-really-training/

47 Gallo, C. (2011, December, 1). 7 ways to tell stories with PowerPoint. Forbes. Retrieved from http://www.forbes.com/sites/carminegallo/2011/12/01/7-ways-to-tell-stories-with-powerpoint/

48 Are narrated PowerPoint presentations really training? (2013, April 15). Retrieved from http://training-force.com/are-narrated-powerpoint-presentations-really-training/

49 Shank, P. (2012, June 21). Making online PowerPoint content engaging: Preparing for high-quality narration. Retrieved from http://www.facultyfocus.com/articles/teaching-with-technology-articles/making-online-powerpoint-content-engaging-preparing-for-high-quality-narration/#sthash.4KDA5CR1.dpuf

50 Foshay, W. & Silber, K. (2009). *Handbook of improving performance in the workplace, instructional design and training delivery.* (1st ed.). San Francisco, CA: John Wiley & Sons.

51 Introduction to developing online learning content. (n.d.) Retrieved from http://ep.jhu.edu/faculty/ teach-and-tech/learning-roadmap-for-new-online-instructors/content-types-and-best-practices

52 Toshiba. (2005). Toshiba computer systems increases marketing efficiency with WebEx. Retrieved from http://static.webex.com/fileadmin/webex/documents/enterprise/pdf/high_tech/casestudy_toshiba. pdf

53 Hipsman, I. (2009). Best practices for producing highly effective webinar replays. Retrieved from http:// www.brainshark.com/brainshark/vu/view.asp?pi=696696145

54 Jackson, M., Anderson, A. H., McEwan, R., & Mullin, J. (2000). Impact of video frame rate on communication behavior in two-and four-party groups. Paper presented at the 2000 ACM Conference on Computer Supported Cooperative Work, Philadelphia, PA.

55 Brenner, R. (2008). Virtual presentations. Retrieved from http://www.chacocanyon.com/pointlookout/ 080604.shtml

56 Brenner, R. (2008). Virtual presentations. Retrieved from http://www.chacocanyon.com/pointlookout/ 080604.shtml

57 Webinar Presentation Tips (2011, June 23). Article posted to http://www.howtowebinar.com/162/ webinar-presentation-tips/

58 Stourk, J., & Sproull, L. (1995). Through a glass darkly: What do people learn in videoconferences? *Human Communication Research, 22,* 197–219.

59 Mark, G., Grudin, J., & Poltrock, S. (1999). Meeting at the desktop: An empirical study of virtually collocated teams. Paper presented at European Conference on Computer-Supported Cooperative Work, Copenhagen, Denmark.

60 Talley, C. (2005). Ten tips from a distance learning trainer. *Online Classroom, 4, 3.*

61 1080 Group (2009). Engage! How to avoid the seven sins of live, online presentations: A 1080 paper prepared for Citrix online. Retrieved from http://www.workshifting.com/downloads/downloads/ G2MC_1080Group_SevenSinsofOnline Presentations-1.pdf

62 Courville, R. (n.d.) Three things speakers should know about virtual presenting. Article posted to http:// www.speakingaboutpresenting.com/presentation-skills/three-things-virtual-presenting/#more-3117

63 Dummies. (n.d.). Preparing for the virtual presentation. Retrieved from http://www.dummies.com/ how-to/content/preparing-for-a-virtual-presentation.html

64 Boyd, S. (2008, March 12). Speaking to an international audience [Web log message]. Retrieved from http://www.speaking-tips.com/Articles/Speaking-To-An-International-Audience.aspx

65 The Total Communicator. (2004). Time for your videoconference close-up: What now? Retrieved from http://totalcommunicator.com/vol2_3/video.html

66 Daley, R. (2011). Bostonian group communicates their benefit platforms with brainshark. Retrieved from http://www.brainshark.com/ideas-blog/customer-articles/Bostonian-Group-Communicates-Their-Benefit-Platforms-with-Brainshark.aspx

67 Gallo, C. (2010). Record voice for your next presentation. Retrieved from http://www.businessweek.com/smallbiz/content/jan2010/sb2010016_891182.htm

68 Bozarth, J. (2010, May 4). Nuts and bolts: Principles of multimedia learning. Retrieved from http://www.learningsolutionsmag.com/articles/453/nuts-and-bolts-principles-of-multimedia-learning

69 Talley, C. (2005). Ten tips from a distance learning trainer. *Online Classroom, 4*, 3.

70 Milne-Tyte, A. (2011, September, 26). Seeking work? Ready your webcam. *New York Times.* Retrieved from http://online.wsj.com

71 Dummies. (n.d.). Preparing for the virtual presentation. Retrieved from http://www.dummies.com/how-to/content/preparing-for-a-virtual-presentation.html

72 Anderson, S., Alrajeh, N., Cordray, D., Gigante, J. (2002). Learning about screening using an online or live lecture: Does it matter? *Journal of General Internal Medicine, 17*(7), 540–545.

73 Richards, B. (2011, April 26). How much Narration in your PowerPoint? Retrieved from http://blogs.missouristate.edu/techtalk/2011/04/26/how-much-narration-in-your-powerpoint/

74 Bozarth, J. (2010, May 4). Nuts and bolts: Principles of multimedia learning. Retrieved from http://www.learningsolutionsmag.com/articles/453/nuts-and-bolts-principles-of-multimedia-learning

Chapter 15

1 Business leadership conferences still in demand and growing despite economic recession. (2009, January 26). Retrieved from http://www.webershandwick.com/Default.aspx/AboutUs/PressReleases/2009/BusinessLeadershipConferencesStillInDemandandGrowingDespiteEconomicRecessionAccoring-toNewWeberShandwickStudy

2 Gallo, C. (2009, January 20). How to handle tough questions. *BusinessWeek.* Retrieved from http://www.businessweek.com/smallbiz/content/jan2009/sb20090120_668348.htm

3 Giuliano, P. (2005). Ask the expert: Team or group presentations. *The Total Communicator, 3.* Retrieved from http://totalcommunicator.com/vol3_1/expert2.html

4 Use the backchannel during your Q&A. (2009, December 2). Article posted to http://www.socialtimes.com/2009/12/8-tips-for-managing-the-twitter-backchannel-during-your-presentation/

5 Bruff, D. (2009, January 19). The backchannel by Cliff Atkinson. Article posted to http://derekbruff.com/teachingwithcrs/?p=467

6 Atkinson, C. (2009). *The backchannel: How audiences are using twitter and social media and changing presentations forever.* Berkeley, CA: New Riders Press.

7 How to present while people are twittering. (2009, February 23). Article posted to http://pistachioconsulting.com/twitter-presentations/

8   Atkinson, C. (2009). *The backchannel: How audiences are using twitter and social media and changing presentations forever.* Berkeley, CA: New Riders Press.

9   Extending your presentations through the backchannel. (2010, February 5). Article posted to http://www.ducttapemarketing.com/blog/2010/02/05/extending-your-presentations-through-the-backchannel/

10 Warren, G. (n.d.) How to have a successful Q&A session in your online meeting. Retrieved from http://mobileoffice.about.com/od/conferencing-and-collaboration/a/online-meetings-and-presentations-q-and-a-sessions.htm

11 Warren, G. (n.d.) How to have a successful Q&A session in your online meeting. Retrieved from http://mobileoffice.about.com/od/conferencing-and-collaboration/a/online-meetings-and-presentations-q-and-a-sessions.htm

12 Mitchell, O. (2009.) How to present with Twitter (and other backchannels). Retrieved from http://www.speakingaboutpresenting.com/wp-content/uploads/Twitter.pdf

13 Mitchell, O. (2009.) How to present with Twitter (and other backchannels). Retrieved from http://www.speakingaboutpresenting.com/wp-content/uploads/Twitter.pdf

14 Mitchell, O. (2009.) How to present with Twitter (and other backchannels). Retrieved from http://www.speakingaboutpresenting.com/wp-content/uploads/Twitter.pdf

15 Mitchell, O. (2009.) How to present with Twitter (and other backchannels). Retrieved from http://www.speakingaboutpresenting.com/wp-content/uploads/Twitter.pdf

16 Boyd, S. D. (2004). The presentation after the presentation. *Techniques, 79,* 42–43.

17 Warren, G. (n.d.) How to have a successful Q&A session in your online meeting. Retrieved from http://mobileoffice.about.com/od/conferencing-and-collaboration/a/online-meetings-and-presentations-q-and-a-sessions.htm

18 Warren, G. (n.d.) How to have a successful Q&A session in your online meeting. Retrieved from http://mobileoffice.about.com/od/conferencing-and-collaboration/a/online-meetings-and-presentations-q-and-a-sessions.htm

INDEX

A

ABC Evening News 178
Academic journals, supporting materials 131–132
Academic Search Premier 131
Active agreement 205
Adaptation of audiences 39–42
  direct methods 40–41
  indirect methods 41–42
Adaptors 236
Ad hominem 212
Adobe Connect 312
Adobe Presenter 311
Age, audience analysis and 24
Aids, presentation 243–266
  asynchronous presentation 297–298
  audio/video 252
  clarity and retention in 244–245
  defined 244
designing tips 260–262
diagrams 251
effectiveness and 245
maps 252
multimedia 253–259
numerical charts 246–250
photographs 251
types of 246–252
using, tips for 263–265
Alcoba, Gabriel 135
Allen, M. 197, 224
American Journal of Preventive Medicine 134
American Medical Association 181
American Obesity Association 9
American Psychological Association (APA) 8, 144
Americas Competitiveness Forum in Atlanta 86
Analogical reasoning 217–219
  defined 217–218
  tips for using 218

Analogies, in quasi-scientific explanations 176–180
Anderson, P.A. 236, 237, 238
Anxiety 51
    speaking and 14–19. *See also* Communication apprehension
APA. *See* American Psychological Association (APA)
Appearance, physical 238–239
Apple 188
Apple, Inc. 194, 240, 253, 310, 311, 312
Apprehension 14–19. *See also* Anxiety, speaking
Argument ad hominem 212, 220
Arguments, order of in persuasive presentation 204
    primacy effect 204
    recency effect 204
Aristotle 212, 213
Army Wives 80
ArticleFirst 131
Assertion-evidence model 257
Associated Press 7
Asynchronous presentation 297–298. *See also* Synchronous presentation
    challenges of 303
    methods for building 299–300
    technology options for 303
    tips for using 300
Atkinson, Cliff 323
Attention, capturing audience 68–77. *See also* Attention-gaining devices; Attention-getters
Attention-gaining devices 68–77. *See also* Attention-getters
    audience analysis and 81
    audience identification 80
    choosing 80–81
    interesting fact or statistic 76
    quotation and 76
    somber tone 81
    stories/narratives 68–76
    strengths as speaker 81
    technology (audio/visual aids) 76–77
    time restrictions 81
    topic development 81–86
Attention-getters 68–77, 77–78, 78–80, 80–81, 84, 86–87, 89. *See also* Attention-gaining devices
    audience participation 78
    compliment the audience 77
    hypothetical situations and 79–80
    jokes and 79
    outside classroom 77–78
    questions and 78–79
    recent events, referring 77–78
    referring back 86
    to avoid 78–80
Attire, clothing. *See* Appearance, physical
Attitude 192–193
    creating 194
    reinforcing 194

Attitudes, of audience 28–29
    favorable 29
    hostile 30–31
    neutral 31
Audience analysis 21–44
    adaptation and. *See* Adaptation of audiences
    demographic 23–26. *See also* Demographic audience analysis
    environment and 36–39. *See also* Environmental audience analysis
    importance 22–23
    persuasive speaking and 190
    psychology and 27–35. *See also* Psychological factors
Audience-centered speaking 5
Audiences
    adaptation. *See* Adaptation of audiences
    analysis. *See* Audience analysis
    attention capturing 68–77. *See also* Attention-gaining devices; Attention-getters
    attitudes of 28–29. *See also* Attitudes, of audience
    commitment 29
    difficult member of 321–322
    establishing common ground with 214
    favorable (friendly) 29
    geographical location 25
    hostile 30–31
    identification with 22, 80
    inoculation 29
    involvement 29
    knowledge 34–35
    motivation 31–33
    neutral 31
    obstacles to understanding presentation 173–174
    participation 78
    passive 31
    persuasive speaking and 189–190
    responding to 5
    virtual 19
    voluntary 33
Audio/video, as presentation aid 252, 313
Audio/visual aids 76–77
Authoritarian decision making 270

B

Backchannel 322–325
    defined 322
Backchannel, The 323
    online question-and-answer session 324–325
Backup plan 263
Balance
    in main points of presentation 101–102
    in outline 139

Bandwagon 220–221
Bar chart 248–249
Bar-Zvi, M. 19
BDO Seidman 285
Behavior 193
Belief 192
Beloit College 24
Big Ten football 2
Bingham, Karen 302
Blue Phenomenon 262
BMC Cancer 217
Boogard, Derek 32
Books, supporting materials 128
  citation of 134
Boyd, Stephen D. 322
Brady, Sarah 198
Brief example 115
Broadcast Outlets 129–131
Brogan, Chris 322
Build feature, software presentation program 258
Bulleted lists 257–258
Bureau of Labor Statistics 135
BusinessWeek 53, 184

C

Camera angles 290–291
Campbell, Jennifer 159
Cancer Research UK 165
Captive audiences 32
Carbon emissions, online presentation and 286
Career success 3
Carrell, L. J. 240, 241
Catalono, Charles 39
Cato Institute 7
Causal design 100
Causal pattern 100, 200
Causal reasoning 218–219
  defined 218
  post hoc, ergo propter hoc 219
  tips for using 219
CBS Evening News 167, 168
CBS News 168
Census Bureau 52, 53, 123, 131
Centers for Disease Control 8, 56, 124, 126, 142, 181, 235
Central route to persuasion 195, 196, 197, 198
Chalkboard use, avoiding 263
Change, target in persuasion 194–195
Chart 246–250
Chester, Ryan 172, 173
Chronological pattern 99
CIA World Factbook 129
Cingular/AT&T 230

Cisco 298, 309
Citation, of sources 134–135, 144, 146
  books 134
  interviews 135
  journal/magazine articles 134
  newspapers 134–135
  news releases 135
  Web sites 135
Clincher, ending with 86–87, 91
Closed-ended questions 40
Closure, Q&A session 326
CNN 51, 55, 62, 92, 183, 186
Coffee drinkers 217
Cognitive restructuring (cognitive modification) 18
Colors to avoid 291
Color use 262
  culture and 262
Columbia Club of Indianapolis 82
Column charts 249–250
Comic Sans 261
Communication apprehension 14
  cognitive restructuring and 18–20
  defined 14
  situational 14
  skills deficit and 15
  skills training and 15
  systemic desensitization and 15–17
  traitlike 14
  visualization and 18–19
Communication skills 2, 3
Comprehensiveness, news presentations and 164–165
Comprehensive Online Research Education (CORE) 121
Conclusion, in presentation, 85, 85–89, 89–91
  call to action 87
  common pitfalls 88–89
  drawing out 88
  ending abruptly 88
  ending with clincher/memorable thought 86–87
  example of 90–91
  introducing new arguments and points 88
  leaving implicit 88–89
  objectives 85–89
  quotation 87
  referring back to attention-getter 86
  thesis and main points, restating 86
Conclusion, of deductive argument 215–216
Conflict, in group 268–269
Connotative meaning 295
Consensus decision making 269
Contingency plan 276
Coordination 142–143
  online presentation and 287
Copyright 11
CORE. *See* Comprehensive Online Research Education (CORE)

Cost, online presentation 286
Courier new 261
Create, attitudes and beliefs in persuasive presentation 194
Credibility 213–214
  aiding, supporting evidence and 111
  derived 214
  establishing 82–83
  initial 213
  of Web sites, evaluating 124, 125, 130
  terminal 214
Credibility statement 82–83, 84, 90, 145
Culture, color use and 262. See Color use
Cultures
  high-context 294
  low-context 294
Current events, in topic selection 51–52
Cut-and-paste plagiarism 8

D

Dallas Friday Group 78
Daniels, Mitch 220
Davies, Sally 158
Davis, Scott 86
Decision-making, group 270
  types 270
Decision-making, online presentation and 287–288
Decision rules 195
Deductive reasoning 215–216
  defined 215
  syllogism 215
  tips for using 215–216
Delaney, Kim 80
Delayed translation 239–240
Delicious 128
Delivery cues 148
Delivery methods 230–233
  extemporaneous 233
  impromptu 230–231
  manuscript 232
  memorized 232
Delivery, of presentation 228–229
  challenges 305
  characteristics of effective 229–230
  group presentation 268–269
  importance of 228–229
  methods of 230–233
  physical 236–240
  practicing 240–241
  style 229–230
  vocal 233–236
Delivery, physical 236–240
  appearance and 238–239
  eye contact 237–238
    facial expression in 238
    gestures 236–237
    movement in 237
    translator and 239–240
Delivery, vocal 233–236
  defined 233
  enunciation in 235
  nonfluencies in 235
  paralanguage 233
  pauses in 235
  pitch in 234
  pronunciation in 235–236
  rate in 234
  variety in 233–236
  volume in 233–234
Democratic decision-making 270
Demographic audience analysis 23–26
  age 24
  common 26
  dangers 27
  defined 23
  geographical location 25
  group affiliation 25
  sex and gender 24–25
  socioeconomic factors 26
Demonstration presentations. See Instructional presentations
Denotative meaning 295
Derived credibility 214
Desired state in instructional presentations 166
Dewey, John 271
Diagrams 251
Dickinson, H. 269
Dipboye, R. L. 96, 228
Directional transitions 104–105, 143, 180
Direct methods, in audience analysis 40–41
Direct question 78
Distance education 87, 285
Distributed audience 284, 285, 286, 308
Diversity 281–282
Dockterman, Eliana 134
Drawing conclusion, in induction 216–217
Dropbox 274
Dryden, John 86

E

Effectiveness, of presentational speaking 4–11
  audience-centered 5
  characteristics 4–11
  ethics and 6
  factors for 4–11
  goal-directed 5
Efficacy 224, 270
Ego-involvement 198

Einstein's Principle of Relativity 172
Elaboration 195
Elaboration Likelihood Model ELM 195–198
    central route to persuasion 197
    decision rules and 195
    defined 195
    motivation of audience 195
    one-sided vs. two-sided messages 197
    peripheral route to persuasion 195, 197
    principles of 197–198
    processing message and 195
Electronic Arts 33
Elevator pitch presentation 184
Eli Lilly & Co. 78
Ellen Degeneres Show 228
ELM. *See* Elaboration Likelihood Model (ELM)
Elucidating explanation 175, 176, 186
Emblems, as gesture 236–237
Encyclopedia Britannica 129
Enunciation 235
Environmental audience analysis 36–39
    occasion 36–37
    order of speakers 37
    physical setting 36
    technology and 38–39
    time/length of presentation 38
    time of day 37
Environmental constraints, online presentation 306
Environmental Health Perspectives 216
Esztergom Basilica 245
Ethics 11, 75, 190, 225
    persuasive speaking and 190
    presentational speaking and 5
Ethos 212–225
    credibility 213
    derived credibility 214
    expertise 213
    initial credibility 213
    terminal credibility 214
    trustworthiness 213
Evaluation, of supporting materials. *See* Supporting materials,
        evaluation of
Evidence identification, outlining and 139
Evidence, supporting. *See* Supporting evidence
Examples, as supporting evidence 115–116
    brief 115
    describe in detail 117
    extended 116, 117
    hypothetical 116
    selection 117
    tips for using 117–118
Excessive collaboration 10
Expertise 13, 23, 33, 34, 46, 50, 82, 111, 120, 132, 183, 213
Expert testimony 72, 118, 119, 126, 128

Explanatory presentation 167–181
    elucidating 175, 176, 177
    informatory vs. 159–160
    quasi-scientific 167, 177, 179, 180
    transformative 158, 180, 181
Explanatory presentation, obstacles to understanding
        presentation 173–174
    complex structures/processes 174
    concept/term use 174
    hard-to-believe phenomena 174
Explanatory speaking 159, 160, 168, 174
Expressiveness, recall and 228
Extemporaneous delivery 4, 147, 233, 299, 301
Extended example 116, 117
Eye contact 229, 232, 233, 236, 237–238, 321

F

Fabrication 11
Façade of Duomo 245
Facebook 41, 42, 56, 57, 110, 119, 126, 127, 128, 297
Facial expression 222, 224, 228, 229, 238, 308
Fact, in persuasive presentation 199–201
    causal pattern in 200
    refutative pattern in 200
Factuality, news presentations and 164
Fajen, B. R. 96, 104
Fallacy 219, 220, 221, 222
    argument ad hominem 220
    bandwagon 220–221
    false dilemma 221
    hasty generalization 217
    invalid analogy 11, 218
    post hoc, ergo propter hoc 219
    red herring 222
    slippery slope 221
    straw person 222
False dilemma, or false dichotomy 221
Farook, Syad 188
Favorable (friendly) audiences 29
FBI 188
Fear appeals 224
FedStats 131
Feedback 140
Fehnel, Jay 30, 97, 180
Findlay, Ian 118
Flexibility, presentation outlining and 140
Focus group 40, 41
Fonts, choosing 260–261
    studies on 261
Forbes 69, 244, 284
FOX 212
Foxx, Jamie 22
Framework 148

Framing 291
  headroom 291
Franklin, Ben 76
Full-sentence headline
  advantages 255
  using effectively 255

G

Gallo, Carmine 238, 308, 319
Gallo Communications 238
Gallup polls 14
Gates, Robert 80
General purpose, of topic 58
General purpose statement 63
Geographical location, audience 23, 25, 26
Gerard, Clare, Dr. 74, 75
Gestures 236–237, 296
  adaptors 236
  emblems 237
  illustrators 237
Gillespie, G. 96, 104
Gill Sans 261
Global audience 294–297
  constructing 295
  delivering 295–297
  presenting to 294–297
  supporting material 295
Global warming 175
Goad, David 309
Goal-directed speaking 5
Goals
  of group presentation 270–272
  of persuasion 193–195
Golden Globe Awards 22
Good Morning America 158, 228
Google 52, 54, 55, 62, 123, 133, 186, 310, 312, 313
Google+ 312, 313
Google Docs 274
Google Hangouts 274
Google News 51
Government documents, supporting materials 131
Grebe, Stephanie 304
Greenwald, Alan 3
Gross, Richard 163
Group affiliation 25
Group efficacy 270
Group meeting 269, 273
Group presentation 268–282
  actual 277
  conflict in 268–269
  delivering 268–269
  design format 275–276

goal establishment 270–272
  leader/point person, choosing 269–270
  multicultural 281–282
  preparing 269–276
  research in 272
  tasks in 272–273, 274
  template development 274–275
Guggenheim Museum 252
Guilt appeals 224

H

Handouts 264
Harvard University 6
Hashtag 323
Hasty generalization 217, 220
Heart and Stroke Foundation of Canada 159
Heritage Foundation 7
Hersman, Deborah A. P. 74
High-context cultures 294, 295
Hitler, Adolph 225
Hodges, L. F. 19
Honesty, in presentation 8, 10, 213, 224
Hornstine, Blair 6
Hostile audiences 30–31
"How to" presentations. *See* Instructional presentations
How to Present with Twitter (and Other Backchannels) 325
HTML 310
Huffington Post 55, 123, 127, 142
Humane Society 10
Humor 79, 296
Hunters Feed the Hungry 114
Hypothetical examples 116
Hypothetical situations 79–80

I

Identification, with audience 22, 80
Illustrators, as gesture 237
Impromptu speaking 230–231
  defined 230
  guidelines for 231
Incremental plagiarism 8, 9
Indirect methods, of audience analysis 41–42
Inductive reasoning 216–217
  defined 216
  hasty generalization 217
  tips for using 217
Infinitive phrase 59
Informative presentation 58
Informative speaking 159–160
  defined 159
  explanatory. *See* Explanatory presentation

informatory. *See* Informatory presentations
types 159–160
Informatory presentations 160–167
  explanatory vs. 162, 163
  instructional 165–167
  news. *See* News presentations
Informatory speaking 159–160
Infrastructure, online presentation 307
Initial credibility 213, 214, 287
Inoculation 29
Inoculation theory 31
Instagram 56
Instructional feedback, presentation outlining and 140
Instructional presentations 165–167
  defined 165
  desired state 166
  four states of 167
  interim state 166
  prerequisite state 166
  unwanted state 166
Interactivity, of speaker/audience 305–316, 309–316
Interim state, in instructional presentations 166, 167
Internal previews 105
Internal reviews 143, 180
Internal summaries 105–106
International Olympic Committee 268
Internet 7, 8, 38, 54, 73, 76, 99, 126, 132, 135, 166, 174,
       180, 252, 287, 298, 312, 313, 323
  evaluating information from 122
  plagiarism and 6–11
  searches 54
  traditional research skills and 126
InterNIC 125
Interviews 40
  citation of 135
  supporting materials 122
Introductions, of presentation 67, 67–85, 89–90, 150, 275
  attention-gaining devices in. *See* Attention-gaining devices
  credibility statement 82–83
  example of 79–80, 84–85
  importance 67
  objectives of 67–85
  previewing main points 84–85
  Relevance statement 83, 85, 90, 92, 93
  topic, announcing 84–85
invalid analogy 11, 218, 220
Involvement, audience 32
IOC. *See* International Olympic Committee (IOC)
Italy's National Commission for Forecasting and Predicting
       Great Risks 173
Item comparison, bar charts and 249–250
iTunes 218, 288, 312

J

JAMA 217
Jelphs, K. 269
Jobs, Steve 230, 240, 319
JobWeb 3
Johns Hopkins University Libraries 124
Johnson, Kelley 228
Jokes 79, 296
Journal & Courier 220, 343
Journalist's Resource 131
Journal of the American Medical Association 181
Journals, citation of 134
JSTOR 131

K

Kaiser Family Foundation 124
Keller, J. M. 46
Kelly, Megyn 212
Kennedy, John F. 199
Keynote slides 250
Keynote Tweet 323
Key, Tim 165
King, Martin Luther 46
Knowledge, of audience 34–35
Koenders, Oscar 286
Kyodo News International 131

L

L'Aquila, Italy 173
Latitude of acceptance 198, 199
Latitude of non-commitment 198
Latitude of rejection 198
Lay summary 175
LCD. *See* Liquid crystal display (LCD)
Leader in group presentation 269–270
Lechleiter, John C. 78, 87
LexisNexis Academic 73, 93, 129, 130
Liberty National Award 80
Liberty University 46
Libraries, supporting materials 121–122
Library research 131
Lighting 290
  fill light 290
  key light 290
Lindell, Michael K. 173
Line charts 249–250
Liquid crystal display (LCD) 253
Live presentation 287, 304, 313
Localizing 52, 83, 113–115

Logos 215–219
  analogical reasoning 217–218
  causal reasoning 218–219
  deductive reasoning 215–216
  inductive reasoning 216–217
Lopez-Alt, J. Kenji 158
Los Angeles Times 163
Low-context cultures 294
Lynne, Jeff 7

M

Mackiewicz, Jo 261
Made to Stick: Why Some Ideas Survive and Others Die 96
Magazines, supporting materials 129–131
  citation of 134
Magna Corporation 272
Main points 61, 63, 67, 97–102. *See also* Outline
  characteristics 101–102
  introducing, conclusion and 88
  number of 98
  organization of 98–101
  previewing 84–85
  restating 86
  transitioning 106
Major premise 216
Manuscript delivery 232
  defined 232
Maps 251
Martin Luther King Day 46
Marvin Gaye's estate 7
Mashable blog 126
Mass media, scientific explanation in 177
Materials, supporting. *See* Supporting materials
McCroskey, James 14
McDonald's 112
McGuire 31
Media, credibility of 130
Memorable thought, ending with, 86–87
Memorized delivery 232
Menzel 240
Metaphors, in quasi-scientific explanations 176–180
Michigan State 2
Milestones 279–280
Miller, Will 38
Minimalist instruction 167
Minor premise 215, 216
Misrepresentation 7–8
Miss America pageant 228
Miss Colorado 228
Mitchell, Olivia 325
Monroe, Alan 206, 207

Monroe's motivated sequence 206, 278
  defined 206
  using 207
Moore, Russell 46
Mortenson, Greg 75
Motivated audience 31–33, 77, 78, 204
MotorBoating magazine 131
Movement, in presentation 237
MSNBC 51, 130
Multicultural groups 281–282
Multimedia presentation 253–259
  design principles and 259
  Keynote slides 253, 257
  PowerPoint 253, 254, 255
  software, advantages of 253
  using effectively 254–260
Murray, David 68
Musser, MaryEm 285

N

NACE. *See* National Association of Colleges and Employers (NACE)
Narratives, as attention-getting device 68–76
Narrative transport 71
NASA 175
National Association of Colleges and Employers (NACE) 2, 277
National Center for Public Policy Research 124
National Highway Transportation Safety Administration 90
National Hockey League (NHL) 32
National Public Radio (NPR) 26, 51
National Rifle Association (NRA) 30, 198
National security 188
National Sleep Foundation (NSF) 133
National Transportation Safety Board 74
Need, of policy in persuasive presentation 203–210
Net Worth 272
Neuroscience 69, 171
Neutral audiences 31
New England Journal of Medicine 142, 180
Newsletters, topic selection and 52–54
Newspaper Source 131
Newspapers, supporting materials 129–131
  citation of 134–135
News presentations 160–165
  comprehensiveness 164–165
  factuality 164
  relevancy, to audience 161
  surprise value in 161–163
News releases
  citation of 135–136
  sources for 52
  supporting materials 128
  topic selection and 52–54

News services, topic selection and 52–54
New York Times 54, 55, 96, 123, 130, 131, 133, 135, 162, 170
Nikodijevic, Jelena 3
Note cards, speaking outline on 148
NRA. *See* National Rifle Association (NRA)
Numerical charts 246–250
  bar 248–249
  line and column 249–250
  pie 247–248

O

Obama, Barack 182, 188
Ohio State 2
O'Keefe 213, 224, 342
On-demand presentation 288, 302, 308
Online presentation 284–288
  asynchronous 297–298
  benefits of 285–287
  challenges 303
  coordination 287
  cost savings of 286
  faster decision-making 287
  goals of 285
  green 286
  knowledge transference in 311
  live 284
  on-demand 285
  preparing for 285
  skype 313–314
  slide presentation 310
  steps in creating 277–278
  synchronous 288
  time savings 286
  tools for 309
  types of 287–288
Online questions and answer session 324
Open-ended questions 40
Organizational pattern 98
Organization, of presentation 13, 96, 97–106
  balance in 101–102
  body 97–106
  causal pattern in 100
  chronological pattern in 99
  directional transitions 104–105
  importance of 96
  internal previews 105
  internal summaries 105–106
  main points in 97–102
  parallel wording and 102
  persuasive speaking and 200–201
  problem-solution design 99–100
  signposts 105

  spatial pattern in 98–99
  supporting evidence 102–103
  topical pattern in 100–101
  transitions 104–106
Oswald, Lee Harvey 199
Outline, presentation 13, 138–156
  balances in 139
  creating 144–146
  donating to Soles4Souls 150–156
  evidence identification 139
  flexibility and 140
  formatting preparation outline. *See* Preparation outline, formatting
  importance of 138–140
  instructional feedback and 140
  organization assurance 139
  quantity assessment 139
  speaking outline. *See* Speaking outline

P

Palin, Sarah 138
Papageorgis 31
Paralanguage 233
Parallel wording 102
Parkinson's disease 217
Participation, audience 78
Passive agreement 204, 205
Passive audience 31, 306
Pathos 212, 222–225, 225
  delivery 224
  enhancing 225
  language 223
  supporting evidence 223–224
  visual aids 225
Paul, Rand 7
Pauses, in vocal delivery 235
Peer testimony 118–119
People for the Ethical Treatment of Animals (PETA) 202
Performance, practice and 241
Peripheral route 195, 197
Personal experience, topic selection from 50–51
Personal interests, topic selection and 51
Personal Report of Public Speaking Anxiety (PRPSA) 14, 16, 17
Persuasion 58, 189–210
  attitudes and 192–193
  behavior and 193
  beliefs and 192
  defined 190
  Elaboration Likelihood Model (ELM) 195–198
  goals of 193–195
  organizing presentation 199–208
  process of 191

Social Judgment Theory 198–199
targets of 191–193
Persuasive message 189, 191, 193, 196, 216
Persuasive presentation
facts and 199–201
policy and 203–208
three types 199–208
value and 201–203
vs. informative 189–190
Persuasive presentation, stategies for
ethos and 212, 213–214
logos and 212, 215–219
pathos and 212, 222–225
Persuasive theory
Elaboration Likelihood Model (ELM) 195–198
Social Judgment 198–199. *See also* Social Judgment Theory
PETA. *See* People for the Ethical Treatment of Animals (PETA)
Petty, Tom 7
Pew Research Center 121, 130
Photographs, as presentation aid 244, 252, 258
locating 252
Phrase headlines 255–256
Physical delivery 236–240. *See also* Delivery, physical
Pie chart 247–248
Pinterest 128, 297
Pitch, in vocal delivery 234
Pittsburgh Post-Gazette 3
Plagiarism 6–11
consequences of 6–7
copyright issues 11
cut-and-paste 8
defined 6
excessive collaboration 10
incremental 8–9
misrepresentation 7–8
resources on 8
types of 7–11
Plan
of policy inn persuasive presentation 203
Q&A session 319
Podcasts 312
Policy, in persuasive presentation 203–208
active agreement 205
need, of proposal 203
passive agreement 204
plan, of proposal 203
practicality, of proposal 203
Popular Science magazine 179
Post hoc, ergo propter hoc 219, 220
PowerPoint 11, 36, 66, 69, 244, 250, 252, 253, 254, 255, 259, 261, 263, 264, 265, 273, 274, 275, 276, 287, 297, 298, 299, 300, 304, 307, 308, 309, 310, 311, 312
narrated 298, 302, 310
PowerPoint Twitter Tools 323

Practicality, of policy in persuasive presentation 203
Practice 240–241
extended examples and 117
group presentation 276
online presentation 303–316
performance and 241
sessions, guidelines 240
using presentation aids 263–265
Preparation outline
checklist for 147
speaking outline and 148
Preparation outline, formatting 140–144
appropriate symbolization 141
coordinated points 142–143
effective subordination 141–142
full sentences 140–141
reference page 144
specific purpose and thesis statements 143
transitions 143–144
Prerequisite state, in instructional presentations 166
Presentation
aids 244–266
audience analysis and. *See* Audience analysis
conclusion in. *See* Conclusion, in presentation
effective 3
group 268–269
informative 58
informative speaking in. *See* Informative speaking
introductions in. *See* Introductions, of presentation
organization of. *See* Organization
outline. *See* Outline
persuasive 58
presentational speaking overview. *See* Presentational speaking
purpose of 58, 59–60
question and answer session in 318–326
special occasion speaking in. *See* Special occasion speaking
supporting evidence and research. *See* Supporting evidence
topic and purpose selection in. *See* Topic; Topic selection
Presentation aids 244–266. *See also* Aids, presentation
Presentational skills, importance of 2
Presentational speaking 2–20
audience size and 4
career success and 3
defined 3–4
effectiveness of. *See* Effectiveness of presentational speaking
inclusivity in 3–4
informality in 4
interactivity in 4
vs. public speaking 3
Presentation process 12–13
organization 13
practice 13
purpose 12

research 12–13
  topic selection 12
Presentation Secrets of Steve Jobs: How to Be Insanely Great in Front of Any Audience 319
Presidential election 212
Prestige testimony 119
Previewing
  importance 84
  main points 84–85
Preview statement 84, 85
Prezi slides 244, 253, 257, 298, 310
Primacy effect 66
  in arguments 204
PR Newswire 52, 128
Problem-cause-solution designs 205
Problem-solution design 99, 206
Problem-solving approach 271
Process conflict 268, 269
Process, presentation. *See* Presentation process
Procter & Gamble 66
Project Information Literacy 110, 126
Pronunciation 235–236
Proquest Research Library 131
PRPSA. *See* Personal Report of Public Speaking Anxiety (PRSPA)
Psychological factors, of audience analysis 27–35
  attitudes of audience 28–29
  audience motivation 31–33
  knowledge of audience 34–35
Public speaking 3, 3–4
  fear of 3
Purdue Cultural Awareness Committee 272
Purdue University 49, 56, 63, 135, 144, 206
Purpose, of presentation 58

Q

Q&A session 324. *See* Question-and- answer (Q&A), session
Q&A session. See Question-and-answer (Q&A), session 139
Quasi-scientific explanation 167, 170, 177, 179, 180, 186
Question-and-answer (Q&A), session 276–278, 318–326
  answering questions 319–322
  backchannel 322–325
  closure and 326
  guidelines for 318–326
  preparing for 318–319
Questionnaires 41, 241
Questions 78–79
  direct 78
  of fact 199–201
  of policy 203–208
  of value 201–203
  rhetorical 78
Quotations 76, 87

R

Radiation 176
Rana, Dr. Jamal S. 134
Rate, in vocal delivery 234
Real Estate Masters Guild 66, 140, 223, 276
Recall, expressiveness and 228
Recency effect 66
  in arguments 204
Redford, Robert 119, 183
Red herring 222
Reference page 144
Reference works, supporting materials 129
Reflective thinking 271
Refutative pattern 197, 200, 278
Reinforce, attitudes and beliefs in persuasive presentation 194
Relationship conflict 268
Relaxation techniques 15
Relevance statement 81, 83, 161
Relevancy, for audience news presentations and 161
Repetition, in quasi-scientific explanations 179
Research 8, 50
  in group presentation 272
  supporting 110–111. *See also* Supporting materials
Resource interdependent 272
Rhetorical question 78
Rhetoric (Aristotle) 212
Rickards, J.P. 104
Risi, Jennifer 284
Rothbaum, B.O. 19
Rowan, Kathy 159
Rueff, Rusty 33
Rule of thirds 291

S

Safir, M. P. 19
Sans Serif font 258, 260, 261
Santorum, Rick 114
Schiferl, Michael 263
Schiro, James 297
Schizophrenia 176
Science Daily 53, 186
Scientific explanation, in mass media 177
Seattle Post-Intelligencer 131
September 11, 2001 24, 49, 194, 232
Serif 260, 261
Seven46 268
Sex and gender, audience analysis and 24–25
Shaw, D. E. 51
Shorenstein Center 131
Sigman, Stan 230
Signposts 105, 143

Simultaneous translation 239
Situational apprehension 14
60 Minutes 51, 75
Skills deficit 15
Skills training, for addressing apprehension 15
Skype 274, 309, 312, 313, 314, 315, 324
Slate magazine 131
SlideRocket 252
Slideshare 312
Slippery slope 221
Smith, Harry K. 167
Smith, Paul 66
Smith, Sam 7
Snapchat 112, 132
Social bookmarking sites 128
Social Judgment Theory 198–199
    applying 198–199
    defined 198
    ego-involvement and 198
    latitude of acceptance in 198
    latitude of noncommitment in 198
    latitude of rejection in 198
Social media 56–57, 126–128, 128
Social Times 323
Software, presentation 253–259
    advantages 253
    effective use of 254–259
Spatial pattern 98–99
Speaker transitions 275
Speaking outline 147–149
    brief 147
    delivery cues 148
    frameworks vs. outlines 148–149
    guidelines 148
    legibility 147
    on note cards 148
    preparation outline and, 147
    sample 153–156
    supporting materials and 147
Special effects, avoiding 250, 259
Special occasion speaking 182–185
    speech of acceptance 184
    speech of introduction 182–183
    speech of recognition 185
    speech of welcome 185
Specific purpose statement 59–60, 63, 143, 144
    as declarative statement 59–60
    as infinitive phrase 60
    clear and precise 60
    qualities 59–60
Speech of acceptance, special occasion speeches 184
Speech of introduction, special occasion speeches 182–183
Speech of recognition, special occasion speeches 185
Speech of welcome, special occasion speeches 185
Starks, Cynthia J. 82, 87

Statistics, as attention-gaining devices 76
Statistics, as supporting evidence 112–115, 115
    explaining 113
    limiting 114
    localize 113–115
    mean 113
    median 113
    outlier 113
    representative 112
    rounding off 114
    sources of 114–115
    tips 112–115
    understanding 113
Status report 278–281
Stereotyping 25, 26, 27
Stoehr, Amy 66, 140, 223, 276
Stories, as attention-getting device 68–76
Straw person 222
Streaming, audio/video 287, 288, 310, 312
Subordination, preparation outline and 141–142
Subpoints 10, 72, 97, 102, 103, 105, 106, 140, 141, 142, 145
Sullivan, J. F. 96, 104
Summer Olympics 268
Sundance Film Festival 119
Sundance Institute 119
SunGard 286, 353
Supporting evidence 102–103, 110–136
    aiding credibility 111
    importance 110–111
    supporting materials. *See* Supporting materials
Supporting materials
    consistent and complementary 121
    evaluation of. *See* Supporting materials, evaluation of
    locating. *See* Supporting materials, locating
    speaking outline and 147–150
    tips on using 120–121
    types. *See* Supporting materials, types of
    variety of sources for 121
Supporting materials, evaluation of 132–133
    accuracy 132
    authority 132
    credibility 133
    current 132
    level 133
    objectivity 133
    relevancy 133
    variety of sources 133
Supporting materials, locating 121–133
    academic journals 131–132
    books 128
    evaluating 132–133
    government documents 131
    interviews 122
    libraries 121–122
    magazines, newspapers, and broadcast outline 129–131

news releases 128
references works 129
social media 126–128
Weblogs 123–126
Websites 123
Supporting materials, types of 111–121
examples. *See* Examples
statistics. *See* Statistics
testimony. *See* Testimony
Suprise value, in news presentations 161–163
Surveys 41
Swanson's Unwritten Rules of Management 7
Swanson, William 7
Syllogism 215
conclusion 215
major premise 215
minor premise 215
Symbolization, preparation outline and 141
Synchronous presentation 288. *See also* Asynchronous
presentation
backgrounds 291
behavior 293–294
camera angles 290–291
challenges of 303
color and wardrobe 291–292
content 292
delivering 293–294
delivering online 310
eye contact 293
framing 291
lighting 290
movement 293
planning 289–292
posture 293
setting 290–292
technology options for 312
tips for using 289
voice 293
Systemic desensitization, for addressing apprehension 15–17

T

Tarantino, Quentin 22
Target, in persuasive presentation 191–193
Task conflict 269
Teamwork skill 3
Technical skill 303–316
Technology
attention-gaining devices (attention-getter) 76–77
limitations 303–316
TED 3
TED talk series 244

10-Minute Rule 275
Terminal credibility 214, 287
Testimony, as supporting evidence 118–119, 119–120
citing credentials of sources 120
expert 118
peer 118–119
prestige 119
quote/paraphrase accurately 119
tips for using 119–120
from unbiased sources 119–120
Text charts 250
Thesis, restating 86
Thesis statement 13, 46, 61, 61–63, 62, 63, 67, 81, 84, 85,
90, 92, 93, 97, 99, 100, 101, 110, 143, 144, 145, 150,
162, 163, 186, 200, 202, 205, 255
anatomy 62–63
general purpose 63
guidelines 61–62
qualities 61
specific purpose statement 63
Thicke, Robin 7
Thomas, Lawrence 2
Three Cups of Tea 75, 334
Time series comparisons, column/line charts and 249–250
Times New Roman 261
Today Show, The 158, 228
Topic
announcing 84–85
general purpose of 58
narrowing 51, 57–63
selection. *See* Topic selection
specific purpose statement. *See* Specific purpose statement
thesis statement. *See* Thesis statement
Topical pattern 100, 176
Topic selection 12, 46–64
anxiety in 51
audience appropriate 49
current events and 51–52
fresh 48
interesting 47
internet searches 54
news releases, news services, and newsletters and 52–54
other sources 57
personal experience and 50–51
personal interests and 51
qualities of 47–50
relevance of 47
research and 50
significant 48
social media 56–57
strategies 50–57
timeliness of 48–49
weblogs 54–56

Toshiba Computer Systems 286
Towler, A. J. 96, 228
Toyota Prius 89
Trait-like apprehension 14
Transformative explanation 180–181
Transitions 104–106, 143–144
    directional 104–105, 143
    donating to Soles4Souls, example 150–156
    impact of 104
    in quasi-scientific explanations 176–180
    internal previews 105
    internal summaries 105–106
    signposts 105, 143
    transitioning 106
Translator/translation 239–240
    delayed 239
    simultaneous 239
Trump, Donald 46, 138, 212
Trust, in distributed groups 287
Trustworthiness 213–214
Tufte, Edward 255
Twain, Mark 14, 76
Twitter 40, 41, 42, 44, 56, 110, 126, 127, 128, 136, 288, 306, 322, 323, 325

U

University of Oxford 165
Unwanted state 166
UPS 86, 151
USA Today 131, 152
U.S. Geological Survey 163
USOC. *See* U. S. Olympic Committee (USOC)

V

Values 28
    in persuasive presentation 201–203
Varley, Nick 268
Video/audio, as presentation aid 252, 313
Video conference 284–285, 287, 302
Virginia-based Network Solutions 125
Virtual audiences 19
Virtual environment 289
Virtual presentation 89, 287, 288, 292, 306
Virtual visualization 19
Visual aids 76–77, 225–226, 296
    in quasi-scientific explanations 164, 172
Visual Composing: Document Design for Print and Digital Media 261
Visualization
    for addressing apprehension 15, 18–19
    virtual 19
Vital Speeches of the Day 68
Vocal delivery 233–236. *See also* Delivery, vocal

Vocal fillers 235, 300
Vocal nonfluencies 235
Vocal variety 233–236
Voice over Internet Protocol (VoIP) service 313
VoIP. *See* Voice over Internet Protocol (VoIP) service
Volume, in vocal delivery 233–234
Voluntary audiences 33
Vox 175

W

Wallach, H. S. 19
Wall Street Journal 2, 3, 66, 131, 133
Wandless, Jessica 284
Washington Business Journal 14
Washington Post 123, 131, 133, 135
Web conferences 287, 311
Weber Shandwick 284, 318, 323
WebEx 278, 284, 312, 313
Webinars 284, 286, 288, 312
Weblogs 54–56, 110
    supporting materials 123–126
Web misinformation 180
Web presentation. *See* Online presentation
Websites, as supporting evidence 123
    citation of 135
    citations 125
    evaluating credibility 124, 125
    external links 125
    site credentials 124
    timeliness of information 125
    URL 124
Williams, Pharrell 7
Wilson, Steven R. 135
Winfrey, Oprah 119
Witte, Kim 224
Word selection 23
World Almanac 129
World Health Organization 124, 135, 165
Wright, Frank Lloyd 252

X

Y

Yahoo 51, 52, 186
YouTube 56, 166, 297, 311, 312, 315

Z

Zee, Ginger 178
Zimand E. 19
Zurich Financial Services 297

FORMS AND ASSIGNMENTS

A

NAME: _____

COM114 Information Sheet

Please complete this form and return it to your instructor.

1. Name: _____

2. Phone: _____

3. E-mail Address: _____

4. Major: _____

5. Year in College: _____

6. Please list previous speech courses taken in high school:

7. Please list previous speech and/or communication courses taken at other colleges or universities and/or any public speaking experience outside the classroom.

8. Please list hobbies, extracurricular activities, and interests.

9. Please list your specific goals for improving your presentation skills.

10. How do you anticipate applying the knowledge learned in this course in your major or career?

11. I have read and understand the syllabus and course policy statement for the course. I understand and agree to abide by the course policies and procedures as noted in the syllabus and policy statement.

Student Signature: _____   Date: _____

NAME: _____

Tell a Narrative

Point Value: 40

Length: 1–2 minutes

Assignment Overview

In this presentation, you will choose a complete narrative with a beginning, middle, and end to share with the class. You will need to utilize your delivery skills in order to present this narrative in a manner that moves your audience. When choosing a narrative to share with the class, some aspects to consider are (1) Does the story include a significant action? (2) Is the story engaging? (3) Will the audience be able to relate to your story? (4) Can you effectively share the story with your audience in the time allowed? (5) Is the story simple (i.e., not overly complex while also developed and detailed)? (6) Does the story adequately utilize pacing? (7) Does the story illustrate or support the topic of your Persuasive presentation?

You will use a narrative that you wish to incorporate into your Persuasive presentation later in the semester. While you will share the complete narrative during this presentation, you may wish to use the first portion of it for your persuasive attention-getter and/or the resolution for the clincher in your persuasive, or all of the narrative as support for a main point in the persuasive presentation. You cannot use hypothetical examples for your narrative and the narrative must come from someone else. For example, if your grandfather served in the Vietnam War and your persuasive topic relates to donations for veterans, you could interview your grandfather and use that story. If you do not have someone to interview, you may utilize a narrative that you have found in a news article or on your persuasive topic's organization's website (for example, a veteran's story from the *New York Times* or a story posted on Paralyzed Veterans of America's website). Since you have already chosen the topic that you plan to do your Persuasive presentation on, all you need to do is find a narrative that relates to that topic. However, know that you are not required to include the narrative you present this time during your Persuasive presentation if you find a narrative later that works better with your topic or you change to a completely different topic and your narrative no longer works with it. Please contact your instructor with any questions about this.

This assignment emphasizes delivery. It is important that you present the story in a complete fashion with a beginning, middle, and ending. This will help your audience to follow along with your story and to comprehend the story as a whole. Simple presentations such as this are an excellent opportunity to become comfortable speaking in front of an audience. They also provide opportunities to practice such delivery techniques as eye contact, hand gestures, tone, and volume without having to worry about sharing large volumes of knowledge. The focus is on extemporaneous delivery in which you have prepared and practiced, but are not delivering a memorized presentation or reading it to the class. Presenting in an extemporaneous style allows you to not only adapt your narrative for your audience as you go along, but also provides you the opportunity to present in a dynamic manner that engages your audience which is a huge factor in this presentation.

*Your topics for your Narrative and Persuasive assignments must be approved by your instructor.

Specific Requirements

- ◎ Inform your students of a complete story that is compelling and will captivate them as an audience member.

- ◎ Approved topic. You will not be allowed to submit an assignment if your instructor has not approved your topic in writing. If you fail to receive written approval for your topic from your instructor before your assigned speaking day, you will lose your opportunity to speak and will receive a ZERO on this assignment.

- ◎ Time limit: 1–2 minutes. If your speech fails to meet the time requirements, you will be penalized 5 points so practice!

- ◎ You must create and submit a simple framework by the date assigned by your instructor. A framework template is provided. If you do not submit a framework, you will not be allowed to present and will receive a zero for the assignment. Failure to submit a complete framework by the deadline will result in a 5-point deduction from your speech grade.

- ◎ You must orally cite your source. Failure to do so is a 10% deduction.

- ◎ Your framework will be run through the plagiarism detector SafeAssign. Plagiarized frameworks will be penalized and must be redone.

- ◎ Use an extemporaneous speaking style. This means that you are not to read your story or to memorize your story word-for-word, but are to talk to the audience. You are allowed one side of one 5 × 7 note card to use for this presentation. Your instructor will collect your note card after you present.

- ◎ Organize your story to have a beginning, middle, and end.

- ◎ Deliver your narrative on the assigned day. Speakers who miss their assigned day will receive a zero. See the syllabus and instructor policy statement for more information. You, not your instructor, are responsible for knowing the date of your presentation.

Evaluation

1. Analysis of the topic and audience
2. Organization of the story
3. Use of emotive and simple language
4. Refined delivery
5. Focus on garnering empathy from your audience

NAME: _____

Topic Worksheet

Narrative/Persuasive Presentations ————————

Read the assignment sheets for the Narrative presentation and the Persuasive presentation before completing this topic form.

First, decide the topic of your Persuasive presentation. Remember, this must be related to an organization. You are persuading me to take part in an organization or in an activity sponsored by that organization. This is a speech of policy.

1. The organization/organization event I want to persuade people to join/attend, etc. is

   _____

   _____

   _____

   _____

2. The specific action I want people to take is (donate $10 to feed one child for a month, sign this peti-tion to bring this person to campus, volunteer one Saturday a month to restock shelves at the food pantry, etc.)

   _____

   _____

   _____

   _____

3. This organization/event is worthy because

   _____

   _____

   _____

   _____

Next decide the topic of your Narrative presentation. This will be a 1–2 minute story that evokes pathos for your organization. It later will be used (in a shortened version) as the attention-getter or support in your Persuasive Presentation.

4.   The narrative I plan to use is

_____

_____

_____

_____

5.   I obtained this narrative by (interviewing a friend, from the organization's webpage, from a newspaper article, etc.)

_____

_____

_____

6.   This will be an effective attention-gaining device/support for my persuasive presentation because

_____

_____

_____

7.   This narrative relates to the persuasive presentation topic by (for example, this person received help from this organization, this person volunteers for this organization, etc.)

_____

_____

_____

_____

NAME: _____

Narrative Framework

1. What is the beginning of your narrative? How do you plan to lay the foundation for your audience?

    _____

    _____

    _____

    _____

2. What is the middle (the action)?

    _____

    _____

    _____

    _____

3. What is the ending (the resolution)?

    _____

    _____

    _____

    _____

4. What is the narrative's relationship to your topic? (I'm telling this story because ….)

    _____

    _____

    _____

    _____

5. What reference(s) did you use? List in APA format as you would on a reference page, even if you conducted a personal interview.

    _____

    _____

    _____

    _____

NAME: _____

Narrative Presentation Evaluation Form

Speaker: _____ **Date:** _____

Topic: _____ **Time:** _____

Structure and Content (25 Points)

1. Story has clear beginning ____ yes ____ somewhat ____ no
2. Story has a distinct middle ____ yes ____ somewhat ____ no
3. Story has a definite conclusion (end) ____ yes ____ somewhat ____ no
4. Includes significant action ____ yes ____ somewhat ____ no
5. Organization is tied to story ____ yes ____ somewhat ____ no
6. Source is cited ____ yes ____ somewhat ____ no
7. Simple, descriptive, emotive language is used ____ yes ____ somewhat ____ no
8. Story has clear beginning ____ yes ____ somewhat ____ no

Comments:

Delivery (15 Points)

1. Used effective vocal delivery (appropriate rate and volume, clear articulation, varied inflection, no vocal fillers) ____ yes ____ somewhat ____ no
2. Used effective physical delivery (eye contact, hand gestures, avoided distracting mannerisms, etc.) ____ yes ____ somewhat ____ no
3. Speech appeared practiced ____ yes ____ somewhat ____ no

Comments:

COM114 Presentation Peer Evaluation

Narrative Evaluation

Speaker Name: _____   **Speaker Topic:** _____

You must provide objective, evidence-based feedback. Draw upon the textbook and information gleaned in class to support each comment (both strengths and opportunities for feedback).

Delivery Evaluation

One area the speaker could improve on:

One area the speaker did well:

Content Evaluation

(You may comment on any area of the content: topic, thesis, organization, support, transitions, citations, introduction elements, conclusion elements.)

One area the speaker could improve on:

One area the speaker did well:

I was affected by the narrative: _____ yes   _____ no

Explain:

NAME: _____

COM114 Presentation Peer Evaluation

Narrative Evaluation ———————————————————

Speaker Name: _____ **Speaker Topic:** _____

You must provide objective, evidence-based feedback. Draw upon the textbook and information gleaned in class to support each comment (both strengths and opportunities for feedback).

Delivery Evaluation

One area the speaker could improve on:

One area the speaker did well:

Content Evaluation

(You may comment on any area of the content: topic, thesis, organization, support, transitions, citations, introduction elements, conclusion elements.)

One area the speaker could improve on:

One area the speaker did well:

I was affected by the narrative: _____ yes _____ no

Explain:

NAME: _____

COM114 Presentation Peer Evaluation

Narrative Evaluation ───────────────────────

Speaker Name: _____   **Speaker Topic:** _____

You must provide objective, evidence-based feedback. Draw upon the textbook and information gleaned in class to support each comment (both strengths and opportunities for feedback).

Delivery Evaluation

One area the speaker could improve on:

One area the speaker did well:

Content Evaluation

(You may comment on any area of the content: topic, thesis, organization, support, transitions, citations, introduction elements, conclusion elements.)

One area the speaker could improve on:

One area the speaker did well:

I was affected by the narrative: _____ yes   _____ no

Explain:

Simple Explanation

Point Value: 60

Time Limit: 1–2 minutes

Assignment Overview

In today's information age we are often faced with presenting difficult or challenging information to an audience who may have little experience with the ideas we are presenting. It becomes particularly important that we can take these ideas and express them in an understandable way to audiences with varying levels of knowledge.

You will want your audience to be able to grasp and remember the material in your explanation after hearing it only once. In order to do this effectively it is important that you draw analogies between your audiences' experiences and the material you are presenting in your explanation.

This assignment requires excellent audience analysis in order to provide information at a level the audience can process and understand. It is your job to analyze your audience effectively so that your explanation is effective.

Topic

You should select a topic for your simple explanation that can then be included in your instructional asynchronous presentation. (For additional reference, see assignment specifications for the asynchronous presentation.) You will present your simple explanation in class and you will also incorporate it into your asynchronous presentation. For example, if your simple explanation is to explain the process of fermentation, your asynchronous presentation could be about how to make sangria. Or, if your simple explanation is about explaining the qualities of high-quality soil, your asynchronous presentation could be about how to make a raised-bed garden because one of the advantages of a raised-bed garden is better soil quality.

* Your topic for both your Simple Explanation and your Asynchronous Presentation must be approved by your instructor prior to your presentation. If you do not receive **written** approval of your topics, you will not be allowed to speak. You must submit a completed topic form, and receive an OK from your instructor, before you can speak on a topic.

Visual Aids

You must include one visual aid in your explanation. It should be a PowerPoint (or Prezi) slide that utilizes the assertion evidence model. The visual aid should be relevant, professional, and enhance your audience's understanding of your topic. Additionally, you should explain your visual aid clearly.

Analogy/Metaphor/Definition

Depending on if your Simple Explanation is of a process (Quasi-Scientific) or a concept (Elucidating Explanation), you will need to use an analogy or example/definition to help your audience understand your explanation.

References/Citations/Supporting Material

At least one source will be needed for the explanation. Wikipedia does not count as a source nor do other crowd-sourced websites. Also websites such as "How Stuff Works" and "E-How" are not considered reliable sources. If you doubt the legitimacy of a source, please check it with your instructor before you submit the final project. It is best to use sources that are also in print (*New York Times,* etc.).

Frame Work

A typed, **complete** framework must be submitted to Blackboard by the assigned date or you will not be allowed to present. A framework template is provided.

Specific Requirements

- ◎ Time Limit: 1–2 minutes. If your speech does not meet the time criteria, you will be penalized 5 points.
- ◎ Complete framework submitted to Blackboard by date assigned by instructor. A framework template is provided. If you do not submit a framework, you will not be allowed to present and will receive a zero for the assignment. You must include your references. If you fail to submit a completed framework by the due date, you will be penalized 5 points.
- ◎ Adequately explain the idea.
- ◎ Relate unfamiliar ideas to what the audience knows and values.
- ◎ Demonstrate skillful use of transitions.
- ◎ Use an effective analogy/metaphor/example.
- ◎ Refined delivery: Your speaking style should be extemporaneous. This means that you are not to read your explanation or to memorize your speech, but are to talk to the audience and adapt to the audience as you speak. Work for both effective physical and vocal delivery.
- ◎ Create informative visual aid that utilizes the assertion evidence model. Professionally use the visual aid.
- ◎ Choose an interesting topic. Your topic must be approved by your instructor in writing before you can deliver your explanation. If you fail to receive written approval for your topic from your instructor before your assigned speaking day, you will lose your opportunity to speak and will receive a **zero** on this assignment.
- ◎ You must orally cite your source. Failure to do so is a 10% deduction.
- ◎ You must also meet any additional requirements as outlined in class by your instructor.
- ◎ Deliver your explanation on the assigned day. Speakers who miss their assigned day will receive a zero. See the syllabus and instructor policy statement for more information. You, not your instructor, are responsible for knowing the date of your presentation.

Evaluation

1. Analysis of the topic and audience
2. Organization of the explanation
3. Use of simple language
4. Use of examples, analogies
5. Refined delivery
6. Creation of visual aid
7. Use of visual aid

Topic Worksheet

Simple Explanation/Asynchronous (Narrated Powerpoint) Presentations

Read the assignment sheets for the Simple Explanation Presentation and the Asynchronous (Narrated PowerPoint) Presentation before completing this topic form.

First, decide the topic of your Asynchronous Presentation (the Narrated PowerPoint). This is an instructional presentation. See Chapter 8 of your textbook. This should be a sequential (steps) presentation that instructs an audience how to do something. Pick a topic that you can see someone going to Google and typing in (nobody Googles how to make a sandwich). But you must be able to fully demonstrate the task in 3–5 minutes. Think narrowly (you cannot show me how to build a computer in 3–5 minutes). Think of your hobbies, your interests, your major if you aren't sure what to do. What do you know how to do that you can share?

1. My topic for my how-to Asynchronous Presentation (the Narrated PowerPoint) is

   _____

   _____

   _____

   _____

2. Someone might search for this how-to because

   _____

   _____

   _____

   _____

Next, you will need to decide the topic of the Simple Explanation. This will be an explanation of one scientific or mechanical or technical component of your how-to. This is not a step in your how-to. This is not a reason/reasons why your how-to is important. Your how-to instructs. Your simple explanation explains. Think of it as how something works vs. how to do something.

3. In my simple explanation I will explain how

   _____

   _____

   _____

   _____

4. This will be useful in my how-to because

_____

_____

_____

_____

5. Where will this be placed in the NPP?

_____

_____

_____

_____

NAME: _____

Simple Explanation Framework

1. What are you explaining?

   _____

   _____

   _____

   _____

   _____

   _____

2. What is your thesis?

   _____

   _____

   _____

   _____

   _____

   _____

3. Main point I:

   _____

   _____

   _____

   _____

   _____

   _____

4. Main point II:

   _____

   _____

   _____

   _____

   _____

5. What is your analogy, example, etc.?

_____

_____

_____

_____

_____

_____

6. What is your visual aid? How will it add to understanding?

_____

_____

_____

_____

_____

_____

7. What reference(s) did you use? List in APA format as you would on a reference page, even if you conducted a personal interview.

_____

_____

_____

_____

_____

_____

*Add key points as needed, although you should limit to four key points.

NAME: _____

Simple Explanation Evaluation Form

Speaker: _____   **Date:** _____

Topic: _____   **Time:** _____

Explanation (30 Points) ————————————————

1. Clear thesis with main points previewed   ____ yes   ____ somewhat   ____ no
2. Adequately explained the idea, concept, phenomena   ____ yes   ____ somewhat   ____ no
3. Related unfamiliar ideas to what the audience knows and values   ____ yes   ____ somewhat   ____ no
4. Defined unfamiliar terms and concepts   ____ yes   ____ somewhat   ____ no
5. Effectively used an analogy, quasi-scientific explanation, etc.   ____ yes   ____ somewhat   ____ no
6. Orally cited at least one source   ____ yes   ____ somewhat   ____ no

Additional Comments:

Delivery (15 Points) ————————————————

1. Used adequate and inclusive eye contact   ____ yes   ____ somewhat   ____ no
2. Used effective vocal delivery (appropriate rate and volume, clear articulation, varied inflection, and no vocal fillers)   ____ yes   ____ somewhat   ____ no
3. Delivery was extemporaneous (did not memorize, did not rely on notes)   ____ yes   ____ somewhat   ____ no
4. Explanation appeared well rehearsed and practiced   ____ yes   ____ somewhat   ____ no

Additional Comments:

Visual Aid (15 Points)

1. Used relevant, professional visual aid that
   enhanced audience understanding of topic _____ yes _____ somewhat _____ no
2. Applied assertion evidence model _____ yes _____ somewhat _____ no
3. Clearly explained visual aid _____ yes _____ somewhat _____ no

Additional Comments:

Comments/Suggestions for Improvement:

NAME: _____

COM114 Presentation Peer Evaluation

Simple Explanation Evaluation ————————————

Speaker Name: _____ **Speaker Topic:** _____

You must provide objective, evidence-based feedback. Draw upon the textbook and information gleaned in class to support each comment (both strengths and opportunities for feedback).

Delivery Evaluation

One area the speaker could improve on:

One area the speaker did well:

Content Evaluation

(You may comment on any area of the content: topic, thesis, organization, support, transitions, citations, introduction elements, conclusion elements.)

One area the speaker could improve on:

One area the speaker did well:

Visual Aid Evaluation

(You may comment on aid that was chosen, use of the aid, etc.)

One area the speaker could improve on:

One area the speaker did well:

I understood the explanation: _____ yes _____ no

Explain:

NAME: _____

COM114 Presentation Peer Evaluation

Simple Explanation Evaluation ————————————————

Speaker Name: _____ **Speaker Topic:** _____

You must provide objective, evidence-based feedback. Draw upon the textbook and information gleaned in class to support each comment (both strengths and opportunities for feedback).

Delivery Evaluation

One area the speaker could improve on:

One area the speaker did well:

Content Evaluation

(You may comment on any area of the content: topic, thesis, organization, support, transitions, citations, introduction elements, conclusion elements.)

One area the speaker could improve on:

One area the speaker did well:

Visual Aid Evaluation

(You may comment on aid that was chosen, use of the aid, etc.)

One area the speaker could improve on:

One area the speaker did well:

I understood the explanation: _____ yes _____ no

Explain:

NAME: _____

COM114 Presentation Peer Evaluation

Simple Explanation Evaluation ————————————————

Speaker Name: _____   **Speaker Topic:** _____

You must provide objective, evidence-based feedback. Draw upon the textbook and information gleaned in class to support each comment (both strengths and opportunities for feedback).

Delivery Evaluation

One area the speaker could improve on:

One area the speaker did well:

Content Evaluation

(You may comment on any area of the content: topic, thesis, organization, support, transitions, citations, introduction elements, conclusion elements.)

One area the speaker could improve on:

One area the speaker did well:

Visual Aid Evaluation

(You may comment on aid that was chosen, use of the aid, etc.)

One area the speaker could improve on:

One area the speaker did well:

I understood the explanation: _____ yes   _____ no

Explain:

NAME: _____

Instructional Asynchronous Presentation

Topic: Instructional

Point Value: 100

Time limit: 3–5 minutes

This assignment asks you to develop an instructional, asynchronous presentation using the narration tool in Microsoft PowerPoint or Prezi. As technology continues to advance, the format of presentations continue to evolve. You will not always be standing directly in front of your audience, so it is important for you to be able to skillfully present information in a computer-mediated format.

Topic Selection

Instructing audiences, groups, and teams is something that occurs regularly in professional and social situations.

Topic selection is quite important for this presentation insofar that you will need to select a topic to instruct your audience about something they do not already know how to do. Again, your audience for this presentation is not necessarily your classmates, but anyone who might type in "How to …" on Google. This could be something technical, something related to your major, or something you enjoy. For instance, your audience is highly likely to know how to make a peanut butter and jelly sandwich or how to carve a pumpkin. However, they may not know how to recognize poisonous plants or insects, which would be a better topic for this assignment. In other words, trivial subject matter would not be appropriate for this assignment. Avoid simple recipe-related topics.

The topic must be something you can talk about and teach about using presentational software. With that in mind, if your topic has more than approximately 15 steps, it is likely too complicated to be able to adequately demonstrate in a 3–5 minute presentation.

* Your topic for your Simple Explanation assignment and your Asynchronous Assignment must be approved by your instructor

Visual Aids

Visual aids are another key element of this presentation. Your audience only has the slides you create to look at while you are speaking. Not only do your slides need to be attractive and professional, but they are the means by which you will show your audience how to perform the different steps of your topic. Image-based slides should follow the Assertion-Evidence model discussed in your textbook. Remember any animation you choose to use should be tasteful and should function solely to direct your audience's attention to the relevant aspect of the slide.

References/Citations/Supporting Material

At least three sources will be needed for the presentation. One of the three sources can be the same as the one required for the Simple Explanation. Wikipedia does not count as a source nor do other crowd-sourced websites. Sites such as "How Stuff Works" and "E-How" also are not acceptable references. If you doubt the legitimacy of a source, please check it with your instructor before you submit the final project. It is best to use sources that are also in print (*New York Times,* etc.). These sources will need to be cited orally within the audio of your narration.

Organization

Organization is a key element stressed in this presentation. Do you present information clearly and comprehensively? Is the information easy for an audience to follow? Do you present all four steps of instructional presentations concisely?

Framework

A typed framework must be submitted to Blackboard by the assigned date or you will not be allowed to present. A framework is provided.

Specific Requirements

◎ Approved topic. You will not be allowed to submit an assignment if your instructor has not approved your topic in writing. If you fail to receive written approval for your topic from your instructor before your assigned speaking day, you will lose your opportunity to speak and will receive a **zero** on this assignment.

◎ Framework submitted to Blackboard by assigned date. A framework template is provided. If you do not submit a framework to Blackboard, you will not be allowed to present and will receive a zero for the assignment. A late framework or incomplete framework will result in a 10-point deduction from your grade.

◎ Asynchronization works and is narrated.

◎ Assignment submitted to instructor by deadline. If you fail to submit your presentation by the deadline, you will receive a zero. Do not wait until the last minute. You, not your instructor, are responsible for technology malfunctions.

◎ Time limit is met–between 3 and 5 minutes (going over or under will result in a 10-point deduction).

◎ Develop a clear thesis that meets criteria in the book.

◎ Includes the four components of an instructional presentation.

◎ Organization is clear and easy to follow.

◎ Appropriate development of introduction and conclusion.

◎ Skillfully uses the Assertion Evidence Model.

◎ Incorporates an abbreviated form of your simple explanation in a manner that aids in a better understanding of the instructional presentation.

◎ Use source material well to support ideas and cite sources correctly (who, where, date).

◎ Include source material on slides.

◎ Orally cite all your sources. Failure to do so will result in a 10% deduction.

◎ Demonstrate skillful use of transitions.

◎ Good use of supporting information.

◎ Refined delivery (no vocal fillers, background noise, appropriate rate and volume).

◎ Audio is professional.

Evaluation

1. Analysis of the topic and audience
2. Organization of the presentation
3. Use of all four steps of an instructional presentation
4. Use of simple language
5. Use of examples, analogies
6. Refined delivery in narration
7. Audio is professional
8. Presentation is professional
9. Time limit is met
10. Proper number of sources used.
11. Sources were reliable

NAME: _____

Instructional Asynchronous Presentation Framework

1. What is your topic?

   _____

   _____

   _____

   _____

   _____

   _____

2. What are your thesis and main points?

   _____

   _____

   _____

   _____

   _____

   _____

3. In what step will you use your Simple Explanation?

   _____

   _____

   _____

   _____

   _____

4. What is your desired state? Identify the steps in your presentation that will fall under this state.

   _____

   _____

   _____

   _____

   _____

5. What is your prerequisite state? Identify the steps in your presentation that will fall under this state.

_____

_____

_____

_____

_____

6. What is your interim state? Identify the steps in your presentation that will fall under this state.

_____

_____

_____

_____

_____

_____

7. What is your unwanted state? Identify the steps in your presentation that will fall under this state.

_____

_____

_____

_____

_____

_____

8. What reference(s) did you use? List in APA format as you would on a reference page, even if you conducted a personal interview.

_____

_____

_____

_____

_____

_____

NAME: _____

Instructional Asynchronous Presentation Evaluation Form

Speaker: _____ **Time:** _____

Topic: _____

Content and Organization (20 Points)

1. Presentation is focused on main idea   ____ yes   ____ somewhat   ____ no
2. Credibility statement   ____ yes   ____ somewhat   ____ no
3. Thesis statement   ____ yes   ____ somewhat   ____ no
4. Incorporated all four steps of instructional presentation   ____ yes   ____ somewhat   ____ no
5. Presentation was well organized   ____ yes   ____ somewhat   ____ no
6. Transitions used effectively   ____ yes   ____ somewhat   ____ no

Comments:

Support (30 Points)

1. Used source material well, supported ideas, and cited it correctly (who, where, date)   ____ yes   ____ somewhat   ____ no
2. Used minimum required number of sources   ____ yes   ____ somewhat   ____ no
3. Incorporated simple explanation, seamlessly   ____ yes   ____ somewhat   ____ no
4. Provided adequate detail   ____ yes   ____ somewhat   ____ no
5. All necessary steps were included and explained   ____ yes   ____ somewhat   ____ no
6. Steps were described at novice level   ____ yes   ____ somewhat   ____ no
7. Narration adds support to text   ____ yes   ____ somewhat   ____ no

Comments:

Delivery (15 Points)

1. Used effective vocal delivery (appropriate rate and volume, clear articulation, varied inflection, and no vocal fillers)   _____ yes   _____ somewhat   _____ no
2. Audio is clear   _____ yes   _____ somewhat   _____ no

Comments:

Visual Aid

1. Effectively used the Assertion Evidence model where appropriate   _____ yes   _____ somewhat   _____ no
2. Slides are professional, relevant, and enhance audience understanding, and appropriate   _____ yes   _____ somewhat   _____ no

Comments:

Other

1. Presentation demonstrated effective audience analysis   _____ yes   _____ somewhat   _____ no
2. Presentation accomplished objectives in time allotted   _____ yes   _____ somewhat   _____ no
3. Viewers can complete task after viewing   _____ yes   _____ somewhat   _____ no

Comments:

12345678910111213

NAME: _____

Persuasive Presentation

Topic: Supporting a nonprofit/club

Point Value: 100

Length: 3–5 minutes

Assignment Overview

For this presentation you are going to persuade your classmates to support or join a charity or nonprofit organization, or a specific event put on by such an organization, or a Purdue club or organization (Greek organizations are not allowed). You are going to persuade your audience to join, volunteer their time, donate money or other tangible goods, or take some other action (sign a petition, etc.). First choose your organization/event. Next choose your goal. Then choose an organizational pattern. For example, you could use a problem-solution format. You would first explain what the problem is and then explain why your audience should support the organization you chose to help that problem. For example, you might want to persuade your audience to volunteer at a local animal shelter. You would first talk about the problem of pet overpopulation and then explain how being a volunteer can help solve that problem. You can also talk about the personal benefits one might get from supporting the cause you chose. These can be national or local organizations or events. You do not have to be personally involved; however, it is often easier if you are.

It is likely that your area of interest has many such organizations. For example those of you with an interest in engineering may want to persuade your audience to become involved with a project of the Purdue chapter of Engineers Without Borders. You would first talk about the a problem the chapter is involved with (citizens need an alternative fuel source in Nakyenyi, Uganda) and then explain how joining Purdue EWB chapter to help with the design of a biogas digester can help to solve that problem. Other such organizations include: Engineers for a Sustainable World, EPICS at Purdue, or the Global Design Team at Purdue. Check to see what kind of organizations are in your department or area of interest.

Remember:

◎ Please avoid stale topics such as donating blood or the Purdue University Dance Marathon.

◎ This is a speech of policy. You are trying to persuade your audience to do something. This is not a speech of value or fact. Make sure you focus on the action you want me to take.

◎ Persuasion is a process. Your instructor will not approve controversial topics that you could not possibly sway opinion on in 3–5 minutes.

Specific Requirements

◎ Choose an interesting topic. Your topic must be approved by your instructor before you can deliver your explanation. If you fail to have your topic approved by your instructor before your assigned speaking day, you will lose your opportunity to speak and will receive a **zero** on this assignment.

◎ Submit a full complete outline to Blackboard by the date assigned by your instructor. If you do not submit an outline by the required date, you will not be allowed to present and will receive a zero for the assignment. An outline template is provided. A late outline will received a 10-point deduction.

◎ Choose an appropriate organizational pattern and appeal (you may use problem/solution, fear appeals, etc.).

◎ Have at least four sources. This material should be current. All these sources must be cited correctly within your presentation. Failure to orally cite your sources will result in a 10% deduction.

◎ Time limit: 3–5 minutes. If your speech does not meet the time criteria, you will be penalized 10 points.

◎ Use extemporaneous delivery.

◎ Develop a thesis that meets the criteria discussed in class

◎ Develop two main points that meet class criteria and fit one of the organization patterns discussed in class.

◎ Develop a strong introduction and conclusion that meet class criteria.

◎ Demonstrate skillful use of transitions.

◎ Use a visual aid.

◎ Use a narrative (story) as either your AG device or support in the body of your presentation.

◎ Include a call to action in your conclusion. Remember, the goal is to encourage your audience to engage in a behavior.

◎ Deliver your presentation on the assigned day. Speakers who miss their assigned day will receive a zero. See the syllabus and instructor policy statement for more information. You, not your instructor, are responsible for knowing the date of your presentation.

Evaluation

1. Analysis of the topic and audience
2. Organization of the presentation
3. Use of persuasive language
4. Refined delivery
5. Use of evidence and appeals
6. Effective use of a visual aid.

NAME: _____

Persuasive Presentation Outline Template

Presentation Topic: _____

- ◎ Outline template needs to be completed in full sentences.
- ◎ Remember to include in-text citations; remember to orally cite your references. *(It's a –10 deduction in your speech if you fail to orally cite your sources.)*
- ◎ Remember that each element of your body will be only one sentence. This is an outline, not a text of your presentation.

Introduction

I.   Attention-Getter (this would be a good place for your Narrative or even just the start of your Narrative)

II. Credibility Statement

III. Relating to the Audience

IV. Thesis Statement (we should clearly hear your two MPs, the problem, and your proposed solution for that problem)

Transition:

Body

I.   Main Point I (This is your problem.)
   A. Supporting Point (Remember if you have an A you must also have a B.)
      1. Sub-subpoints (Remember to use a variety of sources: statistics, peer testimony.)
      2. Sub-subpoints (Remember to include your oral citations, According to a 2015 article in the New York Times, more than 50 million ….)
   B. Supporting Point (Remember all elements of the outline body are just one sentence.)

Directional Transition: (Summary/Preview)

II. Main Point II (This is your solution.)
   A. Supporting Point (Make sure you tell me specifically HOW: How to donate, how much to donate, exactly what the money will go for, how money is used now, etc.)
      1. Sub-subpoints (Remember if you have a 1, you need to have a 2.)
      2. Sub-subpoints
   B. Supporting Point (It's a good idea here to have testimony from someone who has benefited or volunteered.)

Transition: (Summary/Preview)

Conclusion

I. Restate Thesis:
II. Closing Statement or Clincher: (This would be a good place to provide the end of your Narrative if you only used the start in your AG.)

References

(Your references will be in APA Style on a new page.)

NAME: _____

Speech Evaluation Form A

Persuasive Presentation ————————————————

Speaker: _____   **Time Limit:** _____

Topic: _____   **Length of Speech:** _____

Introduction

_____ 1. Captured attention

_____ 2. Stated thesis

_____ 3. Related topic to audience

_____ 4. Established speaker credibility

_____ 5. Previewed main points

_____ 6. Provided transition to body

7. Other comments:

Body

_____ 1. Organized main points clearly and logically

_____ 2. Included transitions between main points

_____ 3. Used accurate, relevant, and timely supporting materials in sufficient quantity

_____ 4. Cited sources accurately in speech

_____ 5. Used well-reasoned arguments

_____ 6. Avoided logical fallacies

_____ 7. Used relevant, professional visual aids that enhanced audience understanding

_____ 8. Explained visual aids clearly

_____ 9. Used persuasive language

_____ 10. Used an oral language style that was appropriate to topic and audience

_____ 11. Used a variety of supporting material (statistics, examples, narratives)

12. Other comments:

Conclusion

_____ 1. Provided transition to conclusion

_____ 2. Restated thesis

_____ 3. Summarized main points

_____ 4. Ended with a memorable final thought (clincher)

5. Other comments:

Delivery

_____ 1. Used adequate and inclusive eye contact

_____ 2. Used effective vocal delivery (appropriate rate and volume, clear articulation, varied inflection, and no vocal fillers)

_____ 3. Used effective physical delivery (posture, gestures, movement)

_____ 4. Delivery was extemporaneous

_____ 5. Presentation appeared well-rehearsed and practiced

6. Other comments:

Topic

_____ 1. Presentation demonstrated effective audience analysis

_____ 2. Presentation incorporated Narrative Presentation well

3. Other comments:

Comments

Major Strengths:

Areas Needing Improvement:

Suggested Goals for Next Speech:

Overall Evaluation:

Total Points/Grade:

NAME: _____

Speech Evaluation Form A

Persuasive Presentation

Speaker: _____   **Time Limit:** _____

Topic: _____   **Length of Speech:** _____

Introduction

_____ 1. Captured attention
_____ 2. Stated thesis
_____ 3. Related topic to audience
_____ 4. Established speaker credibility
_____ 5. Previewed main points
_____ 6. Provided transition to body
7. Other comments:

Body

_____ 1. Organized main points clearly and logically
_____ 2. Included transitions between main points
_____ 3. Used accurate, relevant, and timely supporting materials in sufficient quantity
_____ 4. Cited sources accurately in speech
_____ 5. Used well-reasoned arguments
_____ 6. Avoided logical fallacies
_____ 7. Used relevant, professional visual aids that enhanced audience understanding
_____ 8. Explained visual aids clearly
_____ 9. Used persuasive language
_____ 10. Used an oral language style that was appropriate to topic and audience
_____ 11. Used a variety of supporting material (statistics, examples, narratives)
12. Other comments:

Conclusion

_____ 1. Provided transition to conclusion
_____ 2. Restated thesis
_____ 3. Summarized main points
_____ 4. Ended with a memorable final thought (clincher)
5. Other comments:

Delivery

_____ 1. Used adequate and inclusive eye contact

_____ 2. Used effective vocal delivery (appropriate rate and volume, clear articulation, varied inflection, and no vocal fillers)

_____ 3. Used effective physical delivery (posture, gestures, movement)

_____ 4. Delivery was extemporaneous

_____ 5. Presentation appeared well-rehearsed and practiced

6. Other comments:

Topic

_____ 1. Presentation demonstrated effective audience analysis

_____ 2. Presentation incorporated Narrative Presentation well

3. Other comments:

Comments

Major Strengths:

Areas Needing Improvement:

Suggested Goals for Next Speech:

Overall Evaluation:

Total Points/Grade:

NAME: _____

Speech Evaluation Form B

Persuasive Presentation ————————————————

Speaker: _____ **Time Limit:** _____

Topic: _____ **Situation/Audience:** _____

Introduction

(Captured attention, stated thesis, relevance, credibility, transition)

Strengths:

Weaknesses:

Body

(Organization, transitions, sources, visual aids, language, arguments, avoided fallacies)

Strengths:

Weaknesses:

Conclusion

(Transition, restated thesis, clincher)

Strengths:

Weaknesses:

Delivery

(Eye contact, vocal variety, physical delivery, extemporaneous, rehearsed)

Strengths:

W e a k n e s s e s :

Other

(Audience analysis, use of Narrative Presentation)

Strengths:

Weaknesses:

Comments

Major Strengths:

Areas Needing Improvement:

Total Points/Grade:

NAME: _____

Speech Evaluation Form B

Persuasive Presentation ————————————————

Speaker: _____   **Time Limit:** _____

Topic: _____   **Situation/Audience:** _____

Introduction

(Captured attention, stated thesis, relevance, credibility, transition)

Strengths:

Weaknesses:

Body

(Organization, transitions, sources, visual aids, language, arguments, avoided fallacies)

Strengths:

Weaknesses:

Conclusion

(Transition, restated thesis, clincher)

Strengths:

Weaknesses:

Delivery

(Eye contact, vocal variety, physical delivery, extemporaneous, rehearsed)

Strengths:

Weaknesses:

Other

(Audience analysis, use of Narrative Presentation)

Strengths:

Weaknesses:

Comments

Major Strengths:

Areas Needing Improvement:

Total Points/Grade:

NAME: _____

COM114 Presentation Peer Evaluation

Persuasive Evaluation ————————————————————

Speaker Name: _____ **Speaker Topic:** _____

You must provide objective, evidence-based feedback. Draw upon the textbook and information gleaned in class to support each comment (both strengths and opportunities for feedback).

Delivery Evaluation

One area the speaker could improve on:

One area the speaker did well:

Content Evaluation

(You may comment on any area of the content: topic, thesis, organization, support, transitions, citations, introduction elements, conclusion elements.)

One area the speaker could improve on:

One area the speaker did well:

Visual Aid Evaluation ————————————————

(You may comment on aid that was chosen, use of the aid, etc.)

One area the speaker could improve on:

One area the speaker did well:

I was persuaded by this presentation: ———— yes   ———— no

Explain:

NAME: _____

COM114 Presentation Peer Evaluation

Persuasive Evaluation —————————————————

Speaker Name: _____   **Speaker Topic:** _____

You must provide objective, evidence-based feedback. Draw upon the textbook and information gleaned in class to support each comment (both strengths and opportunities for feedback).

Delivery Evaluation

One area the speaker could improve on:

One area the speaker did well:

Content Evaluation

(You may comment on any area of the content: topic, thesis, organization, support, transitions, citations, introduction elements, conclusion elements.)

One area the speaker could improve on:

One area the speaker did well:

Visual Aid Evaluation

(You may comment on aid that was chosen, use of the aid, etc.)

One area the speaker could improve on:

One area the speaker did well:

I was persuaded by this presentation: _____ yes _____ no

Explain:

NAME: _____

COM114 Presentation Peer Evaluation

Persuasive Evaluation

Speaker Name: _____ **Speaker Topic:** _____

You must provide objective, evidence-based feedback. Draw upon the textbook and information gleaned in class to support each comment (both strengths and opportunities for feedback).

Delivery Evaluation

One area the speaker could improve on:

One area the speaker did well:

Content Evaluation

(You may comment on any area of the content: topic, thesis, organization, support, transitions, citations, introduction elements, conclusion elements.)

One area the speaker could improve on:

One area the speaker did well:

Visual Aid Evaluation

(You may comment on aid that was chosen, use of the aid, etc.)

One area the speaker could improve on:

One area the speaker did well:

I was persuaded by this presentation: _____ yes   _____ no

Explain:

NAME: _____

COM114 Presentation Peer Evaluation

Persuasive Evaluation —————————————————————

Speaker Name: _____   **Speaker Topic:** _____

You must provide objective, evidence-based feedback. Draw upon the textbook and information gleaned in class to support each comment (both strengths and opportunities for feedback).

Delivery Evaluation

One area the speaker could improve on:

One area the speaker did well:

Content Evaluation

(You may comment on any area of the content: topic, thesis, organization, support, transitions, citations, introduction elements, conclusion elements.)

One area the speaker could improve on:

One area the speaker did well:

Visual Aid Evaluation

(You may comment on aid that was chosen, use of the aid, etc.)

One area the speaker could improve on:

One area the speaker did well:

I was persuaded by this presentation: _____ yes   _____ no

Explain:

NAME: _____

Small Group Persuasive Presentation

Point Value: _____

Length: 15 Minutes. Q&A: 10 Minutes

My Group's Presentation Day: _____

For this assignment you will need to take everything you have learned this semester and apply it to this presentation. You will draw on your delivery skills, organizational abilities, reasoning and argumentation skills, critiquing skills, as well as your ability to interact and communicate effectively in small groups. This presentation will require some role-playing.

The Situation

Purdue's president controls the distribution of funds from an incentive grant pool. These grants are used to improve campus or campus-community relations. One purpose is to encourage students to become more actively involved in their local community by either solving problems or offering useful services. Previously, presidents funded a proposal to create the Purdue Cultural Awareness Committee to help unite various campus ethnic groups and promote diversity. Another funded proposal involved the creation of video public service announcements and posters to promote exposure to Purdue's Sexual Harassment Network. These grants award a maximum of $1,500 to each recipient.

You are part of a group who has a particular campus concern but has lacked the funds necessary to address the problem. Your group sees these incentive grants as an opportunity to bring some of your ideas to the public forefront and actually make a difference here on campus or in the local community. The president will be entertaining several proposals from other groups. Your group will essentially be competing for this grant against the other groups in your section. The guidelines for this grant money follow:

1. The proposal should clearly identify a campus or community concern or problem and present a solution to this problem.
2. You can pair with an existing Purdue student organization or form a new group to solve this issue.
3. The proposed plan, program, or event must be completed during the current academic year.
4. The proposal should include a budget that does not exceed $1,500.
   a. Funds can be used to purchase project materials, supplies, and promotional materials.
   b. Funds cannot be used to hold an event to raise more funds or cover salaries.

Remember, you will be competing for the resources, so your proposal must be compelling and persuasive. You will present your proposal to the president's appointed committee and your instructor. The committee will be comprised of other classmates. While your instructor will be responsible for grading the assignment, the committee will have input in the final appraisal of the proposal.

Specific Requirements

You and four or five other classmates will form a group and identify a campus/community concern or problem and propose a solution to that problem. Each group should select a distinct problem. Each group should get their problem approved by their instructor to ensure that each group's problem is distinct. Problems will be approved on a first-come, first-served basis.

- Every person in the group should take a speaking part in the presentation and have knowledge of the proposal.
- Each presentation will follow the problem-solution format discussed in class. Pay particular attention to the need, plan, and practicality issues related to questions of policy.
- The last part of the presentation will consist of a question and answer session with the selection committee (members of the class). The committee should try their best to find problems with the proposal. So, the presenting group must cover every possible angle of the problem and solution. Be sure you are prepared to defend health, social, economic, environmental, etc. concerns.
- The group must stay within the time limit for the presentation and question-and-answer session.
- Every class member will also serve on a selection committee. As a member of this committee, you will be required to ask very thoughtful and knowledgeable questions about other groups' proposals and provide a critique of the proposals.
- Every class member not presenting or serving on a committee will be critiquing group presentations.

If there is a shirker in your group, you (**not** your instructor) will need to deal with him/her. That is, it will be the responsibility of the group to set up rules pertaining to attending planning meeting(s), who will do what, sanctions for not doing what was expected, etc. The group will sign a group contract, and every member will be held to the behavioral guidelines as outlined by that contract. Get these issues settled as soon after group formation as possible so that on presentation day, when Joe Blow doesn't show up or shows up unprepared, the group will have a known procedure for dealing with Joe!!!!

Receiving Credit

Point breakdown will be provided by your instructor.

Criteria for Group Presentation

All group members will receive the same score for this portion of the assignment.

1. Presentation and Group Effectiveness
   a. Creativity and vividness of presentation.
   b. How well you engaged the audience. The best way to fulfill this criteria is to use a variety of methods to present your ideas–rather than rely solely on a lecture approach, use videos, have handouts, **anything** to break the monotony of a string of individual presentations.
   c. Perceived productivity of the group. Did you accomplish your task? How informative and persuasive is the information? Was the presentation well-organized?

NAME: _____

    d. Perceived cohesiveness of the group. How well did the group members seem to work together? Did everyone take an active part?

    e. Elements of effective speaking. (All those things we have talked about all semester long.)

        i.   Organization

        ii. Effective use of evidence

        iii. Refined delivery

        iv. Audience analysis

        v.   Appropriate use of visual aids

2. Executive summary of the proposal. This is just the outline of the presentation.

3. Feedback from the committee members.

Criteria for Individual Evaluation

Individual scores will be assigned for this portion.

1. Individual presentation skills. Basically, your instructor will be evaluating your delivery on the presentation, how well you answered questions from the committee, and your overall demeanor during your group's presentation.

2. Committee member responsibilities. Were you prepared with thoughtful and thorough questions during one other group's presentation? Did you provide a thorough and honest critique of the other group's proposal and presentation.

The instructor reserves the right to lower any student's final grade on this assignment based on group feedback and level of participation in the project.

Small Group Persuasive Presentation

Diversity Program Grant

Point Value: _____

Length: 15 Minutes. Q&A: 5 Minutes

My Group's Presentation Day: _____

For this assignment, you will need to take everything you have learned this semester and apply it to this presentation. You will draw on your delivery skills, organizational abilities, reasoning and argumentation skills, critiquing skills, as well as your ability to interact and communicate effectively in small groups. This presentation will require some role-playing.

The Situation

Purdue's College of Liberal Arts Diversity Action Committee is sponsoring a $500 Diversity Program Grant for undergraduate student organizations. Funded by the Dean of the College of Liberal Arts, the purpose of the grant is to encourage students to more actively promote diversity and cultural awareness. The guidelines for the grant money follow:

1. The student organization must be officially recognized by Purdue University.
2. The proposal should clearly promote diversity awareness or cultural awareness.
3. The proposed plan, program, or event must be completed during the 2016–2017 academic year.
4. The proposal should include a budget that does not exceed $500.

You are part of a group that has an innovative and promising plan but lacks the funds necessary to complete it. Your group sees this grant as an opportunity to bring some of your ideas to the public forefront and actual make a difference here on campus. The Dean will be entertaining several proposals from other groups. Your group will essentially be competing for this grant against the other groups in your COM114 section.

Your Task

Your group will need to identify a specific Purdue student organization and present a unique plan for promoting diversity or cultural awareness.

Remember, you will be competing for the resources, so your proposal must be compelling and persuasive. You will present your proposal to an appointed committee and your instructor. The committee will be comprised of other classmates. While your instructor will be responsible for grading the assignment, the committee will have an input in the final appraisal of your proposal.

Specific Requirements

You and four or five other classmates will form a group and identify a way in which to promote diversity through a Purdue University student organization. Each group should select a specific student organization and unique plan of action. Each group should get their organization and topic approved by their instructor to ensure that each group's problem is distinct. Topics will be approved on a first-come, first-served basis.

◎ Every person in the group should take a speaking part in the presentation and have knowledge of the proposal.

◎ Each presentation will follow the problem-solution format discussed in class. Pay particular attention to the need, plan, and practicality issues related to questions of policy.

◎ The last part of the presentation will consist of a question and answer session with the selection committee (members of the class). The committee should try their best to find problems with the proposal. So, the presenting group must cover every possible angle of the problem and solution. Be sure you are prepared to defend cultural, social, economic, health, environmental, etc. concerns.

◎ The group has the entire class period for the presentation and question and answer session.

◎ Every class member will also serve on a selection committee. As a member of this committee, you will be required to ask very thoughtful and knowledgeable questions about other groups' proposals and provide a critique of the proposals.

If there is a shirker in your group, you (**not** your instructor) will need to deal with him/her. That is, it will be the responsibility of the group to set up rules pertaining to attending/planning meeting(s), who will do what, sanctions for not doing what was expected, etc. The group will sign a group contract, and every member will be held to the behavioral guidelines as outlined by that contract. Get these issues settled as soon after group formation as possible so that on your presentation day, when Joe Blow doesn't show up or shows up unprepared, the group will have a known procedure for dealing with Joe!!!!

NAME: _____

Receiving Credit ————————————————

Point breakdown will be provided by our instructor.

Criteria for Group Presentation

All group members will receive the same score for this portion of the assignment.

1. Presentation and Group Effectiveness
   a. Creativity and vividness of presentation.
   b. How well you engaged the audience. The best way to fulfill this criterion is to use a variety of methods to present your ideas—rather than rely solely on a lecture approach, use videos, have handouts, **anything** to break the monotony of a string of individual presentations.
   c. Perceived productivity of the group. Did you accomplish your task? How informative and persuasive is the information? Was the presentation well-organized?
   d. Perceived cohesiveness of the group. How well did the group members seem to work together? Did everyone take an active part?
   e. Elements of effective speaking. (All those things we have talked about all semester long).
      i. Organization
      ii. Effective use of evidence
      iii. Refined delivery
      iv. Audience analysis
      v. Appropriate use of visual aids
2. Executive summary of the proposal: This is just the outline of the presentation.
3. Feedback from the committee members.

Criteria for Individual Evaluation

Individual scores will be assigned for this portion.

1. Individual presentation skills. Basically, your instructor will be evaluating your delivery on the presentation, how well you answered questions from the committee, and your overall demeanor during your group's presentation.
2. Committee member responsibilities. Were you prepared with thoughtful and thorough questions during one other group's presentation? Did you provide a thorough and honest critique of the other group's proposal and presentation.

The instructor reserves the right to lower any student's final grade on this assignment based on group feedback and level of participation in the project.

NAME: _____

Small Group Presentation

Group Evaluation Form

Speaker: _____   **Time Limit:** _____

Topic: _____   **Situation/Audience:** _____

Introduction

_____ 1. Captured attention
_____ 2. Stated thesis
_____ 3. Related topic to audience
_____ 4. Established credibility

_____ 5. Previewed main points
_____ 6. Provided transition to body
7. Other comments:

Body

_____ 1. Organized main points clearly and logically
_____ 2. Included transitions between main points
_____ 3. Used accurate, relevant, and timely supporting materials in sufficient quantity
_____ 4. Cited sources accurately in speech
_____ 5. Used relevant, professional visual aids that enhanced audience understanding
_____ 6. Used visual aids appropriately
_____ 7. Used an oral language style appropriate to topic and audience
8. Other comments:

Conclusion

_____ 1. Provided transition to conclusion
_____ 2. Restated thesis
_____ 3. Summarized main points

_____ 4. Ended with a memorable final thought (clincher)
5. Other comments:

Question and Answer Section

_____ 1. Rephrased questions
_____ 2. Answered questions clearly and completely
_____ 3. Answered questions succinctly

_____ 4. Q&A was well-organized and professional
5. Other comments:

Overall Group Assessment

_____ 1. Project demonstrated creativity

_____ 2. Accomplishment of group persuasive and informative goals

_____ 3. Presentation demonstrated group cohesiveness

_____ 4. Transitioning from one speaker to another was smooth

5. Other comments:

Evaluation of Proposal

_____ 1. Proposal clearly identified and defined campus issue/problem

_____ 2. Proposal presented a clear plan for dealing with issue

_____ 3. Proposal presented a practical solution

4. Other comments:

Status Reports

_____ 1. Status report followed format outlined in textbook

_____ 2. Status report was complete

_____ 3. Status report was professional

Comments

Major Strengths:

Areas Needing Improvement:

Overall Evaluation:

Total Points/Grade:

Presentation Score _____

Executive Summary _____

Committee Evaluation _____

Total Group Score _____

NAME: _____

Small Group Presentation

Individual Evaluation Form ————————————

Name: _____   **Group:** _____

Individual Delivery

_____ 1. Used adequate and inclusive eye contact (extemporaneous delivery)

_____ 2. Used effective vocal delivery (appropriate rate and volume, clear articulation, varied inflection, and no vocal fillers)

_____ 3. Used effective physical delivery (posture, gestures, movement)

_____ 4. Actively engaged during group presentation

5. Comments:

Total Points: _____

Committee Member Responsibilities

_____ 1. Asked well-informed questions

_____ 2. Attentive during the presentation

_____ 3. Provided honest, thorough feedback on the group critique form

Total Points: _____

Individual Score

Individual Delivery: _____   Total: _____

Committee Member: _____

Total Project Score

Individual Score: _____   Total Score: _____

Group Score: _____

NAME: _____

COM114 Presentation Peer Evaluation

Group Evaluation ———————————————————————

Your Name: _____   **Group Topic:** _____

Group Number: _____

You must provide objective, evidence-based feedback. Draw upon the textbook and information gleaned in class to support each comment (both strengths and opportunities for feedback).

Delivery Evaluation

(You may comment on the overall delivery of the group: Did they seem cohesive? Did they use speaker transitions? Did they begin strongly and end strongly? etc.)

One area the group could improve on:

One area the group did well:

Content Evaluation

(You may comment on any area of the content: topic, thesis, organization, support, transitions, citations, introduction elements, conclusion elements.)

One area the group could improve on:

One area the group did well:

Visual Aid Evaluation

(You may comment on aid/aids that was/were chosen, use of the aids, aids that would have been more helpful, etc.)

One area the group could improve on:

One area the group did well:

I was persuaded by this presentation: _____ yes _____ no

Explain:

NAME: _____

COM114 Presentation Peer Evaluation

Group Evaluation

Your Name: _____   **Group Topic:** _____

Group Number: _____

You must provide objective, evidence-based feedback. Draw upon the textbook and information gleaned in class to support each comment (both strengths and opportunities for feedback).

Delivery Evaluation

(You may comment on the overall delivery of the group: Did they seem cohesive? Did they use speaker transitions? Did they begin strongly and end strongly? etc.)

One area the group could improve on:

One area the group did well:

Content Evaluation

(You may comment on any area of the content: topic, thesis, organization, support, transitions, citations, introduction elements, conclusion elements.)

One area the group could improve on:

One area the group did well:

Visual Aid Evaluation

(You may comment on aid/aids that was/were chosen, use of the aids, aids that would have been more helpful, etc.)

One area the group could improve on:

One area the group did well:

I was persuaded by this presentation: _____ yes _____ no

Explain:

NAME: _____

COM114 Presentation Peer Evaluation

Group Evaluation ————————————————————

Your Name: _____   Group Topic: _____

Group Number: _____

You must provide objective, evidence-based feedback. Draw upon the textbook and information gleaned in class to support each comment (both strengths and opportunities for feedback).

Delivery Evaluation

(You may comment on the overall delivery of the group: Did they seem cohesive? Did they use speaker transitions? Did they begin strongly and end strongly? etc.)

One area the group could improve on:

One area the group did well:

Content Evaluation

(You may comment on any area of the content: topic, thesis, organization, support, transitions, citations, introduction elements, conclusion elements.)

One area the group could improve on:

One area the group did well:

Visual Aid Evaluation

(You may comment on aid/aids that was/were chosen, use of the aids, aids that would have been more helpful, etc.)

One area the group could improve on:

One area the group did well:

I was persuaded by this presentation: _____ yes   _____ no

Explain:

NAME: _____

Group Member Feedback Status Report I

First Status Report: Overall Status

Overall: This is the overall status of a project. Remember, a status report is actually part of a group project. It should be professional and coordinated. Your first status report should include the following elements of an overall status report presented in a succinct and professional manner (1–3 minutes total):

The project name and description: Explain the problem your group has chosen and what research you have to justify this is a relevant and substantial problem. Explain your solution. Is your solution practical? Feasible? Does it completely solve the problem?

_____

_____

_____

_____

_____

The overall project status: As part of this answer, specifically include who has been assigned what part of the project. Who will be delivering in the introduction? The body? The conclusion?

_____

_____

_____

_____

_____

How much of the project you planned to have completed by this time: As part of this answer, specifically include a rough draft of your budget, since that is a first step in any project. Remember, you cannot go over your budget.

_____

_____

_____

_____

_____

How much of the project you have actually completed by this time: Be specific here. ("A lot" and "some" are not acceptable answers.) You need to provide specifics.

_____

_____

_____

_____

_____

How far behind, or ahead, you are: Again, be specific. As part of this answer, what took longer/less time than you anticipated?

_____

_____

_____

_____

_____

_____

Group Member Feedback Status Report II

Second Status Report: Milestones

Milestones: By this time in your preparation for your group project you should have reached (or hoped to reach) several milestones to report. Remember, a status report is actually part of a group project. It should be professional and coordinated. Your second status report should include the following elements of a status report focused on milestones presented in a succinct, professional manner (1–3 minutes):

Milestone name: Talk about three milestones (e.g., final budget, complete rough draft of outline, completed visual aids, etc.)

_____

_____

_____

_____

_____

The percent complete of the milestone: Again, be specific.

_____

_____

_____

_____

_____

The planned start and the planned finish:

_____

_____

_____

_____

_____

The actual start and the actual finish:

_____

_____

_____

_____

_____

_____

You may choose to include elements of an issues status report here as well. For example, did you fail to reach a milestone because of a specific issue (minor or major)? Who is working to resolve that issue?

NAME: _____

Group Member Feedback Status Report Final

Please provide feedback on your fellow group members. This is an optional form that carries no point value. However, comments made could be taken in account when the instructor distributes group points.

Group Member Name: _____

How many meetings did this member attend? _____

How many did they miss? _____

What role did this group member play? _____

Please provide written feedback on this group member's performance.

_____

_____

_____

Group Member Name: _____

How many meetings did this member attend? _____

How many did they miss? _____

What role did this group member play? _____

Please provide written feedback on this group member's performance.

_____

_____

_____

Group Member Name: _____

How many meetings did this member attend? _____

How many did they miss? _____

What role did this group member play? _____

Please provide written feedback on this group member's performance.

_____

_____

_____

Group Member Name: _____

How many meetings did this member attend? _____

How many did they miss? _____

What role did this group member play? _____

Please provide written feedback on this group member's performance.

_____

_____

_____

Group Member Name: _____

How many meetings did this member attend? _____

How many did they miss? _____

What role did this group member play? _____

Please provide written feedback on this group member's performance.

_____

_____

_____